THE BOOK OF DAILY PRAYER

The Book of Daily Prayer

Compiled by

Robert E. Webber

William B. Eerdmans Publishing Company
Grand Rapids, Michigan

Library of Congress Cataloging-in-Publication Data

The Book of daily prayer / compiled by Robert E. Webber.
p.   cm.
ISBN 0-8028-3753-0. — ISBN 0-8028-0678-3 (pbk.)
1. Church year — Prayer-books and devotions — English.
2. Devotional calendars. 3. Prayer — Christianity. I. Webber, Robert.
BV4812.A1B66   1993
242'.3 — dc20   93-26627
CIP

Contents

How to Pray with This Book

By picking *The Book of Daily Prayer* up into your hands and determining that you are going to have a regular prayer life, you have set in motion a spiritual discipline that can change your spiritual life. All it takes is some understanding of the principles which underlie the approach to prayer taken in this book, a determination to stick to it, and a mind, heart, and will that is open to God.

You will agree with me, I'm sure, that Christians are called to pray. Our Lord frequently prayed, leaving us an example to do likewise. Then there is the earliest Christian community, which is described by Luke as a praying church (Acts 2:42). Finally, all throughout church history we have examples of women and men of God who saw great things happen because of prayer.

If prayer is such a central activity of the church and of God's people, we must ask ourselves, "Why do so many of us find it difficult to pray?"

WHY IS IT SO DIFFICULT TO PRAY?

Recently I heard a Christian statesman speak on the subject of prayer. He spoke honestly and directly about his experience and in doing so connected squarely with the problems many Christians experience in prayer. Allow me to reiterate his points.

First, he said, *"For me prayer is the most difficult of the Christian practices."* He went on to say, "I can attend church happily, I can tithe, care for the needs of the poor, help someone in need, counsel a friend

1

or a stranger, but when it comes to prayer my lips still form the words 'Lord, teach me to pray.'"

Next he confessed, *"When I'm at prayer my mind wanders."* He touched a real nerve with almost everyone present when he told us how he had tried to read the Bible through in a year, meditate on a psalm every day, read through a whole book at one sitting, and keep a prayer journal. While each of these approaches met with a degree of success, he was still in search, he said, of a way to organize his prayer life to be consistent and fruitful.

Finally, he admitted: *"I find my prayer and meditation time to be too intellectual."* By "intellectual" he meant, as he said, that his prayer was too much from the head and not enough from the heart and will. His desire was to go beyond a mere understanding of scripture into a deeper level of feeling and action.

I believe this person's experience is altogether typical of the prayer life of many Christians. It is my purpose in *The Book of Daily Prayer* to address these problems and offer a way of praying that can be consistent and fruitful.

HOW *THE BOOK OF DAILY PRAYER* CAN ASSIST YOUR PRAYER LIFE

First, *The Book of Daily Prayer* makes the habit of daily prayer less difficult because it *offers a convenient guide to prayer on a day-to-day basis throughout the year.* God has made us in such a way that we need visible and tangible helps to guide our thoughts and direct our ways. Prayer is often difficult because it is the one area in life where some Christians feel that external guides and directions are *not* necessary. But *The Book of Daily Prayer* takes into account the need we all have for guidance and leadership in prayer. Therefore, it organizes in one small volume readings and prayers from the whole Bible that provide strong spiritual direction. By organizing psalms, prayers, and scripture into a consistent daily pattern of prayer, this book carries the believer into a Christian experience that puts each day into a spiritual context.

Next, *The Book of Daily Prayer* is designed to guide a believer's thoughts in such a way that wandering of the mind is minimized. You don't have to ask "What shall I do next?" or "What shall I pray for?" Instead the daily prayers are organized to carry you from one step to the next in a very natural way. The prayers for each day are organized around

a threefold approach to prayer: preparation; hearing God speak; respond-
ing to God. Here is the typical order of prayer. Note how you are to
progress through each stage of prayer:

The Order of the Daily Prayers	How the Order Organizes Your Internal Experience of Prayer
1. Preparation: Theme, *Anti- phon, and Opening Prayer	1. These three parts of prayer in- tend to quiet the heart and ready you to hear God speak.
2. Hearing God Speak: The Scrip- ture Reading	2. The theme of each meditation is especially struck in the scrip- ture reading. Let God speak.
3. Response: Responsorial Psalm, Prayer, Closing Psalm Prayer	3. The responsorial psalm confesses something about God; the prayer is focused on confession, adoration, thanks- giving, or prayer; the closing Psalm prayer (or "O" prayer) is oriented toward a sense of hope or a call to action.

*Varies slightly during Lent and Easter

Third, *The Book of Daily Prayer* overcomes the problem we experience in organizing prayer throughout the year. It orders your prayer
life around the life of Christ as it finds expression through the Christian
year. For some people who know little about the Christian year a brief
explanation is in order. The main principle you need to know is that the
Christian year is the way we celebrate time Christianly. In America we
all live by two approaches to time: the civil year, which begins in January,
and the academic year, which begins in September. Unfortunately many
Christians organize their spiritual time around these two calendars and
fail to realize that they are attempting to practice their spirituality in a
secular framework of time. The Christian year is organized around
Advent, Christmas, Epiphany, Lent, Holy Week, Easter, and Pentecost.
Let me illustrate these three calendars so you have a sense of time from
a Christian perspective:

The Civil Year	The Academic Year	The Christian Year
New Year's Day	September: School Starts	Advent: Anticipation of Christ's Coming
President's Day	December: Winter Break	Christmas: Christ's Birth
Martin Luther King Day	March: Spring Break	Epiphany: Manifestation of Christ to the World
Mother's Day	June: Graduation	Lent: Preparation for Christ's Death
Father's Day	July–August: Summer Break	Holy Week: Last Week of Christ's Life
Memorial Day		Easter: Celebrating the Resurrection
Fourth of July		Pentecost: Celebrating the Holy Spirit and the Beginning of the Church
Labor Day		
Thanksgiving Day		

There is nothing wrong with organizing our time around the civil year and the academic year. Life simply requires it. But as Christians we have one more way of marking time — a spiritual way, the Christian year. While the Christian year has seven seasons we are all aware that the two climactic events of the Christian year are Christmas and Easter. Our spiritual life is organized around the two events of the birth and death-resurrection of Jesus in the following manner: preparation, fulfillment, response. For example, we prepare for the coming of Christ during Advent; the fulfillment of his coming occurs at Christmas; the response to his coming is expressed during Epiphany. The same pattern is seen in the time organized around the death and resurrection of Christ. During Lent we prepare for Christ's death and resurrection; in Easter the fulfillment comes; during Pentecost the response to his death and resurrection regulates our prayer.

	Birth	Death-Resurrection
Preparation:	Advent	Lent, Holy Week
Fulfillment:	Christmas	Easter
Response:	Epiphany	Pentecost

One of the underlying assumptions of *The Book of Daily Prayer* is that our spiritual health is greatly improved by bringing the practice of prayer and scriptural meditation up into the life of Christ through the seasons of time that are marked by his birth, life, death, and resurrection. This is a strong medicine against secularism! The prayers of each season are designed to carry you into the experience of Christ, to let you feel the anticipation of Advent, the fulfillment of Christmas, and the joyful response of Epiphany. The Christian year will become a habit of life, a way to spiritually live and breathe through the months of every year.

Finally, *The Book of Daily Prayer is designed to overcome the problem of making prayer time too intellectual.* My own experience with the prayers in this book is that they are best prayed with the mind, the heart, and the will: First, read the daily prayer with the mind and ask "What is being said in the scripture and the prayers?"; second, read the prayers again with the heart and ask "What is God saying to me today?"; finally, read the prayer with the will and ask "What does God want me to do today?" You may find that it will be most beneficial to you to pray with a pen and paper in hand, jotting down how God speaks to your mind, your heart, and your will. Here is a fourfold approach that I take to these prayers. The time I spend ranges from ten to thirty minutes.

Step I   Pray the entire Daily Prayer.
Step II Pray with the mind. Go over the entire prayer, seeking to understand how it proclaims Christ and spiritual truth. How does it fit into the Christian year? What is being said? How do the various parts connect?
Step III Pray with the heart. Go over the entire prayer again, looking for that verse or phrase that will jump out at you and speak to your heart. Focus on that passage. Mull it over in your heart. Let it enter into your heart and take up residence.
Step IV Pray with the will. Look over the prayer again until a particular passage speaks to you regarding something you ought to do.

You will find that the impact will vary from day to day. Some days you will feel that you have accomplished very little, other days you will be struck with one or another passage either in the mind, the heart, or the will. And on other days, hopefully many, you will be touched in your whole person by your prayer time.

Of course it is easy to get discouraged, to lapse, and to give up entirely. To prevent failure:

1. Have a set time each day when you pray.
2. Have a set place where you pray.
3. Have a spouse or friend who prays *The Book of Daily Prayer* (not necessarily with you) who will meet with you periodically for discussion and mutual support.

HOW TO FIGURE OUT THE DATES

The fact that *The Book of Daily Prayer* is organized around the Christian year and not the civil year will pose some slight difficulty for people who are not well acquainted with the Christian year. However, I want to stress that the difficulty is slight, and that I have taken great care throughout the book to offer simple direction to guide the reader from day to day. The problem is this: certain dates of the Christian year are moveable. Christmas always falls on December 25th and Epiphany on January 6th. But the beginning date of Advent, Lent, Easter, and Pentecost all change from year to year. Therefore you will have to depend (1) on the simple chart of dates that follows (p. 8) and (2) directions given at crucial points in the text of *The Book of Daily Prayer*. These are all simple enough that with a little determination you should not have any problems. Here are some basic guidelines:

1. Start with Advent, the beginning of the Christian year, which begins four Sundays before Christmas (see the chart of dates on p. 8). As you pray through Advent watch for the note that sends you to December 17th. This will vary from year to year depending on the starting date of Advent. The days between December 17th and January 6th remain the same from year to year.
2. After Epiphany you will do daily readings that will take you to the first Sunday after Epiphany. For example, if Epiphany falls on a Wednesday you will do the prayers for three days after Epiphany and then proceed to the first Sunday after Epiphany.
3. The number of weeks after Epiphany depend on the length of time between Epiphany and Ash Wednesday, the first day of Lent. There can be as few as four full weeks and as many as seven full weeks. For example, on the Saturday of the fifth week after Epiphany a note at the bottom of the page tells you "In 1994, 1999, and 2010, go to the last Sunday after Epiphany (p. 141) tomorrow." The last week after Epiphany contains readings for the Sunday, Monday, and Tuesday before Ash Wednesday.

4. The dates of Ash Wednesday are in the chart on p. 8. You will begin with prayers for Wednesday, Thursday, Friday, and Saturday. Then you will commence with the first week in Lent. There are five weeks in Lent before Holy Week. This always remains the same. Holy Week completes the Lenten cycle.

5. The dates of Easter are in the chart. There are always seven weeks of Easter, ending with Pentecost day. The date of Pentecost is in the chart.

6. Each week of readings in the season from Pentecost to Advent, that is, to the beginning of the Christian year, is indicated by this formula: "Week of the Sunday closest to [date]." On Pentecost Sunday commence your prayers for this season with the Sunday closest in date to Pentecost Sunday.

7. As you approach late November, check on the chart on p. 8 for the date of the Sunday on which Advent — and a new year — begins.

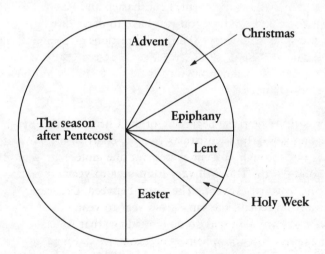

Dates that seasons of the Christian year begin with through 2013-14

YEAR	Advent	Lent	Holy Week	Easter	Pentecost
1992-93	November 29	February 24	April 4	April 11	May 30
1993-94	November 28	February 16	March 27	April 3	May 22
1994-95	November 27	March 1	April 9	April 16	June 4
1995-96	December 3	February 21	March 31	April 7	May 26
1996-97	December 1	February 12	March 23	March 30	May 18
1997-98	November 30	February 25	April 5	April 12	May 31
1998-99	November 29	February 17	March 28	April 4	May 23
1999-2000	November 28	March 8	April 16	April 23	June 11
2000-01	December 3	February 28	April 8	April 15	June 3
2001-02	December 2	February 13	March 24	March 31	May 19
2002-03	December 1	March 5	April 13	April 20	June 8
2003-04	November 30	February 25	April 4	April 11	May 30
2004-05	November 28	February 9	March 20	March 27	May 15
2005-06	November 27	March 1	April 9	April 16	June 4
2006-07	December 3	February 21	April 1	April 8	May 27
2007-08	December 2	February 6	March 16	March 23	May 11
2008-09	November 30	February 25	April 5	April 12	May 31
2009-10	November 29	February 17	March 28	April 4	May 23
2010-11	November 28	March 9	April 17	April 24	June 12
2011-12	November 27	February 22	April 1	April 8	May 27
2012-13	December 2	February 13	March 24	March 31	May 19
2013-14	December 1	March 5	April 13	April 20	June 8

*Christmas and Epiphany are omitted because they always begin on the same dates, December 25 and January 6. Ascension day is always ten days before Pentecost and thirty-nine days after Easter.

Advent

The first thing we must know about Advent is that it represents the beginning of the Christian year, where our spiritual journey begins. During this time we enter into the anticipation of Israel — the longing shared by Abraham, Moses, David, and the prophets. What we long for is the coming of the Messiah and all that his coming means for the world.

Second, we should know that for the Christian, Advent not only means the coming of the Messiah at Bethlehem, but the coming of Christ at the end of the age. During Advent we look to Christ to establish his kingdom, to create the new heavens and the new earth. Therefore, the Readings and Prayers of Advent center around the twofold theme of his coming. Sometimes the prayers will focus on one or the other coming and sometimes both the coming of Christ in Bethlehem and his coming at the end of history are contained in the same reading.

Third, it is important that we look not only at the fact of Christ's coming at Bethlehem and his coming again, but also at the *meaning* of his comings. As you pray keep in mind the truth that Christ became one of us in order to restore us and his creation to its original condition. In the pre-Christian era Israel longed for the restoration of the whole creation (Isaiah 65:17-25). Today we Christians still long for the same restoration (Romans 8:18-24). We confess that Christ, who conquered the power of evil, will come again in great glory to put away the powers forever. He will rid the earth of pain, sorrow, and death. The nations will no longer war with each other. Swords will be turned into plowshares. The lamb will lie down with the lion (Isaiah 2:4; 11:6-9). Advent brings these themes of the first and the second comings together, and calls us to meditate on the salvation brought to the whole world through the babe born in Bethlehem.

9

Fourth, Advent calls us not only to long for this day, but also to prepare for it. Thus, in the midst of great joy, there is also the need for repentance. We are to clean house, to ready ourselves for his coming by the renewal of our spiritual condition.

Finally, the overall structure of the Advent readings and prayers is designed to lead us from longing for the second coming and the renewal of the universe into an increasingly intense expectation of Christ's coming in Bethlehem. Week by week and day by day the prayers are designed to lead us nearer to Christ, to his birth and coming again, and to the meaning Christ holds for our lives. The following summary of themes shows this progression:

Week I	Vigilant waiting for the second coming of the Lord
Week II	Preparation for both comings of the Lord
Week III	The Messianic Age is near
Dec. 17-23	His coming is announced
Dec. 24	His arrival is imminent

The daily devotions for Advent are designed to help us experience the mood of repentance and joy. The theme of preparation through repentance is expressed in every devotion as is the theme of joy.

One final word of instruction. What we want to accomplish spiritually is this: We want to allow these devotions to shape our inner experience of preparation for Christ's coming. We want to let God birth within us an expectation of his presence and power in our life, and in the life of the world. Pray for this to happen to you as you pray these prayers day by day.

Advent: Day 1   First Week: Sunday

Theme: The cry "Prepare the way of the Lord!" calls us to ready ourselves for the second coming of the Lord by walking in his ways.

Antiphon and Opening Prayer

Be strong, do not fear!
Here is your God.

He will come. . . .
He will come and save you. Isaiah 35:4

Lord, help me to prepare for the coming of your Son.
May he find me waiting and watching in joyful anticipation.
Through Christ, I pray.

Scripture Reading

A voice cries out:
"In the wilderness prepare the way of the LORD,
make straight in the desert a highway for our God.
Every valley shall be lifted up,
and every mountain and hill be made low;
the uneven ground shall become level,
and the rough places a plain.
Then the glory of the LORD shall be revealed,
and all people shall see it together,
for the mouth of the LORD has spoken." Isaiah 40:3-5
optional: Matthew 24:31-44

Responsorial Psalm

To you, O LORD, I lift up my soul.
O my God, in you I trust;
do not let me be put to shame;
do not let my enemies exult over me.
Do not let those who wait for you be put to shame.
Psalm 25:1-3a

Prayers, pp. 529-32

Closing Psalm Prayer

Lord Jesus Christ, as I await your coming
show me your ways,
teach me your paths.
For you are the God of my salvation.
On you I wait all the day. adapted from Psalm 25:4-5

Advent: Day 2   First Week: Monday

Theme: When the Lord comes again, he will gather all the nations of
the world under his rule. Then there will be peace in the world.

Antiphon and Opening Prayer

Hear the word of the LORD, O nations,
and declare it in the coastlands far away;
say, "He who scattered Israel will gather him,
and will keep him as a shepherd a flock."   Jeremiah 31:10

Lord, you come to bring peace to all nations
and to gather a people in your name.
Grant me your peace.

Scripture Reading

In days to come
the mountain of the LORD's house
shall be established . . .
all the nations shall stream to it. . . .
He shall judge between the nations,
and shall arbitrate for many peoples;
they shall beat their swords into plowshares,
and their spears into pruning hooks;
nation shall not lift up sword against nation,
neither shall they learn war any more.   Isaiah 2:2, 4
                              optional: Matthew 8:5-11

Responsorial Psalm

Pray for the peace of Jerusalem:
"May they prosper who love you.
Peace be within your walls,
and security within your towers."
For the sake of my relatives and friends
I will say, "Peace be within you."

For the sake of the house of the LORD our God,
    I will seek your good.   Psalm 122:6-9

Prayers, pp. 529-32

Closing Psalm Prayer

Lord, as I wait for your coming judgment,
may my feet stand in the gates of Jerusalem.
May I experience peace in your house of prayer,
and let me be glad when they say,
"Let us go into the house of the Lord."
             adapted from Psalm 122:1-2

Advent: Day 3   First Week: Tuesday

Theme: When Christ rules over the world, the power of evil will be
destroyed. He will rule with justice and equity for all. We are
called to live in this hope.

Antiphon and Opening Prayer

Then the LORD my God will come. . . .
    And the LORD will become king over all the earth; on that day
the LORD will be one and his name one.
             Zechariah 14:5, 9

Lord, you who have come to be king over all the earth,
reign in my life through Jesus Christ my Lord.

Scripture Reading

He shall not judge by what his eyes see,
    or decide by what his ears hear;
but with righteousness he shall judge the poor,
    and decide with equity for the meek of the earth;

he shall strike the earth with the rod of his mouth,
  and with the breath of his lips he shall kill the wicked.

Isaiah 11:3b-4
optional: Luke 10:21-24

Responsorial Psalm

Blessed be the LORD, the God of Israel,
  who alone does wondrous things.
Blessed be his glorious name forever;
  may his glory fill the whole earth.
    Amen and Amen.   Psalm 72:18-19

Prayers, pp. 529-32

Closing Psalm Prayer

Lord, through me deliver the needy, the poor also.
Redeem their life from oppression and violence.

adapted from Psalm 72:12-14

Advent: Day 4   First Week: Wednesday

Theme: In the Messianic Age we will gather at the Table of the Lord
    and feast with him. Now we are to live in the expectation of
    this joyous day.

Antiphon and Opening Prayer

Therefore do not pronounce judgment before the time, before the
Lord comes, who will bring to light the things now hidden in
darkness and will disclose the purposes of the heart.

I Corinthians 4:5

Lord God,
grant that I may be ready for Christ when he comes in glory,
and grant that I may share in the banquet of heaven.

Scripture Reading

On this mountain the LORD of hosts will make for all peoples
    a feast of rich food, a feast of well-aged wines,
    of rich food filled with marrow, of well-aged wines strained
      clear. . . .
It will be said on that day,
    Lo, this is our God; we have waited for him,
      so that he might save us.
    This is the LORD for whom we have waited;
    let us be glad and rejoice in his salvation.   Isaiah 25:6, 9
                                optional: Matthew 15:29-37

Responsorial Psalm

You prepare a table before me;
    in the presence of my enemies;
you anoint my head with oil;
    my cup overflows.
Surely goodness and mercy shall follow me
    all the days of my life,
and I shall dwell in the house of the LORD
    my whole life long.   Psalm 23:5-6

Prayers, pp. 529-32

Closing Psalm Prayer

Lord, lead me beside the still waters.
Restore my soul,
and lead me in the paths of righteousness
for your name's sake.   adapted from Psalm 23:2-3

Advent: Day 5   First Week: Thursday

Theme: Only those persons and nations that have been just will enter
        into the Messianic Age. Repent and turn your life toward right
        living.

Antiphon and Opening Prayer

Yet you are near, O LORD,
    and all your commandments are true.
Long ago I learned from your decrees
    that you have established them forever.   Psalm 119:151-152

Father God, forgive me.
For I have not always walked in obedience to your
commandments.
Through Jesus, I pray.

Scripture Reading

Open the gates,
    so that the righteous nation that keeps faith
    may enter in.
Those of steadfast mind you keep in peace —
    in peace because they trust in you.
Trust in the LORD forever,
    for in the LORD GOD
    you have an everlasting rock.
For he has brought low
    the inhabitants of the height;
    the lofty city he lays low.
He lays it low to the ground,
    casts it to the dust.   Isaiah 26:2-5
                                    optional: Matthew 7:21-27

Responsorial Psalm

O give thanks to the LORD, for he is good;
    his steadfast love endures forever!
It is better to take refuge in the LORD
    than to put confidence in mortals.
It is better to take refuge in the LORD
    than to put confidence in princes.   Psalm 118:1, 8-9

Prayers, pp. 529-32

Closing Psalm Prayer

I thank you that you have answered me
    and have become my salvation.
Blessed is the one who comes in the name of the LORD!

Psalm 118:21, 26a

Advent: Day 6   First Week: Friday

Theme: The blind will see the coming Messianic Age. The Lord who
    causes the blind to see will enlighten your path today.

Antiphon and Opening Prayer

They grope in the dark without light;
    he makes them stagger like a drunkard.   Job 12:25

Lord Jesus, you who are the Light of the World,
reveal the darkness within me, and dispel my sin.
O Light of Life.

Scripture Reading

On that day the deaf shall hear
    the words of a scroll,
and out of their gloom and darkness
    the eyes of the blind shall see.
The meek shall obtain fresh joy in the LORD,
    and the neediest people shall exult in the Holy One
    of Israel. . . .
They will sanctify my name;
they will sanctify the Holy One of Jacob,
    and will stand in awe of the God of Israel.

Isaiah 29:18-19, 23b
optional: Matthew 9:27-31

Responsorial Psalm

The LORD is my light and my salvation;
    whom shall I fear?
The LORD is the stronghold of my life;
    of whom shall I be afraid?
Though an army encamp against me,
    my heart shall not fear;
though war rise up against me,
    yet I will be confident.   Psalm 27:1, 3

Prayers, pp. 529-32

Closing Psalm Prayer

One thing I have desired of you, O Lord, and that will I seek:
That I may dwell in your house all the days of my life.

                                        adapted from Psalm 27:4

Advent: Day 7   First Week: Saturday

Theme: Waiting can be tedious. We can lose heart. God calls us to be
       diligent in our waiting by walking in his ways. Diligence results
       in praise.

Antiphon and Opening Prayer

Restore us, O God;
    let your face shine, that we may be saved.   Psalm 80:3

Lord Jesus Christ,
I give my heart to you,
for salvation is in no other name.
Your face only do I seek.
Let me trust in you, I pray.

Scripture Reading

Though the Lord may give you the bread of adversity and the water of affliction, yet your Teacher will not hide himself any more, but your eyes shall see your Teacher. And when you turn to the right or when you turn to the left, your ears shall hear a word behind you, saying, "This is the way; walk in it."

Isaiah 30:20-21, 23-26
optional: Matthew 9:35–10:8

Responsorial Psalm

The Lord builds up Jerusalem;
    he gathers the outcasts of Israel.
He heals the brokenhearted,
    and binds up their wounds.
He determines the number of the stars;
    he gives to all of them their names.   Psalm 147:2-4

Prayers, pp. 529-32

Closing Psalm Prayer

Lord, you take pleasure in those who fear you,
in those who hope in your mercy.
I will sing to you with thanksgiving;
as I wait I will sing praises to your name.

adapted from Psalm 147:7, 11

Advent: Day 8   Second Week: Sunday

Theme: In view of Christ's coming in Bethlehem and his coming at the
        end of history, we should prepare our hearts and commit our-
        selves to help the poor.

Antiphon and Opening Prayer

I will extol you, my God and King,
    and bless your name forever and ever.   Psalm 145:1

Lord, prepare my heart for the coming of your Son.
Pardon my iniquity;
comfort my spirit and save my life.

Scripture Reading

But the LORD of hosts is exalted by justice,
    and the Holy God shows himself holy by righteousness.
Then the lambs shall graze as in their pasture,
    fatlings and kids shall feed among the ruins. . . .
Ah, you who call evil good
    and good evil,
who put darkness for light
    and light for darkness,
who put bitter for sweet
    and sweet for bitter!   Isaiah 5:16-17, 20
                                        optional: Matthew 3:1-12

Responsorial Psalm

For he delivers the needy when they call,
    the poor and those who have no helper.
He has pity on the weak and the needy,
    and saves the lives of the needy.
From oppression and violence he redeems their life;
    and precious is their blood in his sight.   Psalm 72:12-14

Prayers, pp. 529-32

Closing Psalm Prayer

Lord, guide me in the path of righteousness.
Teach me justice,
give me a heart for the poor,
save the children of the needy,
and break the back of the oppressor.   adaptation of Psalm 72:1-4

Advent: Day 9   Second Week: Monday

Theme: When Christ comes at Bethlehem and again at the end of history,
he comes to redeem us. Let us rejoice in God's salvation today.

Antiphon and Opening Prayer

Be strong, do not fear!
Here is your God. . . .
He will come and save you.   Isaiah 35:4

Lord, you who are soon to come,
save me from my sin;
cleanse me and make me whole.

Scripture Reading

A highway shall be there,
and it shall be called the Holy Way. . . .
The redeemed shall walk there.
And the ransomed of the LORD shall return,
and come to Zion with singing;
everlasting joy shall be upon their heads;
they shall obtain joy and gladness,
and sorrow and sighing shall flee away.   Isaiah 35:8, 9, 10
optional: Luke 5:17-26

Responsorial Psalm

Will you not revive us again,
so that your people may rejoice in you?
Show us your steadfast love, O LORD,
and grant us your salvation.   Psalm 85:6-7

Prayers, pp. 529-32

Closing Psalm Prayer

> Lord, let me hear what you will speak.
> For you speak peace to your people and your saints.
> Surely your salvation is near.   adapted from Psalm 85:8-9

Advent: Day 10   Second Week: Tuesday

Theme: Today we meditate on the coming of Christ at the end of history.
      We live in the hope that all things will be made new.

Antiphon and Opening Prayer

> On that day living waters shall flow out from Jerusalem.
>
> Zechariah 14:8

> Lord Jesus,
> come and renew me.
> Renew my heart, my spirit,
> my spiritual life and my relationship. In Jesus' name.

Scripture Reading

> See, the Lord GOD comes with might,
>   and his arm rules for him;
> his reward is with him,
>   and his recompense before him.
> He will feed his flock like a shepherd;
>   he will gather the lambs in his arms,
> and carry them in his bosom,
>   and gently lead the mother sheep.   Isaiah 40:10-11
>   optional: Matthew 18:12-14

Responsorial Psalm

> Let the heavens be glad, and let the earth rejoice;
>   let the sea roar, and all that fills it . . .
>   for he is coming to judge the earth.

He will judge the world with righteousness,
   and the peoples with his truth.   Psalm 96:11, 13b

Prayers, pp. 529-32

Closing Psalm Prayer

I will sing to the Lord a new song!
O sing to the Lord, all the earth.
Sing to the Lord, bless his name.
Proclaim the good news of his salvation from day to day.
                    adapted from Psalm 96:1-2

Advent: Day 11   Second Week: Wednesday

Theme: Sometimes we grow weary in waiting and lose the vision for
      which we wait. But the Lord promises that he will renew our
      strength.

Antiphon and Opening Prayer

Make a joyful noise to the LORD, all the earth.
   Worship the LORD with gladness;
   come into his presence with singing.
Know that the LORD is God.   Psalm 100:1-3a

Most merciful God,
restore the vision of your redemption within me
and strengthen my inner person
as I wait upon you.

Scripture Reading

Have you not known? Have you not heard?
The LORD is the everlasting God,
   the Creator of the ends of the earth.
He does not faint or grow weary;

his understanding is unsearchable. . . .
Those who wait for the LORD shall renew their strength,
    they shall mount up with wings like eagles,
they shall run and not be weary,
    they shall walk and not faint.   Isaiah 40:28, 31
                      optional: Matthew 11:28-30

Responsorial Psalm

For as the heavens are high above the earth,
    so great is his steadfast love toward those who fear him;
as far as the east is from the west,
    so far he removes our transgressions from us.
As a father has compassion for his children,
    so the LORD has compassion for those who fear him.
                            Psalm 103:11-13

Prayers, pp. 529-32

Closing Psalm Prayer

Bless the LORD, O my soul,
    and do not forget all his benefits —
who forgives all your iniquity,
    who heals all your diseases,
who redeems your life from the Pit.   Psalm 103:2-4a

Advent: Day 12   Second Week: Thursday

Theme: While we wait for Christ's coming at Bethlehem and again at
        the end of history, he will give us his help and we will know
        that the Lord is full of mercy.

Antiphon and Opening Prayer

> I will praise you with an upright heart. . . .
> I will observe your statutes;
> > do not utterly forsake me.   Psalm 119:7a, 8

> Lord, give me the joy of your love.
> Help me to serve you and others,
> as I wait for your coming.

Scripture Reading

> For I, the LORD your God,
> > hold your right hand;
> it is I who say to you, "Do not fear,
> > I will help you." . . .
> So that all may see and know,
> > all may consider and understand,
> that the hand of the LORD has done this,
> > the Holy One of Israel has created it.   Isaiah 41:13, 20
> > > > optional: Matthew 11:11-15

Responsorial Psalm

> I will extol you, my God and King,
> > and bless your name forever and ever.
> Every day I will bless you,
> > and praise your name forever and ever.
> Great is the LORD, and greatly to be praised;
> > his greatness is unsearchable.   Psalm 145:1-3

Prayers, pp. 529-32

Closing Psalm Prayer

> Lord, you are gracious and full of compassion,
> slow to anger and great in mercy.
> You are good to all,
> and your tender mercies are over all your works.
> > > > adapted from Psalm 145:8-9

Advent: Day 13   Second Week: Friday

Theme: We can prepare ourselves for both comings of Christ by keeping
his commandments. Observe his law today and meditate on it
continually.

Antiphon and Opening Prayer

Happy are those whose delight is in the law of the Lord.
In his law they meditate day and night. adapted from Psalm 1:1-2

All-powerful Father,
I await the healing power of Christ.
Do not let me be discouraged by weakness,
but keep me steadfast in your law while I await his coming.

Scripture Reading

Thus says the LORD,
    your Redeemer, the Holy One of Israel:
I am the LORD your God,
    who teaches you for your own good,
    who leads you in the way you should go.
O that you had paid attention to my commandments!
    Then your prosperity would have been like a river,
    and your success like the waves of the sea.   Isaiah 48:17-19
                                   optional: Matthew 11:16-18

Responsorial Psalm

Happy are those
    who do not follow the advice of the wicked,
or take the path that sinners tread,
    or sit in the seat of scoffers;
but their delight is in the law of the LORD,
    and on his law they meditate day and night.   Psalm 1:1-2

Prayers, pp. 529-32

Closing Psalm Prayer

Lord, may I be like a tree planted by the rivers of water.
It brings forth its fruit in its season.
Its leaf will not wither. adapted from Psalm 1:3

In 1995, 2006, and 2007 continue with the Dec. 17th (p. 36) devotion tomorrow.

Advent: Day 14 Second Week: Saturday

Theme: Elijah will come to prepare the way of the Lord. He calls us
into repentance from sin and into a renewal of life as we await
the Messiah.

Antiphon and Opening Prayer

Give ear, O Shepherd of Israel. . . .
Stir up your might,
and come to save us. Psalm 80:1a, 2b

Lord, you who will come soon,
make me ready for your appearing,
that I may receive your coming with great joy.

Scripture Reading

Lo, I will send you the prophet Elijah before the great and terrible
day of the LORD comes. He will turn the hearts of parents to their
children and the hearts of children to their parents, so that I will not
come and strike the land with a curse.

Malachi 4:5-6
read also Matthew 17:10-13

Responsorial Psalm

You brought a vine out of Egypt;
    you drove out the nations and planted it.
You cleared the ground for it;
    it took deep root, and filled the land.   Psalm 80:8-9

Prayers, pp. 529-32

Closing Psalm Prayer

Give us life, and we will call on your name.
Restore us, O LORD God of Hosts;
    let your face shine, that we may be saved.   Psalm 80:18b, 19

In 1995, 2000, and 2006 continue with the Dec. 17th devotion (p. 36) tomorrow.

Advent: Day 15   Third Week: Sunday

Theme: The day of the Lord is coming closer. He will soon appear in
      power and great glory. Our longing for his coming intensifies
      as the day draws near.

Antiphon and Opening Prayer

O God, you are my God, I seek you,
    my soul thirsts for you.   Psalm 63:1a

Father,
as the day of your appearing draws closer,
create within me a longing for your arrival.

Scripture Reading

Wail, for the day of the LORD is near. . . .
    Cruel, with wrath and fierce anger,
to make the earth a desolation,
    and to destroy its sinners from it.

For the stars of the heavens and their constellations
> will not give their light:
the sun will be dark at its rising,
> and the moon will not shed its light.   Isaiah 13:6, 9-10
>
> read also Mark 1:1-8

Responsorial Psalm

O God, you are my God, I seek you,
> my soul thirsts for you;
my flesh faints for you,
> as in a dry and weary land where there is no water.
So I have looked upon you in the sanctuary,
> beholding your power and glory.   Psalm 63:1-2

Prayers, pp. 529-32

Closing Psalm Prayer

Because your steadfast love is better than life,
> my lips will praise you.
So I will bless you as long as I live;
> I will lift up my hands and call on your name.   Psalm 63:3-4

In 2001, 2007, and 2012 continue with the Dec. 17th devotion (p. 36) tomorrow.

Advent: Day 16   Third Week: Monday

Theme: The star will soon rise out of Jacob. As the day draws near, our
> commitment to follow his teaching and to walk in his ways
> deepens.

Antiphon and Opening Prayer

To you, O LORD, I lift up my soul.
O my God, in you I trust. . . .
Make me to know your ways, O LORD.   Psalm 25:1-2a, 4a

Lord,
I long to walk with you,
to follow your teaching,
to await your coming,
to receive you into my life.

Scripture Reading

The oracle of one who hears the words of God,
    and knows the knowledge of the Most High,
who sees the vision of the Almighty,
    who falls down, but with his eyes uncovered:
I see him, but not now;
    I behold him, but not near —
a star shall come out of Jacob,
    and a scepter shall rise out of Israel.   Numbers 24:16-17a

Responsorial Psalm

Turn to me, and be gracious to me,
    for I am lonely and afflicted.
Relieve the troubles of my heart,
    and bring me out of my distress.
Consider my affliction and my trouble,
    and forgive all my sins.   Psalm 25:16-18

Prayers, pp. 529-32

Closing Psalm Prayer

Make me to know your ways, O LORD;
    teach me your paths.
Lead me in your truth, and teach me,
    for you are the God of my salvation;
    for you I wait all the day long.   Psalm 25:4-5

In 1996, 2002, and 2013 continue with the Dec. 17th devotion (p. 36) tomorrow.

Advent: Day 17   Third Week: Tuesday

Theme: The whole remnant of Israel waits for the coming of the Lord.
        We bless the name of the coming one and wait in peace.

Antiphon and Opening Prayer

O magnify the LORD with me,
and let us exalt his name together.
His praise shall continually be in my mouth.

                              adapted from Psalm 34:1, 3

I bless you Father,
I bless you Son,
I bless you Holy Spirit.
Bless me now as I await your coming in glory.

Scripture Reading

I will deal with all your oppressors
    at that time.
And I will save the lame
    and gather the outcast,
and I will change their shame into praise
    and renown in all the earth.
At that time I will bring you home,
    at the time when I gather you;
for I will make you renowned and praised
    among all the peoples of the earth,
when I restore your fortunes
    before your eyes, says the LORD.   Zephaniah 3:19-20
                                        read also Luke 21:29-38

Responsorial Psalm

When the righteous cry for help, the LORD hears,
    and rescues them from all their troubles.
The LORD is near to the brokenhearted,
    and saves the crushed in spirit.
Many are the afflictions of the righteous,
    but the LORD rescues them from them all.   Psalm 34:17-19

Prayers, pp. 529-32

Closing Psalm Prayer

Lord, as I await your coming,
may I keep my tongue from evil
and my lips from speaking guile.
May I depart from evil, do good, seek peace, and pursue it.

adapted from Psalm 34:13-14

In 1997, 2003, 2008, and 2014 continue with the Dec. 17th devotion (p. 36) tomorrow.

Advent: Day 18   Third Week: Wednesday

Theme: When Christ comes the heavens will open, and justice and peace
will flow forth. The peace of his coming now surrounds us.

Antiphon and Opening Prayer

Let me hear what God the LORD will speak,
for he will speak peace to his people,
to his faithful, to those who turn to him in their hearts.

Psalm 85:8

Lord, open my ears that I may hear your words of peace.
Open my heart that I may do your works of peace.

Scripture Reading

I am the LORD, and there is no other;
besides me there is no god. . . .
I form light and create darkness,
I make weal and create woe;
I the LORD do all these things.
Shower, O heavens from above,
and let the skies rain down righteousness;
let the earth open, that salvation may spring up,

and let it cause righteousness to sprout up also;
I the LORD have created it.   Isaiah 45:5a, 7-8
                                        read also Luke 7:18-23

Responsorial Psalm

LORD, you were favorable to your land;
   you restored the fortunes of Jacob.
You forgave the iniquity of your people;
   you pardoned all their sin.
You withdrew all your wrath;
   you turned from your hot anger.   Psalm 85:1-3

Prayers, pp. 529-32

Closing Psalm Prayer

Steadfast love and faithfulness will meet;
   righteousness and peace will kiss each other. . . .
The LORD will give what is good . . .
   and will make a path for his steps.   Psalm 85:10, 12, 13b

In 1998, 2009, and 2015 continue with the Dec. 17th devotion (p. 36) tomorrow.

Advent: Day 19   Third Week: Thursday

Theme: When Christ comes he will rescue us from sin. He will heal us
   and turn our mourning into a dance of joy.

Antiphon and Opening Prayer

For you have drawn me up,
   and did not let my foes rejoice over me.   Psalm 30:1

Lord, you who have lifted me up.
I lift up your name.

For you have rescued me from sin and darkness.
You are coming to save me.

Scripture Reading

Do not fear, for you will not be ashamed;
    do not be discouraged, for you will not suffer disgrace. . . .
For the LORD has called you
    like a wife forsaken and grieved in spirit,
like the wife of a man's youth when she is cast off,
    says your God. . . .
But with everlasting love I will have compassion on you,
    says the LORD, your Redeemer.   Isaiah 54:4a, 6, 8b
                                            read also Luke 7:24-30

Responsorial Psalm

I will extol you, O LORD, for you have drawn me up,
    and did not let my foes rejoice over me.
O LORD my God, I cried out to you for help,
    and you have healed me.
O LORD, you brought up my soul from Sheol,
    restored me to life from among those gone down to the Pit.
                                            Psalm 30:1-3

Prayers, pp. 529-32

Closing Psalm Prayer

Lord, I sing praises to you,
and give thanks at the remembrance of your holy name.
For weeping may endure for a night,
but joy comes in the morning.   adapted from Psalm 30:4-5

In 1993, 1999, 2004, and 2010 continue with the Dec. 17th devotion (p. 36) tomorrow.

Advent: Day 20   Third Week: Friday

Theme: As the day of Christ's coming draws near, Jerusalem becomes a
house of prayer. Our longing also turns into a prayer. And we
are blessed.

Antiphon and Opening Prayer

May God be gracious to us and bless us
and make his face to shine upon us,
that your way may be known upon earth.   Psalm 67:1-2a

Lord, I pray that my life may be a living prayer to you.
Let me wait upon your coming in prayerful anticipation.

Scripture Reading

Maintain justice, and do what is right,
for soon my salvation will come,
and my deliverance will be revealed.
Happy is the mortal who does this,
the one who holds it fast,
who keeps the Sabbath, not profaning it,
and refrains from doing any evil. . . .
For my house shall be called a house of prayer
for all peoples.   Isaiah 56:1-2, 7b
read also John 5:33-36

Responsorial Psalm

How awesome are your deeds!
Because of your great power, your enemies cringe before you.
All the earth worships you;
they sing praises to you,
sing praises to your name.   Psalm 66:3-4

Prayers, pp. 529-32

Closing Psalm Prayer

Lord, I will make a joyful shout to you;
I will sing out the honor of your name.
I will say blessed be God,
who has not turned away my prayer
nor his mercy from me!   adapted from Psalm 66:1, 2, 20

December 17

Theme: The genealogy of the one who is to come goes all the way back
to the beginning of history. He comes into our midst as one of
us.

Antiphon and Opening Prayer

Blessed be the LORD, the God of Israel,
who alone does wondrous things. . . .
May his glory fill the whole earth.   Psalm 72:18, 19b

Lord, you who created all and entered into the history of your
creation,
in the line of David,
let me, your servant, enter into the longing for your sure coming.

Scripture Reading

The son of David, the son of Abraham. . . .
And Jacob the father of Joseph the husband of Mary, of whom
Jesus was born, who is called the Messiah.
So all the generations from Abraham to David are fourteen
generations; and from David to the deportation to Babylon, fourteen
generations; and from the deportation to Babylon to the Messiah,
fourteen generations.
Matthew 1:1, 16-17

Responsorial Psalm

May he have dominion from sea to sea,
    and from the River to the ends of the earth.
May his foes bow down before him,
    and his enemies lick the dust.
May all kings fall down before him,
    all nations give him service.   Psalm 72:8, 9, 11

Prayers, pp. 529-32

Closing "O" Prayer

O Wisdom,
O Holy Word of God,
you govern all creation with your strong and tender care to me,
and show your people the way to salvation.

December 18

Theme: The one who is to come is born of a woman, Mary. His name
        is above every name. At his name every knee shall bow.

Antiphon and Opening Prayer

May his name endure forever,
    his fame continue as long as the sun.
May all nations be blessed in him;
    may they pronounce him happy.   Psalm 72:17

Lord, as the day of your appearing draws near,
increase within me a love for that name that is above every name.

Scripture Reading

. . . Before they [Joseph and Mary] lived together, she was found to
be with child from the Holy Spirit. Her husband Joseph, being a
righteous man and unwilling to expose her to public disgrace,

planned to dismiss her quietly. But . . . an angel of the Lord appeared
to him in a dream and said, "Joseph, son of David, do not be afraid
to take Mary as your wife, for the child conceived in her is from the
Holy Spirit. . . . You are to name him Jesus."

Matthew 1:18b-21

Responsorial Psalm

May his name endure forever,
  his fame continue as long as the sun. . . .
Blessed be the LORD, the God of Israel,
  who alone does wondrous things.
Blessed be his glorious name forever;
  may his glory fill the whole earth.   Psalm 72:17a, 18-19

Prayers, pp. 529-32

Closing "O" Prayer

O sacred Lord of ancient Israel,
who showed yourself to Moses in the burning bush,
who gave him the holy law in Sinai mountain,
come, stretch out your mighty hand to set us free.

December 19

Theme: John the Baptist precedes the coming of Christ. He goes before
       Christ to turn the hearts of the people toward the coming
       Messiah.

Antiphon and Opening Prayer

For you are my rock and my fortress.
For you, O Lord, are my hope.
My praise is continually of you.   adapted from Psalm 71:3, 5, 6

Lord, quicken my heart to anticipate your coming.
Prepare it as an abiding place for your Son Jesus.

Scripture Reading

Then there appeared to him an angel of the Lord. . . . But the
angel said to him, "Do not be afraid, Zechariah, for your prayer
has been heard. Your wife Elizabeth will bear you a son, and you
will name him John. . . . He will be great in the sight of the
Lord. . . . He will turn many of the people of Israel to the Lord
their God. With the spirit and power of Elijah he will go before
him, to turn the hearts of parents to their children."

Luke 1:11a, 13, 15a, 16-17a

Responsorial Psalm

O God, do not be far from me;
 O my God, make haste to help me. . . .
But I will hope continually,
 and will praise you yet more and more.
My mouth will tell of your righteous acts,
 of your deeds of salvation all day long.   Psalm 71:12, 14-15a

Prayers, pp. 529-32

Closing "O" Prayer

O flower of Jesse's stem, you have been raised up as a sign to all
peoples.
Kings stand in your presence.
The nations bow down in worship before you.
Let nothing keep you from coming to our aid.

December 20

Theme: Mary is told that she will bring forth Jesus, who will reign over
 the world forever. The earth and all things belong to him.

Antiphon and Opening Prayer

Lift up your heads, O gates!
that the King of glory may come in.
Who is the King of Glory?
The LORD of hosts, he is the King of Glory. Psalm 24:7, 8, 10

Lord, as you are about to enter the world you created,
may I, your creature, receive you with gladness of heart.

Scripture Reading

. . . Greetings, favored one! The Lord is with you. . . . Do not be afraid, Mary, for you have found favor with God. And now, you will conceive in your womb and bear a son, and you will name him Jesus. He will be great, and will be called the Son of the Most High. . . . He will reign over the house of Jacob forever, and of his kingdom there will be no end.

Luke 1:28, 30-32a, 33

Responsorial Psalm

Who shall ascend the hill of the LORD?
And who shall stand in his holy place?
Those who have clean hands and pure hearts,
who do not lift up their souls to what is false,
and do not swear deceitfully.
They will receive blessings from the LORD,
and vindication from the God of their salvation. Psalm 24:3-5

Prayers, pp. 529-32

Closing "O" Prayer

O key of David, O royal power of Israel,
come break down the prison walls of death
for those who dwell in darkness and the shadows of death.
Lead your captive people into freedom.

December 21

Theme: Mary visits Elizabeth. Elizabeth confirms that Mary is blessed
        among women. The whole earth is about to be blessed through
        him.

Antiphon and Opening Prayer

Our soul waits for the LORD. . . .
Our heart is glad in him,
        because we trust in his holy name.   Psalm 33:20-21

Lord, my soul waits and longs for your coming.
Let me trust in you so that, when you appear, my heart may
rejoice.

Scripture Reading

When Elizabeth heard Mary's greeting, the child leaped in her womb.
And Elizabeth was filled with the Holy Spirit and exclaimed with a
loud cry, "Blessed are you among women, and blessed is the fruit of
your womb. . . . And blessed is she who believed that there would
be a fulfillment of what was spoken to her by the Lord."
                                                        Luke 1:41-42, 45

Responsorial Psalm

Truly the eye of the LORD is on those who fear him,
        on those who hope in his steadfast love,
to deliver their soul from death,
        and to keep them alive in famine. . . .
Let your steadfast love, O LORD, be upon us,
        even as we hope in you.   Psalm 33:18, 19, 22

Prayers, pp. 529-32

Closing "O" Prayer

O radiant Dawn, Splendor of Eternal Light, Sun of Justice,
shine on those who dwell in darkness and the shadow of death.

December 22

Theme: Mary blessed the Lord because he had done great things. We
join with Mary to bless and extol God, who brings us his
redemption.

Antiphon and Opening Prayer

There is none holy like the Lord,
for there is none besides you,
nor is there any rock like our God.

Lord, you who do great things,
I extol and magnify your holy name.
For you are the God of my salvation.

Scripture Reading

My soul magnifies the Lord,
    and my spirit rejoices in God my Savior,
for he has looked with favor on the lowliness of his servant . . .
for the Mighty One has done great things for me,
    and holy is his name.
His mercy is for those who fear him
    from generation to generation.   Luke 1:46-50

Responsorial Psalm

Praise the LORD! Praise, O servants of the LORD,
    praise the name of the LORD!
Blessed be the name of the LORD
    from this time on and forevermore.
From the rising of the sun to its setting
    the name of the LORD is to be praised.   Psalm 113:1-3

Prayers, pp. 529-32

Closing "O" Prayer

O King of all nations,
the only joy of every human heart;
O keystone of the mighty arch of humankind,
come and save your creature,
fashioned from the dust.

December 23

Theme: The birth of John the Baptist assures us that the birth of Christ
is soon. He will come to set us free and save us.

Antiphon and Opening Prayer

O my God, in you I trust;
    for you are the God of my salvation;
    for you I wait all day long.   Psalm 25:2a, 5b

Lord,
as the day of your coming approaches,
let my soul be lifted up,
let my heart sing,
for you are the God of my salvation.

Scripture Reading

Now the time came for Elizabeth to give birth, and she bore a son. . . .
They were going to name him Zechariah after his father. But his
mother said, "No; he is to be called John." . . . Then they began
motioning to his father to find out what name he wanted to give
him. He asked for a writing tablet and wrote, "His name is John."
And all of them were amazed.

Luke 1:57-63

Responsorial Psalm

Who are they that fear the LORD?
He will teach them the way that they should choose.
They will abide in prosperity,
and their children shall possess the land.
The friendship of the LORD is for those who fear him,
and he makes his covenant known to them.   Psalm 25:12-14

Prayers, pp. 529-32

Closing "O" Prayer

O Immanuel, King, and Lawgiver,
desire of all nations,
Savior of all people,
come, and set us free,
O Lord our God.

December 24

Theme: The appointed time has come. The seed of David is about to be
born. The kingdom of God will soon be established.

Antiphon and Opening Prayer

With my mouth I will proclaim your faithfulness
to all generations.
Let the heavens praise your wonders, O LORD.   Psalm 89:1b, 5a

Lord,
may I, like your servants Elizabeth and Mary,
open my heart and life to receive you.

Scripture Reading

Go and tell my servant David: Thus says the LORD. . . . When your
days are fulfilled and you lie down with your ancestors, I will raise

up your offspring after you, who shall come forth from your body, and I will establish his kingdom. He shall build a house for my name, and I will establish the throne of his kingdom forever. I will be a Father to him, and he shall be a son to me.

II Samuel 7:5, 12-14a
read also Luke 1:67-79

Responsorial Psalm

The heavens are yours, the earth also is yours;
the world and all that is in it — you have founded them. . . .
You have a mighty arm;
strong is your hand, high your right hand.   Psalm 89:11, 13

Prayers, pp. 529-32

Closing "O" Prayer

Lord, I will sing of your mercies forever;
with my mouth I will make known your faithfulness.
The heavens will praise your wonders, O Lord;
for who in the heavens can be compared to you, O Lord.
Lord of hosts, you are mighty.   adapted from Psalm 89:1-8

Christmas

The overall theme of Christmas is "God among us." Centuries before the birth of Christ Isaiah wrote: "Therefore the Lord himself will give you a sign. Look, the young woman is with child and shall bear a son, and shall name him Immanuel" (Isaiah 7:14). Matthew translated the word *Immanuel* for his readers, reminding them that it means, "God is with us" (Matthew 1:23).

John also emphasized the theme of "God with us" in the prologue to his Gospel. He tells us that Christ has a preexistent status with the Father: "In the beginning was the Word, and the Word was with God, and the Word was God" (John 1:1). This Word, he reminds us, came into the world as the "Light" of the world. And in him, that is, in Jesus, "the Word became flesh and lived among us, and we have seen his glory, the glory as of the Father's only Son, full of grace and truth" (John 1:14).

The theme of God among us reminds us that Christmas is the time when we celebrate the fulfillment of our Advent longing. The incarnation is the great mystery revealed. It is the mystery of God's love for his world. For in this mystery we celebrate more than the birth of Jesus. We celebrate the mystery of salvation that has begun to take place. For the Babe born in Bethlehem has come to redeem the world, to reconcile an alienated race of people to God and to each other.

For this reason our meditation during Christmas centers around the wonder of who this child is. During the first three days of Christmas our focus is on the incarnation itself, God made flesh, Then during the next four days (which brings us to the end of December) we center on the heavenly nature of Jesus. He is the image of the invisible God, the Creator and Redeemer, the first and the last, the fullness of God. On January 1st our meditation and prayers turn to what Jesus said of himself. We draw on some of the great "I am" passages . . . "I am the light of the world; I am the bread of life; I am the door; I am the way; I am the true vine."

The Psalms chosen for the Christmas season are psalms of response to this one who has become incarnate. They echo the dual sentiment of Christ's rule in the world and our faith and trust in him. The hymns to be sung during Christmas capture the mood as well. . . . "Joy to the World" and "What Child is This?"

The purpose of these devotions is to help us experience the joy of Christ. The four weeks of Advent were weeks of preparation. Now that the Savior has come we are to enjoy his presence. The daily prayers for Christmas will assist us in achieving this sense of joy and will allow God's word to do his work in our hearts and lives.

Christmas Day   December 25

Theme: Today is a great day of rejoicing in heaven and on earth. We
       join the cherubim, the seraphim, and all the angels saying,
       "Glory to God in the highest."

Antiphon and Opening Prayer

[The Lord] said to me, "You are my son;
        today I have begotten you."   Psalm 2:7

Lord Jesus Christ,
on this day you have visited the earth.
May you also be born in my heart.

Scripture Reading

. . . Do not be afraid; for see — I am bringing you good news of great joy for all the people: to you is born this day in the city of David a Savior, who is the Messiah, the Lord. . . . And suddenly there was with the angel a multitude of the heavenly host, praising God and saying,

"Glory to God in the highest heaven,
        and on earth peace among those whom he favors."
                                                   Luke 2:10-11, 13-14

Responsorial Psalm

I will tell of the decree of the LORD:
He said to me, "You are my son;
    today I have begotten you.
Ask of me, and I will make the nations your heritage,
    and the ends of the earth your possession."   Psalm 2:7-8

Prayers, pp. 529-32

Closing Psalm Prayer

Praise the LORD, all you nations!
    Extol him, all you peoples!
For great is his steadfast love toward us. . . .
Praise the LORD!   Psalm 117:1-2

Second Day of Christmas   December 26

Theme: Jesus Christ is the Word made flesh. God became incarnate in
    order to save us from our sin and bring us to the Father.

Antiphon and Opening Prayer

My soul longs, indeed it faints
    for the courts of the LORD;
my heart and my flesh sing for joy
    to the living God.   Psalm 84:2

O Incarnate One,
blessed are you who has come to live in my world,
to share in my life,
and to take me up to heaven.

Scripture Reading

In the beginning was the Word, and the Word was with God, and
the Word was God. . . . In him was life, and the life was the light
of all people. The light shines in the darkness, and the darkness did
not overcome it. . . .

And the Word became flesh and lived among us, and we have
seen his glory, the glory as of a father's only son, full of grace and
truth.

John 1:1, 4-5, 14

Responsorial Psalm

Steadfast love and faithfulness will meet;
    righteousness and peace will kiss each other.
Faithfulness will spring up from the ground,
    and righteousness will look down from the sky. . . .
Righteousness will go before him,
    and will make a path for his steps.   Psalm 85:10-11, 13

Prayers, pp. 529-32

Closing Psalm Prayer

LORD, you were favorable to your land;
    you restored the fortunes of Jacob.
You forgave the iniquity of your people;
    you pardoned all their sin.
You withdrew all your wrath.   Psalm 85:1-3a

Third Day of Christmas   December 27

Theme: The incarnation was no mere appearance. The witness of scrip-
    ture is that Jesus was truly flesh and blood — one of us.

Antiphon and Opening Prayer

And all people shall see it together,
for the mouth of the LORD has spoken.   Isaiah 40:5

Lord Jesus,
you who lived among us,

who took on our grief and sorrows,
come and take up residence in me, your servant.

Scripture Reading

We declare to you what was from the beginning, what we have heard,
what we have seen with our eyes, what we have looked at and
touched with our hands, concerning the word of life . . . we declare
to you what we have seen and heard so that you also may have
fellowship with us; and truly our fellowship is with the Father and
with his Son Jesus Christ. We are writing these things so that our
joy may be complete.
This is the message we have heard from him.

I John 1:1, 3-5a

Responsorial Psalm

Praise the LORD!
Praise, O servants of the LORD;
    praise the name of the LORD!
Blessed be the name of the LORD
    from this time on and forevermore.
From the rising of the sun to its setting
    the name of the LORD is to be praised.   Psalm 113:1-3

Prayers, pp. 529-32

Closing Psalm Prayer

Lord, you are high above all the nations,
and your glory is above the heavens.
Who is like you, O Lord my God?
For you humble yourself to behold the things that
are in heaven and on the earth.   adaptation of Psalm 113:4-6

Fourth Day of Christmas   December 28

Theme: Jesus the man is truly God. The infant is the image of the
invisible God. The babe in Bethlehem is the Creator and Redeemer.

Antiphon and Opening Prayer

Praise the LORD! . . .
Praise the LORD, for the LORD is good;
    sing to his name, for he is gracious.   Psalm 135:1a, 3

Lord Jesus,
you who are one with the Father,
I praise and adore you,
for you have made the invisible God present.

Scripture Reading

For in him all things in heaven and on earth were created, things
visible and invisible, whether thrones or dominions or rulers or
powers — all things have been created through him and for him. He
himself is before all things, and in him all things hold together. He
is the head of the body, the church; he is the beginning, the firstborn
from the dead, so that he might come to have first place in everything.
                                         Colossians 1:16-18

Responsorial Psalm

The heavens are telling the glory of God;
    and the firmament proclaims his handiwork.
Day to day pours forth speech,
    and night to night declares knowledge.
There is no speech, nor are there words;
    their voice is not heard;
yet their voice goes out through all the earth.   Psalm 19:1-4a

Prayers, pp. 529-32

Closing Psalm Prayer

> O brightness of his glory, express image of his person.
> You who uphold all things by the Word of your power.
> You who purge our sins,
> I will sing praises to your name today and always.
>
> adapted from Hebrews 1:3

Fifth Day of Christmas December 29

Theme: This infant who is fully man and fully God has come among us
to call us to himself, to the healing and salvation that he brings.

Antiphon and Opening Prayer

> I call upon the LORD, who is worthy to be praised,
> so I shall be saved from my enemies. Psalm 18:3

> Lord, it is in you I wish to abide.
> You alone are my rock and my fortress.
> In you alone I trust.

Scripture Reading

> . . . While Jesus was standing there, he cried out, "Let anyone who
> is thirsty come to me, and let the one who believes in me drink. As
> the scripture has said, 'Out of this believer's heart shall flow rivers
> of living water.' " . . .
> When they heard these words, some in the crowd said, "This is
> really the prophet." Others said, "This is the Messiah."
>
> John 7:37b-38, 40-41a

Responsorial Psalm

> The LORD is my rock, my fortress, and my deliverer,
> my God, my rock in whom I take refuge,
> my shield, and the horn of my salvation, my stronghold.
> I call upon the LORD, who is worthy to be praised. Psalm 18:2-3

Prayers, pp. 529-32

Closing Psalm Prayer

He drew me out of mighty waters.
He delivered me from my strong enemy. . . .
He brought me out in a broad place;
 he delivered me, because he delighted in me.

Psalm 18:16, 17, 19

Sixth Day of Christmas December 30

Theme: The child in the nativity is no ordinary child. This infant is the
 Alpha and the Omega, the Beginning and the End. He is to be
 worshiped.

Antiphon and Opening Prayer

That will I seek after:
to live in the house of the LORD
all the days of my life. Psalm 27:4

Lord Jesus, you who are the beginning and ending of all things,
may I dwell in you, and you in me forever.

Scripture Reading

. . . I heard behind me a loud voice like a trumpet. . . .
 Then I turned to see whose voice it was that spoke to me. . . .
 When I saw him, I fell at his feet as though dead. But he placed
his right hand on me, saying, "Do not be afraid; I am the First and
the Last."

Revelation 1:10, 12, 17

Responsorial Psalm

His glory is great through your help;
 splendor and majesty you bestow on him.

You bestow on him blessings forever;
    you make him glad with the joy of your presence. . . .
We will sing and praise your power.   Psalm 21:5-6, 13b

Prayers, pp. 529-32

Closing Psalm Prayer

Some trust in chariots and some in horses,
but I will remember the name of the Lord my God.
In him alone will I trust.   adapted from Psalm 20:7

Seventh Day of Christmas   December 31

Theme: In Jesus the fullness of God dwells. He is over all principalities
       and powers. It is he and he alone that all people praise.

Antiphon and Opening Prayer

Bless the LORD, O my soul!
    and all that is within me,
        bless his Holy Name.   Psalm 103:1

Lord Jesus, babe of Bethlehem,
you who are the fullness of God,
come and fill me with your presence,
that I might praise you.

Scripture Reading

. . . The knowledge of God's mystery, that is, Christ himself, in whom
are hidden all the treasures of wisdom and knowledge. . . .
    As you therefore have received Christ Jesus the Lord, continue
to live your lives in him. . . .
    For in him the whole fullness of deity dwells bodily, and you have
come to fullness in him, who is the head of every ruler and authority.
        Colossians 2:2b-3, 6, 9-10

Responsorial Psalm

> Praise the LORD from the heavens;
>   Praise him in the heights!
> Praise him, all his angels;
>   praise him, all his host!
> Praise him, sun and moon;
>   praise him, all you shining stars!
> Praise him.   Psalm 148:1-4a

Prayers, pp. 529-32

Closing Psalm Prayer

> Lord, let your name be exalted and
> your glory be above the earth.
> Let fire, hail, snow, and clouds praise you.
> Let mountains and all hills praise you,
> and let me praise you by my lips and life.
>   adapted from Psalm 148:7-14

Eighth Day of Christmas   January 1

Theme: This child who is the light of the world has come to cast away
       the darkness and calls us to walk in the light.

Antiphon and Opening Prayer

> Whom shall I fear?
> The LORD is the stronghold of my life;
> of whom shall I be afraid?   Psalm 27:1

> Lord Jesus, you who are the light of the world,
> cast your light upon me that I might walk in your ways,
> and delight in your will.

Scripture Reading

. . . "I am the light of the world. Whoever follows me will never walk in darkness, but will have the light of life." Then the Pharisees said to him, "You are testifying on your own behalf; your testimony is not valid." Jesus answered, "Even if I testify on my own behalf, my testimony is valid because I know where I have come from and where I am going."

John 8:12-14

Responsorial Psalm

Great is the LORD and greatly to be praised. . . .
As we have heard, so have we seen
    in the city of the LORD of hosts,
in the city of our God,
    which God establishes forever.   Psalm 48:1a, 8

Prayers, pp. 529-32

Closing Psalm Prayer

Lord, you have established your light in the world.
I will clap my hands,
I will shout with the voice of triumph.
For you, O Lord, are awesome;
you are a great King over all the earth.

adapted from Psalm 47:1-2

Ninth Day of Christmas   January 2

Theme: Jesus is the Bread of Life. No one shall live by bread alone, but by every word that proceeds from Jesus' mouth.

Antiphon and Opening Prayer

Praise the LORD with the lyre. . . .
Sing to him a new song;
>   play skillfully on the strings, with loud shouts! Psalm 33:2a, 3

Lord Jesus, you who are the Bread of Life,
let me feed on you.
Satisfy my hunger and fill me with righteousness.

Scripture Reading

Very truly, I tell you, whoever believes has eternal life. I am the bread
of life. Your ancestors ate the manna in the wilderness, and they
died. This is the bread that comes down from heaven, so that one
may eat of it and not die. I am the living bread that came down
from heaven. Whoever eats of this bread will live forever; and the
bread that I will give for the life of the world is my flesh.

John 6:47-51

Responsorial Psalm

Truly the eye of the LORD is on those who fear him,
>   on those who hope in his steadfast love,
to deliver their soul from death,
>   and to keep them alive in famine.
Let your steadfast love, O LORD, be upon us,
>   even as we hope in you.   Psalm 33:18-19, 22

Prayers, pp. 529-32

Closing Psalm Prayer

Happy are those who take refuge in him.
O fear the LORD, you his holy ones,
>   for those who fear him have no want. . . .
But those who seek the LORD lack no good thing.

Psalm 34:8b-9, 10b

Tenth Day of Christmas   January 3

Theme: This Jesus whom the shepherds worship, who is he? He is the
       door of the sheep. No one can come to the pasture except
       through this door.

Antiphon and Opening Prayer

Blessed be the Lord
    who daily bears us up;
    God is our salvation!   Psalm 68:19

Lord Jesus,
you who entered our life to be the door to heaven,
daily turn me toward yourself
that I may walk in the way of truth.

Scripture Reading

. . . Anyone who does not enter the sheepfold by the gate but climbs
in by another way is a thief and a bandit. The one who enters by
the gate is the shepherd of the sheep. . . .
     . . . Very truly, I tell you, I am the gate for the sheep. . . . I am
the gate. Whoever enters by me will be saved, and will come in and
go out and find pasture.

                                                   John 10:1-2, 7, 9

Responsorial Psalm

Sing to God, O kingdoms of the earth;
    sing praises to the Lord. . . .
Ascribe power to God,
    whose majesty is over Israel;
    and whose power is in the skies. . . .
Blessed be God!   Psalm 68:32, 34, 35b

Prayers, pp. 529-32

Closing Psalm Prayer

Blessed be the LORD, the God of Israel,
    who alone does wondrous things.
Blessed be his glorious name forever;
    may his glory fill the whole earth.
      Amen.   Psalm 72:18-19

Eleventh Day of Christmas   January 4

Theme: The angel told David that Jesus "will save his people from their sins." Now Jesus declares that he alone is the way to the Father.

Antiphon and Opening Prayer

The heavens are yours, the earth also is yours;
    the world and all that is in it.   Psalm 89:11

Lord,
you who are the way, the truth, and the life,
to you belong all things.
I give you myself, Lord.

Scripture Reading

Jesus said to him, "I am the way, and the truth, and the life. No one comes to the Father except through me. If you know me, you will know my Father also. From now on you do know him and have seen him. . . ."

"Believe me that I am in the Father and the Father is in me; but if you do not, then believe me because of the works themselves. . . . If in my name, you ask me for anything, I will do it."

                            John 14:6-7, 11, 14

Responsorial Psalm

But you, O LORD, are a shield around me,
    my glory, and the one who lifts up my head.

I cry aloud to the LORD,
    and he answers me from his holy hill.
I lie down and sleep;
    I wake again, for the LORD sustains me.   Psalm 3:3-5

Prayers, pp. 529-32

Closing Psalm Prayer

Incline your ear, O LORD, and answer me,
    for I am poor and needy.
Preserve my life, for I am devoted to you. . . .
For you, Lord, are good and forgiving,
    abounding in steadfast love to all who call on you.
                            Psalm 86:1-2a, 5

Twelfth Day of Christmas   January 5

Theme: Jesus is the true vine. We are called to abide in him. God has
      given him the nations of the world.

Antiphon and Opening Prayer

I will give thanks to the LORD with my whole heart. . . .
Great are the works of the LORD. . . .
And his righteousness endures forever.   Psalm 111:1a, 2a, 3b

Lord Jesus, you alone are the true vine,
the one in whom the branches find life.
Send your life into me that I may grow in you.

Scripture Reading

I am the true vine, and my Father is the vinegrower. He removes
every branch in me that bears no fruit. Every branch that bears fruit
he prunes, to make it bear more fruit. . . . Abide in me as I abide in
you. Just as the branch cannot bear fruit by itself unless it abides in

the vine, neither can you unless you abide in me. I am the vine, you are the branches.

John 15:1-2, 4-5a

Responsorial Psalm

Serve the LORD with fear,
    with trembling kiss his feet,
or he will be angry, and you will perish in the way;
    for his wrath is quickly kindled.
Happy are all who take refuge in him.   Psalm 2:11

Prayers, pp. 529-32

Closing Psalm Prayer

Rise up, O LORD!
    Deliver me, O my God! . . .
Deliverance belongs to the LORD;
    may your blessing be on your people!   Psalm 3:7a, 8

Epiphany

If we are going to achieve the greatest possible benefit from the prayers during Epiphany we need to know first of all that Epiphany, which means "manifestation," has to do with the manifestation of Jesus to the world as Savior.

The principal New Testament account that captures the meaning of Epiphany is the story of the coming of the Wise Men to worship Jesus. One of the most important facts about these men is their point of origin. They were, the text tells, "from the East." In other words, they were Gentiles. Christ, this text proclaims, is manifested to the Gentiles. The gospel goes beyond the borders of Israel to include the whole world. Christ is the Savior not only of Israel, but of all people everywhere and in every time.

Next, we should approach our prayer life during the season after Epiphany with the realization that the Christ who is manifested to the world will manifest himself to us. Two of the primary accounts which manifest Jesus as Lord are the baptism and the wedding in Cana. In the baptism, Jesus is revealed by the voice from the Father, which proclaims, "This is my Son, the Beloved, with whom I am well pleased" (Matthew 3:17). Then at the wedding feast Jesus reveals his supernatural power by turning the water into wine (John 2:1-11).

Throughout the Epiphany season we are encountered again and again by one manifestation of Christ after another. The readings and prayers carry us through his earthly life clear up to his condemnation.

What we want to accomplish for ourselves during Epiphany is this: First, we want to increase in faith. We want the conviction that *Jesus is* to be deepened in our own mind, heart, and will. Second, as Jesus manifests himself to us, we want to ask how we can manifest him to our friends and neighbors. Epiphany is a good time to take a look at your own witness. Epiphany will truly take effect in your life if you commit yourself to share your faith with at least one person during this season.

January 6

Theme: In the visit of the wise men, Jesus is manifested to the Gentiles.
Through this we understand that Christ's work extends beyond
Israel to the whole world.

Antiphon and Opening Prayer

Here is my servant, whom I uphold,
my chosen, in whom my soul delights;
I have put my spirit upon him.   Isaiah 42:1a

Lord God,
you sent forth your Son for us all.
Grant that we who believe in him
may be encouraged in our faith
and strengthened in our witness.

Scripture Reading

In the time of King Herod, after Jesus was born in Bethlehem of
Judea, wise men from the East came to Jerusalem, asking, "Where
is the child who has been born king of the Jews? For we observed
his star at its rising, and have come to pay him homage." . . .
    On entering the house, they saw the child with Mary his mother;
and they knelt down and paid him homage.

Matthew 2:1-3, 11a
optional: Isaiah 52:7-10

Responsorial Psalm

He has pity on the weak and the needy,
and saves the lives of the needy.

From oppression and violence he redeems their life;
and precious is their blood in his sight.   Psalm 72:13-14

Prayers, pp. 529-32

Closing Psalm Prayer

Blessed be you, Lord God,
God of Israel and Lord of all,
who only does wondrous things.
Blessed be your glorious name,
let the whole earth be filled with your glory.

adapted from Psalm 72:18-19

January 7

Theme: Today Christ is manifested as the one who has power over
nature. We bless him who has come to bless the world.

Antiphon and Opening Prayer

Bless the LORD, O my soul,
and all that is within me,
bless his holy name!   Psalm 103:1

O Lord, I will bless and extol your Holy Name.
For you are manifested in all the world
through your works.

Scripture Reading

On the third day there was a wedding in Cana of Galilee. . . . When
the wine gave out, the mother of Jesus . . . said to the servants, "Do
whatever he tells you.". . . Jesus said to them, "Fill the jars with
water." . . . When the steward tasted the water that had become
wine . . . he said, "You have kept the good wine until now." Jesus

did this, the first of his signs, in Cana of Galilee, and revealed his
glory; and his disciples believed in him.

John 2:1a, 3a, 5, 7, 9-11
optional: Isaiah 52:3-6

Responsorial Psalm

Bless the LORD, O you his angels,
    you mighty ones who do his bidding. . . .
Bless the LORD, all his works,
    in all places of his dominion.
Bless the LORD, O my soul.   Psalm 103:20, 22

Prayers, pp. 529-32

Closing Psalm Prayer

O Lord, you have been mindful of us.
You have blessed the house of Israel.
You have blessed those who fear you.
I will bless you, O Lord,
and praise your name forever!   adapted from Psalm 115:12-13

In 1995, 2006, and 2012 go to the first Sunday after Epiphany (p. 73) tomorrow.

January 8

Theme: Today Christ is manifested as the one who has power over
       illness. We give thanks to God that he has become our salvation.

Antiphon and Opening Prayer

O give thanks to the LORD, for he is good. . . .
The LORD is my strength and my might;
    he has become my salvation.   Psalm 118:1a, 14

Lord, you who manifested your power in Cana of Galilee,
manifest your strength and power in my life.
And let me be a witness to your power.

Scripture Reading

Then [Jesus] came again to Cana in Galilee where he had changed
the water into wine. Now there was a royal official whose son lay
ill in Capernaum. . . . The official said to him, "Sir, come down
before my little boy dies." Jesus said to him, "Go; your son will live."
The man believed the word that Jesus spoke to him and started on
his way. . . . Now this was the second sign that Jesus did after coming
from Judea to Galilee.

John 4:46, 49-50, 54
optional: Isaiah 52:3-6

Responsorial Psalm

The stone that the builders rejected
has become the chief cornerstone.
This is the LORD's doing;
it is marvelous in our eyes.
This is the day that the LORD has made;
let us rejoice and be glad in it. Psalm 118:22-24

Prayers, pp. 529-32

Closing Psalm Prayer

Praise the LORD, all you nations!
Extol him, all you peoples!
For great is his steadfast love toward us,
and the faithfulness of the LORD endures forever.
Praise the LORD! Psalm 117

In 1994, 2000, 2005, and 2011 go to the first Sunday after Epiphany (p. 73) tomorrow.

January 9

Theme: Today Jesus manifests his power over infirmities. Like the ill
man beside the pool, we need to respond in faith to Christ.

Antiphon and Opening Prayer

The LORD will keep your going out and your coming in
    from this time on and forevermore.   Psalm 121:8

Lord Jesus,
you manifested yourself as sent from God.
Manifest yourself in my life,
and let me manifest you in my life.

Scripture Reading

Now in Jerusalem by the Sheep Gate there is a pool, called in Hebrew
Beth-zatha, which has five porticoes. In these lay many invalids —
blind, lame, and paralyzed. One man was there who had been ill for
thirty-eight years. . . . Jesus said to him, "Stand up, take your mat
and walk." At once the man was made well, and he took up his mat
and began to walk. . . .
    The man went away and told the Jews that it was Jesus who
had made him well.

John 5:2-5, 8, 15
optional: Isaiah 63:1-5

Responsorial Psalm

The LORD will keep you from all evil;
    he will keep your life.
The LORD will keep
    your going out and your coming in
    from this time on and forevermore.   Psalm 121:7-8

Prayers, pp. 529-32

Closing Psalm Prayer

[Lord, I acknowledge your power this day]
I lift up my eyes to the hills —
    from where will my help come?
My help comes from the LORD,
    who made heaven and earth.   Psalm 121:1-2

In 1999 and 2010 go to the first Sunday after Epiphany (p. 73) tomorrow.

January 10

Theme: Today Jesus manifests his power over nature in the multiplica-
        tion of the loaves and fishes. Like the crowd, we confess that
        he is the prophet sent of God.

Antiphon and Opening Prayer

All the kings of the earth shall praise you, O Lord.
They shall sing of your ways, for great is your glory.
                        adapted from Psalm 138:4-5

Lord, your glory is great over all the earth.
For you have manifested yourself as the King over nature and all
things.
I bless your holy name.

Scripture Reading

When he looked up and saw a large crowd coming toward him,
Jesus said to Philip, "Where are we to buy bread for these people to
eat?" . . . One of his disciples, Andrew, Simon Peter's brother, said
to him, "There is a boy here who has five barley loaves and two
fish. But what are they among so many people?" . . . Jesus took the
loaves, and when he had given thanks, he distributed them to those
who were seated; so also the fish, as much as they wanted. . . . When

the people saw the sign that he had done, they began to say, "This
is indeed the prophet who is to come into the world."

John 6:5, 8, 11, 14

optional: Isaiah 65:1-9

Responsorial Psalm

I give you thanks, O LORD, with my whole heart . . .
> you have exalted your name and your word
> above everything.
On the day I called, you answered me,
> you increased my strength of soul.   Psalm 138:1a, 2b-3

Prayers, pp. 529-32

Closing Psalm Prayer

Lord, though I walk in the midst
of trouble, you will revive me.
You will stretch out your hand
and perfect that which concerns me.
Your mercy, O Lord, endures forever.

adapted from Psalm 139:7-8

In 1998, 2004, and 2009 go to the first Sunday after Epiphany (p. 73) tomorrow.

January 11

Theme: In the ancient world the raging sea was a symbol of the evil
     powers. When Jesus calmed the sea, this symbolized his power
     over evil.

Antiphon and Opening Prayer

Lord, you are upright,
you are my rock.
There is no unrighteousness in you.   adapted from Psalm 92:15

Lord, you manifest yourself as victor over all powers
in land and sea, and over all the earth.
Let my praises be lifted to you alone, for you are God.

Scripture Reading

When evening came, his disciples went down to the sea, got into a
boat, and started across the sea to Capernaum. . . . The sea became
rough because a strong wind was blowing. . . . They saw Jesus
walking on the sea and coming near the boat, and they were terrified.
But he said to them, "It is I; do not be afraid." Then they wanted
to take him into the boat and immediately the boat reached the land
toward which they were going.

John 6:16-17a, 18, 19b-21
optional: Isaiah 65:13-16

Responsorial Psalm

It is good to give thanks to the Lord,
and to sing praises to your name,
to declare your lovingkindness and your faithfulness.
For you, Lord, have made me glad through your work.

adapted from Psalm 92:1-4

Prayers, pp. 529-32

Closing Psalm Prayer

Lord, I will triumph in the works of your hand;
your works are great,
your thoughts are very deep,
and you, O Lord, are on high forevermore.

adapted from Psalm 92:5-8

In 1997, 2003, and 2014 go to the first Sunday after Epiphany (p. 73) tomorrow.

January 12

Theme: The manifestation of Jesus through his miracles points to one
conclusion and one alone: Jesus is Lord!

Antiphon and Opening Prayer

Make a joyful noise to the LORD, all the earth;
  break forth in joyous song, and sing praises.   Psalm 98:4

Lord, you make the blind to see and the lame to walk.
Surely you are the Lord the Messiah, the King of the universe.
I worship and adore you.

Scripture Reading

As he [Jesus] walked along, he saw a man blind from birth. . . .
[Jesus said,] "As long as I am in the world, I am the light of the
world." When he had said this, he spat on the ground and made
mud with the saliva and spread the mud on the man's eyes, saying
to him, "Go, wash in the pool of Siloam" (which means Sent). Then
he went and washed and came back able to see. . . .
    The Pharisees said to him, "What do you say about him? It was
your eyes he opened." . . .
    The man answered, "If this man were not from God, he could
do nothing."

John 9:1, 5-7, 17, 30a, 33
optional: Isaiah 66:1-2, 22-23

Responsorial Psalm

O sing to the LORD a new song,
  for he has done marvelous things.
His right hand and his holy arm
  have gotten him victory.
The LORD has made known his victory.   Psalm 98:1-2a

Prayers, pp. 529-32

Closing Psalm Prayer

> Lord, I will sing to you with the harp,
> I will shout joyfully before you, the King.
> For you are coming to judge the earth;
> with righteousness you will judge the world
> and the peoples with equity.   adapted from Psalm 98:5-9

First Week after Epiphany   Sunday

Theme: At his baptism, Jesus is publicly proclaimed to be the Son of
       God, the Messiah. We submit ourselves to him as Lord.

Antiphon and Opening Prayer

> Here is my servant, whom I uphold,
>   my chosen, in whom my soul delights;
> I have put my Spirit upon him.   Isaiah 42:1

> Lord Jesus,
> you came among us to bear our sins and save us,
> I confess that you and you alone are the Lord, the Christ.

Scripture Reading

Then Jesus came from Galilee to John at the Jordan, to be baptized
by him. . . . And when Jesus had been baptized, just as he came up
from the water, suddenly the heavens were opened to him and he
saw the Spirit of God descending like a dove and alighting on him.
And a voice from heaven said, "This is my Son, the Beloved, with
whom I am well pleased."

> Matthew 3:13, 16-17
> optional: Genesis 1:1-3

Responsorial Psalm

> You love righteousness and hate wickedness.
> Therefore God, your God, has anointed you
>   with the oil of gladness beyond your companions.   Psalm 45:7

Prayers, pp. 529-32

Closing Psalm Prayer

> Lord Jesus Christ, you are the most handsome of men;
> grace is poured upon your lips;
> therefore God has blessed you forever
> and the peoples fall under you.   adapted from Psalm 45:2, 5

First Week after Epiphany   Monday

Theme: After the Baptism, our Lord is driven into the wilderness. Here
        he demonstrates his power over the temptations of the evil one.

Antiphon and Opening Prayer

> Many are rising against me;
> many are saying to me,
>   "There is no help for you in God."   Psalm 3:1b-2

> Lord Jesus, you who were tempted in all ways,
> deliver me from my temptations
> and grant me the faith to trust in your power over evil.

Scripture Reading

> The beginning of the good news of Jesus Christ, the Son of God. . . .
>   In those days Jesus came from Nazareth of Galilee and was
> baptized by John in the Jordan. . . .
>   And the Spirit immediately drove him out into the wilderness. He

was in the wilderness forty days, tempted by Satan; and he was with
the wild beasts; and the angels waited on him.

Mark 1:1, 9, 12-13
optional: Genesis 2:4-25

Responsorial Psalm

Rise up, O LORD!
    Deliver me, O my God!
For you strike all my enemies on the cheek;
    you break the teeth of the wicked.
Deliverance belongs to the LORD;
    may your blessing be on your people!   Psalm 3:7-8

Prayers, pp. 529-32

Closing Psalm Prayer

Lord, I lay down and sleep,
I awake, for you sustain me.
I will not be afraid of those who set themselves against me.
For you have broken the teeth of the ungodly.

adapted from Psalm 3:5-7

First Week after Epiphany   Tuesday

Theme: Jesus demonstrates his power over the evil one by casting out
        demons at Capernaum. His power is still available today.

Antiphon and Opening Prayer

Turn, O LORD, save my life;
    deliver me for the sake of your steadfast love.
I am weary with my moaning.   Psalm 6:4, 6a

O Lord, you who have the power to deliver all people from evil.
Look on me, your servant, with compassion,
and deliver me from the power of evil for Christ's sake.

Scripture Reading

. . . When the Sabbath came, he entered the synagogue and taught. They were astounded at his teaching, for he taught them as one having authority, and not as the scribes. Just then there was in their synagogue a man with an unclean spirit. . . . Jesus rebuked him, saying, "Be silent, and come out of him." . . . They were all amazed, and they kept on asking one another, "What is this? A new teaching — with authority! He commands even the unclean spirits, and they obey him." At once his fame began to spread throughout the surrounding region of Galilee.

Mark 1:21-23, 25, 27-28
optional: Genesis 3:1-24

Responsorial Psalm

Depart from me, all you workers of evil;
    for the LORD has heard the sound of my weeping.
The LORD has heard my supplication;
    the LORD accepts my prayer.
All my enemies shall be ashamed and struck with terror;
    they shall turn back and in a moment be put to shame.

Psalm 6:8-10

Prayers, pp. 529-32

Closing Psalm Prayer

O Lord, have mercy on me and deliver me from my sins,
for I am weak and my bones are troubled.
O Lord, heal me.   adapted from Psalm 6:2

First Week after Epiphany   **Wednesday**

Theme: The faith of the leper who asked for healing provides us with
      an example of the faith we need to bring to Christ.

Antiphon and Opening Prayer

Happy are those who keep his decrees,
who seek him with their whole heart! Psalm 119:2

Lord Jesus, you manifested yourself as the one who heals all our
infirmities.
Help me to seek you and to long for the healing you bring.

Scripture Reading

A leper came to him begging him, and kneeling he said to him, "If
you choose, you can make me clean." Moved with pity, Jesus
stretched out his hand and touched him, and said to him, "I do
choose. Be made clean!" Immediately the leprosy left him, and he
was made clean. . . . But he went out and began to proclaim it freely,
and to spread the word, so that Jesus could no longer go into a town
openly, but stayed out in the country; and people came to him from
every quarter.

Mark 1:40-42, 45
optional: Genesis 4:1-16

Responsorial Psalm

How can young people keep their way pure?
By guarding it according to your word.
With my whole heart I seek you;
do not let me stray from your commandments.
I treasure your word in my heart,
so that I may not sin against you. Psalm 119:9-11

Prayers, pp. 529-32

Closing Psalm Prayer

Blessed are you, O LORD. . . .
I will meditate on your precepts,
and fix my eyes on your ways.
I will delight in your statutes;
I will not forget your word. Psalm 119:12a, 15, 16

First Week after Epiphany   Thursday

Theme: Not only does Jesus have the power to heal our emotional and
physical infirmities, he also forgives our sin and makes us whole.

Antiphon and Opening Prayer

I love you, O LORD, my strength. . . .
My shield and the horn of my salvation, my stronghold.

Psalm 18:1, 2b

Lord, you are my strength.
In you and in you alone do I trust.
For you are my Savior.
You lighten the path of my life.

Scripture Reading

When he returned to Capernaum after some days, it was reported
that he was at home. So many gathered around that there was no
longer room for them. . . . Then some people came, bringing to him
a paralyzed man. . . . When Jesus saw their faith, he said to the
paralytic, "Son, your sins are forgiven." Now some of the scribes
were sitting there, questioning in their hearts. . . . "Who can forgive
sins but God alone?" . . . [So Jesus] said to them, . . . "So that you
may know that the Son of Man has authority on earth to forgive
sins" — he said to the paralytic — "I say to you, stand up, take your
mat, and go to your home." And he stood up, and immediately took
the mat, and went out . . . so that they were all amazed and glorified
God, saying, "We have never seen anything like this!"

Mark 2:1-2a, 3a, 5-6, 7b, 10-12
optional: Genesis 4:17-26

Responsorial Psalm

The LORD is my rock, my fortress, and my deliverer.
>   my God, my rock in whom I take refuge. . . .
I call upon the LORD, who is worthy to be praised.

Psalm 18:2a, 3a

Prayers, pp. 529-32

Closing Psalm Prayer

The LORD lives! Blessed be my rock,
>   and exalted be the God of my salvation. . . .
For this I will extol you, O LORD . . .
>   and sing praises to your name. Psalm 18:46, 49

First Week after Epiphany Friday

Theme: The ministry of Jesus is not directed toward the self-righteous. He came to those who know they are in need of his help and healing power.

Antiphon and Opening Prayer

Protect me, O God.
For in you I take refuge.
You are my Lord. adapted from Psalm 16:1-2

Lord Jesus, like the sinners and tax collectors,
I come to you with no pretense.
Come to me, Lord,
reside in my home, and heal my infirmities.

Scripture Reading

And as he sat at dinner in Levi's house, many tax collectors and sinners were also sitting with Jesus and his disciples. . . . When the scribes of the Pharisees saw that he was eating with sinners and tax collectors, they said to his disciples, "Why does he eat with tax collectors and sinners?" When Jesus heard this, he said to them, "Those who are well have no need of a physician, but those who are sick; I have come to call not the righteous but sinners."

Mark 2:15-17
optional: Genesis 6:1-8

Responsorial Psalm

Therefore my heart is glad, and my soul rejoices. . . .
You show me the path of life.
> In your presence there is fullness of joy;
> in your right hand are pleasures forevermore. Psalm 16:9a, 11

Prayers, pp. 529-32

Closing Psalm Prayer

Lord, you maintain my lot.
The lines have fallen to me in pleasant places.
Yes, I have a good inheritance.
I will bless you,
I will set you always before me.   adapted from Psalm 16:5-8

First Week after Epiphany   Saturday

Theme: Not everyone who saw the marvelous works of Christ believed in him. Today, as in the first century, we must make a choice for or against him.

Antiphon and Opening Prayer

Be exalted, O LORD, in your strength!
We will sing and praise your power.   Psalm 21:13

Lord Jesus Christ, you are exalted above all others.
I confess that you are my Lord.
Let me not forsake your name or your house of praise.

Scripture Reading

Again he entered the synagogue, and a man was there who had a withered hand. They watched him to see whether he would cure him on the sabbath, so that they might accuse him. And he said to the man who had the withered hand, "Come forward." . . . [Then he] said to the man, "Stretch out your hand." He stretched it out, and his hand was restored. The Pharisees went out and immediately conspired with the Herodians against him, how to destroy him.

Mark 3:1-3, 5b-6
optional: Genesis 5:9-22

Responsorial Psalm

In your strength the king rejoices, O LORD,
    and in your help how greatly he exults!
You have given him his heart's desire,
    and you have not withheld the request of his lips.

Psalm 21:1-2

Prayers, pp. 529-32

Closing Psalm Prayer

Lord, some trust in chariots,
and some in horses.
But I will remember the name of the Lord my God.

adapted from Psalm 20:7

Second Week after Epiphany   Sunday

Theme: Today Jesus is manifested as "the Lamb of God who takes away
      the sin of the world." In him alone we trust for our salvation.

Antiphon and Opening Prayer

I waited patiently for the LORD;
> he inclined to me and heard my cry.   Psalm 40:1

Lord Jesus, you came to reconcile the world to yourself.
Thank you for extending this salvation to me.
May I praise your name forever and ever.

Scripture Reading

The next day he [John] saw Jesus coming toward him and declared, "Here is the Lamb of God who takes away the sin of the world!" . . . And John testified, "I saw the Spirit descending from heaven like a dove, and it remained on him. I myself did not know him, but the one who sent me to baptize with water said to me, 'He on whom you see the Spirit descend and remain is the one who baptizes with the Holy Spirit.' And I myself have seen and have testified that this is the Son of God."

John 1:29, 32-34
optional: Genesis 7:1-23

Responsorial Psalm

You have multiplied, O LORD my God,
> your wondrous deeds and your thoughts toward us;
> none can compare with you.
Were I to proclaim and tell of them,
> they would be more than can be counted.   Psalm 40:5

Prayers, pp. 529-32

Closing Psalm Prayer

Do not, O LORD, withhold your mercy from me;
let your steadfast love and your faithfulness
> keep me safe forever. . . .
You are my help and my deliverer.   Psalm 40:11, 17b

Second Week after Epiphany   Monday

Theme: Word about Jesus' ministry spread rapidly so that crowds of
people followed after him, acknowledging his unusual power
and presence.

Antiphon and Opening Prayer

Sing praises to the LORD, who dwells in Zion!
Declare his deeds among the peoples.   Psalm 9:11

O Lord Jesus, you do marvelous works among the people.
Work in my life and heal my sins and wounds to your glory.

Scripture Reading

Jesus departed with his disciples to the sea, and a great multitude
from Galilee followed him; hearing all that he was doing. . . . He
had cured many, so that all who had diseases pressed upon him to
touch him. Whenever the unclean spirits saw him, they all fell down
before him and shouted, "You are the Son of God!" But he sternly
ordered them not to make him known.

Mark 3:7-8a, 10-12
optional: Genesis 8:6-22

Responsorial Psalm

The LORD is a stronghold for the oppressed,
a stronghold in times of trouble.
And those who know your name put their trust in you,
for you, O LORD, have not forsaken those who seek you.

Psalm 9:9-10

Prayers, pp. 529-32

Closing Psalm Prayer

I will give thanks to the LORD with my whole heart;
I will tell of all your wonderful deeds.

I will be glad and exult in you;
    I will sing praise to your name, O Most High.   Psalm 9:1-2

Second Week after Epiphany   Tuesday

Theme: The scribes claim Jesus' power comes from Satan. But Jesus
claims he has entered Satan's house and bound him.

Antiphon and Opening Prayer

O save your people, and bless your heritage;
    be their shepherd, and carry them forever.   Psalm 28:9

Lord, you cast down the mighty powers and overthrow evil.
Deliver me from the powers and principalities that seek to rule
my life.

Scripture Reading

And the scribes who came down from Jerusalem said, "He has
Beelzebul, and by the ruler of the demons he casts out demons." And
he called them to him and spoke to them in parables, "How can
Satan cast out Satan? If a kingdom is divided against itself, that
kingdom cannot stand. . . . But no one can enter a strong man's
house and plunder his property without first tying up the strong
man; then indeed the house can be plundered."

                                 Mark 3:22-24, 27
                      optional: Genesis 9:1-17

Responsorial Psalm

Do not let the foot of the arrogant tread on me,
    or the hand of the wicked drive me away.
There the evildoers lie prostrate;
    they are thrust down, unable to rise.   Psalm 36:11-12

Prayers, pp. 529-32

Closing Psalm Prayer

To you, O LORD, I call;
>   my rock, do not refuse to hear me. . . .
Hear the voice of my supplication as I cry to you for help.

>   Psalm 28:1a, 2a

Second Week after Epiphany   Wednesday

Theme: Those who follow after Jesus are called to live a life in keeping
>   with his teaching. We are to choose the way of truth every day.

Antiphon and Opening Prayer

Teach me, O LORD, the way of your statutes. . . .
See, I have longed for your precepts;
>   in your righteousness give me life.   Psalm 119:33a, 40

Lord, through your Spirit you have begun the work of salvation
in me.
Keep me in your truth and grant me to show forth works of
praise in your name.

Scripture Reading

Listen! A sower went out to sow. And as he sowed, some seed fell
on the path, and the birds came and ate it up. Other seed fell on
rocky ground. . . . And when the sun rose, it was scorched; and since
it had no root, it withered away. Other seed fell among thorns, and
the thorns grew up and choked it, and it yielded no grain. Other
seed fell into good soil and brought forth grain, growing up and
increasing and yielding thirty and sixty and a hundredfold. Let
anyone with ears to hear listen!

>   Mark 4:3-5a, 6-9
>   optional: Genesis 9:18-29

Responsorial Psalm

I have chosen the way of faithfulness;
    I set your ordinances before me.
I cling to your decrees, O LORD;
    let me not be put to shame.
I run the way of your commandments,
    for you enlarge my understanding.   Psalm 119:30-32

Prayers, pp. 529-32

Closing Psalm Prayer

Lord, I will trust in your word,
I will keep your commandments continually,
I will seek your precepts,
I will speak of your testimonies,
and I will meditate on your statutes.

                adapted from Psalm 119:42-48

Second Week after Epiphany   Thursday

Theme: Jesus describes the kingdom of God and calls people to have
       faith in him — to be like the seed planted in good ground.

Antiphon and Opening Prayer

Commit your way to the LORD;
trust in him, and he will act.   Psalm 37:5

Lord, let me be as the seed that falls into good ground.
May your life within me grow and ripen into a tree that bears
good fruit.

Scripture Reading

He also said, "The kingdom of God is as if someone would scatter seed on the ground, and would sleep and rise night and day, and the seed would sprout and grow, he does not know how. The earth produces of itself, first the stalk, then the head, then the full grain in the head. But when the grain is ripe, at once he goes in with his sickle, because the harvest has come."

Mark 4:26-29

optional: Genesis 11:1-9

Responsorial Psalm

Our steps are made firm by the LORD,
> when he delights in our way;
though we stumble, we shall not fall headlong,
> for the LORD holds us by the hand.

Psalm 37:23-24

Prayers, pp. 529-32

Closing Psalm Prayer

Lord, I will trust in you and do good.
I will delight myself in you.
I will rest in you and wait patiently for you,
and you will give me the desire of my heart.

adapted from Psalm 37:3-5

Second Week after Epiphany   Friday

Theme: Jesus manifests himself as the one in whom the disciples can trust and not be afraid. He calls us to trust in his strength.

Antiphon and Opening Prayer

Be strong, and let your heart take courage,
> all you who wait for the LORD.

Psalm 31:24

Lord, help me to put my trust in you.
For you are the God of my salvation,
you are the Lord of my life,
and you are my true hope.

Scripture Reading

. . . [Jesus] said to them, "Let us go across to the other side." . . . A
great windstorm arose, and the waves beat into the boat. . . . He
woke up and rebuked the wind, and said to the sea, "Peace! be still!"
Then the wind ceased, and there was a dead calm. He said to them,
"Why are you afraid? Have you still no faith?" And they were filled
with great awe and said to one another, "Who then is this, that even
the wind and the sea obey him?"

Mark 4:35b, 37a, 39-41
optional: Genesis 11:27–12:28

Responsorial Psalm

In you, O LORD, I seek refuge;
  do not let me ever be put to shame. . . .
Incline your ear to me;
  rescue me speedily.
Be a rock of refuge for me,
  a strong fortress to save me.   Psalm 31:1a

Prayers, pp. 529-32

Closing Psalm Prayer

You are indeed my rock and my fortress;
  for your name's sake lead me and guide me. . . .
  For you are my refuge.
Into your hand I commit my spirit;
  you have redeemed me, O LORD, faithful God.

Psalm 31:3, 4b-5

Second Week after Epiphany   Saturday

Theme: Jesus demonstrates his power over the demonic. This same
power over evil is available to us today when we confess our
sin.

Antiphon and Opening Prayer

Happy are those whose transgression is forgiven,
     whose sin is covered . . .
     and in whose spirit there is no deceit.   Psalm 32:1, 2b

Lord Jesus Christ,
you have power over the powers of evil,
you put them down, you destroy them.
Search out my heart, Lord,
and cast out the evil within me.

Scripture Reading

When he had stepped out of the boat, immediately a man out of the
tombs with an unclean spirit met him. . . . [The man] shouted at the
top of his voice, "What have you to do with me, Jesus, Son of the
Most High God? I adjure you by God, do not torment me." For he
had said to him, "Come out of the man, you unclean spirit!" Now
there on the hillside a great herd of swine was feeding. . . . The
unclean spirits came out and entered the swine; and the herd,
numbering about two thousand, rushed down the steep bank into
the sea, and were drowned in the sea.

Mark 5:2, 7-8, 11, 13
optional: Genesis 12:9–13:1

Responsorial Psalm

Many are the torments of the wicked,
     but steadfast love surrounds those who trust in the LORD.
Be glad in the LORD and rejoice, O righteous,
     and shout for joy, all you upright in heart.   Psalm 32:10-11

Prayers, pp. 529-32

Closing Psalm Prayer

> [Lord,] I acknowledged my sin to you,
>   and I did not hide my iniquity;
> I said, "I will confess my transgressions to the LORD,"
>   and you forgave the guilt of my sin.   Psalm 32:5

Third Week after Epiphany   Sunday

Theme: Jesus gathers his disciples in the beginning of his ministry. Like
them, we are called to follow after him.

Antiphon and Opening Prayer

> Wait for the LORD;
>   be strong, and let your heart take courage.   Psalm 27:14

> Lord Jesus,
> you called your disciples to leave their nets and follow you.
> So may I, your servant, follow in your way.

Scripture Reading

> As [Jesus] walked by the Sea of Galilee, he saw two brothers, Simon,
> who is called Peter, and Andrew his brother, casting a net into the
> sea'— for they were fishermen. And he said to them, "Follow me,
> and I will make you fish for people." Immediately they left their
> nets and followed him. As he went from there, he saw two other
> brothers, James son of Zebedee, and his brother John, in the boat
> with their father Zebedee, mending their nets, and he called to them.
> Immediately they left the boat and their father, and followed him.
>
>   Matthew 4:18-22
>   optional: Genesis 13:2-18

Responsorial Psalm

> One thing I asked of the LORD,
>   that will I seek after:

to live in the house of the LORD
all the days of my life,
to behold the beauty of the LORD,
and to inquire in his temple.   Psalm 27:4

Prayers, pp. 529-32

Closing Psalm Prayer

Lord, in the time of trouble,
you shall hide me in your pavilion.
In the secret place of your tabernacle,
you shall hide me;
you shall set me high upon a rock.   adapted from Psalm 27:5

Third Week after Epiphany   Monday

Theme: Jesus is asked by Nicodemus to explain the meaning of the New
Birth. Like Nicodemus, we ask the same question.

Antiphon and Opening Prayer

I will give thanks to the LORD with my whole heart;
I will tell of all your wonderful deeds.   Psalm 9:1

Lord God, cause my heart to be full of praise,
and teach me how to give praise
for your wonderful deeds in my life.

Scripture Reading

Nicodemus said to him, "How can anyone be born after having
grown old? Can one enter a second time into the mother's womb
and be born?" Jesus answered, "Very truly, I tell you, no one can
enter the kingdom of God without being born of water and Spirit.
What is born of the flesh is flesh, and what is born of the Spirit is

spirit. Do not be astonished that I said to you, 'You must be born from above.'"

John 3:4-7

optional: Genesis 14:8-24

Responsorial Psalm

O LORD, who may abide in your tent?
    Who may dwell on your holy hill?
Those who walk blamelessly, and do what is right,
    and speak the truth from their heart. . . .
Those who do these things shall never be moved.

Psalm 15:1-2, 5b

Prayers, pp. 529-32

Closing Psalm Prayer

Make me to know your ways, O LORD;
    teach me your paths.
Lead me in your truth, and teach me,
    for you are the God of my salvation;
    for you I wait all day long.   Psalm 25:4-5

Third Week after Epiphany   Tuesday

Theme: Jesus is rejected by the people of his hometown. We may choose
    not to reject him, but to follow him forever.

Antiphon and Opening Prayer

Your throne, O God, endures forever and ever.
Your royal scepter is a scepter of equity.   Psalm 45:6

Lord Jesus Christ,
you were rejected by the people of your own hometown.
May I embrace you, trust in you, and follow after your teaching.

Scripture Reading

On the sabbath he began to teach in the synagogue, and many who heard him were astounded. They said. . . ."Is not this the carpenter?" [But] Jesus said to them, "Prophets are not without honor, except in their hometown, and among their own kin, and in their own house." And he could do no deed of power there, except that he laid his hands on a few sick people and cured them. And he was amazed at their unbelief. Then he went about among the villages, teaching.

Mark 6:2a, 3a, 4-6
optional: Genesis 15:1-21

Responsorial Psalm

You love righteousness and hate wickedness.
Therefore God, your God, has anointed you
    with the oil of gladness beyond your companions. . . .
I will cause your name to be celebrated in all generations;
    therefore the peoples will praise you forever and ever.

Psalm 45:7, 17

Prayers, pp. 529-32

Closing Psalm Prayer

My heart overflows with a goodly theme. . . .
You are the most handsome of men;
    grace is poured upon your lips;
    therefore God has blessed you forever.   Psalm 45:1a, 2

Third Week after Epiphany   Wednesday

Theme: The teaching and works of Jesus are becoming increasingly well known. Herod and others now ask, "Who is this man?"

Antiphon and Opening Prayer

At midnight I rise to praise you. . . .
The earth, O LORD, is full of your steadfast love;
    teach me your statutes.   Psalm 119:62a, 64

Lord Jesus, the people of this world rise up against you.
They seek to kill you and destroy the work of your kingdom.
May I, O Lord, stand in the company of your people and not
theirs.

Scripture Reading

King Herod heard of it, for Jesus' name had become known. Some
were saying, "John the baptizer has been raised from the dead; and
for this reason these powers are at work in him." But others said,
"It is Elijah." And others said, "It is a prophet, like one of the
prophets of old." But when Herod heard of it, he said, "John, whom
I beheaded, has been raised."

Mark 6:14-16
optional: Genesis 16:1-14

Responsorial Psalm

The LORD is my portion;
    I promise to keep your words.
I implore your favor with all my heart;
    be gracious to me according to your promise.
When I think of your ways,
    I turn my feet to your decrees.   Psalm 119:57-59

Prayers, pp. 529-32

Closing Psalm Prayer

Lord, I will remember your word.
I will not turn away from your law,
for your statutes have been my song.
Your word has given me life.
Therefore I will remember your judgments.

adapted from Psalm 119:49-54

Third Week after Epiphany   Thursday

Theme: Jesus manifests his power over nature by multiplying the fish
       and the loaves. We are called to trust in his might, not that of
       ourselves or of others.

Antiphon and Opening Prayer

The mighty one, God the LORD,
speaks and summons the earth
from the rising of the sun to its setting.   Psalm 50:1

Lord God, you are the Mighty One,
the one who does great and wondrous deeds.
You heal the sick; you raise the dead; you renew the earth.
Renew me, O Lord, and fashion me after your will.

Scripture Reading

Then he ordered them to get all the people to sit down in groups on
the green grass. So they sat down in groups of hundreds and of fifties.
Taking the five loaves and the two fish, he looked up to heaven, and
blessed and broke the loaves, and gave them to his disciples to set
before the people; and he divided the two fish among them all. And
all ate and were filled; and they took up twelve baskets full of broken
pieces and of the fish.

                                                    Mark 6:39-43
                                      optional: Genesis 16:15–17:14

Responsorial Psalm

Out of my distress I called on the LORD;
        the LORD answered me and set me in a broad place. . . .
It is better to take refuge in the LORD
        than to put confidence in mortals.
It is better to take refuge in the LORD
        than to put confidence in princes.   Psalm 118:5, 8, 9

Prayers, pp. 529-32

Closing Psalm Prayer

The LORD is my strength and my might;
    he has become my salvation. . . .
I thank you that you have answered me
    and become my salvation. . . .
O give thanks to the LORD, for he is good.   Psalm 118:14, 21, 29

Third Week after Epiphany   Friday

Theme: Jesus demonstrates his power over all kinds of diseases. He who
        has the power to heal infirmities also heals our inner selves.

Antiphon and Opening Prayer

The sacrifice acceptable to God is a broken spirit;
    a broken and contrite heart, O God, you will not despise.
                                  Psalm 51:17

Lord Jesus Christ,
you who have the power to heal
the sick and make them whole, heal me.
Bring me to spiritual wholeness and make me glad.

Scripture Reading

When they got out of the boat, people at once recognized him, and
rushed about that whole region and began to bring the sick on mats
to wherever they heard he was. And wherever he went, into villages
or cities or farms, they laid the sick in the marketplaces, and begged
him that they might touch even the fringe of his cloak; and all who
touched it were healed.

                                      Mark 6:54-56
                          optional: Genesis 17:15-27

Responsorial Psalm

> Create in me a clean heart, O God,
>> and put a new and right spirit within me.
> Do not cast me away from your presence,
>> and do not take your holy spirit from me.
> Restore to me the joy of your salvation,
>> and sustain in me a willing spirit.   Psalm 51:10-12

Prayers, pp. 529-32

Closing Psalm Prayer

> Purge me with hyssop, and I shall be clean;
>> wash me, and I shall be whiter than snow.
> Let me hear joy and gladness. . . .
> Hide your face from my sins,
>> and blot out all my iniquities.   Psalm 51:7, 8a, 9

Third Week after Epiphany   Saturday

Theme: Jesus manifests his power to see beyond the external. He knows
what is on the inside of the heart. We are called to confess our
sin and trust in him.

Antiphon and Opening Prayer

> Give ear to my prayer, O God;
>> do not hide yourself from my supplication.   Psalm 55:1

> Lord Jesus,
> you who can penetrate into the heart
> and can know our innermost thoughts,
> cleanse my mind and my thoughts,
> and let me long for you.

Scripture Reading

... [He] said to them, "Listen to me ... there is nothing outside a person that by going in can defile, but the things that come out are what defile. . . .

"For it is from within, from the human heart, that evil intentions come: fornication, murder, theft, adultery, avarice, wickedness, deceit, licentiousness, envy, slander, pride, folly. All these evil things come from within, and they defile a person."

Mark 7:14-15, 21-23
optional: Genesis 18:1-16

Responsorial Psalm

My heart is in anguish within me,
    the terrors of death have fallen upon me.
Fear and trembling come upon me,
    and horror overwhelms me.
And I say, "O that I had wings like a dove!
    I would fly away and be at rest."   Psalm 55:4-6

Prayers, pp. 529-32

Closing Psalm Prayer

But I call upon God. . . .
Cast your burden on the LORD,
    and he will sustain you;
he will never permit
    the righteous to be moved. . . .
But I will trust in you.   Psalm 55:16a, 22, 23b

Fourth Week after Epiphany   Sunday

Theme: Throughout the Gospels it is clear that our Lord sides with the poor. He calls us to love and care for the poor as well.

Antiphon and Opening Prayer

The LORD is King; let the peoples tremble! . . .
Let them praise your great and awesome name.   Psalm 99:1a, 3a

Lord, you love the poor and show compassion to the weak.
Let your church set aside all claim to wealth and power,
and stand with the poor of the earth.

Scripture Reading

Blessed are the poor in spirit, for theirs is the kingdom of heaven.
Blessed are those who mourn, for they will be comforted.
Blessed are the meek, for they will inherit the earth.
Blessed are those who hunger and thirst for righteousness, for
they will be filled.
Blessed are the merciful, for they will receive mercy.

Matthew 5:3-7
optional: Genesis 18:16-33

Responsorial Psalm

Mighty King, lover of justice,
    you have established equity;
you have executed justice
    and righteousness in Jacob.
Extol the LORD our God;
    worship at his footstool.   Psalm 99:4-5a

Prayers, pp. 529-32

Closing Psalm Prayer

Let the sea roar, and all that fills it;
    the world and those who live in it. . . .
For he is coming
    to judge the earth.
He will judge the world with righteousness,
    and the peoples with equity.   Psalm 98:7, 9

Fourth Week after Epiphany   Monday

Theme: That the kingdom of Jesus is to extend beyond the borders of
        Israel is demonstrated when Jesus heals the daughter of a Gentile
        woman.

Antiphon and Opening Prayer

Be exalted, O God, above the heavens.
   Let your glory be over all the earth.   Psalm 57:11

Lord Jesus, you have been exalted in all the earth.
You have shown your loving kindness to all people.
I will praise your name, for it is above every name.

Scripture Reading

A woman whose little daughter had an unclean spirit immediately
heard about him, and she came and bowed down at his feet. Now
the woman was a Gentile. . . . [Jesus] said to her, "Let the children
be fed first, for it is not fair to take the children's food and throw
it to the dogs." But she answered him, "Sir, even the dogs under the
table eat the children's crumbs." Then he said to her, "For saying
that, you may go — the demon has left your daughter."

                                          Mark 7:25-26a, 27-29
                                          optional: Genesis 19:1-7

Responsorial Psalm

When I am afraid,
   I put my trust in you.
In God, whose word I praise,
   in God I trust; I am not afraid;
   what can flesh do to me?   Psalm 56:3-4

Prayers, pp. 529-32

Closing Psalm Prayer

> I will render thank offerings to you.
> For you have delivered my soul from death,
>   and my feet from falling,
> so that I may walk before God
>   in the light of life.   Psalm 56:12b-13

Fourth Week after Epiphany   **Tuesday**

Theme: The power that Jesus exhibits over illness and over the powers
        of evil manifests him as the Lord, the ruler of the universe.

Antiphon and Opening Prayer

> On God rests my deliverance and my honor;
>   my mighty rock, my refuge is in God.   Psalm 62:7

> Lord, the whole world acknowledges you to be the Lord.
> All powers bow the knee before you.
> Open my mouth that I may sing forth your praises.

Scripture Reading

> They brought to him a deaf man who had an impediment in his
> speech; and they begged him to lay his hand on him. He took him
> aside in private, away from the crowd, and put his fingers into his
> ears, and he spat and touched his tongue. Then looking up to heaven,
> he sighed and said to him, "Ephphatha," that is, "Be opened." And
> immediately his ears were opened, his tongue was released, and he
> spoke plainly.
>
> Mark 7:32-35
> optional: Genesis 21:1-21

Responsorial Psalm

> For God alone my soul waits in silence;
>   from him comes my salvation.

He alone is my rock and my salvation,
my fortress; I shall never be shaken. . . .
For my hope is from him.   Psalm 62:1-2, 5b

Prayers, pp. 529-32

Closing Psalm Prayer

Once God has spoken;
twice have I heard this:
that power belongs to God,
and steadfast love belongs to you, O Lord.
For you repay to all
according to their work.   Psalm 62:11-12

Fourth Week after Epiphany   Wednesday

Theme: The power and light of Christ will be manifested throughout all
the earth to the ends of the world.

Antiphon and Opening Prayer

Blessed be the LORD, the God of Israel,
who alone does wondrous things.   Psalm 72:18

Lord, you who manifest yourself by making the blind to see,
let the knowledge of your great glory
extend to the ends of the earth.

Scripture Reading

They came to Bethsaida. Some people brought a blind man to him
and begged him to touch him. He took the blind man by the hand
and led him out of the village; and when he had put saliva on his
eyes and laid his hands on him, he asked him, "Can you see
anything?" And the man looked up and said, "I can see people, but
they look like trees, walking." Then Jesus laid his hands on his eyes

again; and he looked intently and his sight was restored, and he saw
everything clearly. Then he sent him away to his home.

Mark 8:22-26a
optional: Genesis 22:1-18

Responsorial Psalm

> May he have dominion from sea to sea,
>> and from the River to the ends of the earth. . . .
> For he delivers the needy when they call,
>> the poor and those who have no helper. . . .
> From oppression and violence he redeems their life.

Psalm 72:8, 12, 14a

Prayers, pp. 529-32

Closing Psalm Prayer

> May his name endure forever,
>> his fame continue as long as the sun.
> May all nations be blessed in him;
>> may they pronounce him happy. . . .
> May his glory fill the whole earth.   Psalm 72:17, 19

Fourth Week after Epiphany   **Thursday**

Theme: The manifestation of Jesus to his disciples as the Son of the
living God represents a turning point. Henceforth he will teach
of his death.

Antiphon and Opening Prayer

> In you, O LORD, I take refuge;
> let me never be put to shame.
> Incline your ear to me and save me.   Psalm 71:1, 2b

Lord, you manifest yourself as the Messiah,
who has come to redeem us from our sin.
Like Peter, may we confess that you are the Christ,
the Son of God.

Scripture Reading

Jesus went on with his disciples to the villages of Caesarea Philippi;
and on the way he asked his disciples, "Who do people say that I
am?" And they answered him, "John the Baptist; and others, Elijah;
and still others, one of the prophets." He asked them, "But who do
you say that I am?" Peter answered him, "You are the Messiah."
And he sternly ordered them not to tell anyone about him.

Then he began to teach them that the Son of Man must undergo
great suffering.

Mark 8:27-31a
optional: Genesis 23:1-10

Responsorial Psalm

My mouth will tell of your righteous acts,
of your deeds of salvation all day long,
though their number is past my knowledge.
I will come praising the mighty deeds of the Lord GOD.
I will praise your righteousness, yours alone.   Psalm 71:15-16

Prayers, pp. 529-32

Closing Psalm Prayer

Be to me a rock of refuge,
a strong fortress, to save me. . . .
For you, O Lord, are my hope,
my trust, O LORD, from my youth.
My praise is continually of you.   Psalm 71:3a, 5, 6b

Fourth Week after Epiphany   Friday

Theme: Jesus is transfigured before Peter, James, and John. For one
fleeting moment they see him in the fullness of his glory with
the Father.

Antiphon and Opening Prayer

I will praise the name of God with a song;
I will magnify him with thanksgiving.   Psalm 69:30

Lord Jesus Christ, stretch the vision of my life.
May I see beyond what is
and catch a glimpse of the glory that is to be attained.

Scripture Reading

Six days later, Jesus took with him Peter and James and John, and
led them up a high mountain apart, by themselves. And he was
transfigured before them, and his clothes became dazzling white,
such as no one on earth could bleach them. . . . Then a cloud
overshadowed them, and from the cloud there came a voice, "This
is my Son, the Beloved; listen to him!" Suddenly when they looked
around, they saw no one with them any more, but only Jesus.

Mark 9:2-3, 7-9
optional: Genesis 24:1-27

Responsorial Psalm

Answer me, O LORD, for your steadfast love is good;
according to your abundant mercy, turn to me.
Do not hide your face from your servant. . . .
Draw near to me, redeem me.   Psalm 69:16-17a, 18a

Prayers, pp. 529-32

Closing Psalm Prayer

Let your salvation, O God, protect me.
I will praise the name of God with a song;
I will magnify him with thanksgiving.

adapted from Psalm 69:29-30

Fourth Week after Epiphany   Saturday

Theme: Jesus is near to those in need. We must admit our helplessness
and call on him for his help and strength.

Antiphon and Opening Prayer

We give thanks to you, O God;
    we give thanks; your name is near.
People tell of your wondrous deeds.   Psalm 75:1

Lord, to whom should we turn in the time of trouble?
You, O Lord, are near and ready to help us.
We believed, Lord, in you; help our unbelief, we pray.

Scripture Reading

Someone from the crowd answered him, "Teacher, I brought you my
son; he has a spirit that makes him unable to speak; and whenever
it seizes him, it dashes him down; and he foams and grinds his teeth
and becomes rigid. . . ." And they brought the boy to him. When
the spirit saw him, immediately it convulsed the boy, and he fell on
the ground and rolled about, foaming at the mouth. . . . [The father
said] "if you are able to do anything, have pity on us and help us."
Jesus said to him, "If you are able! — All things can be done for the
one who believes."

Mark 9:17-18a, 20, 22b-23
optional: Genesis 24:28-51

Responsorial Psalm

> The LORD is my light and my salvation;
>> whom shall I fear?
> The LORD is the stronghold of my life;
>> of whom shall I be afraid?
> Though an army encamp against me,
>> my heart shall not fear. Psalm 27:1, 3a

Prayers, pp. 529-32

Closing Psalm Prayer

> He will hide me in his shelter.
> In the day of trouble he will conceal me under the cover of his tent.
> He will set me on a high rock. adapted from Psalm 27:5

In 1997, 2002, 2005, 2008, and 2013 go to the last Sunday after Epiphany (p. 141) tomorrow.

Fifth Week after Epiphany   Sunday

Theme: In the Sermon on the Mount Jesus instructs his disciples to be salt and light. During Epiphany we are called once again to manifest Christ to the world.

Antiphon and Opening Prayer

> Happy are those
>> who do not follow the advice of the wicked. Psalm 1:1

> Lord Jesus, as you called your disciples to be your witnesses,
> so let me this day
> be salt and light in my home and in my place of work.

Scripture Reading

You are the salt of the earth; but if salt has lost its taste, how can its saltiness be restored? It is no longer good for anything, but is thrown out and trampled under foot.

   You are the light of the world. A city built on a hill cannot be hid. No one after lighting a lamp puts it under the bushel basket, but on the lampstand, and it gives light to all in the house. In the same way, let your light shine before others, so that they may see your good works and give glory to your Father in heaven.

Matthew 5:13-16
optional: Genesis 18; 24:50-67

Responsorial Psalm

Happy are those who do not follow the advice of the wicked,
or take the path that sinners tread,
   or sit in the seat of scoffers;
but their delight is in the law of the LORD,
   and on his law they meditate day and night.   Psalm 1:1-2

Prayers, pp. 529-32

Closing Psalm Prayer

Lord, let me be like a tree
planted by the streams of water.
It yields fruit in its season,
and its leaf does not wither.
Whatever such a person does will prosper.

adapted from Psalm 1:3

Fifth Week after Epiphany   Monday

Theme: The glory of God's name is known everywhere. It is proclaimed
in the cup of cold water, in the seas, and in the sky.

Antiphon and Opening Prayer

> Help us, O God of our salvation,
> > for the glory of your name;
> deliver us.   Psalm 79:9

> Lord, you who are everywhere
> and known through all your works,
> may we your servants give the
> cup of cold water in your name
> and share the wonder of your glory.

Scripture Reading

> John said to him, "Teacher, we saw someone casting out demons in
> your name, and we tried to stop him, because he was not following
> us." But Jesus said, "Do not stop him; for no one who does a deed
> of power in my name will be able soon afterward to speak evil of
> me. Whoever is not against us is for us. For truly I tell you, whoever
> gives you a cup of water to drink because you bear the name of
> Christ will by no means lose the reward."
> > > > > Mark 9:38-41
> > > > optional: Genesis 25:19-34

Responsorial Psalm

> Will the Lord spurn forever,
> > and never again be favorable?
> Has his steadfast love ceased forever?
> > Are his promises at an end for all time?
> Has God forgotten to be gracious?
> > Has he in anger shut up his compassion?   Psalm 77:7-9

Prayers, pp. 529-32

Closing Psalm Prayer

> When the waters saw you, O God,
> > when the waters saw you, they were afraid;
> > the very deep trembled.
> The clouds poured out water;
> > the skies thundered.   Psalm 77:16-17a

Fifth Week after Epiphany   Tuesday

Theme: Jesus, being well aware of how Israel sinned against God, warns
his followers to abhor sin and to flee from it.

Antiphon and Opening Prayer

Give ear, O my people, to my teaching;
   incline your ears to the words of my mouth.   Psalm 78:1

Lord, may we who have committed ourselves to follow after you,
shun evil and be saved from the power of darkness.
Grant this through your beloved Son.

Scripture Reading

If your hand causes you to stumble, cut it off; it is better for you to
enter life maimed than to have two hands and to go to hell, to the
unquenchable fire. And if your foot causes you to stumble, cut it off;
it is better for you to enter life lame than to have two feet and to
be thrown into hell. . . . Where their worm never dies, and the fire
is never quenched.

                                                      Mark 9:43-46

Responsorial Psalm

In the sight of their ancestors he worked marvels. . . .
He divided the sea and let them pass through it. . . .
Yet they sinned still more against him,
   rebelling against the Most High in the desert.
They tested God in their heart.   Psalm 78:12a, 13a, 17-18a

Prayers, pp. 529-32

Closing Psalm Prayer

> Then we your people, the flock of your pasture,
> will give thanks to you forever;
> from generation to generation we will recount your praise.
>
> Psalm 79:13

Fifth Week after Epiphany   Wednesday

Theme: Those who come to Jesus and enter into his kingdom must come
as little children. Faith is simple trust and obedience.

Antiphon and Opening Prayer

> Oh, how I love your law!
> It is my meditation all day long. . . .
> For it is always with me.   Psalm 119:97, 98b

> Lord, let me come to you with the trust and faith of a child.
> Let me love your teaching.
> Direct me to follow in the path that you have laid out for me.

Scripture Reading

> People were bringing little children to him in order that he might
> touch them; and the disciples spoke sternly to them. But when Jesus
> saw this, he was indignant and said to them, "Let the little children
> come to me; do not stop them; for it is to such as these that the
> kingdom of God belongs. Truly I tell you, whoever does not receive
> the kingdom of God as a little child will never enter it." And he took
> them up in his arms, laid his hands on them, and blessed them.
>
> Mark 10:13-16
> optional: Genesis 27:1-29

Responsorial Psalm

> Your decrees are wonderful;
>> therefore my soul keeps them.
> The unfolding of your words gives light;
>> it imparts understanding to the simple.
> With open mouth I pant,
>> because I long for your commandments.   Psalm 119:129-131

Prayers, pp. 529-32

Closing Psalm Prayer

> You are my hiding place and my shield;
>> I hope in your word.
> Uphold me according to your promise, that I may live.
>> Psalm 119:114, 116a

Fifth Week after Epiphany   Thursday

Theme: Jesus makes it clear that trust must be placed in him, and him
       alone. Those who hope in him are blessed.

Antiphon and Opening Prayer

> I will praise the LORD as long as I live;
> I will sing praises to my God all my life long.   Psalm 146:2

> Lord, you bring me the joy of salvation and make my life full.
> Do not turn from me nor forsake me.
> Bring me into the fullness of your kingdom for your name's sake.

Scripture Reading

> Then Jesus looked around and said to his disciples, "How hard it
> will be for those who have wealth to enter the kingdom of God! . . .
> It is easier for a camel to go through the eye of a needle than for
> someone who is rich to enter the kingdom of God." They were greatly
> astounded and said to one another, "Then who can be saved?" Jesus

looked at them and said, "For mortals it is impossible, but nor for God; for God all things are possible."

Mark 10:23, 25-27
optional: Genesis 27:30-45

Responsorial Psalm

Do not put your trust in princes,
    in mortals, in whom there is no help.
When their breath departs, they return to the earth;
    on that very day their plans perish.   Psalm 146:3-4

Prayers, pp. 529-32

Closing Psalm Prayer

Happy are those whose help is the God of Jacob,
    whose hope is in the LORD their God,
who made heaven and earth,
    the sea, and all that is in them.   Psalm 146:5-6

Fifth Week after Epiphany   Friday

Theme: Jesus provides his disciples an epiphany of his coming sorrow and suffering. We momentarily enter into that pain.

Antiphon and Opening Prayer

O LORD, God of my salvation. . . .
Let my prayer come before you;
    incline your ear to my cry.   Psalm 88:1a, 2

Lord Jesus Christ,
you suffered a cruel death on the cross for my sake and for the world.
Draw me into that suffering
that I might know the release brought by trust in your strong name.

Scripture Reading

He took the twelve aside again and began to tell them what was to happen to him, saying, "See, we are going up to Jerusalem, and the Son of Man will be handed over to the chief priests and the scribes, and they will condemn him to death; then they will hand him over to the Gentiles; they will mock him, and spit upon him, and flog him, and kill him; and after three days he will rise again."

Mark 10:32b-34
optional: Genesis 27:46–28:22

Responsorial Psalm

For my soul is full of troubles. . . .
I am counted among those who go down to the Pit. . .
    Like the slain that lie in the grave,
like those whom you remember no more,
        for they are cut off from your hand.   Psalm 88:3a, 4a, 5b

Prayers, pp. 529-32

Closing Psalm Prayer

To you I have cried out, O Lord,
in the morning my prayer comes before you.
Lord, why do you cast off my soul?
Why do you hide your face from me?
I am distraught.   adapted from Psalm 88:13-15

Fifth Week after Epiphany   Saturday

Theme: Jesus rewards those who have faith in the midst of affliction and adversity. The meaning of life is in faithfulness to God.

Antiphon and Opening Prayer

> Lord, you have been our dwelling place
>   in all generations.
> From everlasting to everlasting you are God.   Psalm 90:1, 2b

> Lord, I offer my suffering to you
> and ask you to take it into yourself.
> I ask you, O Heavenly One, to take away my reproach
> and establish my work and life to your glory.

Scripture Reading

> . . . As he and his disciples and a large crowd were leaving Jericho,
> Bartimaeus son of Timaeus, a blind beggar, was sitting by the
> roadside. When he heard that it was Jesus of Nazareth, he began to
> shout out and say, "Jesus, son of David, have mercy on me!" . . .
> Then Jesus said to him, "What do you want me to do for you?" The
> blind man said to him, "My teacher, let me see again." Jesus said to
> him, "Go; your faith has made you well."
>
> > Mark 10:46-47, 51-52a
> > optional: Genesis 29:1-20

Responsorial Psalm

> Turn, O LORD! How long?
>   Have compassion on your servants!
> Satisfy us in the morning with your steadfast love,
>   so that we may rejoice and be glad all our days.
> Make us glad as many days as you have afflicted us.
>
> > Psalm 90:13-15a

Prayers, pp. 529-32

Closing Psalm Prayer

> Let the favor of the Lord our God be upon us,
>   and prosper for us the work of our hands —
>   O prosper the works of our hands!   Psalm 90:17

In 1994, 1999, and 2010 go to the last Sunday after Epiphany (p. 141) tomorrow.

Sixth Week after Epiphany   Sunday

Theme: Jesus teaches his disciples that God expects his people to choose
        love as the way of life.

Antiphon and Opening Prayer

God is our refuge and strength,
    a very present help in trouble.
Therefore we will not fear.   Psalm 46:1-2a

Father, my heart too frequently seeks vengeance on my enemies.
Turn me away from my anger and a spirit of hatred.
Let me be still and know that you are God.
Teach me to choose the way of love.

Scripture Reading

You have heard that it was said to those of ancient times, "You shall
not murder"; and "whoever murders shall be liable to judgment."
. . . And if you insult a brother or sister, you will be liable to the
council; and if you say, "You fool," you will be liable to the hell of
fire.

Matthew 5:21, 22b
optional: Genesis 29:20-35

Responsorial Psalm

Come, behold the works of the LORD;
    see what desolations he has brought on the earth.
He makes wars cease to the end of the earth;
    he breaks the bow, and shatters the spear;
    he burns the shields with fire.   Psalm 46:8-9

Prayers, pp. 529-32

Closing Psalm Prayer

> "Be still and know that I am God!
>   I am exalted among the nations,
>   I am exalted in the earth."
> The LORD of hosts is with us;
>   the God of Jacob is our refuge.   Psalm 46:10-11

Sixth Week after Epiphany   Monday

Theme: Jesus is manifested as the Messiah of David in Jerusalem. He
who rules the world calls us to cry Hosanna!

Antiphon and Opening Prayer

> I will sing of your steadfast love, O LORD, forever;
> with my mouth I will proclaim your faithfulness to all generations.
>   Psalm 89:1

> Father, you have sent your Son
> to redeem the world and bring it back to yourself.
> May I, trusting in him,
> join with those who sing his praises forever.

Scripture Reading

> Then they brought the colt to Jesus and threw their cloaks on it; and
> he sat on it. Many people spread their cloaks on the road, and others
> spread leafy branches that they had cut in the fields. Then those who
> went ahead and those who followed were shouting,
>   "Hosanna!
>   Blessed is the one who comes in the name of the Lord!
>   Blessed is the coming kingdom of our ancestor David!
>   Hosanna in the highest heaven!"
>   Mark 11:7-10
>   optional: Genesis 29:20-35

Responsorial Psalm

The heavens are yours, the earth also is yours;
the world and all that is in it — you have founded them. . . .
You have a mighty arm;
    strong is your hand, high your right hand.   Psalm 89:11, 13

Prayers, pp. 529-32

Closing Psalm Prayer

Let the heavens praise your wonders, O LORD,
your faithfulness in the assembly of the holy ones.
For who in the skies can be compared to the LORD?

Psalm 89:5-6

Sixth Week after Epiphany   Tuesday

Theme: Jesus reveals his anger against the corruption of his house. He
    calls us to forsake the idols of our making and turn to him.

Antiphon and Opening Prayer

The LORD is king! Let the earth rejoice;
    let the many coastlands be glad!   Psalm 97:1

Lord, you are the God who reigns over all things.
Free me from the false gods that I worship.
And turn me toward you,
that I may love and serve you continually.

Scripture Reading

Then they came to Jerusalem. And [Jesus] entered the temple and
began to drive out those who were selling and those who were buying
in the Temple, and he overturned the tables of the money changers
and the seats of those who sold doves; and he would not allow
anyone to carry anything through the temple. He was teaching,

saying, "Is it not written,
'My house shall be called a house of prayer for all nations?'
  But you have made it a den of robbers."   Mark 11:15-17
                                          optional: Genesis 31:1-24

Responsorial Psalm

All worshipers of images are put to shame,
  those who make their boast in worthless idols;
  all gods bow down before him. . . .
For you, O LORD, are most high over all the earth;
  you are exalted far above all gods.   Psalm 97:7, 9

Prayers, pp. 529-32

Closing Psalm Prayer

The LORD loves those who hate evil;
  he guards the lives of his faithful. . . .
Rejoice in the LORD, O you righteous,
  and give thanks to his holy name!   Psalm 97:10a, 12

Sixth Week after Epiphany   Wednesday

Theme: Although opposition mounted against the Lord Jesus, he continued to meet it with a firm word and a loving touch.

Antiphon and Opening Prayer

With my mouth I will give great thanks to the LORD;
I will praise him in the midst of the throng.   Psalm 109:30

Lord Jesus, I acknowledge that you are the chief cornerstone of
life.
There is no other beside you.
Deliver me from the snare of the evil one
and bring me into the kingdom of truth and love.

Scripture Reading

[After the parable of the vineyard, Jesus said]
"Have you not read this scripture:
    'The stone that the builders rejected
        has become the cornerstone;
    this was the Lord's doing,
        and it is amazing in our eyes'?"
When they realized that he had told this parable against them,
they wanted to arrest him, but they feared the crowd. So they left
him and went away.   Mark 12:10-12
                                     optional: Genesis 31:24

Responsorial Psalm

Help me, O LORD my God!
    Save me according to your steadfast love.
Let them know that this is your hand;
    you, O LORD, have done it.
Let them curse, but you will bless.   Psalm 109:26-28a

Prayers, pp. 529-32

Closing Psalm Prayer

But you, O LORD my Lord,
    act on my behalf for your name's sake;
    because your steadfast love is good, deliver me.
For I am poor and needy,
    and my heart is pierced within me.   Psalm 109:21-22

Sixth Week after Epiphany   Thursday

Theme: The opposition against Jesus continues to grow. The Pharisees
       seek to trap him, but they cannot. We marvel at his great
       wisdom.

Antiphon and Opening Prayer

O give thanks to the LORD, call on his name,
make known his deeds among the peoples.   Psalm 105:1

Lord, although hell gathers itself against you,
the victory is on your side.
Let me join with those who sing your praises
and acknowledge your great deeds!

Scripture Reading

Then they sent to him some Pharisees and some Herodians to trap
him in what he said. And they came and said to him, "Teacher, we
know that you are sincere, and show deference to no one; for you
do not regard people with partiality, but teach the way of God in
accordance with truth. Is it lawful to pay taxes to the emperor, or
not? Should we pay them, or should we not?" But knowing their
hypocrisy, he said to them, "Why are you putting me to the test?
Bring me a denarius and let me see it." And they brought one. Then
he said to them, "Whose head is this, and whose title?" They
answered, "The emperor's." Jesus said to them, "Give to the emperor
the things that are the emperor's, and to God the things that are
God's." And they were utterly amazed at him.

Mark 12:13-17
optional: Genesis 32:3-21

Responsorial Psalm

He is the LORD our God;
    his judgments are in all the earth.
He is mindful of his covenant forever,
    of the word that he commanded, for a thousand generations,
the covenant that he made with Abraham,
    his sworn promise to Isaac.   Psalm 105:7-9

Prayers, pp. 529-32

Closing Psalm Prayer

> Sing to him, sing praises to him;
>> tell of all his wonderful works.
> Glory in his holy name;
>> let the hearts of those who seek the LORD rejoice.
> Seek the LORD and his strength;
>> seek his presence continually.   Psalm 105:2-4

Sixth Week after Epiphany   Friday

Theme: God calls us to love himself and our neighbor. Our neighbor is
the person next door and the poor and desolate of the world.

Antiphon and Opening Prayer

> O give thanks to the LORD, for he is good;
> for his steadfast love endures forever.   Psalm 107:1

> Lord, make me more aware of my neighbor.
> May I be willing not only to love those like myself,
> but also to love those who differ from me, especially the poor.

Scripture Reading

> One of the scribes came near and . . . asked him, "Which
> commandment is the first of all?" Jesus answered, "The first is, 'Hear,
> O Israel: the Lord our God, the Lord is one; you shall love the Lord
> your God with all your heart, and with all your soul, and with all
> your mind, and with all your strength.' The second is this, 'You shall
> love your neighbor as yourself.'"
>> Mark 12:28-31
>> optional: Genesis 32:22–33:17

Responsorial Psalm

> Let the redeemed of the LORD say so,
>> those he redeemed from trouble

and gathered in from the lands,
  from the east and from the west,
  from the north and from the south.   Psalm 107:2-3

Prayers, pp. 529-32

Closing Psalm Prayer

He raises up the needy out of distress,
  and makes their families like flocks.
The upright see it and are glad;
  and all wickedness stops its mouth.   Psalm 107:41-42

Sixth Week after Epiphany   Saturday

Theme: The person who truly loves the Lord and is filled with spiritual
        joy is willing to give everything to the service of God.

Antiphon and Opening Prayer

Let all the earth fear the LORD;
let all the inhabitants of the world stand in awe of him.

                                              Psalm 33:8

Lord, fill me to overflowing with your love.
Teach me not to grasp after things for myself.
Help me to let go of my prized possessions for your sake.

Scripture Reading

. . . [Jesus] watched the crowd putting money into the treasury.
Many rich people put in large sums. A poor widow came and put
in two small copper coins, which are worth a penny. Then he called
his disciples and said to them, "Truly I tell you, this poor widow has
put in more than all those who are contributing to the treasury. For

all of them have contributed out of their abundance; but she out of
her poverty has put in everything she had, all she had to live on."

Mark 12:41b-44
optional: Genesis 35:1-20

Responsorial Psalm

Rejoice in the LORD. . . .
Praise the LORD with the lyre;
>make melody to him with the harp of ten strings.
Sing to him a new song;
>play skillfully on the strings, with loud shouts. Psalm 33:1a, 3

Prayers, pp. 529-32

Closing Psalm Prayer

Our soul waits for the Lord;
>he is our help and shield.
Our heart is glad in him,
>because we trust in his holy name.   Psalm 33:20-21

In 1996, 1998, 2004, 2007, and 2012 go to the last Sunday after Epiphany
(p. 141) tomorrow.

Seventh Week after Epiphany   Sunday

Theme: God loves all people. He sends the sunshine and rain on all
>equally. Like him, we are called to love everyone.

Antiphon and Opening Prayer

O give thanks to the LORD, for he is good;
his steadfast love endures forever!   Psalm 118:1

Father, forgive me for the anger I hold for my enemy.
As you love us all and gave your Son to redeem all people,

so help me, Lord,
to forgive my enemies and turn toward them with a loving heart.

Scripture Reading

You have heard that it was said, "You shall love your neighbor and hate your enemy." But I say to you, Love your enemies and pray for those who persecute you, so that you may be children of your Father in heaven; for he makes his sun rise on the evil and on the good, and sends rain on the righteous and on the unrighteous.

Matthew 5:43-45
optional: Genesis 37:1-36

Responsorial Psalm

With the LORD on my side, I do not fear.
    What can mortals do to me?
The LORD is on my side to help me;
    I shall look in triumph on those who hate me.   Psalm 118:6-7

Prayers, pp. 529-32

Closing Psalm Prayer

You are my God, and I will give thanks to you;
    You are my God, I will extol you.
O give thanks to the LORD, for he is good.   Psalm 118:28-29a

Seventh Week after Epiphany   Monday

Theme: As Jesus approaches his own impending death, the death of his friend Lazarus foreshadows his own death and resurrection.

Antiphon and Opening Prayer

Blessed be the LORD, the God of Israel,
　　from everlasting to everlasting.
And let all the people say, "Amen!"　　　　　　　Psalm 106:48

Father, you who give life and take it away,
may I see the death of my loved ones in the light of the death
and resurrection of your Son.
Fill my heart with hope.

Scripture Reading

Martha said to Jesus, "Lord, if you had been here, my brother would
not have died. But even now I know that God will give you whatever
you ask of him." . . . Jesus said to her, "I am the resurrection and
the life. Those who believe in me, even though they die, will live,
and everyone who lives and believes in me will never die. Do you
believe this?" She said to him, "Yes, Lord, I believe that you are the
Messiah, the Son of God, the one coming into the world."
　　　　　　　　　　　　　　　　　　　John 11:21-22, 25-27
　　　　　　　　　　　　　　　　　　　optional: Genesis 39:1-23

Responsorial Psalm

Remember me, O LORD, when you show favor to your people;
　　help me when you deliver them;
that I may see the prosperity of your chosen ones . . .
　　that I may glory in your heritage.　　　　　　Psalm 106:4-5

Prayers, pp. 529-32

Closing Psalm Prayer

Save us, O LORD our God,
　　and gather us from among the nations,
that we may give thanks to your holy name
　　and glory in your praise.
Praise the LORD!　　　　　　　　　　　　　Psalm 106:47, 48b

Seventh Week after Epiphany   Tuesday

Theme: The Lord who raised Lazarus from the dead watches over us
        and guards our coming and going.

Antiphon and Opening Prayer

I lift up my eyes to the hills —
    from where will my help come?
My help comes from the LORD.   Psalm 121:1, 2a

Lord, you who raised Lazarus from the dead,
you who watch over your whole creation and care for each
person,
grant me faith and confidence in your will.

Scripture Reading

So they took away the stone. And Jesus looked upward and said,
"Father, I thank you for having heard me. I knew that you always
hear me, but I have said this for the sake of the crowd standing here,
so that they may believe that you sent me." When he had said this,
he cried out with a loud voice, "Lazarus, come out!"

John 11:41-43
optional: Genesis 40:1-23

Responsorial Psalm

He who keeps Israel
    will neither slumber nor sleep.
The LORD is your keeper;
    the LORD is your shade at your right hand.
The sun shall not strike you by day,
    nor the moon by night.   Psalm 121:4-6

Prayers, pp. 529-32

Closing Psalm Prayer

> The LORD will keep you from all evil;
>   he will keep your life.
> The LORD will keep
>   your going out and your coming in
>   from this time on and forevermore.   Psalm 121:7-8

Seventh Week after Epiphany   Wednesday

Theme: At the end of his earthly life our Lord felt the pain of rejection.
         He withdrew to the comfort of his disciples.

Antiphon and Opening Prayer

> Out of the depths I cry to you, O LORD.
>   Lord, hear my voice!
> Let your ears be attentive.   Psalm 130:1-2a

> Lord Jesus, when I am challenged or rejected for being your
> disciple,
> help me to remember that you have gone before me
> on that way of rejection.

Scripture Reading

> So the chief priests and the Pharisees called a meeting of the council,
> and said, "What are we to do? This man is performing many signs."
> . . . So from that day on they planned to put him to death.
>   Jesus therefore no longer walked about openly among the Jews,
> but went from there to the town called Ephraim in the region near
> the wilderness; and he remained there with his disciples.
>   Now the Passover of the Jews was near.
>   John 11:47, 53-55a
>   optional: Genesis 41:1-57

Responsorial Psalm

> I wait for the LORD, my soul waits,
>   and in his word I hope;

my soul waits for the Lord
more than those who watch for the morning,
more than those who watch for the morning.   Psalm 130:5-6

Prayers, pp. 529-32

Closing Psalm Prayer

O Israel, hope in the LORD!
For with the LORD there is steadfast love,
and with him is great power to redeem.
It is he who will redeem Israel
from all its iniquities.   Psalm 130:7-8

Seventh Week after Epiphany   **Thursday**

Theme: Mary ministers to Jesus in the hour of his anguish and need.
Mary is a model of our servanthood to Jesus.

Antiphon and Opening Prayer

But I have calmed and quieted my soul,
like a weaned child with his mother;
my soul is like the weaned child that is with me.   Psalm 131:2

Father, as your servant Mary put Jesus first in her life and
attended to him,
so let me, your servant, place Christ at the center of my life,
to your glory.

Scripture Reading

Six days before the Passover, Jesus came to Bethany. . . . Mary took
a pound of costly perfume made of pure nard, anointed Jesus' feet,
and wiped them with her hair. The house was filled with the fragrance
of the perfume. But Judas Iscariot . . . said, "Why was this perfume
not sold for three hundred denarii and the money given to the poor?"

. . . Jesus said, "Leave her alone. She bought it so that she might keep it for the day of my burial."

John 12:1a, 3, 5, 7
optional: Genesis 42:1-38

Responsorial Psalm

How very good and pleasant it is
    when kindred live together in unity!
It is like the precious oil on the head,
    running down upon the beard of Aaron,
    running down over the collar of his robes.   Psalm 133:1-2

Prayers, pp. 529-32

Closing Psalm Prayer

Come, bless the LORD, all you servants of the LORD,
  . who stand by night in the house of the LORD!
Lift up your hands to the holy place,
    and bless the LORD.   Psalm 134:1-2

Seventh Week after Epiphany   Friday

Theme: Beneath the popularity of Jesus during his last days is the grow-
      ing storm of hostility generated by the religious leaders.

Antiphon and Opening Prayer

With my voice I cry to the LORD. . . .
I pour out my complaint before him;
I tell my trouble before him.   Psalm 142:1a, 2

Father in heaven,
Your Son Jesus endured the pain of rejection and hostility,
May I, your servant, not join with those who this day are hostile
to him.

Scripture Reading

When the great crowd of the Jews learned that he was there, they came not only because of Jesus but also to see Lazarus, whom he had raised from the dead. So the chief priests planned to put Lazarus to death as well, since it was on account of him that many of the Jews were deserting and were believing in Jesus. . . .

It was also because they heard that he had performed this sign that the crowd went to meet him. The Pharisees then said to one another, "You see, you can do nothing. Look, the world has gone after him!"

John 12:9-11, 18-19
optional: Genesis 43:1-34

Responsorial Psalm

No one cares for me.
I cry to you, O LORD;
I say, "You are my refuge,
my portion in the land of the living."
Give heed to my cry,
for I am brought very low.   adapted from Psalm 142:4-6

Prayers, pp. 529-32

Closing Psalm Prayer

Bring me out of prison,
    so that I may give thanks to your name.
The righteous will surround me,
    for you will deal bountifully with me.   Psalm 142:7

Seventh Week after Epiphany   Saturday

Theme: In the final hours of his life our Lord called his disciples to a deep and far-reaching commitment.

Antiphon and Opening Prayer

O LORD, how manifold are your works!
  In wisdom you have made them all;
the earth is full of your creatures.   Psalm 104:24

Father, as your creation finds its meaning in you,
so let me give up my earthly ambition
to lose myself in you and your will for my life.
Through Jesus I pray.

Scripture Reading

Jesus answered them, "The hour has come for the Son of Man to be
glorified. Very truly, I tell you, unless a grain of wheat falls into the
earth and dies, it remains just a single grain; but if it dies, it bears
much fruit. Those who love their life lose it, and those who hate
their life in this world will keep it for eternal life. Whoever serves
me must follow me, and where I am, there will my servant be also."
                                                   John 12:23-26
                                          optional: Genesis 44:1-34

Responsorial Psalm

Bless the LORD, O my soul!
  O LORD my God, you are very great.
You are clothed with honor and majesty,
  wrapped in light as with a garment.
You stretch out the heavens like a tent.   Psalm 104:1-2

Prayers, pp. 529-32

Closing Psalm Prayer

I will sing to the LORD as long as I live;
  I will sing praise to my God while I have being.
May my meditation be pleasing to him,
  for I rejoice in the LORD.   Psalm 104:33-34

In 1995, 2001, 2003, 2006, and 2014 go to the last Sunday after Epiphany
(p. 141) tomorrow.

Eighth Week after Epiphany   Sunday

Theme: The Lord teaches us that our first priority in life is not food,
clothing, and shelter, but the kingdom of God.

Antiphon and Opening Prayer

I will give thanks to the LORD with my whole heart,
    in the company of the upright, in the congregation.

Psalm 111:1

Father, forgive me for failing to keep my priorities right.
Teach me to praise you with my whole heart
and to depend not on my own ingenuity,
but on your tender care.

Scripture Reading

Therefore I tell you, do not worry about your life, what you will eat
or what you will drink, or about your body, what you will wear. Is
not life more than food, and the body more than clothing? . . .
Therefore do not worry, saying, "What will we eat?" or "What will
we drink?" or "What will we wear?" . . . But strive first for the
kingdom of God and his righteousness, and all these things will be
given to you as well.

Matthew 6:25, 31, 33
optional: Genesis 45:1-28

Responsorial Psalm

Great are the works of the LORD,
    studied by all who delight in them.
Full of honor and majesty is his work,
    and his righteousness endures forever.
He has gained renown by his wonderful deeds.   Psalm 111:2-4a

Prayers, pp. 529-32

Closing Psalm Prayer

> The fear of the LORD is the beginning of wisdom;
>> all those who practice it have a good understanding.
> His praise endures forever.   Psalm 111:10

Eighth Week after Epiphany   Monday

Theme: Jesus predicts his death and proclaims that it will result in the
casting down of the evil one.

Antiphon and Opening Prayer

> Answer me when I call. . . .
> Be gracious to me, and hear my prayer.   Psalm 4:1

> Father, you sent your Son to destroy the power of evil,
> to set your creation free, to redeem your people.
> Hear me, Lord, as I offer you my heartfelt praise and adoration.

Scripture Reading

> "Father, glorify your name." Then a voice came from heaven, "I have
> glorified it, and I will glorify it again." The crowd standing there
> heard it and said that it was thunder. Others said, "An angel has
> spoken to him." Jesus answered, "This voice has come for your sake,
> not for mine. Now is the judgment of this world; now the ruler of
> this world will be driven out. And I, when I am lifted up from the
> earth, will draw all people to myself."
>
>> John 12:28-32
>> optional: Genesis 46:1-34

Responsorial Psalm

> How long, you people, shall my honor suffer shame?
>> How long will you love vain words, and seek after lies?
> But know that the LORD has set apart the faithful for himself.
>
>> Psalm 4:2-3a

Prayers, pp. 529-32

Closing Psalm Prayer

Let the light of your face shine on us.
You have put gladness in my heart.
I will both lie down and sleep in peace. adapted from Psalm 4:6-8

Eighth Week after Epiphany   Tuesday

Theme: Jesus calls on the people to humble themselves and believe that
he has come into the world as light in darkness.

Antiphon and Opening Prayer

O LORD, you will hear the desire of the meek;
you will strengthen their heart,
you will incline your ear.   Psalm 10:17

Father in heaven,
I pray that you will find a humble heart and spirit within me.
I believe that you are the light of the world.
Strengthen me in that conviction.

Scripture Reading

Then Jesus cried aloud: "Whoever believes in me believes not in me
but in him who sent me. And whoever sees me sees him who sent
me. I have come as light into the world, so that everyone who believes
in me should not remain in the darkness. I do not judge anyone who
hears my words and does not keep them, for I came not to judge
the world, but to save the world. The one who rejects me and does
not receive my word has a judge."

John 12:44-48a
optional: Genesis 47:1-31

Responsorial Psalm

Rise up, O Lord; O God, lift up your hand;
  do not forget the oppressed.
Why do the wicked renounce God,
  and say in their hearts, "You will not call us to account."

                                                Psalm 10:12, 13

Prayers, pp. 529-32

Closing Psalm Prayer

The Lord is in his holy temple;
  the Lord's throne is in heaven. . . .
For the Lord is righteous;
he loves righteous deeds;
  the upright shall behold his face.   Psalm 11:4a, 7

Eighth Week after Epiphany   Wednesday

Theme: Our Lord washes the feet of his disciples and leaves an example
       of the spirit of life that we are to follow.

Antiphon and Opening Prayer

I will sing to the Lord,
  because he has dealt bountifully with me.   Psalm 13:6

Father, your Son, who is full of your glory,
humbled himself to become one of us,
to live among us, to die for us, and to show us how to live.
So let me follow his example.

Scripture Reading

After he had washed their feet, had put on his robe, and had returned
to the table, he said to them, "Do you know what I have done to
you? You call me Teacher and Lord — and you are right, for that is

what I am. So if I, your Lord and Teacher, have washed your feet, you also ought to wash one another's feet. For I have set you an example, that you also should do as I have done to you. . . . If you know these things, you are blessed if you do them."

John 13:12-15, 17

optional: Genesis 48:1-22

Responsorial Psalm

The promises of the LORD are promises that are pure,
    silver refined in a furnace on the ground,
    purified seven times.
You, O LORD, will protect us;
    you will guard us from this generation forever.   Psalm 12:6-7

Prayers, pp. 529-32

Closing Psalm Prayer

Consider and answer me, O LORD my God!
    Give light to my eyes. . . .
But I trusted in your steadfast love;
    my heart shall rejoice in your salvation.   Psalm 13:3a, 5

Eighth Week after Epiphany   Thursday

Theme: Judas is identified as the one who will betray Jesus. He leaves to set in motion the events that bring Jesus to the cross.

Antiphon and Opening Prayer

The LORD is my rock and my fortress and my deliverer;
my God, my rock in whom I take refuge.

adapted from Psalm 18:2

Father, Judas the betrayer of your Son,
lived with him, heard his teaching, and saw his miracles,

yet turned from him.
O Lord, keep me, your servant, steadfast in the faith.

Scripture Reading

After saying this Jesus was troubled in spirit, and declared, "Very truly, I tell you, one of you will betray me. . . . It is the one to whom I give this piece of bread when I have dipped it in the dish." So when he had dipped the piece of bread, he gave it to Judas son of Simon Iscariot. After he received the piece of bread, Satan entered into him. Jesus said to him, "Do quickly what you are going to do."

John 13:21, 26-27
optional: Genesis 49:1-33

Responsorial Psalm

The cords of death encompassed me;
    the torrents of perdition assailed me;
the cords of Sheol entangled me;
    the snares of death confronted me.
In my distress I called upon the LORD.   Psalm 18:4-6a

Prayers, pp. 529-32

Closing Psalm Prayer

I call upon the LORD, who is worthy to be praised. . . .
From his temple he heard my voice,
    and my cry to him reached his ears.   Psalm 18:3a, 6b

Eighth Week after Epiphany   Friday

Theme: Our Lord, who has shown the meaning of love by his life, now leaves his followers a new command to live by.

Antiphon and Opening Prayer

The LORD is my chosen portion and my cup. . . .
I have a goodly heritage.   Psalm 16:5a, 6b

Father, your Son has commanded us to love one another,
even as he loved us.
Forgive me for my failure,
and set my heart to truly love others and to fulfill the command
of your Son.

Scripture Reading

. . . Jesus said, "Now the Son of Man has been glorified, and God
has been glorified in him. . . . Little children, I am with you only a
little longer. You will look for me; and as I said to the Jews so now
I say to you, 'Where I am going, you cannot come.' I give you a new
commandment, that you love one another. Just as I have loved you,
you also should love one another. By this everyone will know that
you are my disciples, if you have love for one another."

John 13:31, 33-35
optional: Genesis 50:1-14

Responsorial Psalm

If you try my heart, if you visit me by night,
if you test me, you will find no wickedness in me. . . .
I have avoided the ways of the violent.
My steps have held fast to your paths;
my feet have not slipped.   Psalm 17:3a, 4b-5

Prayers, pp. 529-32

Closing Psalm Prayer

Therefore my heart is glad, and my soul rejoices. . . .
You show me the path of life.
In your presence there is fullness of joy;
in your right hand are pleasures forevermore. Psalm 16:9a, 11

Eighth Week after Epiphany   Saturday

Theme: Judas now makes his move. He brings the soldiers to capture
Jesus and to lead him off to his ignoble death.

Antiphon and Opening Prayer

Be exalted, O LORD, in your strength!
We will sing and praise your power.   Psalm 21:13

Father, as the time of your Son's death draws near,
help me to enter into his death,
so that I may identify with him not only in death,
but also in the glorious resurrection.

Scripture Reading

So Judas brought a detachment of soldiers together with police from
the chief priests and the Pharisees, and they came there with lanterns
and torches and weapons. Then Jesus, knowing all that was to
happen to him, came forward and asked them, "Whom are you
looking for?" They answered, "Jesus of Nazareth." Jesus replied, "I
am he." Judas, who betrayed him, was standing with them.

John 18:3-5
optional: Genesis 50:15-26

Responsorial Psalm

The LORD answer you in the day of trouble!
   The name of the God of Jacob protect you!
May he send you help from the sanctuary,
   and give you support from Zion.   Psalm 20:1-2

Prayers, pp. 529-32

Closing Psalm Prayer

Some take pride in chariots, and some in horses,
but our pride is in the name of the LORD our God.
Give victory to the king, O LORD.   Psalm 20:7, 9a

Last Week after Epiphany   Sunday

Theme: Jesus tells his followers that it is no advantage to gain the whole
world and lose our souls.

Antiphon and Opening Prayer

Sing to the LORD a new song,
his praise in the assembly of the faithful.   Psalm 149:1

Father, my heart is so often turned to material gain,
recognition, and success.
Assist me in the ordering of my life,
that I might truly follow after you daily.

Scripture Reading

Then he said to them all, "If any want to become my followers, let
them deny themselves and take up their cross daily and follow me.
For those who want to save their life will lose it, and those who lose
their life for my sake will save it. What does it profit them if they
gain the whole world, but lose or forfeit themselves? Those who are
ashamed of me and of my words, of them the Son of Man will be
ashamed.
Luke 9:23-26a
optional: Deuteronomy 6:1-9

Responsorial Psalm

Let Israel be glad in its Maker;
let the children of Zion rejoice in their King.

Let them praise his name with dancing,
making melody to him with tambourine and lyre.

Psalm 149:2-3

Prayers, pp. 529-32

Closing Psalm Prayer

For the LORD takes pleasure in his people;
he adorns the humble with victory.
Let the faithful exult in glory;
let them sing for joy on their couches. Psalm 149:4-5

Last Week after Epiphany   Monday

Theme: Peter, who has walked with the Lord for three years, denies him
out of fear. Christ calls us to commitment.

Antiphon and Opening Prayer

I will give thanks to the LORD with my whole heart;
I will tell of all your wonderful deeds. Psalm 9:1

Lord, your servant Peter denied you and failed to confess you as
his Lord.
Keep me in your trust and spare me from turning against you,
for the sake of the gospel.

Scripture Reading

Simon Peter and another disciple followed Jesus. . . . He went with
Jesus into the courtyard of the high priest. . . . [Then the servant girl
who stood at the door] said to Peter, "You are not also one of this
man's disciples, are you?" He said, "I am not." Now the slaves and
the police had made a charcoal fire because it was cold, and they
were standing around it and warming themselves. Peter also was
standing with them and warming himself. . . . They asked him, "You

are not also one of his disciples, are you?" He denied it and said, "I am not."

John 18:15, 17-18, 25b
optional: Deuteronomy 6:10-15

Responsorial Psalm

The LORD is a stronghold for the oppressed,
    a stronghold in times of trouble.
And those who know your name put their trust in you,
    for you, O LORD, have not forsaken those who seek you.

Psalm 9:9-10

Prayers, pp. 529-32

Closing Psalm Prayer

O Lord, who may abide in your tent?
    Who may dwell on your holy hill?
Those who walk blamelessly, and do what is right,
    and speak the truth in their heart.   Psalm 15:1-2

Last Week after Epiphany   Tuesday

Theme: Jesus admits to Pilate that he is indeed the King of the Jews.
       But his kingdom is not of this world.

Antiphon and Opening Prayer

Hear the voice of my supplication,
    as I cry to you for help,
as I lift up my hands
    toward your most holy sanctuary.   Psalm 28:2

Father, I confess that your Son is the ruler of the world.
May I not deny this enthronement in my own life.
May I do his will and keep faith with my commitment.

Scripture Reading

Then Pilate . . . summoned Jesus, and asked him, "Are you the King
of the Jews?" . . . Jesus answered, "My kingdom is not from this
world. If my kingdom were from this world, my followers would be
fighting to keep me from being handed over to the Jews. But as it
is, my kingdom is not from here." Pilate asked him, "So you are a
king?" Jesus answered, "You say that I am a king. For this I was
born. . . . Everyone who belongs to the truth listens to my voice."

John 18:33, 36-37
optional: Deuteronomy 6:16-25

Responsorial Psalm

Blessed be the LORD,
   for he has heard the sound of my pleadings.
The LORD is my strength and my shield;
   in him my heart trusts;
so I am helped.   Psalm 28:6-7a

Prayers, pp. 529-32

Closing Psalm Prayer

The LORD is the strength of his people. . . .
O save your people, and bless your heritage;
   be their shepherd, and carry them forever.   Psalm 28:8a, 9

Lent

We have now come to a season of the Christian year that differs significantly from Advent, Christmas, and Epiphany. Before we can think about our spiritual pilgrimage during this season, we need to have some understanding of how the Lenten season differs from the preceding seasons.

Lenten season is the time when we especially identify with the sufferings of Jesus. During Lent we walk the way of the cross. In Advent we longed for the coming of Christ, at Christmas we celebrated his birth, and after Epiphany we encountered Christ in his many manifestations. Now, the entire mood changes. Now in Lent we share in the rejection Christ felt when the religious leaders and others turned from him, rejected him, and plotted his death.

Because we identify with the sufferings of Christ during Lent, Lent is chiefly a time for repentance and renewal. What we want to accomplish during Lent is the opposite of what the Pharisees, the mockers, and doubters did. They rejected Jesus. They were proud, haughty, and confident of their righteousness. Lent is the antithesis of those attitudes. Lent is a time to fall at the feet of Jesus and admit our sinfulness and our need of him. Lent is a time to confess, to cry "Lord, have mercy on me, a sinner!" Lent is a time for humility and repentance. It is a time to get on our knees and get right with God.

Because Lent is an identification with the sufferings of Christ that calls us into repentance and renewal, the church has developed three disciplines that assist us in accomplishing this spiritual concern. They are prayer, fasting, and almsgiving, the threefold theme of Matthew 6.

Our spiritual journey during Lent is related to these three disciplines. First, the *Book of Daily Prayer* provides us with a rich selection of scriptural readings that will help us identify with the suffering of Jesus.

Pray then, as usual, with your mind, your heart, and your will. Next, I urge you to commit yourself to fasting during this Lent. Don't do it to lose weight. That's the wrong motive. Fast in order to identify with the sufferings of Christ. There are many different ways to fast. You can drop a favorite food from your menu, you can choose to fast one day of the week, or you could go on a partial fast for the entire season (except Sunday: Sunday is always a feast day because it celebrates the resurrection, even during Lent). Finally, determine to give to someone in need. Give a gift that goes beyond your normal giving. Let it be a giving that "hurts." That is, you should deprive yourself of something you want in order to help someone else.

Finally, remember that Lent is a time that is crucial to your spiritual health. By taking Lent seriously through prayer, fasting, and almsgiving, you will be able to identify with the sufferings of Jesus in a way that you never have before. And the real spiritual gain of Lent will be experienced during Easter. For by preparing for his death and entering into his suffering you will be able to experience the resurrection joy in a way that you have never experienced it before!

Pray that God will help you maintain your Lenten discipline as you now embark on this period of entering into the sufferings of our Lord.

Ash Wednesday

Theme: In the Old Testament ashes were used as a sign of repentance. Today let ashes remind us that human glamour will come to an end when God calls us before him.

Prayer of Confession

Holy God,
holy and immortal one,
have mercy upon me, a sinner.

Scripture Reading

Yet even now, says the LORD,
    return to me with all your heart,
with fasting, with weeping, and with mourning;

rend your hearts and not your clothing.
Return to the LORD, your God,
    for he is gracious and merciful,
slow to anger, and abounding in steadfast love,
    and relents from punishing.
Who knows whether he will not turn and relent,
    and leave a blessing behind him,
a grain offering and a drink offering
      for the LORD, your God?   Joel 2:12-28;
         read also II Corinthians 5:20–6:6; Matthew 6:1-6, 16-18

Responsorial Psalm

Have mercy on me, O God,
    according to your steadfast love;
according to your abundant mercy
    blot out my transgressions.
Wash me thoroughly from my iniquity,
    and cleanse me from my sin.
For I know my transgressions,
    and my sin is ever before me.   Psalm 51:1-3

Prayers, pp. 529-32

Closing Psalm Prayer

[Lord,] wash me, and I shall be whiter than snow.
Let me hear joy and gladness. . . .
Hide your face from my sins,
    and blot out all my iniquities.
Create in me a clean heart, O God,
    and put a new and right spirit within me.
                Psalm 51:7b, 8a, 9-10

Thursday after Ash Wednesday

Theme: Today's scripture reminds us that life is only gained in its fullness
when we are willing to lose it. Pray that God will teach you
how to lose your life in him.

Prayer of Confession

Against you, you alone, have I sinned,
and done what is evil in your sight.   Psalm 51:4a

Scripture Reading

[Jesus said,] "The Son of Man must undergo great suffering, and be
rejected by the elders, chief priests, and scribes, and be killed, and
on the third day be raised."

Then he said to them all, "If any want to become my followers,
let them deny themselves and take up their cross daily, and follow
me. For those who want to save their life will lose it, and those who
lose their life for my sake will save it. What does it profit them if
they gain the whole world, but lose or forfeit themselves?"

Luke 9:22-25;
read also Deuteronomy 30:15-20

Responsorial Psalm

Happy are those
who do not follow the advice of the wicked,
or take the path that sinners tread,
or sit in the seat of scoffers;
but their delight is in the law of the LORD,
and on his law they meditate day and night.
For the LORD watches over the way of the righteous.

Psalm 1:1-2, 6a

Prayers, pp. 529-32

Closing Psalm Prayer

> Lord, let me be like a tree planted by streams of water.
> It yields its fruit in season.
> Its leaf does not wither.
> Whatever such a person does will prosper.
> Through Jesus Christ I pray.   adapted from Psalm 1:3

Friday after Ash Wednesday

Theme: Today's scripture emphasizes how fasting may unite both the
      rich and the poor: The rich fast in order to give to the poor. In
      this way God blesses both.

Prayer of Confession

> The sacrifice acceptable to God is a broken spirit;
>   a broken and contrite heart, O God, you will not despise.
>   Psalm 51:17

Scripture Reading

> Is not this the fast that I choose:
>   to loose the bonds of injustice,
>   to undo the thongs of the yoke,
> to let the oppressed go free,
>   and to break every yoke?
> Is it not to share your bread with the hungry,
>   and bring the homeless poor into your house;
> when you see the naked, to cover them,
>   and not to hide yourself from your own kin?
> Then your light shall break forth like the dawn,
>   and your healing shall spring up quickly;
> your vindicator shall go before you;
>   the glory of the LORD shall be your rear guard.   Isaiah 58:6-8
>   read also Matthew 9:14-15

Responsorial Psalm

> To you, O LORD, I cried,
>> and to the LORD I made supplication:
> "What profit is there in my death,
>> if I go down to the Pit?
> Will the dust praise you?
>> Will it tell of your faithfulness?
> Hear, O LORD, and be gracious to me!
>> O LORD, be my helper!"   Psalm 30:8-10

Prayers, pp. 529-32

Closing Psalm Prayer

> [Lord,] you have turned my mourning into dancing;
>> you have taken off my sackcloth
>> and clothed me with joy,
> so that my soul may praise you and not be silent.
>> O LORD my God, I will give thanks to you forever.
>   Psalm 30:11-12

Saturday after Ash Wednesday

Theme: During Lent, God especially calls us to a repentance that brings
the renewal of our conversion. We ought to humble ourselves
and admit our need, turning to him.

Prayer of Confession

> I give thanks to you, O Lord my God, with my whole heart,
>> and I will glorify your name forever.
> For great is your steadfast love toward me.   Psalm 86:12-13a

Scripture Reading

After this he went out and saw a tax collector named Levi, sitting at the tax booth; and he said to him, "Follow me." And he got up, left everything, and followed him.

Then Levi gave a great banquet for him in his house; and there was a large crowd of tax collectors and others sitting at the table with them. The Pharisees and their scribes were complaining to his disciples, saying, "Why do you eat and drink with tax collectors and sinners?" Jesus answered, "Those who are well have no need of a physician, but those who are sick; I have come to call not the righteous but sinners to repentance."

Luke 5:27-32
read also Isaiah 58:9-14

Responsorial Psalm

Incline your ear, O LORD, and answer me,
    for I am poor and needy.
Preserve my life, for I am devoted to you;
    save your servant who trusts in you!
You are my God; be gracious to me, O Lord,
    for to you do I cry all day long.
Gladden the soul of your servant,
For to you, O Lord, I lift up my soul.   Psalm 86:1-4

Prayers, pp. 529-32

Closing Psalm Prayer

Give ear, O LORD, to my prayer;
listen to my cry of supplication.
In the day of my trouble I call on you,
for you will answer me.   Psalm 86:6-7

First Week in Lent   **Sunday**

Theme: Today we are reminded that our salvation comes only through
        Jesus Christ. He alone has conquered the power of evil. In his
        strength we are saved.

Prayer of Confession

A king is not saved by his great army;
a warrior is not delivered by his great strength.   Psalm 33:16

Scripture Reading

Then Jesus was led up by the Spirit into the wilderness to be tempted
by the devil. He fasted forty days and forty nights, and afterwards
he was famished. . . .
    Again, the devil took him to a very high mountain and showed
him all the kingdoms of the world and their splendor; and he said
to him, "All these I will give you, if you will fall down and worship
me." Jesus said to him, "Away with you, Satan! For it is written,
    'Worship the Lord your God,
        and serve only him.' "
    Then the devil left him, and suddenly angels came and waited
on him.

Matthew 4:1-2, 8-11
read also Romans 5:12-21

Responsorial Psalm

By the word of the LORD the heavens were made,
    and all their host by the breath of his mouth.
He gathered the waters of the sea as in a bottle;
    he put the deep in storehouses.
Let all the earth fear the LORD;
    let all the inhabitants of the world stand in awe of him.
For he spoke, and it came to be;
    he commanded, and it stood firm.   Psalm 33:6-9

Prayers, pp. 529-32

Closing Psalm Prayer

> Our soul waits for the LORD;
>> he is our help and shield.
> Our heart is glad in him,
>> because we trust in his holy name.
> Let your steadfast love, O LORD, be upon us,
>> even as we hope in you.   Psalm 33:20-22

First Week of Lent   Monday

Theme: God calls us to holiness. However, when we measure ourselves
against his law, we see only our imperfection. Our condition
leads us to Christ, who alone can save us.

Prayer of Confession

> But who can detect their errors?
>> Clear me from hidden faults. . . .
> Do not let them have dominion over me.   Psalm 19:12-13a

Scripture Reading

> The LORD spoke to Moses, saying:
> Speak to all the congregation of the people of Israel and say to
> them: You shall be holy, for I the LORD your God am holy. . . .
> You shall not steal; you shall not deal falsely; and you shall not
> lie to one another. And you shall not swear falsely by my name,
> profaning the name of your God: I am the LORD.
> You shall not defraud your neighbor; you shall not steal; and
> you shall not keep for yourself the wages of a laborer until morning.
> You shall not revile the deaf or put a stumbling block before the
> blind; you shall fear your God: I am the LORD.
> You shall not render an unjust judgment; you shall not be partial
> to the poor, or defer to the great.
>> Leviticus 19:1-2, 11-15
>> read also Matthew 25:31-46

Responsorial Psalm

The law of the LORD is perfect,
    reviving the soul;
The decrees of the LORD are sure,
    making wise the simple;
The precepts of the LORD are right,
    rejoicing the heart;
The commandment of the LORD is clear,
    enlightening the eyes;
The fear of the LORD is pure,
    enduring forever;
The ordinances of the LORD are true
    and righteous altogether.
More to be desired are they than gold. . . .
    In keeping them there is great reward.   Psalm 19:7-10a, 11b

Prayers, pp. 529-32

Closing Psalm Prayer

[Lord Jesus Christ, you who art holy]
Let the words of my mouth and the meditation of my heart
    be acceptable to you,
    O LORD, my rock and my redeemer.   Psalm 19:14

First Week of Lent   Tuesday

Theme: Jesus sets forth the model of holiness in his prayer. We will be
         forgiven as we forgive others. But God will deliver us from evil,
         if we turn to him.

Prayer of Confession

The face of the LORD is against evildoers. . . .
The LORD is near to the brokenhearted,
and saves the crushed in spirit.   Psalm 34:16a, 18

Scripture Reading

Pray then in this way:
Our Father in heaven,
    hallowed be your name.
Your kingdom come.
Your will be done,
    on earth as it is in heaven.
Give us this day our daily bread.
And forgive us our debts,
    as we also have forgiven our debtors.
And do not bring us to the time of trial.
    but rescue us from the evil one.   Matthew 6:9-13
                       read also Isaiah 55:10-11

Responsorial Psalm

Come, O children, listen to me;
    I will teach you the fear of the LORD.
Which of you desires life,
    and covets many days to enjoy good?
Keep your tongue from evil,
    and your lips from speaking deceit.
Depart from evil, and do good;
    seek peace, and pursue it.   Psalm 34:11-14

Prayers, pp. 529-32

Closing Psalm Prayer

O taste and see that the LORD is good;
    happy are those who take refuge in him.
O fear the LORD, you his holy ones,
    for those who fear him have no want.
The young lions suffer want and hunger,
    but those who seek the LORD lack no good thing.
                       Psalm 34:8-10

First Week of Lent   Wednesday

Theme: The power of evil in every generation keeps people from seeing
       signs of God's presence. We need to repent in order that our
       eyes may be opened.

Prayer of Confession

O that my ways may be steadfast
    in keeping your statutes!
Then I shall not be put to shame,
    having my eyes fixed on all your commandments.

Psalm 119:5-6

Scripture Reading

. . . He began to say, "This generation is an evil generation; it asks for
a sign, but no sign will be given to it except the sign of Jonah. For
just as Jonah became a sign to the people of Nineveh, so the Son of
Man will be to this generation. The queen of the South will rise at
the judgment with the people of this generation and condemn them,
because she came from the ends of the earth to listen to the wisdom
of Solomon, and see, something greater than Solomon is here! The
people of Nineveh will rise up at the judgment with this generation
and condemn it, because they repented at the proclamation of Jonah,
and see, something greater than Jonah is here!"

Luke 11:29-32
read also Jonah 3:1-10

Responsorial Psalm

How can young people keep their way pure?
    By guarding it according to your word.
With my whole heart I seek you;
    do not let me stray from your commandments.
I treasure your word in my heart,
    so that I may not sin against you.
Blessed are you, O LORD!
    teach me your statutes.   Psalm 119:9-12

Prayers, pp. 529-32

Closing Psalm Prayer

> Open my eyes, so that I may behold
> wondrous things out of your law. . . .
> My soul is consumed with longing
> for your ordinances at all times. . . .
> Take away from me their scorn and contempt,
> for I have kept your decrees.   Psalm 119:18, 20, 22

First Week of Lent   **Thursday**

Theme: The Lord who knows us, knows our needs. He will not turn his
        back on us. Therefore, we are to do to others what God does
        for us.

Prayer of Confession

> O LORD, you have searched me and known me.
> You know when I sit down and when I rise up;
>   you discern my thoughts from far away.   Psalm 139:1-2

Scripture Reading

> So I say to you, Ask, and it will be given you; search, and you will
> find; knock, and the door will be opened for you. For everyone who
> asks receives, and everyone who searches finds, and for everyone
> who knocks, the door will be opened. Is there anyone among you
> who, if your child asks for a fish, will give a snake instead of a fish?
> Or if the child asks for an egg, will give a scorpion? If you then,
> who are evil, know how to give good gifts to your children, how
> much more will the heavenly Father give the Holy Spirit to those
> who ask him!"
>
>   Luke 11:9-12
>   read also Esther 4:1-15

Responsorial Psalm

I give you thanks, O LORD, with my whole heart. . . .
All the kings of the earth shall praise you, O LORD,
    for they have heard the words of your mouth.
They shall sing of the ways of the LORD,
    for great is the glory of the LORD.
For though the LORD is high, he regards the lowly;
    but the haughty he perceives from far away.

Psalm 138:1a, 4-6

Prayers, pp. 529-32

Closing Psalm Prayer

Though I walk in the midst of trouble,
    you preserve me against the wrath of my enemies;
you stretch out your hand,
    and your right hand delivers me.
The LORD will fulfill his purpose for me;
    your steadfast love, O LORD, endures forever.

Psalm 138:7-8a

First Week of Lent   Friday

Theme: Lent is a time to heal broken relationships. While the heart cries
        for reconciliation, the spirit is often stubborn and unrepentant.
        Act now to receive God's mercy.

Prayer of Confession

Out of the depths I cry to you, O LORD.
    Lord, hear my voice!
Let your ears be attentive
    to the voice of my supplications!   Psalm 130:1-2

Scripture Reading

So when you are offering your gift at the altar, if you remember that your brother or sister has something against you, leave your gift there before the altar and go; first be reconciled to your brother or sister, and then come and offer your gift. Come to terms quickly with your accuser while you are on the way to court with him, or your accuser may hand you over to the judge, and the judge to the guard, and you will be thrown into prison. Truly I tell you, you will never get out until you have paid the last penny.

Matthew 5:23-26
read also Ezekiel 18:21-28

Responsorial Psalm

If you, O LORD, should mark iniquities,
     Lord, who could stand?
But there is forgiveness with you,
     so that you may be revered.
I wait for the LORD, my soul waits,
     and in his word I hope;
my soul waits for the Lord
     more than those who watch for the morning,
     more than those who watch for the morning.   Psalm 130:3-6

Prayers, pp. 529-32

Closing Psalm Prayer

O Lord, my hope is in you,
because with you there is steadfast love,
and great power to redeem.
It is you who will redeem Israel — and me — from all iniquities.
Thanks be to God!   adapted from Psalm 130:7-8

First Week of Lent   Saturday

Theme: God calls us to love our neighbors. Even here we fall short of
his expectations. Repent today and be reconciled with that
person with whom you are angry.

Prayer of Confession

I will praise you with an upright heart,
when I learn your righteous ordinances.
I will observe your statutes;
do not utterly forsake me.   Psalm 119:7b-8

Scripture Reading

You have heard that it was said, "You shall love your neighbor and
hate your enemy." But I say to you, Love your enemies and pray for
those who persecute you, so that you may be children of your Father
in heaven; for he makes his sun rise on the evil and on the good,
and sends rain on the righteous and on the unrighteous. For if you
love those who love you, what reward do you have? . . . Do not
even the tax collectors do the same? . . . Be perfect, therefore, as
your heavenly Father is perfect."

Matthew 5:43-46, 48
read also Deuteronomy 26:16-19

Responsorial Psalm

Happy are those whose way is blameless,
who walk in the law of the LORD!
Happy are those who keep his decrees,
who seek him with their whole heart,
who also do no wrong,
but walk in his ways.
You have commanded your precepts
to be kept diligently.   Psalm 119:1-4

Prayers, pp. 529-32

Closing Psalm Prayer

> I delight in the way of your decrees,
>   as much as in all riches.
> I will meditate on your precepts,
>   and fix my eyes on your ways.
> I will delight in your statutes:
>   I will not forget your word.   Psalm 119:14-16

Second Week of Lent   Sunday

Theme: Today God calls us to see beyond the sufferings of Jesus to his
        glorification. The transfiguration is the revelatory event through
        which we see his glory.

Prayer of Confession

> The Lord reigns:
> let the peoples tremble!
> Holy is he!   adapted from Psalm 99:1, 3

Scripture Reading

> Six days later, Jesus took with him Peter and James and his brother
> John and led them up on a high mountain by themselves. . . . While
> he was still speaking, suddenly a bright cloud overshadowed them,
> and from the cloud a voice said, "This is my Son, the Beloved; with
> him I am well pleased; listen to him!" When the disciples heard this,
> they fell to the ground and were overcome by fear. But Jesus came
> and touched them, saying, "Get up and do not be afraid." And when
> they looked up, they saw no one except Jesus himself alone.
>   Matthew 17:1, 5-8
>   read also Romans 5:12-29

Responsorial Psalm

> Extol the LORD our God;
>   worship at his footstool.

Holy is he!
Moses and Aaron were among his priests. . . .
They cried to the LORD, and he answered them.
He spoke to them in the pillar of cloud;
    they kept his decrees,
    and the statutes that he gave them.   Psalm 99:5-7

Prayers, pp. 529-32

Closing Psalm Prayer

O Lord, our God, you answered them.
You were a forgiving God to them.
I will exalt you and worship at your holy hill.
For you, Lord, are holy;
You alone are the Lord.   adapted from Psalm 99:8-9

Second Week of Lent   Monday

Theme: God calls us to forsake our sins and turn toward him. We are
      to love our enemies, resist judgmental attitudes, and be generous
      in forgiveness.

Prayer of Confession

Do not remember against us the iniquities of our ancestors;
    let your compassion come speedily to meet us,
      for we are brought very low.   Psalm 79:8

Scripture Reading

But love your enemies, do good, and lend, expecting nothing in
return. Your reward will be great, and you will be children of the
Most High; for he is kind to the ungrateful and the wicked. Be
merciful, just as your Father is merciful.

Do not judge, and you will not be judged; do not condemn, and
you will not be condemned. Forgive, and you will be forgiven; give,

and it will be given to you. A good measure, pressed down, shaken together, running over, will be put into your lap; for the measure you give will be the measure you get back.

Luke 6:35-38
read also Daniel 9:4-10

Responsorial Psalm

How long, O LORD? Will you be angry forever?
    Will your jealous wrath burn like fire? . . .
Help us, O God of our salvation,
    for the glory of your name;
deliver us, and forgive our sins,
    for your name's sake.   Psalm 79:5, 9

Prayers, pp. 529-32

Closing Psalm Prayer

Lord, we your people and sheep of your pasture,
will give you thanks forever;
we will show forth your praise to all generations.
We will turn to you in faith and obey your Word.

adapted from Psalm 79:13

Second Week of Lent   **Tuesday**

Theme: God calls us to turn away from our sin and do right. The conduct
        he desires of us seeks justice and equity for the poor and
        oppressed.

Prayer of Confession

The heavens declare his righteousness,
For God himself is judge.   Psalm 50:6

Scripture Reading

Wash yourselves; make yourselves clean;
  remove the evil of your doings
  from before my eyes;
cease to do evil,
  learn to do good;
seek justice,
  rescue the oppressed,
defend the orphan,
  plead for the widow.
Come now, let us argue it out,
  says the LORD:
though your sins are like scarlet,
  they shall be like snow.

Isaiah 1:16-18
read also Matthew 23:1-12

Responsorial Psalm

But to the wicked God says:
  "What right have you to recite my statutes,
  or take my covenant on your lips? . . .
You give your mouth free rein for evil,
  and your tongue frames deceit.
You sit and speak against your kin;
  you slander your own mother's child.
These things you have done and I have been silent. . . .
But now I rebuke you."

Psalm 50:16, 19-21

Prayers, pp. 529-32

Closing Psalm Prayer

Lord, I will call on you in the day of trouble,
and you will deliver me and glorify me.
I will offer praise to your glory
and I will order my conduct aright.
I will show forth your salvation,
O Lord, my God, and my Redeemer.

adapted from Psalm 50:15, 23

Second Week of Lent   Wednesday

Theme: Today our Lord reveals his forthcoming passion. We bring the
brokenness of our life up into his suffering. There we find his
kindness.

Prayer of Confession

Be gracious to me, O LORD, for I am in distress. . . .
I have become like a broken vessel.   Psalm 31:9a, 12b

Scripture Reading

While Jesus was going up to Jerusalem, he took the twelve disciples
aside by themselves, and said to them on the way, "See, we are going
up to Jerusalem, and the Son of Man will be handed over to the
chief priests and scribes, and they will condemn him to death; then
they will hand him over to the Gentiles to be mocked and flogged
and crucified; and on the third day he will be raised."

But Jesus called them to him and said, ". . . just as the Son of
Man came not to be served but to serve, and to give his life a ransom
for many."

Matthew 20:17-19, 25, 28
read also Jeremiah 18:18-20

Responsorial Psalm

In you, O LORD, I seek refuge;
    do not let me ever be put to shame;
    in your righteousness deliver me.
Incline your ear to me;
    rescue me speedily.
Be a rock of refuge for me,
    a strong fortress to save me.
You are indeed my rock and my fortress.   Psalm 31:1-3a

Prayers, pp. 529-32

Closing Psalm Prayer

Blessed be the LORD,
for he has wondrously shown his steadfast love to me. . . .
I had said in my alarm,
"I am driven far from your sight."
But you heard my supplications
when I cried out to you for help.   Psalm 31:21a, 22

Second Week of Lent   Thursday

Theme: God calls us to inwardness and true values. We are to look at
our hearts, examine our intentions, and bring ourselves back to
the water of life.

Prayer of Confession

Happy are those
who do not follow the advice of the wicked,
or take the path that sinners tread.   Psalm 1:1

Scripture Reading

Thus says the LORD:
Cursed are those who trust in mere mortals
and make mere flesh their strength,
whose hearts turn away from the LORD.
They shall be like a shrub in the desert,
and shall not see when relief comes.
They shall live in the parched places of the wilderness,
in an uninhabited salt land. . . .
The heart is devious above all else;
it is perverse —
who can understand it?
I the LORD test the mind
and search the heart,

to give to all according to their ways,
according to the fruit of their doings.   Jeremiah 17:5-6, 9-10
read also Luke 16:19-31

Responsorial Psalm

The wicked . . . are like chaff that the wind drives away.
Therefore the wicked will not stand in the judgment,
nor sinners in the congregation of the righteous;
for the LORD watches over the way of the righteous,
but the way of the wicked shall perish.   Psalm 1:4-6

Prayers, pp. 529-32

Closing Psalm Prayer

Lord, I will not sit in the seat of the scornful,
but I will delight in your law.
Make me, O Lord, like a tree planted by rivers of water;
may I bring forth fruit, and may my leaf not wither.
adapted from Psalm 1:1-3

Second Week of Lent   Friday

Theme: The Lord wants sinners to be converted to him. Conversion
includes reconciliation with our brothers and sisters. Then we
can rejoice.

Prayer of Confession

If a wicked person turns from all sin,
keeps all my statutes, and does what is right,
that person will surely live.   adapted from Ezekiel 18:21

Scripture Reading

For I tell you, unless your righteousness exceeds that of the scribes and Pharisees, you will never enter the kingdom of heaven.

You have heard that it was said to those of ancient times, "You shall not murder"; and "whoever murders shall be liable to judgment." But I say to you that if you are angry with a brother or sister, you will be liable to judgment. . . . So when you are offering your gift at the altar . . . leave your gift there before the altar and go; first be reconciled to your brother or sister, and then come and offer your gift.

Matthew 5:20-22a, 23-24
read also Ezekiel 18:21-28

Responsorial Psalm

He is the LORD our God;
    his judgments are in all the earth.
He is mindful of his covenant forever,
    of the word that he commanded, for a thousand generations,
the covenant that he made with Abraham,
    his sworn promise to Isaac . . .
    to Israel as an everlasting covenant. . . .
That they might keep his statutes
    and observe his laws.   Psalm 105:7-10, 45

Prayers, pp. 529-32

Closing Psalm Prayer

O give thanks to the LORD, call on his name,
    make known his deeds among the peoples.
Sing to him, sing praises to him;
    tell of all his wonderful works.
Glory in his holy name.   Psalm 105:1-3a

Second Week of Lent   Saturday

Theme: God calls us to be a holy people for himself. His desire is that
       we seek to be perfect. In our seeking we can bless the Lord in
       all places.

Prayer of Confession

> The LORD has compassion for those who fear him.
> For he knows how we were made;
>> he remembers that we are dust.   Psalm 103:13b-14

Scripture Reading

> You have heard that it was said, "You shall love your neighbor and
> hate your enemy." But I say to you, Love your enemies and pray for
> those who persecute you, so that you may be children of your Father
> in heaven; for he makes his sun rise on the evil and on the good,
> and sends rain on the righteous and on the unrighteous. For if you
> love those who love you, what reward do you have? . . . Be perfect,
> therefore, as your heavenly Father is perfect.
>> Matthew 5:43-46a, 48
>> read also Deuteronomy 26:16-19

Responsorial Psalm

> The LORD works vindication
>> and justice for all who are oppressed.
> He made known his ways to Moses,
>> his acts to the people of Israel.
> The LORD is merciful and gracious,
>> slow to anger and abounding in steadfast love.
> He will not always accuse,
>> nor will he keep his anger forever.   Psalm 103:6-9

Prayers, pp. 529-32

Closing Psalm Prayer

> Bless the LORD, all his hosts,
> his ministers that do his will.
> Bless the LORD, all his works,
> in all places of his dominion.
> Bless the LORD, O my soul!   Psalm 103:21-22

Third Week of Lent   Sunday

Theme: In the midst of Lent we are reminded that God gives us the
living water to quench our spiritual thirst and moisten our
parched lips.

Prayer of Confession

> Keep your tongue from evil,
>   and your lips from speaking deceit.
> Depart from evil, and do good.   Psalm 34:13-14a

Scripture Reading

> A Samaritan woman came to draw water, and Jesus said to her, "Give
> me a drink." . . . [She] said to him, "How is it that you, a Jew, ask
> a drink of me, a woman of Samaria?" . . . Jesus said to her, "Everyone
> who drinks of this water will be thirsty again, but those who drink
> of the water that I will give them will never be thirsty. The water
> that I will give will become in them a spring of water gushing up to
> eternal life." The woman said to him, "Sir, give me this water, so
> that I may never be thirsty or have to keep coming here to draw
> water."
>
> John 4:7, 9, 13-14
> read also Exodus 17:3-7

Responsorial Psalm

> O taste and see that the LORD is good;
>   happy are those who take refuge in him.

O fear the LORD, you his holy ones,
>for those who fear him have no want.
The young lions suffer want and hunger,
>but those who seek the LORD lack no good thing.

Psalm 34:8-10

Prayers, pp. 529-32

Closing Psalm Prayer

I will bless the LORD at all times;
>his praise shall continually be in my mouth.
My soul makes its boast in the LORD;
>let the humble hear and be glad.
O magnify the LORD with me,
>and let us exalt his name together.

Psalm 34:1-3

Third Week of Lent   Monday

Theme: God's salvation extends beyond Israel to the ends of the earth.
Even though we are cast down, God will not forget us.

Prayer of Confession

O my God, my soul is cast down within me;
therefore I remember you.

adapted from Psalm 42:6

Scripture Reading

And he said, "Truly I tell you, no prophet is accepted in the prophet's
hometown. But the truth is, there were many widows in Israel in the
time of Elijah, when the heaven was shut up three years and six
months, and there was a severe famine over all the land; yet Elijah
was sent to none of them except to a widow at Zarephath, in Sidon.

There were also many lepers in Israel in the time of the prophet
Elisha, and none of them was cleansed except Naaman the Syrian."

Luke 4:24-27, 30
read also II Kings 5:1-15

Responsorial Psalm

> I say to God, my rock,
> "Why have you forgotten me?
> Why must I walk about mournfully
> because the enemy oppresses me?"
> As with a deadly wound in my body,
> my adversaries taunt me,
> while they say to me continually,
> "Where is your God?"

Psalm 42:9-10

Prayers, pp. 529-32

Closing Psalm Prayer

> O send out your light and your truth;
> let them lead me;
> let them bring me to your holy hill
> and to your dwelling. . . .
> For I shall again praise him,
> my help and my God.

Psalm 43:3, 5b

Third Week of Lent   Tuesday

Theme: God calls us to trust completely in him. For he alone can deliver
us from sin and the power of those who would destroy our
faith.

Prayer of Confession

> Do not remember the sins of my youth or my transgressions;
> according to your steadfast love remember me.

Psalm 25:7

Scripture Reading

King Nebuchadnezzar made a golden statue. . . . And all the officials of the provinces assembled for the dedication of the statue that King Nebuchadnezzar had set up. . . .

Accordingly, at this time certain Chaldeans came forward and denounced the Jews. . . . "There are certain Jews whom you have appointed over the affairs of the province of Babylon: Shadrach, Meshach, and Abednego. These pay no heed to you, O King." . . . Shadrach, Meshach, and Abednego answered the king. . . . "If our God whom we serve is able to deliver us from the furnace of blazing fire and out of your hand, O king, let him deliver us."

Daniel 3:1, 3, 8, 12, 16, 17

read also Matthew 18:21-35

Responsorial Psalm

Who are they that fear the LORD?
He will teach them the way that they should choose.
They will abide in prosperity,
and their children shall possess the land.
The friendship of the LORD is for those who fear him,
and he makes his covenant known to them.
My eyes are ever toward the LORD,
for he will pluck my feet out of the net.   Psalm 25:12-15

Prayers, pp. 529-32

Closing Psalm Prayer

To you, O LORD, I lift up my soul.
O my God, in you I trust. . . .
O guard my life, and deliver me;
    do not let me be put to shame, for I take refuge in you.

Psalm 25:1-2a, 20

Third Week of Lent   Wednesday

Theme: God calls us to fear him and to keep his commandments. Because
        he knows us by our names, our hearts are filled with praise.

Prayer of Confession

The LORD takes pleasure in those who fear him,
in those who hope in his steadfast love.   Psalm 147:11

Scripture Reading

Do not think that I have come to abolish the law or the prophets; I
have come not to abolish but to fulfill. For truly I tell you, until
heaven and earth pass away, not one letter, not one stroke of a letter,
will pass from the law until all is accomplished. Therefore, whoever
breaks one of the least of these commandments, and teaches others
to do the same, will be called least in the kingdom of heaven; but
whoever does them and teaches them will be called great in the
kingdom of heaven.

                                                    Matthew 5:17-19
                                        read also Deuteronomy 4:1, 5-9

Responsorial Psalm

The LORD builds up Jerusalem;
    he gathers the outcasts of Israel.
He heals the brokenhearted,
    and binds up their wounds.
He determines the number of the stars;
    he gives to all of them their names.
Great is our LORD and abundant in power.   Psalm 147:2-5

Prayers, pp. 529-32

Closing Psalm Prayer

Praise the LORD!
How good it is to sing praises to our God;
    for he is gracious, and a song of praise is fitting. . . .

Sing to the LORD with thanksgiving;
> make melody to our God on the lyre. . . .
Praise the LORD!   Psalm 147:1, 7, 20b

Third Week of Lent   Thursday

Theme: We are not to doubt God's power. By trusting in him we are set
> free to rejoice in his salvation and to worship him as our God.

Prayer of Confession

O that today, you would listen to his voice!
> Do not harden your hearts. . . .
For forty years I loathed that generation.   Psalm 95:7a, 8b, 10a

Scripture Reading

Now he was casting out a demon that was mute. . . . But some of
them said, "He casts out demons by Beelzebul. . . ." But he knew
what they were thinking and said to them. . . . "But if it is by the
finger of God that I cast out the demons, then the kingdom of God
has come to you. When a strong man, fully armed, guards his castle,
his property is safe. But when one stronger than he attacks him and
overpowers him, he takes away his armor in which he trusted and
divides his plunder. Whoever is not with me is against me, and
whoever does not gather with me scatters."
>   Luke 11:14a, 15, 17a, 20-23
>   read also Jeremiah 7:23-28

Responsorial Psalm

O come, let us sing to the LORD;
> let us make a joyful noise to the rock of our salvation!
Let us come into his presence with thanksgiving;
> let us make a joyful noise to him with songs of praise!
For the LORD is a great God,
> and a great King above all gods. . . .

The sea is his, for he made it,
 and the dry land, which his hands have formed.

Psalm 95:1-3, 5

Prayers, pp. 529-32

Closing Psalm Prayer

O come, let us worship and bow down,
 let us kneel before the LORD, our Maker!
For he is our God,
 and we are the people of his pasture,
 and the sheep of his hand.

Psalm 95:6-7

Third Week of Lent   Friday

Theme: God calls us to walk in his ways and to love him and one another.
 When we do his will, he delivers us and we shout with joy.

Prayer of Confession

O that my people would listen to me,
 that Israel would walk in my ways!

Psalm 81:13

Scripture Reading

One of the scribes came near and heard them disputing with one another, and seeing that he answered them well, he asked him, "Which commandment is the first of all?" Jesus answered, "The first is, 'Hear, O Israel: the Lord our God, the Lord is one; you shall love the Lord your God with all your heart, and with all your soul, and with all your mind, and with all your strength.' The second is this, 'You shall love your neighbor as yourself.' There is no other commandment greater than these."

Mark 12:28-31
read also Leviticus 19:18

Responsorial Psalm

Hear, O my people, while I admonish you;
   O Israel, if you would but listen to me!
There shall be no strange god among you;
   you shall not bow down to a foreign god.
I am the LORD your God,
   who brought you up out of the land of Egypt.
   Open your mouth wide and I will fill it.   Psalm 81:8-10

Prayers, pp. 529-32

Closing Psalm Prayer

Sing aloud to God our strength;
   shout for joy to the God of Jacob. . . .
In distress you called, and I rescued you;
   I answered you in the secret place of thunder;
   I tested you at the waters of Meribah.   Psalm 81:1, 7

Third Week of Lent   Saturday

Theme: True renewal begins when we call on God to have mercy on us,
        to forgive our sin, and to receive our broken and contrite spirits.

Prayer of Confession

Blot out my transgressions.
Wash me thoroughly from my iniquity,
   and cleanse me from my sin.   Psalm 51:1b-2

Scripture Reading

Two men went up to the temple to pray, one a Pharisee and the other
a tax collector. The Pharisee, standing by himself, was praying thus,
"God, I thank you that I am not like other people: thieves, rogues,
adulterers, or even like this tax collector. I fast twice a week; I give
a tenth of all my income." But the tax collector, standing far off,

would not even look up to heaven, but was beating his breast and saying, "God, be merciful to me, a sinner!" I tell you, this man went down to his home justified rather than the other; for all who exalt themselves will be humbled, but all who humble themselves will be exalted.

Luke 18:10-14

Responsorial Psalm

Create in me a clean heart, O God,
    and put a new and right spirit within me.
Do not cast me away from your presence,
    and do not take your holy spirit from me.
Restore to me the joy of your salvation,
    and sustain in me a willing spirit.
Then I will teach transgressors your ways,
    and sinners will return to you.   Psalm 51:10-13

Prayers, pp. 529-32

Closing Psalm Prayer

O Lord, open my lips,
    and my mouth will declare your praise,
for you have no delight in sacrifice. . . .
The sacrifice acceptable to God is a broken spirit;
    a broken and contrite heart, O God, you will not despise.

Psalm 51:15-16a, 17

Fourth Week of Lent   Sunday

Theme: In the midst of Lent we are reminded that Christ is the Light of
        the world. He will not turn from us when we turn to him in
        faith.

Prayer of Confession

I will come into your house with burnt offerings;
    I will pay you my vows,
those that my lips uttered
    and my mouth promised when I was in trouble.

Psalm 66:13-14

Scripture Reading

For once you were darkness, but now in the Lord you are light. Live
as children of the light — for the fruit of the light is found in all that
is good and right and true. Try to find out what is pleasing to the
Lord. Take no part in the unfruitful works of darkness, but instead
expose them. For it is shameful even to mention what such people
do secretly; but everything exposed by the light becomes visible, for
everything that becomes visible is light. Therefore it says,
    "Sleeper, awake!
        Rise from the dead,
    and Christ will shine on you."

Ephesians 5:8-14
read also John 9:1-41

Responsorial Psalm

Make a joyful noise to God, all the earth;
    sing the glory of his name;
    give to him glorious praise.
Say to God, "How awesome are your deeds!
    Because of your great power, your enemies cringe before you.
All the earth worships you;
    they sing praises to you."   Psalm 66:1-4

Prayers, pp. 529-32

Closing Psalm Prayer

I cried aloud to him. . . .
But truly God has listened;
    he has given heed to the words of my prayer.
Blessed be God,
    because he has not rejected my prayer
    or removed his steadfast love from me.   Psalm 66:17a, 19-20

Fourth Week of Lent   Monday

Theme: Today God reminds us that he will make all things new. He will
        bring us up out of the grave and turn our weeping into joy.

Prayer of Confession

> To you, O LORD, I cried,
>   and to the LORD I made supplication. . . .
> Hear, O LORD, and be gracious to me.   Psalm 30:8, 10a

Scripture Reading

> For I am about to create new heavens
>   and a new earth;
> the former things shall not be remembered
>   or come to mind.
> But be glad and rejoice forever
>   in what I am creating;
> for I am about to create Jerusalem as a joy,
>   and its people a delight.
> I will rejoice in Jerusalem,
>   and delight in my people;
> no more shall the sound of weeping be heard in it,
>   or the cry of distress.   Isaiah 65:17-19
>   read also John 4:41-54

Responsorial Psalm

> I will extol you, O LORD, for you have drawn me up,
>   and did not let my foes rejoice over me.
> O LORD, my God, I cried to you for help,
>   and you have healed me.
> O LORD, you brought up my soul from Sheol,
>   restored me to life from among those gone down to the Pit.
>   Psalm 30:1-3

Prayers, pp. 529-32

Closing Psalm Prayer

> Sing praises to the LORD, you his faithful ones,
>   and give thanks to his holy name.
> For his anger is but for a moment;
>   his favor is for a lifetime.
> Weeping may linger for a night,
>   but joy comes with the morning.   Psalm 30:4-5

Fourth Week of Lent   Tuesday

Theme: Jesus Christ brings new life through faith in him. When we
       repent of our sin and turn to him, we find healing for our lives;
       our inner selves are calmed.

Prayer of Confession

> God is our refuge and strength,
>   a very present help in trouble.
> Therefore we will not fear.   Psalm 46:1, 2a

Scripture Reading

> Now in Jerusalem by the Sheep Gate there is a pool, called in Hebrew
> Beth-zatha, which has five porticoes. In these lay many invalids —
> blind, lame, and paralyzed. One man was there who had been ill for
> thirty-eight years. . . . Jesus said to him, "Stand up, take your mat
> and walk." . . .
>
> Later Jesus found him in the temple and said to him, "See, you
> have been made well! Do not sin any more, so that nothing worse
> happens to you."
>
>   John 5:2-3, 5, 8, 14
>   read also Ezekiel 47:1-9, 12

Responsorial Psalm

> There is a river whose streams make glad the city of God,
>> the holy habitation of the Most High.
> God is in the midst of the city; it shall not be moved;
>> God will help it when the morning dawns.   Psalm 46:4-5

Prayers, pp. 529-32

Closing Psalm Prayer

> "Be still, and know that I am God!
>> I am exalted among the nations,
>> I am exalted in the earth!"
> The LORD of hosts is with us;
>> the God of Jacob is our refuge.   Psalm 46:10-11

Fourth Week of Lent   Wednesday

Theme: The Lord loves his people and gives what is best for them.
Because he is gracious and has not forgotten us, we are to extol
him and bless his holy name.

Prayer of Confession

> The LORD is gracious and merciful,
>> slow to anger and abounding in steadfast love.   Psalm 145:8

Scripture Reading

> Thus says the LORD:
> In a time of favor I have answered you,
>> on a day of salvation I have helped you;
> I have kept you and given you
>> as a covenant to the people,
> to establish the land. . . .

Sing for joy, O heavens, and exult, O earth;
  break forth, O mountains, into singing!
For the LORD has comforted his people,
  and will have compassion on his suffering ones. . . .
See, I have inscribed you on the palms of my hands;
  your walls are continually before me.　　Isaiah 49:8, 13, 16
                                      read also John 5:17-30

Responsorial Psalm

I will extol you, my God and King,
  and bless your name forever and ever.
Every day I will bless you,
  and praise your name forever and ever.
Great is the LORD, and greatly to be praised;
  his greatness is unsearchable. . . .
On the glorious splendor of your majesty,
  and on your wondrous works, I will meditate.
                                      Psalm 145:1-3, 5

Prayers, pp. 529-32

Closing Psalm Prayer

Lord, you who are righteous in all your ways,
and gracious in all your works;
you who are near to all who call upon you,
preserve my love for you.
Let my mouth speak your praise,
and let me bless your holy name forever and ever.
                                      adapted from Psalm 145:17-21

Fourth Week of Lent   Thursday

Theme: The scriptures testify of Jesus. We are to read them in such a
          way that we find Jesus. Then we will be able to triumph in his
          name.

Prayer of Confession

Both we and our ancestors have sinned;
    we have committed iniquity, have done wickedly. Psalm 106:6

Scripture Reading

But I have a testimony greater than John's. The works that the Father
has given me to complete, the very works that I am doing, testify on
my behalf that the Father has sent me. And the Father who sent me
has himself testified on my behalf. You have never heard his voice
or seen his form, and you do not have his word abiding in you,
because you do not believe him whom he has sent.

    You search the scriptures because you think that in them you
have eternal life; and it is they that testify on my behalf.

John 5:36-39
read also Exodus 32:7-14

Responsorial Psalm

O give thanks to the LORD, for he is good. . . .
Who can utter the mighty doings of the LORD,
    or declare all his praise?
Happy are those who observe justice,
    who do righteousness at all times.
Remember me, O LORD, when you show favor to your people;
    that I may glory in your heritage.   Psalm 106:1a, 2-5

Prayers, pp. 529-32

Closing Psalm Prayer

Save me, O Lord, my God,
and I will give thanks to your Holy Name;

I will triumph in your praise;
I will bless you, O Lord God of Israel;
I will bless you from everlasting to everlasting;
I will say Amen! Praise the Lord!   adapted from Psalm 106:48

Fourth Week of Lent   Friday

Theme: As Jesus draws closer to his death, the intensity of his hour
       increases. As we travel with him we are to repent, to believe in
       him, and to exalt his name.

Prayer of Confession

Depart from evil, and do good;
    seek peace, and pursue it. . . .
The face of the LORD is against evildoers.   Psalm 34:14, 16a

Scripture Reading

Then Jesus cried out as he was teaching in the temple, "You know
me, and you know where I am from. I have not come on my own.
But the one who sent me is true, and you do not know him. I know
him, because I am from him, and he sent me." Then they tried to
arrest him, but no one laid hands on him, because his hour had not
yet come. Yet many in the crowd believed in him and were saying,
"When the Messiah comes, will he do more signs than this man has
done?"

John 7:28-31
read also John 7:1-27

Responsorial Psalm

Many are the afflictions of the righteous,
    but the LORD rescues them from them all.
He keeps all their bones;
    not one of them will be broken.
Evil brings death to the wicked,
    and those who hate the righteous will be condemned.

The LORD redeems the life of his servants;
　　none of those who take refuge in him will be condemned.

Psalm 34:19-22

Prayers, pp. 529-32

Closing Psalm Prayer

I will bless the LORD at all times;
　　his praise shall continually be in my mouth.
My soul shall make its boast in the LORD;
　　let the humble hear and be glad.
O magnify the LORD with me,
　　and let us exalt his name together.　　　　　Psalm 34:1-3

Fourth Week of Lent   Saturday

Theme: The forces are gathering against Christ. We, too, who have
　　　　determined to follow him to the cross must battle the forces of
　　　　evil. Call upon him, the Victor, and he will help.

Prayer of Confession

Rise up, O LORD, confront them, overthrow them!
By your sword deliver my life from the wicked.　　　Psalm 17:13

Scripture Reading

. . . Some in the crowd said, "This is really the prophet." Others
said, "This is the Messiah." But some asked, "Surely the Messiah
does not come from Galilee, does he? Has not the scripture said that
the Messiah is descended from David and comes from Bethlehem,
the village where David lived?" So there was division in the crowd
because of him. Some of them wanted to arrest him, but no one laid
hands on him. . . .

Nicodemus, who had gone to Jesus before, and who was one of them, asked, "Our law does not judge people without first giving them a hearing to find out what they are doing, does it?"

John 7:41-44, 50-51

read also Jeremiah 11:18-20

Responsorial Psalm

I call upon you, for you will answer me, O God;
　　incline your ear to me, hear my words.....
Guard me as the apple of the eye;
　　hide me in the shadow of your wings,
from the wicked who despoil me,
　　my deadly enemies who surround me.　　　Psalm 17:6, 8-9

Prayers, pp. 529-32

Closing Psalm Prayer

Lord, test my heart, and try me;
For I have chosen not to transgress
and will keep myself from the paths of the destroyer.
Uphold my steps in your paths,
that my footsteps may not slip.　　　adapted from Psalm 17:3-4

Fifth Week of Lent   Sunday

Theme:　Our time of repentance is not in vain. The God who raises the dead can raise us from our times of trouble. Our hope is in him.

Prayer of Confession

The Lord is just in all his ways,
and kind in all his doings.
The LORD is near to all who call on him.　　　Psalm 145:17-18a

Scripture Reading

Now a certain man was ill, Lazarus of Bethany. . . . When Jesus arrived, he found that Lazarus had already been in the tomb four days. . . . Jesus said to [Martha,] "Your brother will rise again." Martha said to him, "I know that he will rise again in the resurrection on the last day." Jesus said to her, "I am the resurrection and the life. Those who believe in me, even though they die, will live, and everyone who lives and believes in me will never die. Do you believe this?" She said to him, "Yes, Lord, I believe that you are the Messiah, the Son of God, the one coming into the world."

John 11:1a, 17, 23-27
read also Ezekiel 37:12-14

Responsorial Psalm

O LORD, what are human beings that you regard them,
    or mortals, that you think of them?
They are like a breath;
    their days are like a passing shadow.
I will sing a new song to you, O God;
    upon a ten-stringed harp I will play to you.   Psalm 144:3-4, 9

Prayers, pp. 529-32

Closing Psalm Prayer

Lord, while I live I will praise you.
I will sing praises to you while I have my being.
I will not trust in princes;
    my hope is in you, O Lord, my God,
    for you raise those who are bowed down.
You will reign forever!   adapted from Psalm 146:2, 3, 8, 10

Fifth Week of Lent   Monday

Theme: Although God calls us to holiness, he is ready and able to forgive
        when we fall into sin. Therefore we ought not to walk in
        darkness, but in his light.

Prayer of Confession

Who shall ascend the hill of the LORD?
    And who shall stand in his holy place?
Those who have clean hands and pure hearts.   Psalm 24:3-4a

Scripture Reading

They said to him, "Teacher, this woman was caught in the very act
of committing adultery. . . ." [Jesus said,] "Let anyone among you
who is without sin be the first to throw a stone at her." . . . Jesus
straightened up and said to her, "Woman, where are they? Has no
one condemned you?" She said, "No one, sir." And Jesus said,
"Neither do I condemn you. Go your way, and from now on do not
sin again."

   Again Jesus spoke to them, saying, "I am the light of the world.
Whoever follows me will never walk in darkness but will have the
light of life."

                                          John 8:4, 7, 10-12
                              read also Daniel 13:1-9, 15-17, 19-22

Responsorial Psalm

Lift up your heads, O gates!
    and be lifted up, O ancient doors!
    that the King of glory may come in.
Who is the King of glory?
    The LORD, strong and mighty,
    the LORD, mighty in battle. . . .
The LORD of hosts,
    he is the King of glory. Selah.   Psalm 24:7-8, 10b

Prayers, pp. 529-32

Closing Psalm Prayer

Lord, the earth is yours and all its fullness,
the world and all who dwell in it.
For you have founded it on the seas,
and established it on the waters.
Therefore I will not lift up my soul to an idol.
I will seek your face.   adapted from Psalm 24:1, 2, 4, 6

Fifth Week of Lent   Tuesday

Theme: The closer we come to Holy Week, the more intense is Jesus'
witness of himself. Our life finds meaning as we identify with
the sufferings of Jesus.

Prayer of Confession

I hate the work of those who fall away. . . .
No one who practices deceit
    shall remain in my house;
no one who utters lies
    shall continue in my presence.   Psalm 101:3b, 7

Scripture Reading

Again [Jesus] said to them, "I am going away, and you will search
for me, but you will die in your sin. Where I am going, you cannot
come." Then the Jews said, . . . "Who are you?" . . . They did not
understand that he was speaking to them about the Father. So Jesus
said, "When you have lifted up the Son of Man, then you will realize
that I am he, and that I do nothing on my own, but I speak these
things as the Father instructed me. And the one who sent me is with
me; he has not left me alone, for I always do what is pleasing to
him."

John 8:21, 25, 27-29
read also Numbers 21:4-9

Responsorial Psalm

> All day long my enemies taunt me;
>> those who deride me use my name for a curse.
> For I eat ashes like bread,
>> and mingle tears with my drink,
> because of your indignation and anger;
>> for you have lifted me up and thrown me aside.
> My days are like an evening shadow;
>> I wither away like grass.   Psalm 102:8-11

Prayers, pp. 529-32

Closing Psalm Prayer

> Hear my prayer, O LORD;
>> let my cry come to you.
> Do not hide your face from me
>> in the day of my distress.
> Incline your ear to me;
>> answer me speedily in the day when I call.   Psalm 102:1-2

Fifth Week of Lent   Wednesday

Theme: As Jesus comes to the close of his ministry the forces gather
against him. But God is for him. In our troubles we can be
assured of God's presence.

Prayer of Confession

> O Lord, restore my soul,
> and lead me in the paths of righteousness for your name's sake.
>> adapted from Psalm 23:3

Scripture Reading

> They answered him, "Abraham is our father." Jesus said to them, "If
> you were Abraham's children, you would be doing what Abraham

did, but now you are trying to kill me, a man who has told you the truth that I heard from God. This is not what Abraham did. You are indeed doing what your father does." They said to him, "We are not illegitimate children; we have one father — God himself." Jesus said to them, "If God were your Father, you would love me, for I came from God, and now I am here. I did not come on my own, but he sent me."

John 8:39-42
read also Daniel 3:14-28

Responsorial Psalm

The LORD is my shepherd, I shall not want. . . .
Even though I walk through the darkest valley,
    I fear no evil;
for you are with me;
    your rod and your staff —
    they comfort me.

Psalm 23:1, 4

Prayers, pp. 529-32

Closing Psalm Prayer

You anoint my head with oil;
    my cup overflows.
Surely goodness and mercy shall follow me
    all the days of my life,
and I shall dwell in the house of the LORD
    my whole life long.

Psalm 23:5b-6

Fifth Week of Lent   Thursday

Theme: The Pharisees seek to kill Jesus as he reveals more of himself. As Jesus sought strength from his Father, so we, too, are called to rely on him.

Prayer of Confession

> He is the LORD our God;
>> his judgments are in all the earth.
> He is mindful of his covenant forever.   Psalm 105:7-8a

Scripture Reading

"Very truly, I tell you, whoever keeps my word will never see death."
The Jews said to him, "Now we know that you have a demon.
Abraham died, and so did the prophets; yet you say, 'Whoever keeps
my word will never taste death.' Are you greater than our father
Abraham, who died? The prophets also died. Who do you claim to
be?" . . . Jesus said to them, "Very truly, I tell you, before Abraham
was, I am." So they picked up stones to throw at him, but Jesus hid
himself and went out of the temple.

John 8:51-53, 58-59
read also Genesis 17:3-9

Responsorial Psalm

> Seek the LORD and his strength;
>> seek his presence continually.
> Remember the wonderful works he has done,
>> his miracles, and the judgments he uttered,
> O offspring of his servant Abraham,
>> children of Jacob, his chosen ones.   Psalm 105:4-6

Prayers, pp. 529-32

Closing Psalm Prayer

> O give thanks to the LORD, call on his name,
>> make known his deeds among the peoples.
> Sing to him, sing praises to him;
>> tell of all his wonderful works.
> Glory in his holy name.   Psalm 105:1-3a

Fifth Week of Lent   Friday

Theme: Because Jesus has identified himself as God, the pressures are
        building against him. In times of calamity one can trust only in
        God.

Prayer of Confession

The LORD rewarded me according to my righteousness;
    according to the cleanness of my hands he has recompensed me.
                                        Psalm 18:20

Scripture Reading

The Jews took up stones again to stone him. Jesus replied, "I have
shown you many good works from the Father. For which of these
are you going to stone me?" The Jews answered, "It is not for a good
work that we are going to stone you, but for blasphemy, because
you, though only a human being, are making yourself God." Jesus
answered, . . . "If I am not doing the words of my Father, then do
not believe me. But if I do them, even though you do not believe
me, believe the works, that you may know and understand that the
Father is in me, and I am in the Father."
                                John 10:31-33, 37-38
                           read also Jeremiah 20:10-13

Responsorial Psalm

The LORD is my rock, my fortress, and my deliverer,
    my God, my rock in whom I take refuge,
    my shield, and the horn of my salvation, my stronghold.
I call upon the LORD, who is worthy to be praised,
    so I shall be saved from my enemies.   Psalm 18:2-3

Prayers, pp. 529-32

Closing Psalm Prayer

Lord, you sent from above and took me,
you drew me out of many waters.

You delivered me from my enemy;
you gave me the shield of your salvation;
your right hand has held me up.
Therefore I will give thanks to you.

adapted from Psalm 18:16, 17, 35, 49

Fifth Week of Lent   Saturday

Theme: Opposition against our Lord is increasing. While the crowds,
especially the poor and oppressed, follow after him, his enemies
begin to plot his death.

Prayer of Confession

Guard me, O LORD, from the hands of the wicked;
protect me from the violent
who have planned my downfall.   Psalm 140:4

Scripture Reading

So the chief priests and the Pharisees called a meeting of the council,
and said, "What are we to do? This man is performing many signs.
If we let him go on like this, everyone will believe in him, and the
Romans will come and destroy both our holy place and nation." But
one of them, Caiaphas, who was high priest that year, said to them,
"You know nothing at all! You do not understand that it is better
for you to have one man die for the people than to have the whole
nation destroyed.". . . So from that day on they planned to put him
to death.

John 11:47-50, 53
read also Ezekiel 37:21-28

Responsorial Psalm

Those who surround me lift up their heads;
let the mischief of their lips overwhelm them!
Let burning coals fall on them!
Let them be flung into pits, no more to rise!

Do not let the slanderer be established in the land;
    let evil speedily hunt down the violent!   Psalm 140:9-11

Prayers, pp. 529-32

Closing Psalm Prayer

Lord, I know that you will maintain the cause of the afflicted,
and justice for the poor.
The righteous will give thanks to your name.
The upright will dwell in your presence.
Therefore I will praise your name.   adapted from Psalm 140:12-13

Holy Week

We now come to the most spiritually intense week of the entire Christian year. This is the week that our Lord is betrayed, scourged, nailed on the wood of the cross, and laid in a tomb. This is the week in which our sins are forgiven. This is the week when the world is redeemed.

The spiritual significance of this week may be seen by the names given to it throughout church history. It has been called Major Week, Greater Week, Authentic Week, Passion Week, Week of Salvation, Sorrowful Week, and Mournful Week. In the West the name widely used is Holy Week. Indeed, we need to regard it as Holy. That is, it is a week set aside from all other weeks because it is the week when the culminating events of our salvation occurred.

The heart of Holy Week is the three-day commemoration (Triduum) that begins on Thursday evening and ends on Easter Sunday morning. These three days constitute the heart of the church year, for during this time we move through the Last Supper, the denial by Judas, the prayer of our Lord in Gethsemane, and his trial, crucifixion, burial, and resurrection. The days that reenact these events are Maundy Thursday, Good Friday, and Holy Saturday.

What we want to accomplish spiritually through Holy Week is this: We want to enter into the final moments of our Lord's sufferings. The more intensely we share in the sufferings of Jesus, the more joyous will be our experience of the resurrection.

But how do we do this? How can our spiritual pilgrimage be brought up into the sufferings of Christ? Let me suggest two things you can do to intensify your own experience of Christ's suffering and identify with him in his death:

First, take more than your usual time with the prayers in *The Book of Daily Prayer.* Allow enough time each day for yourself to imagine that you are actually there with Jesus in the events of each day. Here is a brief summary of the focus of each day:

Sunday: Jesus' entrance into Jerusalem calls us into a preview of the whole week. Palm Sunday moves from the joy of "Hosanna! Blessed is the one who comes in the name of the Lord!" to the cry "Crucify him!" (Mark 11:9; 15:13).

Monday: Mary's love for Jesus exhibited in the washing of his feet calls us to commitment.

Tuesday: Christ calls us to faith in him.

Wednesday: Here the focus is the betrayal of Judas.

Thursday: We begin the journey into Christ's death as he is taken captive.

Friday: We are taken into his death.

Saturday: We are taken into his grave.

You should note that during Holy Week the optional Old Testament selections are drawn from the servant passages of Isaiah, culminating in the greatest of them, Isaiah 53. The feeling is one of sobriety that leads to pensive meditation on the death of our Lord.

Second, I suggest that you make Thursday, Friday, and Saturday special days of intense spiritual discipline. These are the three most sober days of the Christian experience. In order to help you identify with Christ's suffering and prepare for the resurrection, I suggest you adopt the following disciplines during these three days:

(1) Engage in public worship. Since this is not to be a party time, a time to frolic or play, it may be made more serious by attendance at church services, more strict adherence to fasting, and periods of silence. Many churches have Maundy evening service on Thursday, a service from noon to 3:00 p.m. on Friday, and a service for veneration of the cross on Friday evening. Go to all or as many of these services as possible.

(2) During this time eat simply or perhaps not at all. Let the experience of Christ's death be felt in the stomach.

(3) Observe periods of silence on both Friday and Saturday. Turn off the radio and the TV, take the phone off the hook if possible, and spend blocks of time in absolute silence, prayer, and meditation. These disciplines will help you to prepare for the festive joy that will come later in the resurrection celebration.

Now pray that God will help you to make a spiritual pilgrimage during Holy Week that will intensify your experience of his love and commitment to you, a love that took his son to the cross and the tomb to suffer and die for your sins.

Palm Sunday

Theme: Jesus is proclaimed by the crowds to be the King of Israel. Many
who identify with him today will turn against him by Friday.

Prayer of Confession

Prove me, O LORD, and try me;
test my heart and mind.
For your steadfast love is before my eyes.   Psalm 26:2-3

Scripture Reading

The next day the great crowd that had come to the festival heard
that Jesus was coming to Jerusalem. So they took branches of palm
trees and went out to meet him, shouting,
  "Hosanna!
  Blessed is the one who comes in the name of the Lord —
    the King of Israel!"
Jesus found a young donkey and sat on it; as it is written:
"Do not be afraid, daughter of Zion.
Look, your king is coming,
    sitting on a donkey's colt!"
                                                    John 12:12-15
                                              read also Mark 14:1–15:47

Responsorial Psalm

Ascribe to the LORD, O heavenly beings,
ascribe to the LORD glory and strength.
Ascribe to the LORD the glory of his name;
worship the LORD in holy splendor.   Psalm 29:1-2

Prayers, pp. 529-32

Closing Psalm Prayer

> The LORD is my light and my salvation;
> > whom shall I fear?
> The LORD is the stronghold of my life;
> > of whom shall I be afraid? . . .
> Wait for the LORD;
> > be strong, and let your heart take courage;
> > wait for the LORD!   Psalm 27:1, 14

Monday of Holy Week

Theme: On this day we recall how Mary, the sister of Martha, washed
> the feet of Jesus with fragrant oil. With Mary, we adore Christ.

Prayer of Confession

> Save me, O God. . . .
> > My throat is parched.
> My eyes grow dim
> > with waiting for my God.   Psalm 69:1a, 3

Scripture Reading

> Mary took a pound of costly perfume made of pure nard, anointed
> Jesus' feet, and wiped them with her hair. . . . But Judas Iscariot,
> one of his disciples (the one who was about to betray him), said:
> "Why was this perfume not sold for three hundred denarii and the
> money give to the poor?" (He said this not because he cared about
> the poor, but because he was a thief; he kept the common purse and
> used to steal what was put into it.) Jesus said, "Leave her alone. She
> bought it so that she might keep it for the day of my burial. You
> always have the poor with you, but you do not always have me."
> > > > John 12:3a, 4-8
> > > > read also Isaiah 42:1-9

Responsorial Psalm

> Answer me, O LORD, for your steadfast love is good;
> > according to your abundant mercy, turn to me.
> Do not hide your face from your servant,
> > for I am in distress — make haste to answer me.
> Draw near to me, redeem me,
> > set me free because of my enemies.   Psalm 69:16-18

Prayers, pp. 529-32

Closing Psalm Prayer

> Let heaven and earth praise him,
> > the seas and everything that moves in them.
> For God will save Zion
> > and rebuild the cities of Judah;
> and his servants shall live there and possess it . . .
> > and those who love his name shall live in it.   Psalm 69:34-36

Tuesday of Holy Week

Theme: On this day our Lord is pained by unbelief. Although he calls
on people to believe in him, the words of the prophet Isaiah
come true.

Prayer of Confession

> Be gracious to me, O LORD, for I am languishing;
> > O LORD, heal me, for my bones are shaking with terror.
> > > > > > > > Psalm 6:2

Scripture Reading

> Although he had performed so many signs in their presence, they
> did not believe in him. This was to fulfill the word spoken by the
> prophet Isaiah:

"Lord, who has believed our message,
>   and to whom has the arm of the Lord been revealed?"
And so they could not believe, because Isaiah also said,
"He has blinded their eyes
>   and hardened their heart,
so that they might not look with their eyes,
>   and understand with their heart and turn —
>   and I would heal them."

John 12:37-40
read also Isaiah 49:1-6

Responsorial Psalm

I am weary with my moaning;
>   every night I flood my bed with tears;
>   I drench my couch with my weeping.
My eyes waste away because of grief;
>   they grow weak because of all my foes.
Depart from me, all you workers of evil,
>   for the LORD has heard the sound of my weeping. . . .
The LORD accepts my prayer.   Psalm 6:6-8, 9b

Prayers, pp. 529-32

Closing Psalm Prayer

Lord, do not blind my eyes or harden my heart.
In these days of your Son's suffering deliver me from my sins
and save me for your mercy's sake,
through Jesus Christ your only Son.   adapted from Psalm 6:4

Wednesday of Holy Week

Theme: Today Judas Iscariot is revealed as the one who will betray Jesus.
>   We are not only to enter into the pain of Jesus, but into his trust
>   in the Father.

Prayer of Confession

Be gracious to me, O God, for people trample on me;
all day long foes oppress me.   Psalm 56:1

Scripture Reading

After saying this Jesus was troubled in spirit, and declared, "Very truly, I tell you, one of you will betray me." . . . [Simon Peter] asked him, "Lord, who is it?" Jesus answered, "It is the one to whom I give this piece of bread when I have dipped it in the dish." So when he had dipped the piece of bread, he gave it to Judas son of Simon Iscariot. After he received the piece of bread, Satan entered into him. Jesus said to him, "Do quickly what you are going to do." . . . So, after receiving the piece of bread, he immediately went out. And it was night.

John 13:21, 25-27, 30
read also Isaiah 50:4-9

Responsorial Psalm

My heart is in anguish within me,
the terrors of death have fallen upon me.
Fear and trembling come upon me,
and horror overwhelms me.
And I say, "O that I had wings like a dove!
I would fly away and be at rest;
truly, I would flee far away;
I would lodge in the wilderness."   Psalm 55:4-7

Prayers, pp. 529-32

Closing Psalm Prayer

Give ear to my prayer, O God;
do not hide yourself from my supplication.
Attend to me and hear me.
I will cast my burden on you, Lord.
You will sustain me,
and I will trust in you.   adapted from Psalm 55:1, 22, 23

Maundy Thursday

Theme: Our Lord, knowing that the time of his death is near, and filled
with heaviness of heart, nevertheless picks up the towel to serve
those for whom he will soon die.

Prayer of Confession

For you have lifted me up and thrown me aside.
My days are like an evening shadow;
    I wither away like grass.   Psalm 102:10b-11

Scripture Reading

[Jesus] got up from the table, took off his outer robe, and tied a
towel around himself. Then he poured water into a basin and began
to wash the disciples' feet and to wipe them with the towel that was
tied around him. He came to Simon Peter, who said to him, "Lord,
are you going to wash my feet?" . . . Peter said to him, "You will
never wash my feet." Jesus answered, "Unless I wash you, you have
no share with me." Simon Peter said to him, "Lord, not my feet only
but also my hands and my head!" . . . [Jesus said,] "For I have set
you an example, that you also should do as I have done to you."

John 13:4-6, 8-9, 15
read also Exodus 12:1-14

Responsorial Psalm

For my days pass away like smoke,
    and my bones burn like a furnace.
My heart is stricken and withered like grass;
    I am too wasted to eat my bread.
Because of my loud groaning
    my bones cling to my skin.
I am like an owl of the wilderness,
    like a little owl of the waste places.   Psalm 102:3-6

Prayers, pp. 529-32

Closing Psalm Prayer

Hear my prayer, O LORD;
> let my cry come to you.
Do not hide your face from me
> in the day of distress.
Incline your ear to me;
> answer me speedily in the day when I call.   Psalm 102:1-2

Good Friday

Theme: Today our Lord Jesus Christ is put to death. On this day evil is
conquered, and we are released from the power of sin. Enter
his death so that you may live.

Prayer of Confession

Do not be far from me,
> for trouble is near
> and there is none to help.   Psalm 22:11

Scripture Reading

And carrying the cross by himself, he went out to what is called the
Place of a Skull, which in Hebrew is called Golgotha. There they
crucified him, and with him two others, one on either side, with
Jesus between them. Pilate also had an inscription written and put
on the cross. It read, "Jesus of Nazareth, the King of the Jews." Many
of the Jews read this inscription, because the place where Jesus was
crucified was near the city; and it was written in Hebrew, in Latin,
and in Greek.

John 19:17-20
read also Isaiah 52:13-15; 53:1-12

Responsorial Psalm

> My God, my God, why have you forsaken me? . . .
> All who see me mock at me;
>   they make mouths at me, they shake their heads;
> "Commit your cause to the LORD; let him deliver —
>   let him rescue the one in whom he delights!" . . .
> My hands and feet have shriveled;
> I can count all my bones.
> They stare and gloat over me. . . .
> But you, O LORD, do not be far away!"
>
> Psalm 22:1a, 7-8, 16b-17, 19a

Prayers, pp. 529-32

Closing Psalm Prayer

> You have answered me.
> I will tell of your name to my brothers and sisters:
> All you offspring of Jacob, glorify him;
> Stand in awe of him, all you offspring of Israel.
> He did not hide his face from me,
> But heard when I cried to him.
>
> adapted from Psalm 22:21, 22-24

Holy Saturday

Theme: On this day our Lord Jesus lies in the grave. We, too, have
    journeyed with him into death and now are buried with him.

Prayer of Confession

> For my soul is full of troubles,
>   and my life draws near to Sheol.
> I am counted among those who go down to the Pit.
>
> Psalm 88:3-4

Scripture Reading

After these things, Joseph of Arimathea, who was a disciple of Jesus, though a secret one because of his fear of the Jews, asked Pilate to let him take away the body of Jesus. Pilate gave him permission; so he came and removed his body. . . . They took the body of Jesus and wrapped it with the spices in linen cloths, according to the burial custom of the Jews. Now there was a garden in the place where he was crucified, and in the garden there was a new tomb in which no one had ever been laid. And so, because it was the Jewish day of Preparation, and the tomb was nearby, they laid Jesus there.

John 19:38, 40-42
read also Job 14:1-14

Responsorial Psalm

Every day I call on you, O LORD;
    I spread out my hands to you.
Do you work wonders for the dead?
    Do the shades rise up to praise you?
Is your steadfast love declared in the grave,
    or your faithfulness in Abaddon?
Are your wonders known in the darkness,
    or your saving help in the land of forgetfulness?

Psalm 88:10-12

Prayers, pp. 529-32

Closing Psalm Prayer

O LORD, God of my salvation,
    when, at night, I cry out in your presence,
let my prayer come before you;
    incline your ear to my cry. . . .
O LORD, why do you cast me off?
    Why do you hide your face from me?   Psalm 88:1-2, 14

Easter

During Easter our spirituality and life of prayer shifts from anticipation to fulfillment. For seven long and sober weeks we have been fasting and looking inward at the sin that nailed Jesus to the cross. We have taken the journey into death and we have been buried in the tomb. Now it is time to be released from our imprisonment and resurrected to newness of life.

So newness of life is the theme of our spirituality during Easter. Consequently our prayer life, our relationships, and our spiritual mood will reflect the power of the resurrection experience.

Easter is not just one day. It is a season. For fifty days we celebrate the resurrection of Jesus from the dead and his resurrected presence among us. This season of great joy ends after the ascension on the day of Pentecost, the day that celebrates the coming of the Spirit and the birth of the church.

The focus of our daily readings during Easter season is on the recollection of Jesus' life, ministry, and teaching from the perspective of the resurrection. We must remember that the disciples did not expect a crucified and risen Christ. Consequently, after the resurrection they must have taken time to reflect on the events of Jesus' life in a new and different way. Now they knew who this extraordinary man was. Now they knew that he was God incarnate, come to redeem them from the power of the evil one.

As with the disciples, our spiritual pilgrimage for the next seven weeks will look at various events from the life of Jesus and view them through the resurrection. This new insight should provide us with a wholly different experience of the resurrection event and trigger new dimensions of personal heartfelt praise and thanksgiving to God.

Easter Sunday

Theme: Of all the days of the year, this is the most special, the most
glorious day. It is the day the Lord has made, the day for praise
and rejoicing.

The Lord is Risen, Alleluia!

Lord Jesus Christ,
on this day you rose from the dead.
You conquered evil and set the whole creation free from death.
I will praise your name. Alleluia!

Scripture Reading

When it was evening on that day, the first day of the week, and the
doors of the house where the disciples had met were locked for fear
of the Jews, Jesus came and stood among them and said, "Peace be
with you." After he said this, he showed them his hands and his side.
Then the disciples rejoiced when they saw the Lord. Jesus said to
them again, "Peace be with you. As the Father has sent me, so I send
you." When he had said this, he breathed on them and said to them,
"Receive the Holy Spirit."

John 20:19-22
read also verses 1-18

Responsorial Psalm

Praise the LORD from the heavens;
    praise him in the heights!
Praise him, all his angels;
    praise him, all his host!
Praise him, sun and moon;
    praise him, all you shining stars!
Praise him, you highest heavens.   Psalm 148:1b-4a

Prayers, pp. 529-32

Closing Psalm Prayer

Praise God in his sanctuary;
  praise him in his mighty firmament!
Praise him for his mighty deeds;
  praise him according to his surpassing greatness! . . .
Let everything that breathes praise the LORD.   Psalm 150:1b-2, 6a

Easter Week   Monday

Theme: The resurrection of Jesus Christ kindled the hopes of his disciples
        and filled their lives with new meaning. His resurrection puts a
        new song in the heart.

The Lord is Risen, Alleluia!

Lord Jesus Christ,
you have put a new song in my heart,
for you have demonstrated your power over sin and death.
Grant me the courage and power to live in newness of life.

Scripture Reading

"He is not here; for he has been raised, as he said. Come, see the
place where he lay. Then go quickly and tell his disciples, 'He has
been raised from the dead, and indeed he is going ahead of you to
Galilee; there you will see him.' This is my message for you." So
they left the tomb quickly with fear and great joy, and ran to tell his
disciples. Suddenly, Jesus met them and said, "Greetings!" And they
came to him, took hold of his feet, and worshiped him. Then Jesus
said to them, "Do not be afraid; go and tell my brothers to go to
Galilee; there they will see me."

Matthew 28:6-10
read also Acts 2:14, 22-32

Responsorial Psalm

O sing to the LORD a new song. . . .
Make a joyful noise to the LORD, all the earth;
    break forth into joyous song and sing praises.
Sing praises to the LORD with the lyre,
    with the lyre and the sound of melody.
With trumpets and the sound of the horn;
    make a joyful noise before the King, the LORD.

Psalm 98:1a, 4-6

Prayers, pp. 529-32

Closing Psalm Prayer

I will sing to the Lord a new song!
For he has done marvelous things.
His right hand and his holy arm have gotten him victory!
He has made known his salvation.
All the ends of the earth have seen the salvation of our God.

adapted from Psalm 98:1-3

Easter Week   Tuesday

Theme: The resurrection carries with it the element of surprise. When-
      ever we are surprised by grace, we want to enjoy it forever.

The Lord is Risen, Alleluia!

Lord Jesus Christ, death could not hold you in its grip.
Grant that we might see beyond the grave
and be touched with your resurrected presence.

Scripture Reading

Jesus said to her, "Woman, why are you weeping? Whom are you
looking for?" Supposing him to be the gardener, she said to him,
"Sir, if you have carried him away, tell me where you have laid him,

and I will take him away." Jesus said to her, "Mary!" She turned and said to him in Hebrew, "Rabbouni!" (which means Teacher). Jesus said to her, "Do not hold on to me, because I have not yet ascended to the Father. But go to my brothers and say to them, 'I am ascending to my Father and your Father, to my God and your God.'"

John 20:15-17
read also Acts 2:36-40

Responsorial Psalm

Make a joyful shout to the LORD, all the earth.
> Worship the LORD with gladness;
> come into his presence with singing.

Know that the LORD is God.
> It is he that made us, and we are his;
> we are his people, and the sheep of his pasture. Psalm 100:1-2

Prayers, pp. 529-32

Closing Psalm Prayer

Lord, I will enter your gates with thanksgiving,
and your courts with praise.
I will be thankful to you and bless your name,
for you, O Lord, are good.   adapted from Psalm 100:4-5

Easter Week   **Wednesday**

Theme: The Christ who is resurrected in glory is the same one who was
put to death in shame. By his death and resurrection we are
saved. Trust in him and no other.

The Lord is Risen, Alleluia!

Lord Jesus,
you were rejected and despised.
Yet you became the cornerstone of salvation.

Receive my worship, my praise, my adoration,
and my deep and abiding faith.

Scripture Reading

When he was at the table with them, he took bread, blessed and
broke it, and gave it to them. Then their eyes were opened, and they
recognized him; and he vanished from their sight. They said to each
other, "Were not our hearts burning within us while he was talking
to us on the road, while he was opening the scriptures to us?" That
same hour they got up and returned to Jerusalem; and they found
the eleven and their companions gathered together. They were saying,
"The Lord has risen indeed, and he has appeared to Simon!"

Luke 24:30-34
read also Acts 13:1-10

Responsorial Psalm

O give thanks to the LORD, for he is good. . . .
The stone that the builders rejected
    has become the chief cornerstone.
This is the LORD's doing;
    it is marvelous in our eyes.
This is the day that the LORD has made;
    let us rejoice and be glad in it.   Psalm 118:1a, 22-24

Prayers, pp. 529-32

Closing Psalm Prayer

Blessed is the one who comes in the name of the LORD. . . .
The LORD is God,
and he has give us light. . . .
You are my God, I will extol you.   Psalm 118:26a, 27a, 28b

Easter Week   Thursday

Theme: God in Christ has laid down his life for us to bring us to himself.
Now we are no longer strangers, but friends.

The Lord is Risen, Alleluia!

Risen Lord,
you who laid down your life for me,
come and dwell in me as Lord and friend,
and turn me toward you in love.

Scripture Reading

This is my commandment, that you love one another as I have loved
you. No one has greater love than this, to lay down one's life for
one's friends. You are my friends if you do what I command you. I
do not call you servant any longer, because the servant does not
know what the master is doing; but I have called you friends, because
I have made known to you everything that I have heard from my
Father. You did not choose me, but I chose you. And I appointed
you to go and bear fruit, fruit that will last, so that the Father will
give you whatever you ask him in my name.

John 15:12-16

Responsorial Psalm

Praise the LORD from the heavens;
praise him in the heights!
Praise him, all his angels;
praise him, all his host!
Praise him, sun and moon;
praise him, all you shining stars!
Praise him, you highest heaven.   Psalm 148:1b-4

Prayers, pp. 529-32

Closing Psalm Prayer

> Let them praise the name of the LORD,
>   for his name alone is exalted;
>   his glory is above earth and heaven.
> He has raised up a horn for his people. . . .
> Praise the LORD!   Psalm 148:13, 14

Easter Week   Friday

Theme: Jesus will send the Holy Spirit who will lead his disciples into
        all truth.

The Lord is Risen, Alleluia!

> Lord Jesus,
> you gave us your Holy Spirit
> to make us one family and to guide us in truth.
> Grant us more and more of your Spirit.

Scripture Reading

> If I do not go away, the Advocate will not come to you; but if I go,
> I will send him to you. And when he comes, he will prove the world
> wrong about sin and righteousness and judgment. . . . When the
> Spirit of truth comes, he will guide you into all the truth; for he will
> not speak on his own, but will speak whatever he hears, and he will
> declare to you the things that are to come. He will glorify me, because
> he will take what is mine and declare it to you.
>   John 16:7-8, 13-14

Responsorial Psalm

> O give thanks to the LORD, for he is good;
>   his steadfast love endures forever!
> Let Israel say,
>   "His steadfast love endures forever."
> Let the house of Aaron say,

"His steadfast love endures forever."
Let those who fear the LORD say,
"His steadfast love endures forever."

Psalm 118:1-4

Prayers, pp. 529-32

Closing Psalm Prayer

Open to me the gates of righteousness,
that I may enter through them
and give thanks to the LORD.
This is the gate of the LORD;
the righteous shall enter through it.
I thank you that you have answered me
and have become my salvation.

Psalm 118:19-21

Easter Week   Saturday

Theme: There are always those who insist on proof and signs. Jesus calls
us to follow him in faith, to proclaim his resurrection to others.

The Lord is Risen, Alleluia!

Lord Jesus,
we who have seen you with the eye of faith will follow you.
We will proclaim your praises to the end of the earth.

Scripture Reading

Now after he rose early on the first day of the week, he appeared
first to Mary Magdalene, from whom he had cast out seven
demons. . . . Later he appeared to the eleven themselves as they were
sitting at the table; and he upbraided them for their lack of faith and
stubbornness, because they had not believed those who saw him after
he had risen. And he said to them, "Go into all the world and
proclaim the good news to the whole creation. The one who believes

and is baptized will be saved; but the one who does not believe will
be condemned."

Mark 16:9, 14-16
read also Acts 4:13-21

Responsorial Psalm

All your works shall give thanks to you, O LORD,
>and all your faithful shall bless you.
They shall speak of the glory of your kingdom,
>and tell of your power,
to make known to all people your mighty deeds,
>and the glorious splendor of your kingdom.
Your kingdom is an everlasting kingdom,
>and your dominion endures throughout all generations.

Psalm 145:10-13

Prayers, pp. 529-32

Closing Psalm Prayer

I will praise the LORD as long as I live;
>I will sing praises to my God all my life long. . . .
The LORD will reign forever,
>your God, O Zion, for all generations.
Praise the LORD!

Psalm 146:2, 10

Second Week of Easter   Sunday

Theme: Frequently our hearts are troubled because of this event or that
>person, but the risen Christ calls us to view life from the per-
>spective of our ultimate hope.

The Lord is Risen, Alleluia!

Risen Christ,
you who have gone on before us to prepare a place in your

Father's house,
remember me when you come into your kingdom.

Scripture Reading

"Do not let your hearts be troubled. Believe in God, believe also in
me. In my Father's house are many dwelling places. If it were not
so, would I have told you that I go to prepare a place for you? And
if I go and prepare a place for you, I will come again and will take
you to myself, so that where I am, there you may be also. And you
know the way to the place where I am going." Thomas said to him,
"Lord, we do not know where you are going. How can we know
the way?" Jesus said to him, "I am the way, and the truth, and the
life. No one comes to the Father except through me."

John 14:1-6

optional: Exodus 14:5-22

Responsorial Psalm

Happy are those whose help is the God of Jacob,
    whose hope is in the LORD their God,
who made heaven and earth,
    the sea, and all that is in them;
who keeps faith forever . . .
    who gives food to the hungry.   Psalm 146:5-7

Prayers, pp. 529-32

Closing Psalm Prayer

Praise the LORD!
Praise the LORD, O my soul!
I will praise the LORD as long as I live;
I will sing praises to my God all my life long.   Psalm 146:1-2

Second Week of Easter   Monday

Theme: In the resurrection Jesus calls us to look beyond the moment
with its frustrations and endless tasks to the promise that with
him we will overcome all trials.

The Lord is Risen, Alleluia!

Risen Christ,
you who having been glorified on earth,
now reign in heaven in great glory,
look upon me with your grace and favor.

Scripture Reading

[Jesus] looked up to heaven and said, "Father, the hour has come;
glorify your Son so that the Son may glorify you, since you have
given him authority over all people, to give eternal life to all whom
you have given him. And this is eternal life, that they may know
you, the only true God, and Jesus Christ whom you have sent. I
glorified you on earth by finishing the work that you gave me to do.
So now, Father, glorify me in your own presence with the glory that
I had in your presence before the world existed."

John 17:1-5
optional: Exodus 14:5-22

Responsorial Psalm

Let the light of your face shine on us, O LORD!
You have put gladness in my heart. . . .
I will both lie down and sleep in peace;
for you alone, O LORD, make me lie down in safety.

Psalm 4:6b-7a, 8

Prayers, pp. 529-32

Closing Psalm Prayer

When you are disturbed, do not sin;
ponder it on your beds and be silent.

Offer right sacrifices,
    and put your trust in the LORD.   Psalm 4:4-5

Second Week of Easter   Tuesday

Theme: The resurrected Christ lives in us and through us as we yield to
       him and turn our whole lives over to his service.

The Lord is Risen, Alleluia!

Risen Christ,
you demonstrated that you love righteousness.
Keep me, your servant, upright and just.
May I love truth and justice for your sake and for the sake of the
world.

Scripture Reading

I have given them your word, and the world has hated them because
they do not belong to the world, just as I do not belong to the world.
I am not asking you to take them out of the world, but I ask you
to protect them from the evil one. They do not belong to the world,
just as I do not belong to the world. Sanctify them in the truth; your
word is truth. As you have sent me into the world, so I have sent
them into the world. And for their sakes I sanctify myself, so that
they also may be sanctified in truth.

John 17:14-19
optional: Exodus 15:1-21

Responsorial Psalm

O LORD, you will hear the desire of the meek;
    you will strengthen their heart, you will incline your ear
to do justice for the orphan and the oppressed,
    so that those from earth may strike terror no more.

Psalm 10:17-18

Prayers, pp. 529-32

Closing Psalm Prayer

The LORD is in his holy temple;
   the LORD's throne is in heaven. . . .
For the LORD is righteous;
he loves righteous deeds;
   the upright shall behold his face.   Psalm 11:4a, 7

Second Week of Easter   Wednesday

Theme: The prayer of our Lord Jesus that his church should be one calls
            us to set aside our prejudices and love the whole family of Christ.

The Lord is Risen, Alleluia!

Lord Jesus Christ, you who rose victorious over the grave,
work in me and in all your people here on earth
to create a true love for your church.

Scripture Reading

I ask not only on behalf of these, but also on behalf of those who
will believe in me through their word, that they may all be one. As
you, Father, are in me, and I am in you; may they also be one in us,
so that the world may believe that you have sent me. The glory that
you have given me I have given them, so that they may be one, as
we are one, I in them and you in me, that they may become
completely one, so that the world may know that you have sent me
and have loved them even as you have loved me.
                                        John 17:20-23
                              optional: Exodus 15:22–16:10

Responsorial Psalm

Consider and answer me, O LORD my God!
   Give light to my eyes, or I will sleep the sleep of death,

and my enemy will say, "I have prevailed";
    my foes will rejoice because I am shaken.   Psalm 13:3-4

Prayers, pp. 529-32

Closing Psalm Prayer

But I trusted in your steadfast love;
    my heart shall rejoice in your salvation;
I will sing to the LORD,
    because he has dealt bountifully with me.   Psalm 13:5-6

Second Week of Easter   Thursday

Theme: The resurrection calls us into a new life in Christ. We are to purge ourselves of those evil habits and desires that keep us from living the resurrected life.

The Lord is Risen, Alleluia!

Risen Lord,
as your servant John the Baptist calls us to repentance,
may we heed his call and turn from our sin
to trust in you, the Victor over evil.

Scripture Reading

. . . The Word of God came to John the son of Zechariah. . . . [He] said to the crowds that came out to be baptized by him, "You brood of vipers! Who warned you to flee from the wrath to come? Bear fruits worthy of repentance. Do not begin to say to yourselves, 'We have Abraham as our ancestor'; for I tell you, God is able from these stones to raise up children to Abraham. Even now the axe is lying at the root of the trees; every tree therefore that does not bear good fruit is cut down and thrown into the fire."

Luke 3:2, 7-9
optional: Exodus 16:10-22

Responsorial Psalm

He reached down from on high, he took me;
  he drew me out of mighty waters.
He delivered me from my strong enemy,
  and from those who hated me;
  for they were too mighty for me.
They confronted me in the day of my calamity,
  but the LORD was my support.   Psalm 18:16-18

Prayers, pp. 529-32

Closing Psalm Prayer

You have given me the shield of your salvation,
  and your right hand has supported me;
  your help has made me great.
You gave me a wide place for my steps under me,
  and my feet did not slip.   Psalm 18:35-36

Second Week of Easter   Friday

Theme: When the problems of life overtake us and we feel like a doubt-
        ing Thomas, we need to turn our ears to the voice of the Lord.

The Lord is Risen, Alleluia!

Risen Lord,
let me hear in a new and fresh way
the proclamation from heaven that you are the beloved Son.

Scripture Reading

As the people were filled with expectation, and all were questioning
in the hearts concerning John, whether he might be the Messiah,
John answered all of them by saying, "I baptize you with water; but
one who is more powerful than I is coming; I am not worthy to untie

the thong of his sandals. He will baptize you with the Holy Spirit and fire." . . .

Now when all the people were baptized, and when Jesus also had been baptized and was praying, the heaven was opened, and the Holy Spirit descended upon him in bodily form like a dove. And a voice came from heaven, "You are my Son, the Beloved; with you I am well pleased."

Luke 3:15-16, 21-22
optional: Exodus 16:23-26

Responsorial Psalm

Come, bless the LORD, all you servants of the LORD,
    who stand by night in the house of the LORD!
Lift up your hands to the holy place,
    and bless the LORD.
May the LORD, maker of heaven and earth,
    bless you from Zion!   Psalm 134:1-3

Prayers, pp. 529-32

Closing Psalm Prayer

Praise the name of the LORD;
give praise, O servants of the LORD,
in the courts of the house of our God.
Praise the LORD, for the LORD is good.   Psalm 135:1-3

Second Week of Easter   Saturday

Theme: The same Lord Jesus who defeated Satan in the wilderness is the resurrected Christ who lives in us and fights the devil for us today.

The Lord is Risen, Alleluia!

> Risen Lord,
> you faced the temptation of Satan and sent him in flight.
> Grant me a strong trust in the power of your name.

Scripture Reading

> Then the devil took him to Jerusalem, and placed him on the pinnacle
> of the temple, saying to him, "If you are the Son of God, throw
> yourself down from here, for it is written,
>> 'He will command his angels concerning you,
>>> to protect you,'
>> and
>> 'On their hands they will bear you up,
>>> so that you will not dash your foot against a stone.'"
> Jesus answered him, "It is said, 'Do not put the Lord your God
> to the test.'" When the devil had finished every test, he departed
> from him until an opportune time.

Luke 4:9-13

optional: Exodus 17:1-16

Responsorial Psalm

> The LORD answer you in the day of trouble!
>> The name of the God of Jacob protect you!
> May he send you help from the sanctuary. . . .
> Now I know that the LORD will help his anointed;
>> he will answer him from his holy heaven.   Psalm 20:1-2a, 6a

Prayers, pp. 529-32

Closing Psalm Prayer

> Some take pride in chariots, and some in horses,
>> but our pride is in the name of the LORD our God.
> They will collapse and fall,
>> but we shall rise and stand upright.   Psalm 20:7-8

Third Week of Easter   Sunday

Theme: Like Peter, Jesus calls us to care for and love his sheep. We are
        to turn away from our petty and insignificant grudges and to
        will to love each other.

The Lord is Risen, Alleluia!

Risen Christ,
you called Peter to care for your sheep.
Grant that I, your servant, may love you enough
to love your people everywhere.

Scripture Reading

. . . Jesus said to Simon Peter, "Simon son of John, do you love me
more than these?" He said to him, "Yes, Lord; you know that I love
you." Jesus said to him, "Feed my lambs." A second time he said to
him, "Simon son of John, do you love me?" He said to him, "Yes,
Lord; you know that I love you." Jesus said to him, "Tend my sheep."
He said to him the third time, "Simon son of John, do you love me?"
. . . And he said to him, "Lord, you know everything; you know
that I love you." Jesus said to him, "Feed my sheep."

John 21:15-17
optional: Exodus 18:1-12

Responsorial Psalm

You who fear the LORD, trust in the LORD!
The LORD has been mindful of us;
    he will bless us;
    he will bless the house of Israel;
    he will bless the house of Aaron;
he will bless those who fear the LORD,
    both small and great.   Psalm 115:11-13

Prayers, pp. 529-32

Closing Psalm Prayer

> May the LORD give you increase,
> > both you and your children.
> May you be blessed by the LORD,
> > who made heaven and earth. Psalm 115:14-15

Third Week of Easter Monday

Theme: The poorest people of the world are those who live in indifference to the hunger, suffering, and oppression of others.

The Lord is Risen, Alleluia!

> Risen Lord,
> you came among us to save us and to direct our paths.
> Open my eyes to the poor and oppressed of this world.

Scripture Reading

> When he came to Nazareth, where he had been brought up, he went to the synagogue on the sabbath day, as was his custom. He stood up to read, and the scroll of the prophet Isaiah was given to him. He unrolled the scroll and found the place where it was written:
> > "The Spirit of the Lord is upon me,
> > > because he has anointed me to bring good news to the poor.
> > He has sent me to proclaim release to the captives
> > > and recovery of sight to the blind,
> > > > to let the oppressed go free,
> > to proclaim the year of the Lord's favor."
> > > > Luke 4:16-19

Responsorial Psalm

> To you, O LORD, I lift up my soul.
> O my God, in you I trust. . . .
> Make me to know your ways, O LORD;
> > teach me your paths.

Lead me in your truth, and teach me,
for you are the God of my salvation.   Psalm 25:1-2a, 4-5a

Prayers, pp. 529-32

Closing Psalm Prayer

Good and upright is the LORD;
therefore he instructs sinners in the way.
He leads the humble in what is right,
and teaches the humble his way.   Psalm 25:8-9

Third Week of Easter   **Tuesday**

Theme: Each of us has an unclean demon of one sort or another that
we want left alone. But Jesus can rebuke our demons and free
us.

The Lord is Risen, Alleluia!

Risen Lord,
you command the spirits of evil,
and they flee before your power.
Remove evil from me, O Lord,
and let my life be filled with your spirit.

Scripture Reading

In the synagogue there was a man who had a spirit of an unclean
demon, and he cried out with a loud voice, "Let us alone! What have
you to do with us, Jesus of Nazareth? Have you come to destroy
us? I know who you are, the Holy One of God." But Jesus rebuked
him, saying, "Be silent, and come out of him!" When the demon had
thrown him down before them, he came out of him without having
done him any harm. They were all amazed and kept saying to one

another. . . . "With authority and power he commands the unclean spirits, and out they come!"

Luke 4:33-36
optional: Exodus 19:1-26

Responsorial Psalm

To you, O LORD, I call;
    my rock, do not refuse to hear me,
for if you are silent to me,
    I shall be like those who go down to the Pit.
Hear the voice of my supplication,
    as I cry to you for help,
as I lift up my hands
    toward your most holy sanctuary.   Psalm 28:1-2

Prayers, pp. 529-32

Closing Psalm Prayer

Blessed be the LORD,
    for he has heard the sound of my pleadings. . . .
    In him my heart trusts;
so I am helped, and my heart exults,
    and with my song I give thanks to him.   Psalm 28:6, 7

Third Week of Easter   Wednesday

Theme: Each of us needs to be released from one binding sin, one powerful habit, one painful memory, one thing that keeps us from the fullness of joy.

The Lord is Risen, Alleluia!

Risen Savior,
even as crowds come to you during your earthly sojourn,

so now I, your servant, come to you for strength to live day to day.

Scripture Reading

As the sun was setting, all those who had any who were sick with various kinds of diseases brought them to him; and he laid his hands on each of them and cured them. Demons also came out of many, shouting, "You are the Son of God!" But he rebuked them and would not allow them to speak, because they knew he was the Messiah.

At daybreak he departed and went into a deserted place. And the crowds were looking for him; and when they reached him, they wanted to prevent him from leaving them.

Luke 4:40-42
optional: Exodus 19:16-25

Responsorial Psalm

I have chosen the way of faithfulness;
   I set your ordinances before me.
I cling to your decrees, O LORD;
   let me not be put to shame.
I run the way of your commandments,
   for you enlarge my understanding.   Psalm 119:30-32

Prayers, pp. 529-32

Closing Psalm Prayer

O Lord, all my longing is known to you. . . .
Do not forsake me, O LORD;
   O my God, do not be far from me;
make haste to help me,
   O Lord, my salvation.   Psalm 38:9a, 21-22

Third Week of Easter   Thursday

Theme: We often cling to our own dreams and ambitions when what
God has in mind for us is infinitely more engaging and fulfilling.

The Lord is Risen, Alleluia!

Risen and conquering Lord,
you called Simon to leave his nets and follow you.
Let me, your servant, discover the tasks that you have called me
to do.

Scripture Reading

. . . He said to Simon, "Put out into the deep water and let down
your nets for a catch." Simon answered, "Master, we have worked
all night long but have caught nothing. Yet if you say so, I will let
down the nets." When they had done this, they caught so many fish
that their nets were beginning to break. . . . Then Jesus said to Simon,
"Do not be afraid; from now on you will be catching people." When
they had brought their boats to shore, they left everything and
followed him.

Luke 5:4-6, 10-11
optional: Exodus 20:1-21

Responsorial Psalm

Trust in the Lord and do good;
dwell in the land, and feed on his faithfulness.
Delight yourself also in the Lord,
and he shall give you the desires of your heart.
Commit your way to the Lord; trust also in him.

adapted from Psalm 37:3-5

Prayers, pp. 529-32

Closing Psalm Prayer

Our steps are made firm by the LORD,
when he delights in our way;

though we stumble, we shall not fall headlong,
for the LORD holds us by the hand.   Psalm 37:23-24

Third Week of Easter   Friday

Theme: Sometimes we cannot forgive ourselves for sinful deeds or
words; we let them fester within or harden our hearts to the
release that Christ can bring.

The Lord is Risen, Alleluia!

Lord Jesus Christ,
you who lived, died, and rose again for our sin,
let me hear the words "Your sins are forgiven" in a new way.

Scripture Reading

When Jesus perceived their questionings, he answered them, "Why
do you raise such questions in your hearts? Which is easier, to say
'Your sins are forgiven you,' or to say, 'Stand up and walk'? But so
that you may know that the Son of Man has authority on earth to
forgive sins" — he said to the one who was paralyzed — "I say to
you, stand up and take your bed and go to your home." Immediately
he stood up before them, took what he had been lying on, and went
to his home, glorifying God. Amazement seized all of them.

Luke 5:22-26a
optional: Exodus 24:1-18

Responsorial Psalm

O give thanks to the LORD, call on his name,
make known his deeds among the peoples.
Sing to him, sing praises to him;
tell of all his wonderful works.
Glory in his holy name.   Psalm 105:1-3a

Prayers, pp. 529-32

Closing Psalm Prayer

Let the hearts of those who seek the LORD rejoice.
Seek the LORD and his strength;
  seek his presence continually.
Remember the wonderful works he has done.   Psalm 105:3b-5a

Third Week of Easter   Saturday

Theme: We are each like Matthew, with whom Christ is more than
    willing to eat and drink and to come and rearrange our lives
    and homes.

The Lord is Risen, Alleluia!

Risen Lord,
you can look at me and see into my inner being.
Great physician, you can remove my sins and heal my inner hurts
and pains.
I trust in you.

Scripture Reading

. . . And [Jesus] said to [Levi], "Follow me." And he got up, left
everything, and followed him.

Then Levi gave a great banquet for him in his house; and there
was a large crowd of tax collectors and others sitting at the table
with them. The Pharisees and their scribes were complaining to his
disciples, saying, "Why do you eat and drink with tax collectors and
sinners?" Jesus answered, "Those who are well have no need of a
physician, but those who are sick; I have come to call not the
righteous but sinners to repentance."

Luke 5:27-32
optional: Exodus 25:1-22

Responsorial Psalm

I will extol you, O LORD, for you have drawn me up,
  and did not let my foes rejoice over me.
O LORD my God, I cried to you for help,
  and you have healed me.
O LORD, you have brought up my soul from Sheol. Psalm 30:1-3a

Prayers, pp. 529-32

Closing Psalm Prayer

Sing praises to the LORD, O you his faithful ones,
  and give thanks to his holy name. . . .
  I will give thanks to you forever.   Psalm 30:4, 12b

Fourth Week of Easter   Sunday

Theme: Even though we stumble and fall again and again, the resur-
       rected Christ, who fulfilled the law for us, picks us up and calls
       us to go on in his name.

The Lord is Risen, Alleluia!

Risen Lord,
you lived among us and fulfilled the law on our behalf.
Let me bless your Holy Name
and remember all that you do for me and for all people.

Scripture Reading

Do not think that I have come to abolish the law or the prophets; I
have come not to abolish but to fulfill. . . . Therefore, whoever
breaks one of the least of these commandments, and teaches others
to do the same, will be called least in the kingdom of heaven; but
whoever does them and teaches them will be called great in the
kingdom of heaven. For I tell you, unless your righteousness exceeds

that of the scribes and Pharisees you will never enter the kingdom of heaven.

Matthew 5:17, 19-20

optional: Exodus 28:1-4, 30-38

Responsorial Psalm

Bless the LORD, O you his angels,
  you mighty ones who do his bidding,
  obedient to his spoken word.
Bless the LORD, all his hosts,
  his ministers that do his will.
Bless the LORD, all his works,
  in all places of his dominion.   Psalm 103:20-22

Prayers, pp. 529-32

Closing Psalm Prayer

Bless the LORD, O my soul,
  and all that is within me,
  bless his holy name.
Bless the LORD, O my soul,
  and do not forget all his benefits.   Psalm 103:1-2

Fourth Week of Easter   Monday

Theme: We are the Pharisees who expect everyone to live by the rules
        we set up, but Jesus breaks through our laws and calls us to the
        spirit of life under Christ, who is Lord over all.

The Lord is Risen, Alleluia!

Risen Christ,
you who created the world and rule over it,

uphold me in everything I do,
so that my words and deeds may be to your praise and glory.

Scripture Reading

One sabbath while Jesus was going though the grainfields, his
disciples plucked some heads of grain, rubbed them in their hands,
and ate them. But some of the Pharisees said, "Why are you doing
what is not lawful on the sabbath?" Jesus answered, "Have you not
read what David did when he and his companions were hungry? He
entered the house of God and took and ate the bread of the Presence,
which it is not lawful for any but the priests to eat, and gave some
to his companions?" Then he said to them, "The Son of Man is lord
of the sabbath."

Luke 6:1-5
optional: Exodus 32:1-20

Responsorial Psalm

I trust in the steadfast love of God
    forever and ever.
I will thank you forever,
    because of what you have done.
In the presence of the faithful
    I will proclaim your name, for it is good.   Psalm 52:8b-9

Prayers, pp. 529-32

Closing Psalm Prayer

But you have upheld me because of my integrity,
    and set me in your presence forever.
Blessed be the LORD, the God of Israel,
    from everlasting to everlasting.
        Amen and Amen.

Psalm 41:12-13

Fourth Week of Easter   Tuesday

Theme: Christ chooses us to do his work in the world today through
us. We are his voice, his hands, his feet, his heart to neighbor
and friend.

The Lord is Risen, Alleluia!

Risen Christ,
as you chose your apostles and sent them out with your truth,
grant me the wisdom and power to speak on your behalf today.

Scripture Reading

Now during those days he went out to the mountain to pray; and
he spent the night in prayer to God. And when day came, he called
his disciples and chose twelve of them, whom he also named apostles:
Simon, whom he named Peter, and his brother Andrew, and James,
and John, and Philip, and Bartholomew, and Matthew, and Thomas,
and James son of Alphaeus, and Simon, who was called the Zealot,
and Judas son of James, and Judas Iscariot, who became a traitor.

Luke 6:12-16
optional: Exodus 32:21-34

Responsorial Psalm

Clap your hands, all you peoples;
shout to God with loud songs of joy.
For the LORD, the Most High, is awesome,
a great king over all the earth.
He subdued peoples under us,
and nations under our feet.   Psalm 47:1-3

Prayers, pp. 529-32

Closing Psalm Prayer

God is king over the nations;
God sits on his holy throne.
The princes of the peoples gather

as the people of the God of Abraham.
For the shields of the earth belong to God;
  he is highly exalted.   Psalm 47:8-9

Fourth Week of Easter   **Wednesday**

Theme: We often live as though the teachings of our Lord are irrelevant
        to our lives and our relationships, but he rose to change our
        lives through his life and teaching.

The Lord is Risen, Alleluia!

Risen Savior,
you not only died to redeem me and bring me to heaven,
but you rose to give me a new life.
Let my attitude toward others show you forth.

Scripture Reading

Bless those who curse you, pray for those who abuse you. If anyone
strikes you on the cheek, offer the other also; and from anyone who
takes away your coat do not withhold even your shirt. Give to
everyone who begs from you; and if anyone takes away your goods,
do not ask for them again. Do to others as you would have them
do to you.

  If you love those who love you, what credit is that to you? For
even sinners love those who love them. . . . But love your enemies,
do good, and lend, expecting nothing in return.

                                                    Luke 6:28-32, 35
                                              optional: Exodus 33:1-23

Responsorial Psalm

Do not be afraid when some become rich,
  when the wealth of their houses increases.
For when they die they will carry nothing away;
  their wealth will not go down after them.

Though in their lifetime they count themselves happy . . .
    they will go to the company of their ancestors.

Psalm 49:16-19a

Prayers, pp. 529-32

Closing Psalm Prayer

Your statutes have been my songs. . . .
I remember your name in the night, O LORD,
    and keep your law.
This blessing has fallen to me,
    for I have kept your precepts.   Psalm 119:54a, 55-56

Fourth Week of Easter   Thursday

Theme: Our hopes and ambitions are often material and selfish. We
        build our lives on sand and expect God to bless us because we
        believe the right thing in our heads.

The Lord is Risen, Alleluia!

Risen Christ,
I confess that you are the judge of all the earth.
May I, your servant, hear your voice
and build my house on the Rock.

Scripture Reading

I will show you what someone is like who comes to me, hears my
words, and acts on them. That one is like a man building a house,
who dug deeply and laid the foundation on rock; when a flood arose,
the river burst against that house but could not shake it, because it
had been well built. But the one who hears and does not act is like
a man who built a house on the ground without a foundation. When

the river burst against it, immediately it fell, and great was the ruin
of that house.

Luke 6:47-49

optional: Exodus 34:1-17

Responsorial Psalm

He calls to the heavens above
    and to the earth, that he may judge his people:
"Gather to me my faithful ones,
    who made a covenant with me by sacrifice."
The heavens declare his righteousness,
    for God himself is judge.
Psalm 50:4-6

Prayers, pp. 529-32

Closing Psalm Prayer

Mark this, then, you who forget God. . . .
Those who bring thanksgiving as their sacrifice honor me;
    to those who go the right way
    I will show the salvation of God.
Psalm 50:22-23

Fourth Week of Easter   Friday

Theme: We are the dead — dead in our sins, our attitudes toward other
      people, and our aspirations. To us the risen Lord says, "Arise!"

The Lord is Risen, Alleluia!

Risen Lord,
you touch the sick and disabled, even the dead,
and they rise to life.
Touch my infirmities, O God,
and heal me for your sake.

Scripture Reading

. . . He went to a town called Nain. . . . A man who had died was being carried out. He was his mother's only son, and she was a widow. . . . When the Lord saw her, he had compassion on her and said to her, "Do not weep." Then he came forward and touched the bier, and the bearers stood still. And he said, "Young man, I say to you, rise!" The dead man sat up and began to speak, and Jesus gave him to his mother. Fear seized all of them; and they glorified God, saying, "A great prophet has risen among us!" and "God has looked favorably on his people!" This word about him spread throughout Judea and all the surrounding country.

Luke 7:11-17

optional: Exodus 34:18-35

Responsorial Psalm

I waited patiently for the LORD;
    he inclined to me and heard my cry.
He drew me up from the desolate pit,
    out of the miry bog,
and set my feet upon a rock,
    making my steps secure.   Psalm 40:1-2

Prayers, pp. 529-32

Closing Psalm Prayer

He put a new song in my mouth,
    a song of praise to our God.
Many will see and fear,
    and put their trust in the LORD. . . .
        Great is the LORD!   Psalm 40:3, 16b

Fourth Week of Easter   Saturday

Theme: There is an ultimate point of reference for the pain and rejection
we sometimes feel. Our Lord has experienced our hurts and
offers us his victory.

The Lord is Risen, Alleluia!

Lord, over the grave, when you walked on earth,
you were rejected and despised.
May I, O Lord, find the meaning of my hurts
in the pain you experienced.

Scripture Reading

[The Lord said,] "To what then will I compare the people of this
generation, and what are they like? They are like children sitting in
the marketplace and calling to one another,
    'We played the flute for you, and you did not dance;
        we wailed, and you did not weep.'
For John the Baptist has come eating no bread and drinking no
wine, and you say, 'He has a demon'; the Son of Man has come
eating and drinking, and you say, 'Look, a glutton and a drunkard,
a friend of tax collectors and sinners!'"

Luke 7:31-35
optional: Exodus 40:18-38

Responsorial Psalm

Give ear to my prayer, O God;
    do not hide yourself from my supplication.
Attend to me, and answer me;
    I am troubled in my complaint.
I am distraught by the noise of the enemy,
    because of the clamor of the wicked.
For they bring trouble upon me,
    and in anger they cherish enmity against me.   Psalm 55:1-3

Prayers, pp. 529-32

Closing Psalm Prayer

My heart is in anguish within me,
    the terrors of death have fallen upon me.
Fear and trembling come upon me. . . .
Cast your burden on the LORD,
    and he will sustain you.   Psalm 55:4-5a, 22a

Fifth Week of Easter   Sunday

Theme: We are the ones to whom the Holy Spirit has been sent, but we
        often neither claim the power he brings nor allow ourselves to
        be filled with his presence.

The Lord is Risen, Alleluia!

Risen Lord,
you sent your Spirit among us to help us and to guide us into all
truth.
Guide my life, O Lord,
that I may walk in your ways,
and grow in the power of your Spirit.

Scripture Reading

If you love me, you will keep my commandments. And I will ask the
Father, and he will give you another Advocate, to be with you forever.
This is the Spirit of truth, whom the world cannot receive, because
it neither sees him nor knows him. You know him, because he abides
with you, and he will be in you.

    I will not leave you orphaned; I am coming to you. In a little
while the world will no longer see me, but you will see me; because
I live, you also will live. On that day you will know that I am in my
Father, and you in me, and I in you.

                                    John 14:15-20
                        optional: Leviticus 8:1-36

Responsorial Psalm

Lift up your heads, O gates!
  and be lifted up, O ancient doors!
  that the King of glory may come in.
Who is the King of glory?
  The LORD, strong and mighty,
  the LORD, mighty in battle. . . .
  He is the King of glory.   Psalm 24:7-8, 10b

Prayers, pp. 529-32

Closing Psalm Prayer

The earth is the LORD's and all that is in it,
  the world, and those who live in it;
for he has founded it on the seas,
  and established it on the rivers.   Psalm 24:1-2

Fifth Week of Easter   Monday

Theme: Our hearts are sometimes pained within because this or that
       person misunderstands our purpose, our intentions, and our
       motives.

The Lord is Risen, Alleluia!

Risen and victorious Lord,
by your life you have set an example for me to follow.
Let me not fear those who misunderstand me,
and let me remain faithful to you.

Scripture Reading

And a woman in the city, who was a sinner, having learned that
[Jesus] was eating in the Pharisee's house, brought an alabaster jar
of ointment. She stood behind him at his feet, weeping, and began
to bathe his feet with her tears and to dry them with her hair. Then

she continued kissing his feet and anointing them with the ointment.
Now when the Pharisee who had invited him saw it, he said to
himself, "If this man were a prophet, he would have known who
and what kind of woman this is who is touching him — that she is
a sinner."

Luke 7:37-39

optional: Leviticus 16:1-19

Responsorial Psalm

All day long they seek to injure my cause;
>   all their thoughts are against me for evil.
They stir up strife, they lurk,
>   they watch my steps.
As they hoped to have my life,
>   so repay them for their crime;
>   in wrath cast down the peoples, O God!   Psalm 56:5-7

Prayers, pp. 529-32

Closing Psalm Prayer

. . . When I am afraid,
>   I put my trust in you. . . .
>   In God I trust; I am not afraid;
>   what can flesh do to me?   Psalm 56:3b, 4b

Fifth Week of Easter   Tuesday

Theme: We are the soil on which the seeds fall. We need to clean out
>   the rocks and thorns that will choke the seeds and prevent their
>   growth.

The Lord is Risen, Alleluia!

Risen Lord,
may the seed sown in the soil of my life spring forth into a good

harvest.
For you, O Lord, are my salvation!

Scripture Reading

When a great crowd gathered . . . , he said in a parable: "A sower
went out to sow his seed; and as he sowed, some fell on the path
and was trampled on, and the birds of the air ate it up. Some fell
on the rock; and as it grew up, it withered for lack of moisture. Some
fell among thorns, and the thorns grew with it and choked it. Some
fell into good soil, and when it grew, it produced a hundredfold."
As he said this, he called out, "Let anyone with ears to hear
listen!" . . .
    "Now the parable is this: the seed is the Word of God."

Luke 8:4-8
optional: Leviticus 16:20-34

Responsorial Psalm

For God alone my soul waits in silence. . . .
On God rests my deliverance and my honor;
    my mighty rock, my refuge is in God.
Trust in him at all times, O people;
    pour out your heart before him;
        God is a refuge for us.   Psalm 62:5a, 7-8

Prayers, pp. 529-32

Closing Psalm Prayer

For God alone my soul waits in silence;
    from him comes my salvation.
He alone is my rock and my salvation,
    my fortress; I shall never be shaken.   Psalm 62:1-2

Fifth Week of Easter　　　　　　　　　　Wednesday

Theme: We, the brothers and sisters of Jesus, as we hear his Word and
　　　　live by his teaching, deepen our relationships.

The Lord is Risen, Alleluia!

Risen brother,
you who became one of us that we may become one with you,
let my life be filled with your glory.

Scripture Reading

[Jesus said,] "No one after lighting a lamp hides it under a jar, or
puts it under a bed, but puts it on a lampstand, so that those who
enter may see the light. For nothing is hidden that will not be
disclosed, nor is anything secret that will not become known and
come to light. . . ." Then his mother and his brothers came to him,
but they could not reach him because of the crowd. And he was told,
"Your mother and your brothers are standing outside, wanting to
see you." But he said to them, "My mother and my brothers are
those who hear the Word of God and do it."

Luke 8:16-17, 19-21
optional: Leviticus 19:1-18

Responsorial Psalm

Give the king your justice, O God,
　　　and your righteousness to a king's son.
May he judge your people with righteousness,
　　　and your poor with justice. . . .
May he defend the cause of the poor of the people,
　　　give deliverance to the needy,
　　　and crush the oppressor.　　　　　　　　　　Psalm 72:1-4

Prayers, pp. 529-32

Closing Psalm Prayer

> Blessed be the LORD, the God of Israel,
>   who alone does wondrous things.
> Blessed be his glorious name forever;
>   may his glory fill the whole earth.   Psalm 72:18-19

Fifth Week of Easter   Thursday

Theme: There is no power on earth that can match the power of the
One who frees us to live in the power of the resurrection.

The Lord is Risen, Alleluia!

Risen Savior,
you who demonstrated your power over the demonic of this world
and rose from the grave,
form me after your image.

Scripture Reading

Jesus then asked him, "What is your name?" He said, "Legion"; for
many demons had entered him. They begged him not to order them
to go out into the abyss. . . .

Then the demons came out of the man and entered the swine,
and the herd rushed violently down the steep bank into the lake and
was drowned. . . .

Then people came out to see what had happened, and when they
came to Jesus, they found the man from whom the demons had gone
sitting at the feet of Jesus, clothed and in his right mind. And they
were afraid. . . . [Then Jesus said,] "Return to your home, and
declare how much God has done for you."

                                          Luke 8:30-31, 33, 35, 39
                                          optional: Leviticus 19:26-37

Responsorial Psalm

Be pleased, O God, to deliver me.
O LORD, make haste to help me!
Let those be put to shame and confusion
who seek my life.
Let those be turned back and brought to dishonor
who desire to hurt me. . . .
O LORD, do not delay.   Psalm 70:1-2, 5b

Prayers, pp. 529-32

Closing Psalm Prayer

For you, O Lord, are my hope,
my trust, O LORD, from my youth.
Upon you I have leaned from my birth. . . .
My praise is continually of you.   Psalm 71:5-6

Fifth Week of Easter   Friday

Theme: When we reach out and touch the hem of his garment, the
powers of evil are set in flight and the newness of his Spirit
floods our souls.

The Lord is Risen, Alleluia!

Risen healer,
come and let me touch the hem of your garment.
Heal me, make me whole, and send me forth in peace.

Scripture Reading

Now there was a woman who had been suffering from hemorrhages
for twelve years. . . . She came up behind him and touched the fringe
of his clothes, and immediately her hemorrhage stopped. Then Jesus

asked, "Who touched me?" . . . When the woman saw that she could not remain hidden, she came trembling; and falling down before him, she declared in the presence of all the people why she had touched him, and how she had been immediately healed. He said to her, "Daughter, your faith has made you well; go in peace."

Luke 8:43-45a, 47-48

optional: Leviticus 23:1-22

Responsorial Psalm

O give thanks to the LORD, for he is good;
    for his steadfast love endures forever.
Who can utter the mighty doings of the LORD,
    or declare all his praise?
Happy are those who observe justice,
    who do righteousness at all times.   Psalm 106:1-3

Prayers, pp. 529-32

Closing Psalm Prayer

Remember me, O LORD, when you show favor to your people;
    help me when you deliver them . . .
    that I may glory in your heritage.   Psalm 106:4, 5b

Fifth Week of Easter   Saturday

Theme: Christ gives us power to proclaim his name and boldness to declare for ourselves and others that the new life is real and satisfying.

The Lord is Risen, Alleluia!

O Risen One,
you who called me out of darkness into your marvelous light,
teach me to be the good news and grant me boldness.

Scripture Reading

Then Jesus called the twelve together and gave them power and authority over all demons and to cure diseases, and he sent them out to proclaim the kingdom of God and to heal. He said to them, "Take nothing for your journey, no staff, nor bag, nor bread, nor money — not even an extra tunic. Whatever house you enter, stay there, and leave from there. Wherever they do not welcome you, as you are leaving that town shake the dust off your feet as a testimony against them." They departed and went through the villages, bringing the good news and curing diseases everywhere.

Luke 9:1-6
optional: Leviticus 23:23-44

Responsorial Psalm

One thing I asked of the LORD,
    that will I seek after:
to live in the house of the LORD
    all the days of my life,
to behold the beauty of the LORD,
    and to inquire in his temple.
For he will hide me in his shelter
    in the day of trouble.   Psalm 27:4-5a

Prayers, pp. 529-32

Closing Psalm Prayer

Teach me your way, O LORD. . . .
Wait for the LORD;
    be strong, and let your heart take courage;
    wait for the LORD!   Psalm 27:11a, 14

Sixth Week of Easter   Sunday

Theme: When we allow the kingdom of Christ to rule in our hearts and
         lives, we become the kingdom to people and lift their lives into
         the presence of the King.

The Lord is Risen, Alleluia!

Risen Lord,
you who reign in your kingdom on high,
rule in my life so that it may be known
that you are my Lord and my King.

Scripture Reading

He put before them another parable: "The kingdom of heaven is like
a mustard seed that someone took and sowed in his field; it is the
smallest of all the seeds, but when it has grown it is the greatest of
shrubs and becomes a tree, so that the birds of the air come and
make nests in its branches."

He told them another parable: "The kingdom of heaven is like
yeast that a woman took and mixed in with three measures of flour
until all of it was leavened."

Matthew 13:31-33
optional: Leviticus 25:1-17

Responsorial Psalm

The LORD is king, he is robed in majesty;
    the LORD is robed, he is girded with strength.
He has established the world; it shall never be moved;
    your throne is established from of old;
    you are from everlasting.   Psalm 93:1-2

Prayers, pp. 529-32

Closing Psalm Prayer

The floods have lifted up, O LORD,
    the floods have lifted up their voice. . . .

More majestic than the thunders of mighty waters,
    more majestic than the waves of the sea,
    majestic on high is the LORD!   Psalm 93:3-4

Sixth Week of Easter   Monday

Theme: Christ who lived, died, and rose on earth must be born in our
    hearts, die, and be raised to newness of life within us.

The Lord is Risen, Alleluia!

Risen Lord,
come and dwell in my heart.
Do not forsake me or leave me.
I long for you and desire your healing presence in my life.

Scripture Reading

Once when Jesus was praying alone, with only the disciples near
him, he asked them, "Who do the crowds say that I am?" They
answered, "John the Baptist; but others, Elijah; and still others say
that one of the ancient prophets has arisen." He said to them, "But
who do you say that I am?" Peter answered, "The Messiah of God."

He sternly ordered and commanded them not to tell anyone,
saying, "The Son of Man must undergo great suffering, and be
rejected by the elders, chief priests, and scribes, and be killed, and
on the third day be raised."

Luke 9:18-22
optional: Leviticus 25:35-55

Responsorial Psalm

I cry aloud to God. . . .
Will the Lord spurn forever,
    and never again be favorable?
Has his steadfast love ceased forever?
Are his promises at an end for all time?

Has God forgotten to be gracious?
Has he in anger shut up his compassion?   Psalm 77:1, 7-9

Prayers, pp. 529-32

Closing Psalm Prayer

I will call to mind the deeds of the LORD;
    I will remember the wonders of old.
I will meditate on all your work. . . .
Your way, O God, is holy.
        What god is so great as our God?   Psalm 77:11-13

Sixth Week of Easter   Tuesday

Theme: We are not only to pray the Lord's Prayer, but more, we are to
        let the prayer become the pattern of our experience.

The Lord is Risen, Alleluia!

Risen Lord,
you who taught us how to pray,
come, move into my life and so dwell within me,
that I may become your prayer.

Scripture Reading

Pray then in this way:
Our Father in heaven,
    hallowed be your name.
    Your kingdom come.
    Your will be done,
        on earth as it is in heaven.
    Give us this day our daily bread.
    And forgive us our debts,
        as we also forgive our debtors.

And do not bring us to the time of trial,
   but rescue us from the evil one.   Matthew 6:9-13

Responsorial Psalm

Give ear, O my people, to my teaching;
   incline your ears to the words of my mouth.
I will open my mouth in a parable;
   I will utter dark sayings from of old. . . .
We will not hide them from their children;
   we will tell to the coming generation
the glorious deeds of the LORD, and his might,
   and the wonders that he has done.   Psalm 78:1, 2, 4

Prayers, pp. 529-32

Closing Psalm Prayer

In the sight of their ancestors he worked marvels
      in the land of Egypt. . . .
He divided the sea and let them pass through it. Psalm 78:12a, 13a

Sixth Week of Easter   Wednesday

Theme: Our Lord who invites us to stop worrying about our lives and
       being anxious over things we cannot control, invites us to trust
       him.

The Lord is Risen, Alleluia!

Risen Lord,
forgive me for building my future as though you were not here.
Take away my anxieties and let me learn from the birds of the air.

Scripture Reading

He said to his disciples, "Therefore I tell you, do not worry about your life, what you will eat, or about your body, what you will wear. For life is more than food, and the body more than clothing. Consider the ravens: they neither sow nor reap, they have neither storehouse nor barn, and yet God feeds them. Of how much more value are you than the birds! And can any of you by worrying add a single hour to your span of life? If then you are not able to do so small a thing as that, why do you worry about the rest?

Luke 12:22-26

Responsorial Psalm

Oh, how I love your law!
It is my meditation all the day long.
Your commandment makes me wiser than my enemies,
for it is always with me. . . .
Through your precepts I get understanding;
therefore I hate every false way.   Psalm 119:97-98, 104

Prayers, pp. 529-32

Closing Psalm Prayer

I hold back my feet from every evil way,
in order to keep your word.
I do not turn away from your ordinances,
for you have taught me.
How sweet are your words to my taste,
sweeter than honey to my mouth!   Psalm 119:101-103

Ascension Day   Thursday

Theme: The ascended Lord not only sits on the right of the Father, but lives within us to rule in our heart, control our tongue, and guide our actions.

The Lord is Risen, Alleluia!

Ascended Lord and reigning King,
come as you promised and dwell within me.
Reside in my heart always, even to the end.

Scripture Reading

Now the eleven disciples went away into Galilee, to the mountain to
which Jesus had directed them. When they saw him, they worshiped
him; but some doubted. And Jesus came and said to them, "All
authority in heaven and on earth has been given to me. Go therefore
and make disciples of all nations, baptizing them in the name of the
Father and of the Son and of the Holy Spirit, and teaching them to obey
everything that I have commanded you. And remember, I am with you
always, to the end of the age."

Matthew 28:16-20
optional: Daniel 7:9-14

Responsorial Psalm

God has gone up with a shout,
    the LORD with the sound of a trumpet.
Sing praises to God, sing praises;
    sing praises to our King, sing praises.
For God is the king of all the earth. . . .
God is king over the nations;
    God sits on his holy throne.

Psalm 47:5a, 8

Prayers, pp. 529-32

Closing Psalm Prayer

Clap your hands, all you peoples;
    shout to God with loud songs of joy.
For the LORD, the Most High, is awesome,
    a great king over all the earth. . . .
He is highly exalted.

Psalm 47:1-2, 9b

Sixth Week of Easter   Friday

Theme: God wants to transfigure us into his glory by abiding fully within
us, by permeating our whole life with his presence.

The Lord is Risen, Alleluia!

Ascended Lord,
you gave your disciples a glimpse of your glory.
Fill me with your presence
so that I may be changed from glory to glory.

Scripture Reading

Now about eight days after these sayings Jesus took with him Peter
and John and James, and went up on the mountain to pray. And
while he was praying, the appearance of his face changed, and his
clothes became dazzling white. Suddenly they saw two men, Moses
and Elijah, talking to him. . . . Then from the cloud came a voice
that said, "This is my Son, my Chosen; listen to him!" When the
voice had spoken, Jesus was found alone. And they kept silent and
in those days told no one any of the things they had seen.

Luke 9:28-30, 35-36
optional: I Samuel 2:1-10

Responsorial Psalm

Teach me your way, O LORD,
that I may walk in your truth;
give me an undivided heart to revere your name.
I give thanks to you, O Lord my God, with my whole heart,
and I will glorify your name forever.
For great is your steadfast love toward me.   Psalm 86:11-13a

Prayers, pp. 529-32

Closing Psalm Prayer

Give ear, O LORD, to my prayer;
listen to my cry of supplication.

In the day of my trouble I call on you,
    for you will answer me.   Psalm 86:6-7

Sixth Week of Easter   Saturday

Theme: The Lord can take the spirit that needs to be turned over to
    Jesus, cast it down, destroy it, and release us from its power.

The Lord is Risen, Alleluia!

Ascended Lord,
you discern the evil spirits
and conquer them by your resurrection power.
Take out of me those spirits that keep me from loving and
serving you fully.

Scripture Reading

On the next day, when they had come down from the mountain, a
great crowd met him. Just then a man from the crowd shouted,
"Teacher, I beg you to look at my son; he is my only child. . . ."
Jesus answered, "You faithless and perverse generation, how much
longer must I be with you and bear with you? Bring your son here."
While he was coming, the demon dashed him to the ground in
convulsions. But Jesus rebuked the unclean spirit, healed the boy,
and gave him back to his father.

Luke 9:37-38, 41-42
optional: Numbers 11:16-29

Responsorial Psalm

Lord, you have been our dwelling place
    in all generations.
Before the mountains were brought forth,
    or ever you had formed the earth and the world,
        from everlasting to everlasting you are God. . . .
So teach us to count our days.   Psalm 90:1-2, 12a

Prayers, pp. 529-32

Closing Psalm Prayer

Turn, O LORD! How long?
Have compassion on your servants. . . .
Let the favor of the Lord our God be upon us,
and prosper for us the work of our hands —
O prosper the work of our hands!   Psalm 90:13, 17

Seventh Week of Easter   **Sunday**

Theme: The God who know every intimate detail of our lives, cares for
our hurts, our wants, our needs, and he will not turn away from
us.

The Lord is Risen, Alleluia!

Risen and ascended Christ,
you know my frame, that I am from the dust of the earth.
Do not turn from me or forsake me in my need.

Scripture Reading

What I say to you in the dark, tell in the light; and what you hear
whispered, proclaim from the housetops. . . . Are not two sparrows
sold for a penny? Yet not one of them will fall to the ground apart
from your Father. And even the hairs of your head are all counted.
So do not be afraid; you are of more value than many sparrows.

"Everyone therefore who acknowledges me before others, I also
will acknowledge before my Father in heaven."

Matthew 10:27, 29-32
optional: Exodus 3:1-12

Responsorial Psalm

Make a joyful noise to God, all the earth;
sing the glory of his name;

give to him glorious praise;
Say to God, "How awesome are your deeds! . . .
All the earth worships you;
    they sing praises to you,
        sing praises to your name."   Psalm 66:1-4

Prayers, pp. 529-32

Closing Psalm Prayer

Come and hear, all you who fear God,
    and I will tell what he has done for me. . . .
Blessed be God,
    because he has not rejected my prayer
    or removed his steadfast love from me.   Psalm 66:16, 20

Seventh Week of Easter   Monday

Theme: We are the ones who offer our excuses for not following Jesus,
      but Jesus can free us from our excuses and turn us into disciples.

The Lord is Risen, Alleluia!

Lord Jesus, you who reign on high,
turn me away from the excuses I make against following you,
and fill my heart with a new zeal and passion for you.

Scripture Reading

As they were going along the road, someone said to him, "I will
follow you wherever you go." And Jesus said to him, "Foxes have
holes, and birds of the air have nests; but the Son of Man has nowhere
to lay his head." To another he said, "Follow me." But he said, "Lord,
first let me go and bury my father." . . . Another said, "I will follow
you, Lord; but let me first say farewell to those at my home." Jesus

said to him, "No one who puts a hand to the plow and looks back is fit for the kingdom of God."

Luke 9:57-62
optional: Joshua 1:1-9

Responsorial Psalm

The LORD loves those who hate evil;
> he guards the lives of his faithful;
> he rescues them from the hand of the wicked. . . .
Rejoice in the LORD, O you righteous,
> and give thanks to his holy name!   Psalm 97:10, 12

Prayers, pp. 529-32

Closing Psalm Prayer

The LORD is the king! Let the earth rejoice;
> let the many coastlands be glad. . . .
For you, O LORD, are most high over all the earth. Psalm 97:1, 9a

Seventh Week of Easter   Tuesday

Theme: If we desire a relationship with the Father of our Lord Jesus Christ, it begins by honoring and obeying his only Son, our Lord.

The Lord is Risen, Alleluia!

Risen Christ,
you who are one with the Father and the Holy Spirit,
turn me from my lethargy and build a fire in my soul,
for your sake.

Scripture Reading

> Woe to you, Chorazin! Woe to you, Bethsaida! For if the deeds of power in you had been done in Tyre and Sidon, they would have repented long ago, sitting in sackcloth and ashes. But at the judgment it will be more tolerable for Tyre and Sidon than for you. And you, Capernaum,
>> will you be exalted to heaven?
>> No, you will be brought down to Hades.
>
> Whoever listens to you listens to me, and whoever rejects you rejects me, and whoever rejects me rejects the one who sent me.

Luke 10:13-16
optional: I Samuel 16:1-13a

Responsorial Psalm

> Make a joyful noise to the LORD, all the earth.
>> Worship the LORD with gladness;
>> come into his presence with singing.
> Know that the LORD is God.
>> It is he that made us, and we are his;
>> we are his people, and the sheep of his pasture.

Psalm 100:1-3

Prayers, pp. 529-32

Closing Psalm Prayer

> Enter his gates with thanksgiving. . . .
>> Give thanks to him, bless his name.
> For the LORD is good;
>> his steadfast love endures forever.   Psalm 100:4-5a

Seventh Week of Easter   Wednesday

Theme: The real joy in life is not that we have accomplished this or that in the name of Jesus, but that we live with the promise of an eternal life that starts now.

The Lord is Risen, Alleluia!

Risen Christ,
you have have written my name in heaven.
Protect me from my fleshly pride and turn me to trust wholly in
you.

Scripture Reading

The seventy returned with joy, saying, "Lord, in your name even the
demons submit to us!" He said to them, "I watched Satan fall from
heaven like a flash of lightning. See, I have given you authority to
tread on snakes and scorpions, and over all the power of the enemy;
and nothing will hurt you. Nevertheless, do not rejoice at this, that
the spirits submit to you, but rejoice that your names are written in
heaven."

Luke 10:17-20
optional: I Samuel 4:2-6

Responsorial Psalm

I will sing of loyalty and of justice;
to you, O LORD, I will sing. . . .
I will not set before my eyes
anything that is base.
I hate the work of those who fall away;
it shall not cling to me.
Perverseness of heart shall be far from me;
I will know nothing of evil.   Psalm 101:1, 3-4

Prayers, pp. 529-32

Closing Psalm Prayer

Hear my prayer, O LORD;
let my cry come to you.
Do not hide your face from me
in the day of my distress.
Incline your ear to me;
answer me speedily in the day when I call.   Psalm 102:1-2

Seventh Week of Easter   Thursday

Theme: We find ourselves in the taunting of the young lawyer. Like him
we don't want to pay the price, so we keep diverting the issue.

The Lord is Risen, Alleluia!

Risen and ascended Lord,
you see through my continual attempts to evade your claim on
my life.
Turn me from my devious ways and teach me to walk in your
paths.

Scripture Reading

Just then a lawyer stood up to test Jesus. "Teacher," he said, "what
must I do to inherit eternal life?" He said to him, "What is written
in the law? What do you read there?" He answered, "You shall love
the Lord your God with all your heart, and with all your soul, and
with all your strength, and with all your mind; and your neighbor
as yourself." And he said to him, "You have given the right answer;
do this, and you will live."

But wanting to justify himself, he asked Jesus, "And who is my
neighbor?"

Luke 10:25-29
optional: Zechariah 4:1-14

Responsorial Psalm

O give thanks to the LORD, call on his name,
make known his deeds among the peoples.
Sing to him, sing praises to him;
tell of all his wonderful works.
Glory in his holy name. . . .
Seek his presence continually.   Psalm 105:1-4

Prayers, pp. 529-32

Closing Psalm Prayer

> Remember the wonderful works he has done,
>> his miracles, and the judgments he uttered. . . .
> He is the LORD our God;
>> his judgments are in all the earth.   Psalm 105:5, 7

~

Seventh Week of Easter   Friday

Theme: Like Martha, we sometimes hide our inability to have a personal
relationship with the Lord in our busyness.

The Lord is Risen, Alleluia!

> Risen Jesus,
> you who desire a heart-to-heart relationship with me,
> forgive me for my lack of ease in your presence
> and break through the walls of my defensiveness.

Scripture Reading

> Now as they went on their way, he entered a certain village, where
> a woman named Martha welcomed him into her home. She had a
> sister named Mary, who sat at the Lord's feet and listened to what
> he was saying. But Martha was distracted by her many tasks; so she
> came to him and asked, "Lord, do you not care that my sister has
> left me to do all the work by myself? Tell her then to help me." But
> the Lord answered her, "Martha, Martha, you are worried and
> distracted by many things; there is need of only one thing. Mary has
> chosen the better part, which will not be taken away from her."
>>   Luke 10:38-42
>>   optional: Jeremiah 31:27-34

Responsorial Psalm

> O give thanks to the LORD, for he is good;
>> for his steadfast love endures forever.
> Let the redeemed of the LORD say so,

those he redeemed from trouble
and gathered in from the lands,
    from the east and from the west,
    from the north and from the south.   Psalm 107:1-3

Prayers, pp. 529-32

Closing Psalm Prayer

Long ago you laid the foundation of the earth,
    and the heavens are the work of your hands.
They will perish, but you endure;
    they will all wear out like a garment.
You change them like clothing, and they pass away;
    but you are the same, and your years have no end.

                                              Psalm 102:25-27

Seventh Week of Easter   Saturday

Theme: Our hearts cannot be neutral. Either we are for the Lord or
        against him. But it can clean our house and turn us to him when
        we yield to him.

The Lord is Risen, Alleluia!

Risen and ascended Lord,
look on my heart,
try me and purge me of lukewarmness.
Set my heart on fire for you, Lord.

Scripture Reading

Now if I cast out the demons by Beelzebul, by whom do your
exorcists cast them out? Therefore they will be your judges. But if
it is by the finger of God that I cast out the demons, then the kingdom
of God has come to you. When a strong man, fully armed, guards
his castle, his property is safe. But when one stronger than he attacks
him and overpowers him, he takes away his armor in which he

trusted and divides his plunder. Whoever is not with me is against me, and whoever does not gather with me scatters.

Luke 11:19-23
optional: Ezekiel 36:22-27

Responsorial Psalm

My heart is steadfast, O God, my heart is steadfast;
  I will sing and make melody. . . .
Awake, O harp and lyre!
  I will awake the dawn. . . .
And I will sing praises to you among the nations.
For your steadfast love is higher than the heavens.

Psalm 108:1a, 2, 3b-4a

Prayers, pp. 529-32

Closing Psalm Prayer

Be exalted, O God, above the heavens,
  and let your glory be over all the earth.
Give victory with your right hand, and answer me,
  so that those whom you love may be rescued.   Psalm 108:5-6

The Season after Pentecost

The season after Pentecost has the distinction of being the longest of all the seasons of the Christian year. Because it goes through summer and the long months of fall until the beginning of Advent, it is the season most likely to suffer periods of neglect. Consequently you will have to be extra committed to the discipline of daily prayer to maintain it during these months.

In spite of the length of the season after Pentecost, it can be a very exciting and rewarding time for the spiritual pilgrim. Its central emphasis is on the growth and development of the church as the people of God.

The purpose of our devotion during the season after Pentecost is to allow ourselves to be shaped by the journey of the church during the first century. The New Testament letters were written to living communities of people in various towns of the Roman Empire. Each letter addresses problems and issues that were current in these Christian communities.

Fortunately there is a timelessness to these issues. The problems faced by the early Christians are not different from problems that we face from day to day. These Christians were, like us, people in the process of spiritual growth and maturation. Consequently they were in need of instruction and guidance. These words of wisdom written by and for disciples of Christ are as powerful for us today as they were for the Christians of the first century.

There is a great deal of diversity among liturgical scholars concerning the organization of this material for devotional purposes. I have followed a historical method. My purpose has been to let the New Testament literature of the Acts and the letters flow in the sequence in which it was written. While some will want to follow the historical sequence with

271

some attention, others will prefer to remain indifferent to the sequential pattern. Regardless of the choice, the readings are ordered in such a way that they are not completely dependent on the historical sequence. This allows you to continue the pattern of prayer established in the special seasons of the church year.

The final two weeks of readings are from Revelation and emphasize the coming of Christ. Careful attention to this theme will prepare us for Advent and the beginning again of the spiritual journey which leads us through preparation, anticipation, and response.

For those who wish to follow the historical sequence more closely, an outline of the readings appears below. I have included dates for the events and literature of the New Testament. These are all tentative, as the actual dating of New Testament books does not enjoy unanimous agreement among scholars.

THE GROWING CHURCH, A.D. 30-49

Week of the Sunday closest to May 11	Acts 1–2
Week of the Sunday closest to May 18	Acts 2–3
Week of the Sunday closest to May 25	Acts 4–5
Week of the Sunday closest to June 1	Acts 6
Week of the Sunday closest to June 8	Acts 6–7
Week of the Sunday closest to June 15	Acts 8–9
Week of the Sunday closest to June 22	Acts 10–11
Week of the Sunday closest to June 29	James

THE FIRST MISSIONARY JOURNEY OF PAUL, A.D. 47-48

Week of the Sunday closest to July 6	Acts 12:25–14:28
Week of the Sunday closest to July 13	Galatians

THE SECOND MISSIONARY JOURNEY OF PAUL, A.D. 49-51

Week of the Sunday closest to July 20	Acts 15:36–18:22
Week of the Sunday closest to July 27	I & II Thessalonians

THE THIRD MISSIONARY JOURNEY OF PAUL, A.D. 51-54

Week of the Sunday closest to Aug. 3	Acts 18:23–21:14
Week of the Sunday closest to Aug. 10	I Corinthians
Week of the Sunday closest to Aug. 17	II Corinthians
Week of the Sunday closest to Aug. 24	Romans

PAUL'S ARREST AND REMAINING LIFE, A.D. 54-67

Week of the Sunday closest to Aug. 31	Acts 21:15–28:31

Week of the Sunday closest to Sep. 7   Ephesians
Week of the Sunday closest to Sep. 14   Colossians
Week of the Sunday closest to Sep. 21   Philippians
Week of the Sunday closest to Sep. 28   Philemon & I Timothy
Week of the Sunday closest to Oct. 5   Titus & II Timothy

THE REMAINING LITERATURE OF THE NEW TESTAMENT, A.D. 70-100

Week of the Sunday closest to Oct. 12   I Peter
Week of the Sunday closest to Oct. 19   II Peter & Jude
Week of the Sunday closest to Oct. 26   I, II, III John
Week of the Sunday closest to Nov. 2   Hebrews
Week of the Sunday closest to Nov. 9   Hebrews
Week of the Sunday closest to Nov. 16   Revelation
Week of the Sunday closest to Nov. 23   Revelation

The Day of Pentecost   Sunday

Theme: Almost two thousand years ago the Holy Spirit came upon the new group of believers in Jerusalem. Today he comes to us afresh.

Antiphon and Opening Prayer

I thank you that you have answered me
and have become my salvation.   Psalm 118:21

Spirit of God,
you who come to fill us with the presence and power of your Son,
come and enter my life anew this day.

Scripture Reading

But the Advocate, the Holy Spirit, whom the Father will send in my name, will teach you everything, and remind you of all that I have said to you. Peace I leave with you; my peace I give to you. I do not give to you as the world gives. Do not let your hearts be troubled, and do not let them be afraid. You heard me say to you, "I am going

away, and I am coming to you." If you loved me, you would rejoice
that I am going to the Father, because the Father is greater than I.

John 14:26-28

optional: Deuteronomy 16:9-12

Responsorial Psalm

The stone that the builders rejected
    has become the chief cornerstone.
This is the LORD's doing;
    it is marvelous in our eyes.
This is the day that the LORD has made;
    let us rejoice and be glad in it.   Psalm 118:22-24

Prayers, pp. 529-32

Closing Psalm Prayer

You are my God, and I will give thanks to you;
    you are my God, I will extol you.
O give thanks to the LORD, for he is good,
    for his steadfast love endures forever.   Psalm 118:28-29

Week of the Sunday Closest to May 11   Sunday

Theme: Luke set forth to write an account of the growth of the early
    church that was accurate and is able to guide our lives.

Antiphon and Opening Prayer

The LORD exists forever;
    your word is firmly fixed in heaven.
Your faithfulness endures to all generations;
    You have established the earth, and it stands fast.

Psalm 119:89-90

Lord, by your Holy Spirit you have given us your Word.
Let me hear your truth and guide my footsteps by your teaching.

Scripture Reading

In the first book, Theophilus, I wrote about all that Jesus did and
taught from the beginning until the day when he was taken up to
heaven, after giving instructions through the Holy Spirit to the
apostles whom he had chosen. After his suffering he presented himself
alive to them by many convincing proofs, appearing to them during
forty days and speaking about the kingdom of God.

Acts 1:1-3
optional: Ezekiel 33:1-11

Responsorial Psalm

Your word is a lamp to my feet
  and a light to my path.
I have sworn an oath and confirmed it,
  to observe your righteous ordinances.
I am severely afflicted;
  give me life, O LORD, according to your word.

Psalm 119:105-107

Prayers, pp. 529-32

Closing Psalm Prayer

Let your hand be ready to help me,
  for I have chosen your precepts.
I long for your salvation, O LORD,
  and your law is my delight.
Let me live that I may praise you,
  and let your ordinances help me.   Psal 119:173-175

Week of the Sunday Closest to May 11   Monday

Theme: Pentecost brings us power to witness to Christ as Savior and
       Lord at home and elsewhere.

Antiphon and Opening Prayer

Praise the LORD!
   O give thanks to the LORD, for he is good;
   for his steadfast love endures forever.   Psalm 106:1

Lord, you have called me to share my faith with my friends and
neighbors.
Give me courage and the power of your Holy Spirit.

Scripture Reading

He replied, "It is not for you to know the times or periods that the
Father has set by his own authority. But you will receive power when
the Holy Spirit has come upon you; and you will be my witnesses
in Jerusalem, in all Judea and Samaria, and to the ends of the earth."
When he had said this, as they were watching, he was lifted up, and
a cloud took him out of their sight.
                                                       Acts 1:7-9
                                        optional: Ezekiel 33:12-20

Responsorial Psalm

Remember me, O LORD, when you show favor to your people;
   help me when you deliver them. . . .
   that I may rejoice in the gladness of your nation,
   that I may glory in your heritage.   Psalm 106:4-5

Prayers, pp. 529-32

Closing Psalm Prayer

Save us, O LORD our God,
   and gather us from among the nations,

that we may give thanks to your holy name
and glory in your praise. Psalm 106:47

Week of the Sunday Closest to May 11 Tuesday

Theme: We are the disciples, who, in the absence of the ascended Lord,
return to Jerusalem to await the coming of the Spirit.

Antiphon and Opening Prayer

I lift up my eyes to the hills —
from whence will my help come?
My help comes from the LORD. Psalm 121:1-2a

Lord, my God, I rest in you and in no other.
In peace I wait on you and on the filling of the Holy Spirit.

Scripture Reading

While he was going and they were gazing up toward heaven,
suddenly two men in white robes stood by them. They said, "Men
of Galilee, why do you stand looking up toward heaven? This Jesus,
who has been taken up from you into heaven, will come in the same
way as you saw him go into heaven."

Then they returned to Jerusalem from the mount called Olivet,
which is near Jerusalem, a sabbath day's journey away.

Acts 1:10-12
optional: Ezekiel 33:21-33

Responsorial Psalm

He will not let your foot be moved;
he who keeps you will not slumber.
He who keeps Israel
will neither slumber nor sleep.
The LORD is your keeper;
the LORD is your shade at your right hand. Psalm 121:3-5

Prayers, pp. 529-32

Closing Psalm Prayer

> The LORD will keep
> your going out and your coming in
> from this time on and forevermore.   Psalm 121:8

Week of the Sunday Closest to May 11   Wednesday

Theme: The Holy Spirit comes to those who live in unity and pray in
one accord.

Antiphon and Opening Prayer

> How very good and pleasant it is
> when kindred live together in unity!   Psalm 133:1

> Lord, God of unity,
> you who dwell in one Trinity of persons,
> united in love,
> come and fill me with your Spirit.

Scripture Reading

> Then they returned to Jerusalem from the mount called Olivet, which
> is near Jerusalem, a sabbath day's journey away. When they had
> entered the city, they went to the room upstairs where they were
> staying, Peter, and John, and James, and Andrew, Philip and Thomas,
> Bartholomew and Matthew, James son of Alphaeus, and Simon the
> Zealot, and Judas son of James. All these were constantly devoting
> themselves to prayer, together with certain women, including Mary
> the mother of Jesus, as well as his brothers.
>
>   Acts 1:12-14
>   optional: Ezekiel 34:1-16

Responsorial Psalm

> It is like the precious oil on the head,
>> running down upon the beard,
> on the beard of Aaron,
>> running down over the collar of his robes.
> It is like the dew of Hermon,
>> which falls on the mountains of Zion.
> For there the LORD ordained his blessing,
>> life forevermore.   Psalm 133:2-3

Prayers, pp. 529-32

Closing Psalm Prayer

> Come, bless the LORD, all you servants of the LORD,
>> who stand by night in the house of the LORD!
> Lift up your hands to the holy place,
>> and bless the LORD.
> May the LORD, maker of heaven and earth,
>> bless you from Zion.   Psalm 134:1-3

Week of the Sunday Closest to May 11   Thursday

Theme: God blesses those who wait in the wings of life and prepare
themselves to be called of God.

Antiphon and Opening Prayer

> Happy is everyone who fears the LORD,
> who walks in his ways.   Psalm 128:1

> Lord Jesus, look on me, your servant, with favor.
> Make me ready to respond to your call as it comes to me today.

Scripture Reading

In those days Peter stood up among the believers (together the crowd numbered about one hundred twenty persons) and said, "Friends, the scripture had to be fulfilled, which the Holy Spirit through David foretold concerning Judas, who became a guide for those who arrested Jesus. . . . Then they prayed and said, "Lord, you know everyone's heart. Show us which one of these two you have chosen to take the place in this ministry and apostleship from which Judas turned aside to go to his own place."

Acts 1:15, 16, 24-26
optional: Ezekiel 37:21-28

Responsorial Psalm

You shall eat the fruit of the labor of your hands;
    you shall be happy, and it shall go well with you.
Your wife will be like a fruitful vine
    within your house;
your children will be like olive shoots
    around your table.
Thus shall the man be blessed
    who fears the LORD.   Psalm 128:2-4

Prayers, pp. 529-32

Closing Psalm Prayer

The LORD bless you from Zion.
    May you see the prosperity of Jerusalem
    all the days of your life.
May you see your children's children.
    Peace be upon Israel!   Psalm 128:5-6

Week of the Sunday Closest to May 11   Friday

Theme: When we give our mouths and lips over to the Lord, he will fill us with his Spirit to speak his truth.

Antiphon and Opening Prayer

Let my prayer be counted as incense before you,
and the lifting up of my hands as an evening sacrifice.

Psalm 141:2

Lord, I lift up my hands to you,
I open my mouth and utter words and songs of praise
to you, my God.

Scripture Reading

When the day of Pentecost had come, they were all together in one place. And suddenly from heaven there came a sound like the rush of a violent wind, and it filled the entire house where they were sitting. Divided tongues, as of fire, appeared among them, and a tongue rested on each of them. All of them were filled with the Holy Spirit and began to speak in other languages, as the Spirit gave them ability.

Acts 2:1-4
optional: Ezekiel 39:21-29

Responsorial Psalm

I call upon you, O LORD; come quickly to me;
give ear to my voice when I call to you. . . .
Set a guard over my mouth, O LORD;
keep watch over the door of my lips. . . .
But my eyes are turned toward you, O GOD, my Lord;
in you I seek refuge; do not leave me defenseless.

Psalm 141:1, 3, 8

Prayers, pp. 529-32

Closing Psalm Prayer

Answer me quickly, O LORD;
my spirit fails.
Do not hide your face from me,
or I shall be like those who go down to the Pit.
Let me hear of your steadfast love in the morning,

for in you I put my trust.
Teach me the way I should go,
for to you I lift up my soul.   Psalm 143:7-8

Week of the Sunday Closest to May 11   Saturday

Theme: When God touches the earth or enters into our lives, the leaves
of the tree shake, the mountains go up in smoke.

Antiphon and Opening Prayer

Bow down your heavens, O LORD, and come down;
touch the mountains so that they smoke.   Psalm 144:5

Lord, touch me with your presence and power.
Set my inner self on fire and let me praise your Holy Name!

Scripture Reading

Now there were devout Jews from every nation under heaven living
in Jerusalem. And at this sound the crowd gathered and was
bewildered, because each one heard them speaking in the native
language of each. Amazed and astonished, they asked, "Are not all
these who are speaking Galileans? And how is it that we hear, each
of us, in our own native language? . . . All were amazed and
perplexed, saying to one another, "What does this mean?"
                                                        Acts 2:5-8, 12
                                          optional: Ezekiel 47:1-12

Responsorial Psalm

How could we sing the LORD's song
in a foreign land?
If I forget you, O Jerusalem,
let my right hand wither!
Let my tongue cling to the roof of my mouth,
if I do not remember you,

if I do not set Jerusalem
> above my highest joy.   Psalm 137:4-6

Prayers, pp. 529-32

Closing Psalm Prayer

O LORD, what are human beings that you regard them,
> or mortals that you think them?
They are like a breath;
> their days are like a passing shadow.   Psalm 144:3-4

Week of the Sunday Closest to May 18   Sunday

Theme: The long wait for the coming of the Holy Spirit is over. The
> Spirit has come not only in Jerusalem, but also into our lives.

Antiphon and Opening Prayer

O God, do not be far from me;
> O my God, make haste to help me! . . .
So even to old age and grey hairs,
> O God, do not forsake me,
until I proclaim your might
> to all the generations to come.   Psalm 71:12, 18

Lord, I long for a portion of your Spirit.
As you sent your Spirit to the disciples who waited,
so send your Spirit to me, O Lord.

Scripture Reading

But Peter, standing with the eleven, raised his voice and addressed
them, "Men of Judea and all who live in Jerusalem, let this be known
to you, and listen to what I say. Indeed, these are not drunk, as you
suppose, for it is only nine o'clock in the morning. No, this is what
was spoken through the prophet Joel:

'In the last days it will be, God declares,
that I will pour out my Spirit upon all flesh,
and your sons and your daughters shall prophesy. . . .' "

Acts 2:14-17
optional: Ruth 1:18

Responsorial Psalm

My mouth will tell of your righteous acts,
of your deeds of salvation all day long. . . .
I will come praising the mighty deeds of the LORD God,
I will praise your righteousness, yours alone.   Psalm 71:15a, 16

Prayers, pp. 529-32

Closing Psalm Prayer

My lips will shout for joy
when I sing praises to you;
my soul also, which you have rescued.
All day long my tongue will talk of your righteous help,
for those who tried to do me harm
have been put to shame, and disgraced.   Psalm 71:23-24

Week of the Sunday Closest to May 18   Monday

Theme: Until Christ dies and is risen within us, we will not receive the
        Spirit.

Antiphon and Opening Prayer

Serve the LORD with fear,
with trembling kiss his feet,
or he will be angry, and you will perish in the way;
for his wrath is quickly kindled.
Happy are all who take refuge in him.   Psalm 2:11-12

Lord, you who dwell on high,
you who become incarnate,
you who sent your Spirit,
be born in me today.

Scripture Reading

Since he was a prophet, he knew that God had sworn with an oath
to him that he would put one of his descendants on his throne. . . .
This Jesus God raised up, and of that all of us are witnesses. Being
therefore exalted at the right hand of God, and having received from
the Father the promise of the Holy Spirit, he has poured out this
that you both see and hear.

Acts 2:30, 32-33
optional: Ruth 1:9-18

Responsorial Psalm

He who sits in the heavens laughs;
    the LORD has them in derision.
Then he will speak to them in his wrath,
    and terrify them in his fury, saying,
"I have set my king on Zion, my holy hill."   Psalm 2:4-6

Prayers, pp. 529-32

Closing Psalm Prayer

I will tell of the decree of the LORD:
He said to me, "You are my son;
    today I have begotten you. . . .
Happy are all who take refuge in him.   Psalm 2:7, 12b

Week of the Sunday Closest to May 18   Tuesday

Theme: The message that Christ has risen for me cuts me to the heart,
creates faith, and results in shouts of joy.

Antiphon and Opening Prayer

O LORD, in the morning you hear my voice;
in the morning I plead my case to you, and watch.   Psalm 5:3

Lord Jesus Christ,
let me hear the good news in a new and fresh way,
and may I respond with joy.

Scripture Reading

"Therefore let the entire house of Israel know with certainty that God has made him both Lord and Messiah, this Jesus whom you crucified." Now when they heard this, they were cut to the heart and said to Peter and to the other apostles, "Brothers, what should we do?" Peter said to them, "Repent, and be baptized every one of you in the name of Jesus Christ so that your sins may be forgiven; and you will receive the gift of the Holy Spirit."

Acts 2:36-38
optional: Ruth 1:19; 2:13

Responsorial Psalm

But let all who take refuge in you rejoice;
let them ever sing for joy.
Spread your protection over them,
so that those who love your name may exult in you.
For you bless the righteous, O LORD;
you cover them with favor as with a shield.   Psalm 5:11-12

Prayers, pp. 529-32

Closing Psalm Prayer

Give ear to my words, O LORD;
give heed to my sighing.
Listen to the sound of my cry,
my King and my God,
for to you I pray.   Psalm 5:1-2

Week of the Sunday Closest to May 18   Wednesday

Theme: The presence of the Spirit is found in the life of Christ's body, the church. There we have fullness of joy.

Antiphon and Opening Prayer

I call upon the LORD, who is worthy to be praised,
    so I shall be saved from my enemies.   Psalm 18:3

Lord, I love your church, where you dwell.
Grant me the courage to be all I can to my brothers and sisters.

Scripture Reading

So those who welcomed his message were baptized, and that day about three thousand persons were added. They devoted themselves to the apostles' teaching and fellowship, to the breaking of bread and the prayers. . . . All who believed were together and had all things in common; they would sell their possessions and goods and distribute the proceeds to all, as any had need. Day by day, as they spent much time together in the temple, they broke bread at home and ate their food with glad and generous hearts, praising God and having the goodwill of all people.

        Acts 2:41-42, 44-46
        optional: Ruth 2:14-23

Responsorial Psalm

It is you who light my lamp;
    the LORD, my God, lights up my darkness.
By you I can crush a troop,
    and by my God I can leap over a wall.
This God — his way is perfect;
    the promise of the LORD proves true;
he is a shield for all who take refuge in him.   Psalm 18:28-30

Prayers, pp. 529-32

Closing Psalm Prayer

You have given me the shield of your salvation,
>   and your right hand has supported me;
>   your help has made me great.
You gave me a wide place for my steps under me,
>   and my feet did not slip. Psalm 18:35-36

Week of the Sunday Closest to May 18   Thursday

Theme: Sometimes it seems as though God will never answer our prayer.
Then, when we least expect it, he breaks through to us.

Antiphon and Opening Prayer

How long, O LORD? Will you forget me forever?
>   How long will you hide your face from me? Psalm 13:1

Lord, you who seem to wait in silence.
Hear my longing, my cry,
and come to me to heal my broken life.

Scripture Reading

One day Peter and John were going up to the temple at the hour of
prayer, at three o'clock in the afternoon. And a man lame from birth
was being carried in. People would lay him daily at the gate of the
temple called the Beautiful Gate so that he could ask for alms from
those entering the temple. When he saw Peter and John about to go
into the temple, he asked them for alms. Peter looked intently at
him, as did John, and said, "Look at us." . . . But Peter said, "I have
no silver or gold, but what I have I give you; in the name of Jesus
Christ of Nazareth, stand up and walk."

Acts 3:1-4, 6
optional: Ruth 3:1-18

Responsorial Psalm

> Consider and answer me, O LORD my God!
>> Give light to my eyes, or I will sleep the sleep of death,
> and my enemy will say, "I have prevailed";
>> my foes will rejoice because I am shaken.   Psalm 13:3-4

Prayers, pp. 529-32

Closing Psalm Prayer

> But I trusted in your steadfast love;
>> my heart shall rejoice in your salvation.
> I will sing to the LORD,
>> because he has dealt bountifully with me.   Psalm 13:5-6

Week of the Sunday Closest to May 18   Friday

Theme: The time of refreshing that we all need comes from the Lord
when we turn to him in trust and faith.

Antiphon and Opening Prayer

> Protect me, O God, for in you I take refuge.
> I say to the LORD, "You are my Lord;
>> I have no good apart from you."   Psalm 16:1-2

> Lord, my heart longs to be filled with the peace you alone can
> bring.
> Turn me from my trust in myself to a full reliance on you.

Scripture Reading

> While he clung to Peter and John, all the people ran together to them
> in the portico called Solomon's Portico, utterly astonished. When
> Peter saw it, he addressed the people, "You Israelites, why do you

wonder at this, or why do you stare at us, as though by our own
power or piety we had made him walk? . . . Repent therefore, and
turn to God so that your sins may be wiped out, so that times of
refreshing may come from the presence of the Lord, and that he may
send the Messiah appointed for you, that is, Jesus.

Acts 3:11-12, 19-20
optional: Ruth 4:1-12

Responsorial Psalm

The LORD is my chosen portion and my cup;
>   you hold my lot.
The boundary lines have fallen for me in pleasant places;
>   I have a goodly heritage. . . .
I keep the LORD always before me;
>   because he is at my right hand, I shall not be moved.

Psalm 16:5-6, 8

Prayers, pp. 529-32

Closing Psalm Prayer

Therefore my heart is glad, and my soul rejoices;
>   my body also rests secure.
For you do not give me up to Sheol,
>   or let your faithful one see the Pit.   Psalm 16:9-10

Week of the Sunday Closest to May 18   Saturday

Theme: Following Christ, as the disciples discovered, is not always the
>   most popular course to take. But he is always near.

Antiphon and Opening Prayer

The LORD answer you in the day of trouble!
>   The name of the God of Jacob protect you!   Psalm 20:1

Lord God, in the day of my trouble I cried out to you,
and you heard me.
Hear me now again and come to my aid.

Scripture Reading

While Peter and John were speaking to the people, the priests, the
captain of the temple, and the Sadducees came to them, much
annoyed because they were teaching the people and proclaiming that
in Jesus there is the resurrection of the dead. So they arrested them
and put them in custody until the next day, for it was already evening.
But many of those who heard the word believed; and they numbered
about five thousand.

Acts 4:1-4
optional: Ruth 4:13-22

Responsorial Psalm

Some take pride in chariots, and some in horses,
  but our pride is in the name of the LORD our God.
They will collapse and fall,
  but we shall rise and stand upright.
Give victory to the king, O LORD,
  answer us when we call. Psalm 20:7-9

Prayers, pp. 529-32

Closing Psalm Prayer

Now I know that the LORD will help his anointed;
  he will answer him from his holy heaven
  with mighty victories by his right hand. Psalm 20:6

Week of the Sunday Closest to May 25 Sunday

Theme: Marvelous things are done for God in the power of his name,
the source of power. We praise him.

Antiphon and Opening Prayer

Let them praise the name of the LORD,
    for he commanded and they were created.   Psalm 148:5

Lord, you who do wonderful things by the power of your name,
hear the praise of my voice and the shout of my heart.

Scripture Reading

The next day their rulers, elders, and scribes assembled in Jerusalem. . . . When they had made the prisoners stand in their midst, they inquired, "By what power or by what name did you do this?" Then Peter, filled with the Holy Spirit, said to them, ". . . let it be known to all of you, and to all the people of Israel, that this man is standing before you in good health by the name of Jesus Christ of Nazareth, whom you crucified, whom God raised from the dead. This Jesus is
    'the stone that was rejected by you, the builders;
    it has become the cornerstone.' "

Acts 4:5, 7-8, 10-11
optional: Proverbs 1:1-33

Responsorial Psalm

Praise the LORD!
Praise the LORD from the heavens;
    praise him in the heights!
Praise him, all his angels;
    praise him, all his host!
Praise him, sun and moon;
    praise him, all you shining stars!
Praise him, you highest heavens,
    and you waters above the heavens!   Psalm 148:1-4

Prayers, pp. 529-32

Closing Psalm Prayer

Let them praise the name of the LORD,
    for his name alone is exalted;
    his glory is above earth and heaven.

He has raised up a horn for his people,
>   praise for all his faithful,
>   for the people of Israel who are close to him.
Praise the LORD!   Psalm 148:13-14

Week of the Sunday Closest to May 25   Monday

Theme: When we have been with Jesus, the impact of his life shows not
>   only in our face, but in our actions.

Antiphon and Opening Prayer

To you, O LORD, I lift up my soul.
O my God, in you I trust;
>   do not let me be put to shame;
>   do not let my enemies exult over me.   Psalm 25:1-2

Lord Jesus,
you who came among us and dwelled with us,
grant that I may walk with you and talk of you,
to the glory of your name.

Scripture Reading

Now when they saw the boldness of Peter and John and realized
that they were uneducated and ordinary men, they were amazed and
recognized them as companions of Jesus. . . . So they ordered them
to leave the council while they discussed the matter with one another.
They said, "What will we do with them? For it is obvious to all who
live in Jerusalem that a notable sign has been done through them;
we cannot deny it. But to keep it from spreading further among the
people, let us warn them to speak no more to anyone in this name."
>   Acts 4:13, 15-17
>   optional: Proverbs 3:11-20

Responsorial Psalm

>   Make me to know your ways, O LORD;
>   teach me your paths.
>   Lead me in your truth, and teach me,
>   for you are the God of my salvation;
>   for you I wait all day long.
>   Be mindful of your mercy, O LORD, and of your steadfast love,
>   for they have been from of old.   Psalm 25:4-6

Prayers, pp. 529-32

Closing Psalm Prayer

>   O guard my life, and deliver me;
>   do not let me be put to shame, for I take refuge in you.
>   May integrity and uprightness preserve me,
>   for I wait for you.   Psalm 25:20-21

Week of the Sunday Closest to May 25   Tuesday

Theme: God calls us to be members of his church, a unique body of
    people called to share their lives and possessions.

Antiphon and Opening Prayer

>   Hear the voice of my supplication,
>   as I cry to you for help,
>   as I lift up my hands
>   toward your most holy sanctuary.   Psalm 28:2

>   Father, you have called your church into being
>   and granted me a place in it.
>   Help me to love your people.

Scripture Reading

Now the whole group of those who believed were of one heart and soul, and no one claimed private ownership of any possessions, but everything they owned was held in common. . . . There was not a needy person among them, for as many as owned lands or houses sold them and brought the proceeds of what was sold. They laid it at the apostles' feet, and it was distributed to each as any had need.

Acts 4:32, 34-35
optional: Proverbs 4:1-27

Responsorial Psalm

Blessed be the LORD,
 for he has heard the sound of my pleadings.
The LORD is my strength and my shield;
 in him my heart trusts;
so I am helped, and my heart exults,
 and with my song I give thanks to him.   Psalm 28:6-7

Prayers, pp. 529-32

Closing Psalm Prayer

To you, O LORD, I call;
 my rock, do not refuse to hear me,
for if you are silent to me,
 I shall be like those who go down to the Pit. . . .
O save your people, and bless your heritage;
 be their shepherd, and carry them forever.   Psalm 28:1, 9

Week of the Sunday Closest to May 25   Wednesday

Theme: The power of the Holy Spirit is available to us today. We are the people brought to the apostles for healing.

Antiphon and Opening Prayer

Do not forsake me, O LORD;
    O my God, do not be far from me;
make haste to help me,
    O Lord, my salvation.   Psalm 38:21-22

Lord, I lift up to you the pains of my body and soul.
Stretch forth your hand and touch me with your healing power.

Scripture Reading

The whole assembly kept silence, and listened to Barnabas and Paul
as they told of all the signs and wonders that God had done through
them among the Gentiles. . . . James replied, ". . . Simeon has related
how God first looked favorably on the Gentiles, to take from among
them a people for his name. This agrees with the words of the
prophets, as it is written,
    'After this I will return,
      and I will rebuild the dwelling of David which has fallen;
        from its ruins I will rebuild it, and I will set it up.' "
                              Acts 15:12, 14, 15-16
                          optional: Proverbs 6:1-19

Responsorial Psalm

I am utterly bowed down and prostrate;
    all day long I go around mourning.
For my loins are filled with burning,
    and there is no soundness in my flesh.   Psalm 38:6-7

Prayers, pp. 529-32

Closing Psalm Prayer

My heart throbs, my strength fails me;
    as for the light of my eyes — it also has gone from me. . . .
But it is for you, O LORD, that I wait;
    it is you, O LORD my God, who will answer.
                              Psalm 38:10, 15

Week of the Sunday Closest to May 25   Thursday

Theme: Sometimes our troubles are so overwhelming that we see no end
         in sight, but the Lord knows our frame, he watches our step.

Antiphon and Opening Prayer

Trust in the LORD, and do good;
     so you will live in the land, and enjoy security.   Psalm 37:3

Father in heaven,
you who protected the people of your early church,
come to my assistance.

Scripture Reading

Then the high priest took action; he and all who were with him (that
is, the sect of the Sadducees), being filled with jealousy, arrested the
apostles and put them in the public prison. But during the night an
angel of the Lord opened the prison doors, brought them out, and
said, "Go, stand in the temple and tell the people the whole message
about this life." When they heard this, they entered the temple at
daybreak and went on with their teaching.
                                                    Acts 5:17-21
                                          optional: Proverbs 7:1-27

Responsorial Psalm

Refrain from anger, and forsake wrath.
     Do not fret — it leads only to evil. . . .
Wait for the LORD, and keep to his way,
     and he will exalt you to inherit the land;
     you will look on the destruction of the wicked.
                                              Psalm 37:8, 34

Prayers, pp. 529-32

Closing Psalm Prayer

> Our steps are made firm by the LORD,
> > when he delights in our way;
> though we stumble, we shall not fall headlong,
> > for the LORD holds us by the hand.　　　　Psalm 37:23-24

Week of the Sunday Closest to May 25　　　　Friday

Theme:　There are those who would steer away from obedience to God,
　　　　but God will vindicate our obedience to him alone.

Antiphon and Opening Prayer

> Then my tongue shall tell of your righteousness
> > and of your praise all day long.　　　　Psalm 35:28

> Lord, my soul is troubled
> by those who tempt me to forsake your ways and your will.
> Keep me steadfast in your truth, O God.

Scripture Reading

> Then someone arrived and announced, "Look, the men whom you
> put in prison are standing in the temple and teaching the people!" . . .
> 　　When they had brought them, they had them stand before the
> council. The high priest questioned them, saying, "We gave you strict
> orders not to teach in this name, yet here you have filled Jerusalem
> with your teaching and you are determined to bring this man's blood
> on us." But Peter and the apostles answered, "We must obey God
> rather than any human authority."

> > > > > Acts 5:25, 27-29
> > > > > optional: Proverbs 8:1-21

Responsorial Psalm

> Contend, O LORD, with those who contend with me;
> > fight against those who fight against me!

Take hold of shield and buckler,
>   and rise up to help me!
Draw the spear and javelin
>   against my pursuers;
say to my soul,
>   "I am your salvation."   Psalm 35:1-3

Prayers, pp. 529-32

Closing Psalm Prayer

Wake up! Bestir yourself for my defense,
>   for my cause, my God and my LORD!
Vindicate me, O LORD, my God,
>   according to your righteousness,
>   and do not let them rejoice over me.   Psalm 35:23-24

Week of the Sunday Closest to May 25   Saturday

Theme: If the work we do be merely human, then it will fail. But if it
>   is of God, it will succeed in the way that God defines success.

Antiphon and Opening Prayer

Sing praises to the LORD, O you his faithful ones,
>   and give thanks to his holy name.   Psalm 30:4

Lord, look on the work I do for you.
Bless it in the manner in which you choose,
to your glory and the benefit of your church.

Scripture Reading

But a Pharisee in the council named Gamaliel, a teacher of the law,
respected by all the people, stood up and ordered the men to be put
outside for a short time. . . . [He said,] "So in the present case, I tell
you, keep away from these men and let them alone; because if this

plan or this undertaking is of human origin, it will fail; but if it is
of God, you will not be able to ovethrow them — in that case you
may even be found fighting against God!"

Acts 5:34, 38-39
optional: Proverbs 8:22-36

Responsorial Psalm

I will extol you, O LORD, for you have drawn me up,
    and did not let my foes rejoice over me.   Psalm 30:1-3

Prayers, pp. 529-32

Closing Psalm Prayer

To you, O LORD, I cried,
    and to the LORD I made supplication. . . .
"Hear, O LORD, and be gracious to me!
    O LORD, be my helper!" . . .
so that my soul may praise you and not be silent.
    O LORD my God, I will give thanks to you forever.

Psalm 30:8, 10, 12

Week of the Sunday Closest to June 1   Sunday

Theme: Even when we are rejected and misunderstood for the sake of
    the gospel, the Holy Spirit fills us with rejoicing.

Antiphon and Opening Prayer

Bless the LORD, O my soul,
    and all that is within me,
        bless his holy name.   Psalm 103:1

O Holy Spirit,
you who filled the apostles with overflowing joy,

fill my heart with gladness,
and let my lips praise the name of the Lord.

Scripture Reading

. . . And when they had called in the apostles, they had them flogged.
Then they ordered them not to speak in the name of Jesus, and let
them go. As they left the council, they rejoiced that they were
considered worthy to suffer dishonor for the sake of the name. And
every day in the temple and at home they did not cease to teach and
proclaim Jesus as the Messiah.

Acts 5:40-42
optional: Proverbs 9:1-12

Responsorial Psalm

Bless the LORD, O my soul,
    and do not forget all his benefits —
who forgives all your iniquity,
    who heals all your diseases,
who redeems your life from the Pit,
    who crowns you with steadfast love and mercy.

Psalm 103:2-4

Prayers, pp. 529-32

Closing Psalm Prayer

Bless the LORD, O you his angels,
    you mighty ones who do his bidding,
        obedient to his spoken word.
Bless the LORD, all his hosts,
    his ministers that do his will.
Bless the LORD, all his works,
    in all places of his dominion.
Bless the LORD, O my soul.

Psalm 103:20-22

Week of the Sunday Closest to June 1   Monday

Theme: As the church grows, then and now, God chooses his leaders
out of those who are full of the Holy Spirit.

Antiphon and Opening Prayer

Not to us, O LORD, not to us, but to your name give glory,
for the sake of your steadfast love and your faithfulness.

Psalm 115:1

O Holy Spirit,
fill me with your presence and power,
so that, when God calls me to do his work,
my heart and hands will be ready.

Scripture Reading

Now during those days, when the disciples were increasing in
number, the Hellenists complained against the Hebrews because their
widows were being neglected in the daily distribution of food. And
the twelve called together the whole community of the disciples and
said, "It is not right that we should neglect the word of God in order
to wait on tables. Therefore, friends, select from among yourselves
seven men of good standing, full of the Spirit and of wisdom, whom
we may appoint to this task, while we, for our part, will devote
ourselves to prayer and to serving the word." What they said pleased
the whole community, and they chose Stephen, a man full of faith
and the Holy Spirit, together with Philip, Prochorus, Nicanor, Timon,
Parmenas, and Nicolaus, a proselyte of Antioch.

Acts 6:1-5
optional: Proverbs 10:1-12

Responsorial Psalm

O Israel, trust in the LORD!
He is their help and their shield.
O house of Aaron, trust in the LORD!
He is their help and their shield.
You who fear the LORD, trust in the LORD!
He is their help and their shield.   Psalm 115:9-11

Prayers, pp. 529-32

Closing Psalm Prayer

> May the LORD give you increase,
>   both you and your children.
> May you be blessed by the LORD,
>   who made heaven and earth.

Psalm 115:14-15

Week of the Sunday Closest to June 1   Tuesday

Theme: While God is characterized by righteousness, his enemies are devious and given to falsehood and cunning. But God is to praised.

Antiphon and Opening Prayer

> Great is the LORD and greatly to be praised
>   in the city of our God.

Psalm 48:1

> Lord, see how they turn against me and do not tell the truth.
> In you I will always trust.
> In your name I will glory.

Scripture Reading

Stephen, full of grace and power, did great wonders and signs among the people. Then some of those who belonged to the synagogue of the Freedmen (as it was called), Cyrenians, Alexandrians, and others of those from Cilicia and Asia, stood up and argued with Stephen. But they could not withstand the wisdom and the Spirit with which he spoke. Then they secretly instigated some men to say, "We have heard him speak blasphemous words against Moses and God." They stirred up the people as well as the elders and the scribes; then they suddenly confronted him, seized him, and brought him before the council.

Acts 6:8-12
optional: Proverbs 15:16-33

Responsorial Psalm

Your name, O God, like your praise,
    reaches to the ends of the earth.
Your right hand is filled with victory.
    Let Mount Zion be glad,
let the towns of Judah rejoice
    because of your judgments.   Psalm 48:10-11

Prayers, pp. 529-32

Closing Psalm Prayer

Great is the LORD and greatly to be praised
    in the city of our God. . . .
Then the kings assembled,
    they came on together.   Psalm 48:1, 4

Week of the Sunday Closest to June 1   Wednesday

Theme: Stephen reminded the Pharisees that God called Abraham to a
    life of faith and trust in him. So God calls us.

Antiphon and Opening Prayer

My mouth shall speak wisdom;
    the meditation of my heart shall be understanding.
                                               Psalm 49:3

Lord, you called your servant Abraham
to leave his roots and follow you.
Help me to have that kind of faith and trust in you.

Scripture Reading

Then the high priest asked him, "Are these things so?" And Stephen
replied:

"Brothers and fathers, listen to me. The God of glory appeared to our ancestor Abraham when he was in Mesopotamia, before he lived in Haran, and said to him, 'Leave your country and your relatives and go to the land that I will show you.' . . . He did not give him any of it as a heritage, not even a foot's length, but promised to give it to him as his possession and to his descendants after him, even though he had no child.

Acts 7:1-3, 5
optional: Proverbs 17:1-20

Responsorial Psalm

The LORD is my portion;
　　I promise to keep your words.
I implore your favor with all my heart;
　　be gracious to me according to your promise,
When I think of your ways,
　　I turn my feet to your decrees;
I hurry and do not delay
　　to keep your commandments.

Psalm 119:57-60

Prayers, pp. 529-32

Closing Psalm Prayer

When I think of your ways,
　　I turn my feet to your decrees;
I hurry and do not delay
　　to keep your commandments.

Psalm 119:59-60

Week of the Sunday Closest to June 1　　　Thursday

Theme: Stephen reminded the Pharisees that God took care of Joseph in spite of the treachery of his brothers. So God cares for us.

Antiphon and Opening Prayer

The mighty one, God the LORD,
    speaks and summons the earth
    from the rising of the sun to its setting.   Psalm 50:1

Lord, you lift me up and guide me by your Holy Spirit.
Do not forsake me or leave me to my own inclinations.

Scripture Reading

The patriarchs, jealous of Joseph, sold him into Egypt; but God was
with him, and rescued him from all his afflictions, and enabled him
to win favor and to show wisdom when he stood before Pharaoh,
king of Egypt, who appointed him ruler over Egypt and over all his
household. . . . Then Joseph sent and invited his father Jacob and
all his relatives to come to him, seventy-five in all; so Jacob went
down to Egypt. He himself died there as well as our ancestors.

Acts 7:9-10, 14-15
optional: Proverbs 21:20

Responsorial Psalm

Mark this, then, you who forget God,
    or I will tear you apart, and there will be no one to deliver,
Those who bring thanksgiving as their sacrifice honor me;
    to those who go the right way
    I will show the salvation of God.   Psalm 50:22-23

Prayers, pp. 529-32

Closing Psalm Prayer

"Gather to me my faithful ones,
    who made a covenant with me by sacrifice!"
The heavens declare his righteousness,
    for God himself is judge.   Psalm 50:5-6

Week of the Sunday Closest to June 1 Friday

Theme: Stephen reminds the Pharisees and us that God hears the cries of the oppressed and comes to them with salvation.

Antiphon and Opening Prayer

Save me, O God, by your name,
> and vindicate me by your might. Psalm 54:1

Lord, I have cried out to you and you have heard me.
Hear me now, I pray, and do not turn a deaf ear to me.

Scripture Reading

So he argued in the synagogue with the Jews and the devout persons, and also in the marketplace every day with those who happened to be there. Also some Epicurean and Stoic philosophers debated with him. Some said, "What does this babbler want to say?" Others said, "He seems to be a proclaimer of foreign divinities." (This was because he was telling the good news about Jesus and the resurrection.) So they took him and brought him to the Areopagus and asked him, "May we know what this new teaching is that you are presenting? It sounds rather strange to us, so we would like to know what it means."

Acts 17:17-20
optional: Proverbs 23:19–24:2

Responsorial Psalm

For the insolent have risen against me,
> the ruthless seek my life;
> they do not set God before them.
But surely, God is my helper;
> the Lord is the upholder of my life.
He will repay my enemies for their evil.
> In your faithfulness, put an end to them. Psalm 54:3-6

Prayers, pp. 529-32

Closing Psalm Prayer

With a freewill offering I will sacrifice to you;
    I will give thanks to your name, O LORD, for it is good.
For he has delivered me from every trouble,
    and my eye has looked in triumph on my enemies.

Psalm 54:6-7

Week of the Sunday Closest to June 1   Saturday

Theme: The encounter Moses had with God calls us to be aware of the
        unusual ways in which God may seek to communicate to us.

Antiphon and Opening Prayer

I give you thanks, O LORD, with my whole heart;
    before the gods I sing your praise.   Psalm 138:1

Lord, let me be attentive to the signals of life through which you
speak to me.
Ready my heart and incline my ears to your voice.

Scripture Reading

When he was forty years old, it came into his heart to visit his
relatives, the Israelites. When he saw one of them being wronged,
he defended the oppressed man and avenged him by striking down
the Egyptian. . . . When he heard this, Moses fled and became a
resident alien in the land of Midian. There he became the father of
two sons.
    Now when forty years had passed, an angel appeared to him in
the wilderness of Mount Sinai, in the flame of a burning bush.

Acts 7:23-24, 29-30
optional: Proverbs 25:15-28

Responsorial Psalm

All the kings of the earth shall praise you, O LORD,
 for they have heard the words of your mouth.
They shall sing of the ways of the LORD,
 for great is the glory of the LORD,
For though the LORD is high, he regards the lowly;
 but the haughty he perceives from far away. Psalm 138:4-6

Prayers, pp. 529-32

Closing Psalm Prayer

On the day I called, you answered me,
 you increased my strength of soul. . . .
The LORD will fulfill his purpose for me;
 your steadfast love, O LORD, endures forever.
Do not forsake the work of your hands. Psalm 138:3, 8

Week of the Sunday Closest to June 8   Sunday

Theme: God speaks to us, reminding us that the ground we walk on is
   holy ground, and he calls us to follow where he leads.

Antiphon and Opening Prayer

My heart became hot within me.
While I mused, the fire burned;
 then I spoke with my tongue. Psalm 39:3

Lord God,
all the earth and its fullness is yours.
May I see your hand in all events and places of life,
to your glory.

Scripture Reading

When Moses saw it [the burning bush], he was amazed at the sight; and as he approached to look, then came the voice of the Lord: "I am the God of your ancestors. . . ." Moses began to tremble and did not dare to look. Then the Lord said to him, "Take off the sandals from your feet, for the place where you are standing is holy ground. I have surely seen the mistreatment of my people who are in Egypt. . . . Come now, I will send you to Egypt."

Acts 7:31-34
optional: Ecclesiastes 1:1-11

Responsorial Psalm

LORD, let me know my end,
    and what is the measure of my days;
    let me know how fleeting my life is.
You have made my days a few handbreadths,
    and my lifetime is as nothing in your sight.
Surely everyone stands as a mere breath.   Psalm 39:4-5

Prayers, pp. 529-32

Closing Psalm Prayer

Hear my prayer, O LORD,
    and give ear to my cry;
    do not hold your peace at my tears.
For I am your passing guest,
    an alien, like all my forebears.   Psalm 39:12

Week of the Sunday Closest to June 8   Monday

Theme: Sometimes God calls us into the wilderness experience to be taught by him before he sends us to do his work.

Antiphon and Opening Prayer

Happy are those whom you choose and bring near
to live in your courts. Psalm 65:4

Lord, you brought forth your Son in the likeness of Moses.
Work in me to do your bidding with great joy.

Scripture Reading

It was this Moses whom they rejected . . . and whom God now sent
as both ruler and liberator. . . . He led them out, having performed
wonders and signs in Egypt, at the Red Sea, and in the wilderness
for forty years. This is the Moses who said to the Israelites, "God
will raise up a prophet for you from your own people as he raised
me up." Acts 7:35-37

Responsorial Psalm

By awesome deeds you answer us with deliverance,
O God of our salvation. . . .
Those who live at earth's farthest bounds are awed by your signs;
you make the gateways of the morning and the evening shout for
joy. Psalm 65:5a, 8

Prayers, pp. 529-32

Closing Psalm Prayer

Praise is due to you,
O God, in Zion;
and to you shall vows be performed. . . .
We shall be satisfied with the goodness of your house,
your holy temple. Psalm 65:1, 4

Week of the Sunday Closest to June 8   Tuesday

Theme: Stephen's sermon reminds us how tempted we are to return to the security of the gods of our own making.

Antiphon and Opening Prayer

Hear my cry, O God . . .
   when my heart is faint.
Lead me to the rock
   that is higher than I.   Psalm 61:1-2

Lord, you know my frame,
how easily I wander from you and your truth.
My heart is full of remorse;
bring me back to you.

Scripture Reading

Our ancestors were unwilling to obey [Moses]; instead they pushed him aside, and in their hearts they turned back to Egypt, saying to Aaron, "Make gods for us who will lead the way for us; as for this Moses who led us out from the land of Egypt, we do not know what has happened to him." At that time they made a calf, offered a sacrifice to the idol, and reveled in the works of their hands.

Acts 7:39-41
optional: Ecclesiastes 2:1-15

Responsorial Psalm

For you are my refuge,
   a strong tower against the enemy.
Let me abide in your tent forever,
   find refuge under the shelter of your wings.
For you, O God, have heard my vows;
   you have given me the heritage of those who fear your name.

Psalm 61:3-5

Prayers, pp. 529-32

Closing Psalm Prayer

> Listen to my prayer.
> From the end of the earth I call to you,
> > when my heart is faint. . . .
> So I will always sing praises to your name,
> > as I pay my vows day after day.　　Psalm 61:1a, 2, 8

Week of the Sunday Closest to June 8　　Wednesday

Theme: We are reminded that instead of worshiping the God who is
everywhere, we make false gods with our own hands.

Antiphon and Opening Prayer

> Sing aloud to God our strength;
> > shout for joy to the God of Jacob.
> Raise a song, sound the tambourine.　　Psalm 81:1-2a

> O Lord, my God, how often I create my own god
> and turn to it for consolation.
> Return me to yourself.
> Open my mouth and fill me, O God.

Scripture Reading

> Our ancestors had the tent of testimony in the wilderness. . . . but
> it was Solomon who built a house for him. Yet the Most High does
> not dwell in houses made with human hands; as the prophet says,
> > "Heaven is my throne,
> > > and the earth is my footstool.
> > What kind of house will you build for me? says the Lord,
> > > or what is the place of my rest?
> > Did not my hand make all these things?"
> > > > > Acts 7:44, 47

Responsorial Psalm

Hear, O my people, while I admonish you;
    O Israel, if you would but listen to me!
There shall be no strange god among you;
    you shall not bow down to a foreign god.
I am the LORD your God,
    who brought you up out of the land of Egypt.

Psalm 81:8-10a

Prayers, pp. 529-32

Closing Psalm Prayer

O that my people would listen to me,
    that Israel would walk in my ways!
Then I would quickly subdue their enemies. . . .
Open your mouth wide and I will fill it.   Psalm 81:13-14a, 10

Week of the Sunday Closest to June 8   Thursday

Theme: At the conclusion of Stephen's sermon he reminds Israel how
    they rejected God's reaching out to them in love.

Antiphon and Opening Prayer

Restore us again, O God of our salvation,
    and put away your indignation toward us. . . .
    that his glory may dwell in our land.   Psalm 85:4, 9

O Lord, God of my salvation,
how often have I been indifferent to your voice.
Turn me away from my idols and let me return to you.

Scripture Reading

You stiff-necked people, uncircumcised in heart and ears, you are
forever opposing the Holy Spirit, just as your ancestors used to do.
Which of the prophets did your ancestors not persecute? They killed

those who foretold the coming of the Righteous One, and now you have become his betrayers and murderers. . . .

When they heard these things, they became enraged and ground their teeth at Stephen.

Acts 7:51-52, 54
optional: Ecclesiastes 3:16–4:3

Responsorial Psalm

LORD, you were favorable to your land;
 you restored the fortunes of Jacob.
You forgave the iniquity of your people;
 you pardoned all their sin.
You withdrew all your wrath;
 you turned from your hot anger.   Psalm 85:1-3

Prayers, pp. 529-32

Closing Psalm Prayer

Let me hear what God the LORD will speak,
 for he will speak peace to his people,
 to his faithful, to those who turn to him in their hearts. . . .
Steadfast love and faithfulness will meet;
 righteousness and peace will kiss each other.   Psalm 85:8, 10

Week of the Sunday Closest to June 8   Friday

Theme: When Stephen told the truth, the religious leaders turned against
    him with vengeance, but God opened heaven to receive him.

Antiphon and Opening Prayer

You who live in the shelter of the Most High,
 who abide in the shadow of the Almighty.
will say to the LORD, "My refuge and my fortress;
 my God, in whom I trust."   Psalm 91:1-2

Lord of the church,
teach me not to be a pleaser of people,
but to speak the truth always,
and to depend on your love and grace.

Scripture Reading

But filled with the Holy Spirit, [Stephen] gazed into heaven and saw
the glory of God and Jesus standing at the right hand of God. "Look!"
he said, "I see the heavens opened and the Son of Man standing at
the right hand of God!" But they covered their ears, and with a loud
shout all rushed together against him. Then they dragged him out
of the city and began to stone him.

Acts 7:55-58
optional: Ecclesiastes 5:1-7

Responsorial Psalm

For he will deliver you from the snare of the fowler
    and from the deadly pestilence;
he will cover you with his pinions,
    and under his wings you will find refuge;
    his faithfulness is a shield and buckler.
You will not fear the terror of the night.   Psalm 91:3-5a

Prayers, pp. 529-32

Closing Psalm Prayer

When they call to me I will answer them;
    I will be with them in trouble,
    I will rescue them and honor them. . . .
    and show them my salvation.   Psalm 91:15, 16b

Week of the Sunday Closest to June 8   Saturday

Theme: Sometimes God does not give us what we want. But God knows
what is best for the work of his kingdom.

Antiphon and Opening Prayer

Lord, you have been our dwelling place
    in all generations. . . .
From everlasting to everlasting, you are God.   Psalm 90:1, 2b

O Lord, like Stephen of old,
give me faith in the midst of adversity and trials
that will sustain me come what may.

Scripture Reading

. . . The witnesses [to Stephen's death] laid their coats at the feet of
a young man named Saul. While they were stoning Stephen, he
prayed, "Lord Jesus, receive my spirit." Then he knelt down and
cried out in a loud voice, "Lord, do not hold this sin against them."
When he had said this, he died. And Saul approved of their killing
him.

Acts 7:58b-60; 8:1
optional: Ecclesiastes 5:8-20

Responsorial Psalm

For a thousand years in your sight
    are like yesterday when it is past,
      or like a watch in the night.
You sweep them away; they are like a dream,
    like grass that is renewed in the morning. . .
      in the evening it fades and withers.   Psalm 90:4-6

Prayers, pp. 529-32

Closing Psalm Prayer

> Let the favor of the Lord our God be upon us,
> > and prosper for us the work of our hands —
> > O prosper the work of our hands!   Psalm 90:17

Week of the Sunday Closest to June 15   Sunday

Theme: Saul's fight against the church reminds us that the gates of hell cannot prevail against the church or against those who align themselves with Christ.

Antiphon and Opening Prayer

> Your decrees are very sure;
> > holiness befits your house,
> > O LORD, forevermore.   Psalm 93:5

> O Lord, how often the waves of opposition beat against my soul
> and lure me into their evil.
> Protect me, Lord, by your mighty power.

Scripture Reading

> That day a severe persecution began against the church in Jerusalem, and all except the apostles were scattered throughout the countryside of Judea and Samaria. Devout men buried Stephen and made loud lamentation over him. But Saul was ravaging the church by entering house after house; dragging off both men and women, he committed them to prison.
> > Acts 8:1-3
> > optional: Ecclesiastes 6:1-12

Responsorial Psalm

> The floods have lifted up, O LORD,
> > the floods have lifted up their voice;
> > the floods lift up their roaring.

More majestic than the thunders of mighty waters,
more majestic than the waves of the sea,
majestic on high is the LORD! Psalm 93:3-4

Prayers, pp. 529-32

Closing Psalm Prayer

The LORD is king. . . .
He has established the world; it shall never be moved;
your throne is established from of old;
you are from everlasting. Psalm 93:1-2

Week of the Sunday Closest to June 15 Monday

Theme: Sometimes trouble is the source of great blessing for the church
and for us who wait on the Lord for his strength and direction.

Antiphon and Opening Prayer

Restore us, O God;
let your face shine, that we may be saved. Psalm 80:3

Lord Jesus,
as you sent your disciples forth from persecution to proclaim
your power,
so deliver me from my turmoil and grant me peace.

Scripture Reading

Now those who were scattered went from place to place, proclaiming
the Word. Philip went down to the city of Samaria and proclaimed
the Messiah to them. The crowds with one accord listened eagerly
to what was said by Philip, hearing and seeing the signs that he did,
for unclean spirits, crying with loud shrieks, came out of many who

were possessed; and many others who were paralyzed or lame were
cured. So there was great joy in that city.

Acts 8:4-8
optional: Ecclesiastes 7:1-14

Responsorial Psalm

Give ear, O Shepherd of Israel,
  you who lead Joseph like a flock!
You who are enthroned upon the cherubim, shine forth
  before Ephraim and Benjamin and Manasseh.
Stir up your might,
  and come to save us!   Psalm 80:1-2

Prayers, pp. 529-32

Closing Psalm Prayer

But let your hand be upon the one at your right hand,
  the one whom you made strong for yourself. . . .
Give us life, and we will call on your name.   Psalm 80:17, 18b

Week of the Sunday Closest to June 15   Tuesday

Theme: Sometimes when we are waiting for God to come and encounter
        us, a serendipitous event brings the realization of our longing.

Antiphon and Opening Prayer

For God alone my soul waits in silence,
  for my hope is from him.
He alone is my rock and my salvation.   Psalm 62:5, 6a

Lord, I wait patiently for you to fulfill your will in my life.
Send a message to me, Lord, that I may do your bidding.

Scripture Reading

Then an angel of the Lord said to Philip, "Get up and go toward the south. . . ." Now there was an Ethiopian eunuch, a court official. . . . He had come to Jerusalem to worship and was returning home; seated in his chariot, he was reading the prophet Isaiah. . . . Then Philip began to speak . . . he proclaimed to him the good news about Jesus. As they were going along the road, they came to some water; and the eunuch said, "Look, here is water. What is to prevent me from being baptized?" He commanded the chariot to stop, and both of them, Philip and the eunuch, went down into the water and Philip baptized him.

Acts 8:26a, 27-28, 35-38
optional: Ecclesiastes 8:14–9:10

Responsorial Psalm

For God alone my soul waits in silence;
    from him comes my salvation.
He alone is my rock and my salvation,
    my fortress; I shall never be shaken. . . .
On God rests my deliverance and my honor;
    my mighty rock, my refuge is in God.   Psalm 62:1, 2, 7

Prayers, pp. 529-32

Closing Psalm Prayer

Once God has spoken;
    twice have I heard this:
that power belongs to God,
    and steadfast love belongs to you, O Lord.   Psalm 62:11-12

Week of the Sunday Closest to June 15   Wednesday

Theme: Sometimes those who fight God the most severely are turned completely around to become his committed servants.

Antiphon and Opening Prayer

> Be pleased, O God, to deliver me.
> O LORD, make haste to help me!   Psalm 70:1

> O Lord, my God,
> as you delivered Saul into your own hands and redeemed his life,
> come and do your good work within me.

Scripture Reading

> Meanwhile Saul, still breathing threats and murder against the
> disciples of the Lord, went to the high priest and asked him for letters
> to the synagogues at Damascus, so that if he found any who belonged
> to the Way, men or women, he might bring them bound to Jerusalem.
> Now as he was going along and approaching Damascus, suddenly
> a light from heaven flashed around him. He fell to the ground and
> heard a voice saying to him, "Saul, Saul, why do you persecute me?"
> He asked, "Who are you, Lord?" The reply came, "I am Jesus, whom
> you are persecuting. But get up and enter the city, and you will be
> told what you are to do."

> Acts 9:1-6
optional: Ecclesiastes 9:11-18

Responsorial Psalm

> Let those be put to shame and confusion
>   who seek my life.
> Let those be turned back and brought to dishonor
>   who desire to hurt me. . . .
> Let all who seek you
>   rejoice and be glad in you. . . .
> God is great!   Psalm 70:2, 4

Prayers, pp. 529-32

Closing Psalm Prayer

> But I am poor and needy;
>   hasten to me, O God!

You are my help and my deliverer;
O LORD, do not delay!   Psalm 70:5

Week of the Sunday Closest to June 15   Thursday

Theme: When the Lord chooses us to do a good work through us, he
leads us step by step and day by day.

Antiphon and Opening Prayer

In you, O LORD, I take refuge;
    let me never be put to shame. . . .
    for you are my rock and my fortress.   Psalm 71:1, 3

O Lord, as you chose Saul to become your servant,
so choose me to do your work.
Give me the joy of your presence and a song in my heart.

Scripture Reading

Now there was a disciple in Damascus named Ananias. The Lord
said to him in a vision, "Ananias." He answered, "Here I am, Lord."
The Lord said to him, "Get up and go to the street called Straight,
and at the house of Judas look for a man of Tarsus named Saul. At
this moment he is praying, and he has seen in a vision a man named
Ananias come in and lay his hands on him so that he might regain
his sight."

Acts 9:10-12
optional: Ecclesiastes 11:1-8

Responsorial Psalm

For you, O Lord, are my hope,
    my trust, O LORD, from my youth.
Upon you I have leaned from my birth;
    it was you who took me from my mother's womb.
My praise is continually of you. . . .
My mouth is filled with your praise.   Psalm 71:5-6, 8a

Prayers, pp. 529-32

Closing Psalm Prayer

> I will also praise you with the harp. . . .
> I will sing praises to you with the lyre,
>> O Holy One of Israel.
> My lips will shout for joy
>> when I sing praises to you.   Psalm 71:22-23a

Week of the Sunday Closest to June 15   Friday

Theme: If Jesus can meet a Saul of Tarsus and turn him into Paul the
        apostle, he can meet us and change us into his image.

Antiphon and Opening Prayer

> It is good to give thanks to the LORD,
>> to sing praises to your name, O Most High.   Psalm 92:1

Lord God, you who convert and renew people after the image of
your Son,
send your Spirit into my life and use me to your glory.

Scripture Reading

. . . Immediately [Saul] began to proclaim Jesus in the synagogues,
saying, "He is the Son of God." All who heard him were amazed
and said, "Is not this the man who made havoc in Jerusalem among
those who invoked this name? And has he not come here for the
purpose of bringing them bound before the chief priests?" Saul
became increasingly more powerful and confounded the Jews who
lived in Damascus by proving that Jesus was the Messiah.

                                                      Acts 9:20-23
                                    optional: Ecclesiastes 11:9–12:14

Responsorial Psalm

The righteous flourish like the palm tree,
    and grow like a cedar in Lebanon. . . .
In old age they still produce fruit;
    they are always green and full of sap,
showing that the LORD is upright;
    he is my rock, and there is no unrighteousness in him.

Psalm 92:12, 14-15

Prayers, pp. 529-32

Closing Psalm Prayer

It is good to give thanks to the LORD. . . .
to the music of the lute and harp,
    to the melody of the lyre.
For you, O LORD, have made me glad by your work.

Psalm 92:1a, 3-4a

Week of the Sunday Closest to June 15   Saturday

Theme: The proper response to God's action in history and to his action
        in our lives is, "O give thanks to the Lord."

Antiphon and Opening Prayer

O give thanks to the LORD, for he is good,
    for his steadfast love endures forever.   Psalm 136:1

Lord, for your work in the life of Saul,
and in the great cloud of witnesses who stand by me today,
I give you thanks.

Scripture Reading

When [Saul] had come to Jerusalem, he attempted to join the
disciples; and they were all afraid of him, for they did not believe

that he was a disciple. But Barnabas took him, brought him to the apostles, and described for them how on the road he had seen the Lord, who had spoken to him, and how in Damascus he had spoken boldly in the name of Jesus. So he went in and out among them in Jerusalem, speaking boldly in the name of the Lord.

Acts 9:26-28
optional: Numbers 3:1-13

Responsorial Psalm

O give thanks to the Lord . . .
who made the great lights —
the sun to rule over the day,
the moon and stars to rule over the night . . .
who divided the Red Sea in two . . .
It is he who remembered us in our low estate,
    for his steadfast love endures forever.

adapted from Psalm 136:1, 7-9, 13, 23

Prayers, pp. 529-32

Closing Psalm Prayer

O give thanks to the God of gods. . . .
O give thanks to the Lord of lords . . .
who alone does great wonders,
who by understanding made the heavens,
    for his steadfast love endures forever. Psalm 136:2a, 3a, 4a, 5

Week of the Sunday Closest to June 22   Sunday

Theme: The fervent prayers of Cornelius resulted in the spread of the gospel beyond Israel to include the Gentiles. God does reward our persistence!

Antiphon and Opening Prayer

May God be gracious to us and bless us . . .
that your way may be known upon earth,
      your saving power among all nations.   Psalm 67:1, 2

O Lord, my God, sustain me in my fervent prayer
that I may see your hand at work in my life.

Scripture Reading

In Caesarea there was a man named Cornelius. . . . He was a devout
man who feared God with all his household. . . . One afternoon at
about three o'clock he had a vision in which he clearly saw an angel
of God. . . . He stared at him in terror and said, "What is it, Lord?"
He answered, "Your prayers and your alms have ascended as a
memorial before God. Now send men to Joppa for a certain Simon
who is called Peter."

                                        Acts 10:1-5
                            optional: Numbers 6:22-27

Responsorial Psalm

Let the peoples praise you, O God;
      let all the peoples praise you.
Let the nations be glad and sing for joy,
      for you judge the peoples with equity
      and guide the nations upon earth.
Let all the peoples praise you.   Psalm 67:3-4, 5b

Prayers, pp. 529-32

Closing Psalm Prayer

Let all the peoples praise you. . . .
The earth has yielded its increase;
      God, our God, has blessed us.
May God continue to bless us;
      let all the ends of the earth revere him.   Psalm 67:5-7

Week of the Sunday Closest to June 22   Monday

Theme: Sometimes the Lord asks us to do something we never thought
we could do. But he gives us the strength and courage to act in
his name.

Antiphon and Opening Prayer

The LORD is king! Let the earth rejoice;
let the many coastlands be glad!   Psalm 97:1

Lord, even as you called Peter to love the Gentiles,
help me to reach out and love those who are unlovely to me.

Scripture Reading

About noon the next day, . . . Peter went up on the roof to pray. . . .
He saw the heaven opened and something like a large sheet coming
down, being lowered to the ground by its four corners. In it were
all kinds of four-footed creatures and reptiles and birds of the air.
Then he heard a voice saying, "Get up, Peter; kill and eat." But Peter
said, "By no means, Lord; for I have never eaten anything that is
profane or unclean." The voice said to him again, a second time,
"What God has made clean, you must not call profane."
                                        Acts 10:9, 11-15
                                  optional: Numbers 9:15-23

Responsorial Psalm

Mighty King, lover of justice,
    you have established equity;
you have executed justice
    and righteousness in Jacob.
Extol the LORD our God;
    worship at his footstool.
    Holy is he!   Psalm 99:4-5

Prayers, pp. 529-32

Closing Psalm Prayer

> O LORD our God, you answered them;
>> you were a forgiving God to them. . . .
> Extol the LORD our God,
>> and worship at his holy mountain;
>> for the LORD our God is holy. Psalm 99:8a, 9

Week of the Sunday Closest to June 22 Tuesday

Theme: We can always trust the Lord to accomplish what he sets out to do in the heavens, on the earth, and in our lives.

Antiphon and Opening Prayer

> I will sing of your steadfast love, O LORD, forever;
>> with my mouth I will proclaim your faithfulness to all
>> generations. Psalm 89:1

> Lord, you who rule in the heavens
> and spread your arms out over the earth,
> guide me by your loving and gracious hand.

Scripture Reading

Now while Peter was greatly puzzled about what to make of the vision that he had seen, suddenly the men sent by Cornelius appeared. They were asking for Simon's house and were standing by the gate. . . . So Peter went down to the men and said, "I am the one you are looking for; what is the reason for your coming?" They answered, "Cornelius . . . was directed by a holy angel to send for you to come to his house and to hear what you have to say."

Acts 10:17, 21-22
optional: Numbers 11:1-23

Responsorial Psalm

The heavens are yours, the earth also is yours;
    the world and all that is in it — you have founded them.
The north and the south — you created them. . . .
    Strong is your hand, high your right hand.

Psalm 89:11-12a, 13b

Prayers, pp. 529-32

Closing Psalm Prayer

The heavens will praise your wonders, O Lord,
your faithfulness in the congregation of the saints.
For who in the heavens can be compared to the Lord?

adapted from Psalm 89:5-6

Week of the Sunday Closest to June 22   Wednesday

Theme: Although God's way is the perfect way for us to walk, he
       sometimes has to blaze the trail before we see where he wants
       us to travel.

Antiphon and Opening Prayer

I will sing of loyalty and of justice;
    to you, O LORD, I will sing.   Psalm 101:1

Lord, you who lighten the path of my journey
and lead me day by day and step by step,
open new doors to me today.

Scripture Reading

The following day they came to Caesarea. . . . On Peter's arrival
Cornelius met him, and falling at his feet, worshiped him. But Peter
made him get up, saying, "Stand up; I am only a mortal." And as
he talked with him, he went in and found that many had assembled;

and he said to them, "You yourselves know that it is unlawful for a Jew to associate with or to visit a Gentile; but God has shown me that I should not call anyone profane or unclean."

Acts 10:24a, 25-28
optional: Numbers 11:24-35

Responsorial Psalm

I will look with favor on the faithful in the land,
>   so that they may live with me;
whoever walks in the way that is blameless
>   shall minister to me.
No one who practices deceit
>   shall remain in my house. . . .
I will study the way that is blameless.   Psalm 101:6-7a, 2a

Prayers, pp. 529-32

Closing Psalm Prayer

I will study the way that is blameless.
>   When shall I attain it?
I will walk with integrity of heart
>   within my house. . . .
Whoever walks in the way that is blameless
>   shall minister to me.   Psalm 101:2, 6

Week of the Sunday Closest to June 22   Thursday

Theme: When we are obedient to the voice of the Lord, he will do things for us and others far beyond our expectations and dreams.

Antiphon and Opening Prayer

O give thanks to the LORD, call on his name,
>   make known his deeds among the peoples.   Psalm 105:1

O Lord, you who are marvelous in all your works,
you who do great wonders,
turn me to trust in you and to hope in your grace.

Scripture Reading

Cornelius replied, "Four days ago at this very hour . . . a man in dazzling clothes stood before me. He said, 'Cornelius . . . send therefore to Joppa and ask for Simon, who is called Peter. . . .' Therefore I sent for you immediately, and you have been kind enough to come. So now all of us are here in the presence of God to listen to all that the Lord has commanded you to say."

Then Peter began to speak to them: "I truly understand that God shows no partiality, but in every nation anyone who fears him and does what is right is acceptable to him. . . . Everyone who believes in him receives forgiveness of sins through his name."

Acts 10:30-35, 43
optional: Numbers 12:1-16

Responsorial Psalm

Remember the wonderful works he has done,
   his miracles, and the judgments he uttered,
O offspring of his servant Abraham. . . .
He is the LORD our God;
   his judgments are in all the earth.
He is mindful of his covenant forever.   Psalm 105:5-6a, 7-8a

Prayers, pp. 529-32

Closing Psalm Prayer

Sing to him, sing praises to him;
   tell of all his wonderful works.
Glory in his holy name. . . .
Seek the LORD and his strength;
   seek his presence continually.   Psalm 105:2-3a, 4

Week of the Sunday Closest to June 22   Friday

Theme: When the Lord does a wonderful work for us or someone else,
the appropriate response is one of enthusiasm and thanks!

Antiphon and Opening Prayer

O give thanks to the LORD, for he is good;
    for his steadfast love endures forever.   Psalm 107:1

Lord, you who have worked marvelous deeds among the peoples
of the earth,
work in my life to your praise and glory.

Scripture Reading

While Peter was still speaking, the Holy Spirit fell upon all who
heard the word. The circumcised believers who had come with Peter
were astounded that the gift of the Holy Spirit had been poured out
even on the Gentiles, for they heard them speaking in tongues and
extolling God. Then Peter said, "Can anyone withhold the water for
baptizing these people who have received the Holy Spirit just as we
have?" So he ordered them to be baptized in the name of Jesus Christ.

Acts 10:44-48
optional: Numbers 13:1-30

Responsorial Psalm

Let the redeemed of the LORD say so,
    those he redeemed from trouble
and gathered in from the lands,
    from the east and from the west,
from the north and the south. . . .
For he satisfies the thirsty.   Psalm 107:2-3, 9a

Prayers, pp. 529-32

Closing Psalm Prayer

Let them thank the LORD for his steadfast love. . . .
Let them extol him in the congregation of the people,
    and praise him in the assembly of the elders.

Psalm 107:31-32

Week of the Sunday Closest to June 22   Saturday

Theme: Sometimes God will do a work that seems out of character with
          the way we understand things, but we are to trust in him and
          accept his will.

Antiphon and Opening Prayer

Rejoice in the LORD, O you righteous.
    Praise befits the upright.   Psalm 33:1

O Lord, my God, deliver me from the restrictions that I put on
your work in the world
and teach me to expect the unexpected.

Scripture Reading

Now the apostles and the believers who were in Judea heard that
the Gentiles had also accepted the word of God. So when Peter went
up to Jerusalem, the circumcised believers criticized him, saying,
"Why did you go to uncircumcised men and eat with them?" Then
Peter began to explain it to them. . . . When they heard this, they
were silenced. And they praised God, saying, "Then God has given
even to the Gentiles the repentance that leads to life."

Acts 11:1-4, 18; Numbers 13:31–14:25

Responsorial Psalm

Praise the LORD with the lyre;
    make melody to him with the harp of ten strings.
Sing to him a new song;

play skillfully on the strings, with loud shouts.
For the word of the LORD is upright,
    and all his work is done in faithfulness.   Psalm 33:2-4

Prayers, pp. 529-32

Closing Psalm Prayer

Our soul waits for the LORD;
    he is our help and our shield.
Our heart is glad in him,
    because we trust in his holy name.
Let your steadfast love, O LORD, be upon us.   Psalm 33:20-22a

Week of the Sunday Closest to June 29   Sunday

Theme: Our trials and tribulations, instead of being times of grumbling,
    can be turned into times of great victory and personal growth.

Antiphon and Opening Prayer

I will extol you, my God and King,
    and bless your name forever and ever.   Psalm 145:1

O Lord God, my maker and redeemer,
turn my trials and difficult times into occasions for growth and
great joy.

Scripture Reading

James, a servant of God and of the Lord Jesus Christ,
To the twelve tribes in the Dispersion:
Greetings.
    My brothers and sisters, whenever you face trials of any kind,
consider it nothing but joy, because you know that the testing of
your faith produces endurance; and let endurance have its full effect,
so that you may be mature and complete, lacking in nothing. . . .

Blessed is anyone who endures temptation. Such a one has stood the test and will receive the crown of life that the Lord has promised to those who love him.

James 1:1-4, 12
optional: Numbers 14:26-45

Responsorial Psalm

All your works shall give thanks to you, O Lord,
   and your faithful shall bless you.
They shall speak of the glory of your kingdom,
   and tell of your power. . . .
Your kingdom is an everlasting kingdom,
   your dominion endures throughout all generations.

Psalm 145:10-11, 13

Prayers, pp. 529-32

Closing Psalm Prayer

Every day I will bless you,
   and praise your name forever and ever.
Great is the Lord, and greatly to be praised.   Psalm 145:2-3a

Week of the Sunday Closest to June 29   Monday

Theme: It is an easy thing simply to *believe* the right things, but it is much harder to *live* the Christian life.

Antiphon and Opening Prayer

Praise the Lord!
   O give thanks to the Lord, for he is good;
   for his steadfast love endures forever.   Psalm 106:1

Lord, how easy it is for me simply to believe in you.
Turn my faith into action
and let me do your work to your glory.

Scripture Reading

But be doers of the word, and not merely hearers who deceive themselves. For if any are hearers of the word and not doers, they are like those who look at themselves in a mirror; for they look at themselves and, on going away, immediately forget what they were like. But those who look into the perfect law, the law of liberty, and persevere, being not hearers who forget but doers who act — they will be blessed in their doing.

James 1:22-25
optional: Numbers 16:1-19

Responsorial Psalm

Remember me, O LORD, when you show favor to your people;
help me when you deliver them;
that I may see the prosperity of your chosen ones,
that I may rejoice in the gladness of your nation,
that I may glory in your heritage.   Psalm 106:4-5

Prayers, pp. 529-32

Closing Psalm Prayer

Save us, O LORD our God . . .
that we may give thanks to your holy name,
and glory in your praise.
Blessed be the LORD, the God of Israel,
from everlasting to everlasting.   Psalm 106:47-48

Week of the Sunday Closest to June 29   Tuesday

Theme: We do not understand what it means to be poor and oppressed
until in some circumstance we are the victim of partiality.

Antiphon and Opening Prayer

Those who trust in the LORD are like Mount Zion,
which cannot be moved.   Psalm 125:1

Lord Jesus, you of all men on earth were victimized by the
partiality of hateful and wicked forces.
Teach me to live by your example.

Scripture Reading

My brothers and sisters, do you with your acts of favoritism really
believe in our glorious Lord Jesus Christ? . . . Listen. . . . Has not
God chosen the poor in the world to be rich in faith and to be heirs
of the kingdom that he has promised to those who love him? But
you have dishonored the poor. . . .

You do well if you really fulfill the royal law according to the
scripture, "You shall love your neighbor as yourself." But if you show
partiality, you commit sin and are convicted by the law as
transgressors.

James 2:1, 5-6a, 8-9
optional: Numbers 16:20-35

Responsorial Psalm

Blessed be the LORD. . . .
We have escaped like a bird
from the snare of the fowlers;
the snare is broken,
and we have escaped.
Our help is in the name of the LORD,
who made heaven and earth.   Psalm 124:6-8

Prayers, pp. 529-32

Closing Psalm Prayer

> The LORD is your keeper;
> > the LORD is your shade at your right hand.
> The sun shall not strike you by day,
> > nor the moon by night. . . .
> > He will keep your life. Psalm 121:5-6, 7b

Week of the Sunday Closest to June 29 Wednesday

Theme: The Lord, who puts actions behind his words, calls us to be like
him and to show the truth of our words by our deeds.

Antiphon and Opening Prayer

> Praise the LORD!
> > Praise the name of the LORD;
> > give praise, O servants of the LORD. Psalm 135:1

> O Lord, you who acted on my behalf to restore and renew my
> life,
> bring my words and deeds into union for your sake.

Scripture Reading

> What good is it, my brothers and sisters, if you say you have faith
> but do not have works? Can faith save you? If a brother or sister is
> naked and lacks daily food, and one of you says to them, "Go in
> peace; keep warm and eat your fill," and yet you do not supply their
> bodily needs, what is the good of that? So faith by itself, if it has
> not works, is dead. . . .
> > You see that a person is justified by works and not by faith
> alone.

> James 2:14-17, 24
> optional: Numbers 16:36-50

Responsorial Psalm

For I know that the LORD is great;
  our Lord is above all gods. . . .
He it was who struck down the firstborn of Egypt,
  both human beings and animals;
he sent signs and wonders
  into your midst, O Egypt. . . .
Your name, O LORD, endures forever.   Psalm 135:5, 8-9a, 13

Prayers, pp. 529-32

Closing Psalm Prayer

O house of Israel, bless the LORD!
  O house of Aaron, bless the LORD!
O house of Levi, bless the LORD!
  You that fear the LORD, bless the LORD!
Blessed be the LORD from Zion,
  he who resides in Jerusalem.
Praise the LORD!   Psalm 135:19-21

Week of the Sunday Closest to June 29   Thursday

Theme: The tongue is one of the most difficult members of our body to
        control, but with the help of the Holy Spirit, it can be tamed.

Antiphon and Opening Prayer

Lord, hear my voice!
Let your ears be attentive
  to the voice of my supplications.   Psalm 130:2

Lord God, my Father,
you have given me my tongue to be an instrument of praise.
Let me turn away from evil talk and glorify you.

Scripture Reading

Not many of you should become teachers, my brothers and sisters, for you know that we who teach will be judged with greater strictness. For all of us make many mistakes. Anyone who makes no mistakes in speaking is perfect, able to keep the whole body in check with a bridle. . . . Or look at ships: though they are so large . . . they are guided by a very small rudder wherever the will of the pilot directs. So also the tongue is a small member, yet it boasts of great exploits.

James 3:1-2, 4-5
optional: Numbers 17:1-11

Responsorial Psalm

If you, O LORD, should mark iniquities,
    Lord, who could stand?
But there is forgiveness with you,
    so that you may be revered.
I wait for the LORD, my soul waits,
    and in his word I hope;
my soul waits for the Lord.   Psalm 130:3-6a

Prayers, pp. 529-32

Closing Psalm Prayer

O Israel, hope in the LORD!
    For with the LORD there is steadfast love,
    and with him is great power to redeem.
It is he who will redeem Israel
    from all its iniquities.   Psalm 130:7-8

Week of the Sunday Closest to June 29   Friday

Theme: The only way to control the tongue is to resist the devil, submit
to the Lord, and call on him to set a guard over our mouths.

Antiphon and Opening Prayer

Let my prayer be counted as incense before you,
>   and the lifting up of my hands as an evening sacrifice.

>   Psalm 141:2

Lord, turn my tongue away from the evil power of gossip.
Let my mouth utter your praise,
and my lips speak of your worth.

Scripture Reading

Submit yourselves therefore to God. Resist the devil, and he will flee
from you. . . .

>   Do not speak evil against one another, brothers and sisters.
Whoever speaks evil against another or judges another, speaks evil
against the law and judges the law; but if you judge the law, you are
not a doer of the law but a judge. There is one lawgiver and judge
who is able to save and to destroy. So who, then, are you to judge
your neighbor?

>   James 4:7, 11-12
>   optional: Numbers 20:1-13

Responsorial Psalm

But my eyes are turned toward you, O GOD, my Lord;
>   in you I seek refuge; do not leave me defenseless.
Keep me from the trap that they have laid for me,
>   and from the snares of evildoers.   Psalm 141:8-9

Prayers, pp. 529-32

Closing Psalm Prayer

I call upon you, O LORD; come quickly to me;
>   give ear to my voice when I call to you. . . .
Set a guard over my mouth, O LORD;
>   keep watch over the door of my lips.   Psalm 141:1, 3

Week of the Sunday Closest to June 29   Saturday

Theme: The majestic works of the Lord are seen in the lives he touches
to heal and fill with great gladness.

Antiphon and Opening Prayer

Bless the LORD, O my soul.
O LORD my God, you are very great.
You are clothed with honor and majesty.   Psalm 104:1

Lord, when I observe your works throughout the world and in
my life,
my heart cries out to praise your holy and glorious name.

Scripture Reading

Are any among you suffering? They should pray. Are any cheerful?
They should sing songs of praise. Are any among you sick? They
should call for the elders of the church and have them pray over
them, anointing them with oil in the name of the Lord. The prayer
of faith will save the sick, and the Lord will raise them up; and
anyone who has committed sins will be forgiven. Therefore confess
your sins to one another, and pray for one another, so that you may
be healed.

James 5:13-16
optional: Numbers 20:14-29

Responsorial Psalm

You set the earth on its foundations,
so that it shall never be shaken.
You cover it with the deep as with a garment;
the waters stood above the mountains.
At your rebuke they flee;
at the sound of your thunder they take to flight.

Psalm 104:5-7

Prayers, pp. 529-32

Closing Psalm Prayer

> O LORD, how manifold are your works!
>   In wisdom you have made them all;
>   the earth is full of your creatures. . . .
> Bless the LORD, O my soul!
> Praise the LORD!   Psalm 104:24, 35b

Week of the Sunday Closest to July 6   Sunday

Theme: The first missionary journey of Paul and Barnabas begins in
       Antioch about A.D. 48 after fasting and prayer for guidance.

Antiphon and Opening Prayer

> I will praise the LORD as long as I live;
>   I will sing praises to my God all my life long.   Psalm 146:2

> O Lord, you who lead and guide your servants,
> teach me to fast and pray in expectation of your answer and
> blessing.

Scripture Reading

> Then after completing their mission Barnabas and Saul returned to
> Jerusalem and brought with them John, whose other name was Mark.
>   Now in the church at Antioch there were prophets and
> teachers. . . . While they were worshiping the Lord and fasting, the
> Holy Spirit said, "Set apart for me Barnabas and Saul for the work
> to which I have called them." Then after fasting and praying they
> laid their hands on them and sent them off.
>   Acts 12:25–13:1a, 2-3
>   optional: Numbers 21:4-9, 21-35

Responsorial Psalm

> . . . The LORD opens the eyes of the blind.
> The LORD lifts up those who are bowed down; .

the LORD loves the righteous.
The LORD watches over the strangers;
   he upholds the orphan and the widow,
      but the way of the wicked he brings to ruin.   Psalm 146:8-9

Prayers, pp. 529-32

Closing Psalm Prayer

Happy are those whose help is the God of Jacob,
   whose hope is in the LORD their God,
who made heaven and earth,
      the sea, and all that is in them.   Psalm 146:5-6

Week of the Sunday Closest to July 6   Monday

Theme: We are called to declare good tidings to people everywhere, to
        declare that Jesus is Lord of all.

Antiphon and Opening Prayer

Answer me when I call. . . .
   Be gracious to me, and hear my prayer.   Psalm 4:1

Lord, you who came to rescue humanity from enslavement to sin,
to set us free,
create in me a passion to proclaim your glorious deeds.

Scripture Reading

. . . But they went on from Perga and came to Antioch in Pisidia.
And on the sabbath day they went into the synagogue and sat down.
After the reading of the law and the prophets, the officials of the
synagogue sent them a message, saying, "Brothers, if you have any
word of exhortation for the people, give it." So Paul stood up with
a gesture began to speak:

"You Israelites, and others who fear God, listen. . . . We bring you the good news that what God promised to our ancestors he has fulfilled for us."

Acts 13:14-16, 32
optional: Numbers 32:1-27

Responsorial Psalm

I will tell of the decree of the LORD:
He said to me, "You are my son;
   today I have begotten you.
Ask of me, and I will make the nations your heritage. . . ."
Happy are all who take refuge in him.   Psalm 2:7, 8a, 12b

Prayers, pp. 529-32

Closing Psalm Prayer

Serve the LORD with fear,
   with trembling kiss his feet,
or he will be angry. . . .
Happy are all who take refuge in him.   Psalm 2:11-12

Week of the Sunday Closest to July 6   Tuesday

Theme: We ought to receive the Word of the Lord with glad and thankful
        hearts, lest we be turned away.

Antiphon and Opening Prayer

Lead me, O LORD, in your righteousness
   because of my enemies;
   make your way straight before me.   Psalm 5:8

Lord, my Savior, let me hear your word with an open and
receiving heart,
and do not turn your grace from me.

Scripture Reading

The next sabbath almost the whole city gathered to hear the word of the Lord. But when the Jews saw the crowds, they were filled with jealousy; and blaspheming, they contradicted what was spoken by Paul. Then both Paul and Barnabas spoke out boldly, saying, "It was necessary that the word of God should be spoken first to you. Since you reject it and judge yourselves to be unworthy of eternal life, we are now turning to the Gentiles."

Acts 13:44-46
optional: Numbers 35:1-34

Responsorial Psalm

Give ear to my words, O LORD;
    give heed to my sighing.
Listen to the sound of my cry,
    my King and my God,
    for to you I pray.
O LORD, in the morning you hear my voice.   Psalm 5:1-3

Prayers, pp. 529-32

Closing Psalm Prayer

But let all who take refuge in you rejoice;
    let them ever sing for joy.
Spread your protection over them,
    so that those who love your name may exult in you.

Psalm 5:11-12

Week of the Sunday Closest to July 6   Wednesday

Theme: Whenever the Word of God is at work in our lives, Satan works doubly to draw us into his snares and traps.

Antiphon and Opening Prayer

But I trusted in your steadfast love. . . .
I will sing to the LORD,
    because he has dealt bountifully with me.   Psalm 13:5a, 6

Lord, my Redeemer,
you who have begun a good work in me,
maintain it to your glory and my benefit.

Scripture Reading

Thus the word of the Lord spread throughout the region. But the
Jews incited the devout women of high standing and the leading men
of the city, and stirred up persecution against Paul and Barnabas,
and drove them out of their region. So they shook the dust off their
feet in protest against them, and went to Iconium. And the disciples
were filled with joy and with the Holy Spirit.

Acts 13:49-52
optional: Deuteronomy 1:1-18

Responsorial Psalm

Fools say in their hearts, "There is no God." . . .
The LORD looks down from heaven on humankind
    to see if there are any who are wise,
    who seek after God. . . .
    There is no one who does good,
    no, not one.   Psalm 14:1-3

Prayers, pp. 529-32

Closing Psalm Prayer

How long, O LORD? . . .
Consider and answer me, O LORD, my God!
    Give light to my eyes, or I will sleep the sleep of death.
Psalm 13:1a, 3

Week of the Sunday Closest to July 6   Thursday

Theme: The Word of the Lord, like a two-edged sword, cuts both ways in our hearts and lives.

Antiphon and Opening Prayer

I call upon the LORD, who is worthy to be praised,
    so I shall be saved from my enemies.   Psalm 18:3

Lord, you who are the Word of Life,
penetrate into my heart and life,
and turn me in faith and love toward you.

Scripture Reading

The same thing occurred in Iconium, where Paul and Barnabas went into the Jewish synagogue and spoke in such a way that a great number of both Jews and Greeks became believers. . . . So they remained for a long time, speaking boldly for the Lord, who testified to the word of his grace by granting signs and wonders to be done through them. But the residents of the city were divided.

Acts 14:1, 3-4a
optional: Deuteronomy 3:18-28

Responsorial Psalm

It is you who light my lamp;
    the LORD, my God, lights up my darkness.
By you I can crush a troop,
    and by my God I can leap over a wall.
This God — his way is perfect;
    the promise of the LORD proves true;
    he is a shield for all who take refuge in him.   Psalm 18:28-30

Prayers, pp. 529-32

Closing Psalm Prayer

I love you, O LORD, my strength. . . .
     my rock in whom I take refuge,
     my shield, and the horn of my salvation, my stronghold.

                                        Psalm 18:1, 2b

Week of the Sunday Closest to July 6   Friday

Theme: Faith needs to reach out beyond the seemingly impossible and
        hopeless to grasp the power of God.

Antiphon and Opening Prayer

But you, O LORD, do not be far away.
     O my help, come quickly to my aid!   Psalm 22:19

Lord, you who were forsaken by us
and experienced the silence of your Father,
speak your life-changing word into my life.

Scripture Reading

In Lystra there was a man sitting who could not use his feet and had
never walked, for he had been crippled from birth. He listened to
Paul as he was speaking. And Paul, looking at him intently and seeing
that he had faith to be healed, said in a loud voice, "Stand upright
on your feet." And the man sprang up and began to walk. . . .
     But Jews came there from Antioch and Iconium and won over
the crowds. Then they stoned Paul and dragged him out of the city,
supposing that he was dead.

                                        Acts 14:8-10, 19
                              optional: Deuteronomy 31:7–32:4

Responsorial Psalm

My God, my God, why have you forsaken me?
     Why are you so far from helping me, from the words of my

groaning?
O my God, I cry by day, but you do not answer;
    and by night, but find no rest.   Psalm 22:1-2

Prayers, pp. 529-32

Closing Psalm Prayer

Yet you are holy,
    enthroned on the praises of Israel.
In you our ancestors trusted;
    they trusted, and you delivered them.
To you they cried, and were saved.   Psalm 22:3-5a

Week of the Sunday Closest to July 6   Saturday

Theme: When we are faithful to God and his will, he will open the door
      of faith for us and for others.

Antiphon and Opening Prayer

Be exalted, O LORD, in your strength!
We will sing and praise your power.   Psalm 21:13

Lord God, as you guided Paul and Barnabas by your Spirit,
fill me with your Spirit
and direct my feet on the path of your will.

Scripture Reading

After [Paul and Barnabas] had proclaimed the good news to [Derbe]
and had made many disciples, they returned to Lystra, then on to
Iconium and Antioch. There they strengthened the souls of the
disciples and encouraged them to continue in the faith, saying, "It is
through many persecutions that we must enter the kingdom of God."

When they arrived, they called the church together and related all that God had done with them, and how he had opened a door of faith for the Gentiles.

Acts 14:21, 22, 27
optional: Deuteronomy 34:1-12

Responsorial Psalm

He asked you for life; you gave it to him —
　　length of days forever and ever.
His glory is great through your help. . . .
For the king trusts in the LORD,
　　and through the steadfast love of the Most High he shall not
　　be moved.   Psalm 21:4-5a, 7

Prayers, pp. 529-32

Closing Psalm Prayer

In your strength the king rejoices, O LORD. . . .
You have given him his heart's desire,
　　and have not withheld the request of his lips.   Psalm 21:1-2

Week of the Sunday Closest to July 13   Sunday

Theme: When God takes complete charge of a life and turns it toward serving him, it is to his praise and glory!

Antiphon and Opening Prayer

Praise the LORD!
Praise God in his sanctuary;
　　praise him in his mighty firmament.   Psalm 150:1

Lord Jesus, as you met Paul and turned him into your anointed servant,
so anoint me for the task that lies ahead.

Scripture Reading

You have heard, no doubt, of my earlier life in Judaism. I was violently persecuting the church of God and was trying to destroy it. . . . But when God, who had set me apart before I was born and called me through his grace, was pleased to reveal his Son to me, so that I might proclaim him among the Gentiles. . . .

Then I went into the regions of Syria and Cilicia, and I was still unknown by sight to the churches of Judea that are in Christ; they only heard it said, "The one who formerly was persecuting us is now proclaiming the faith he once tried to destroy."

Galatians 1:13, 15-16, 21-23
optional: Joshua 1:1-18

Responsorial Psalm

Praise him for his mighty deeds;
    praise him according to his surpassing greatness!
Praise him with trumpet sound;
    praise him with lute and harp!
Praise him with tambourine and dance;
    praise him with strings and pipes!   Psalm 150:2-4

Prayers, pp. 529-32

Closing Psalm Prayer

Praise him with clanging cymbals;
    praise him with loud clashing cymbals!
Let everything that breathes praise the LORD!
Praise the LORD!   Psalm 150:5-6

Week of the Sunday Closest to July 13   Monday

Theme: God calls us, as he did Paul, to discover the secret of living fully
        and completely in Christ and Christ alone.

Antiphon and Opening Prayer

> To you, O LORD, I lift up my soul.
> O my God, in you I trust. Psalm 25:1-2a
>
> O Lord, my God,
> let me turn from all reliance on works and upright living
> to trust wholly and completely in you.

Scripture Reading

> . . . Yet we know that a person is justified not by the works of the law but through faith in Jesus Christ. And we have come to believe in Christ Jesus, so that we might be justified by faith in Christ, and not by doing the works of the law, because no one will be justified by the works of the law. . . . I have been crucified with Christ, and it is no longer I who live, but it is Christ who lives in me. And the life I now live in the flesh I live by faith in the Son of God, who loved me and gave himself for me.
> Galatians 2:16, 19b-20
> optional: Joshua 2:1-14

Responsorial Psalm

> Good and upright is the LORD;
>   therefore he instructs sinners in the way.
> He leads the humble in what is right,
>   and teaches the humble his way.
> All the paths of the LORD are steadfast love and faithfulness,
>   for those who keep his covenant and his decrees.
> Psalm 25:8-10

Prayers, pp. 529-32

Closing Psalm Prayer

> Make me to know your ways, O LORD;
>   teach me your paths.
> Lead me in your truth, and teach me,
>   for you are the God of my salvation;
>   for you I wait all day long. Psalm 25:4-5

Week of the Sunday Closest to July 13   Tuesday

Theme: Now that we have come to faith in Jesus Christ, the law is no longer able to terrorize us by its demands.

Antiphon and Opening Prayer

The LORD is my light and my salvation. . . .
The LORD is the stronghold of my life;
    of whom shall I be afraid?   Psalm 27:1

O Lord, my God,
you who through your Son has freed me from having to earn my salvation,
let me trust in him and him alone.

Scripture Reading

Why then the law? . . . But the scripture has imprisoned all things under the power of sin, so that what was promised through faith in Jesus Christ might be given to those who believe.

Now before faith came, we were imprisoned and guarded under the law until faith would be revealed. Therefore the law was our disciplinarian until Christ came, so that we might be justified by faith. But now that faith has come, we are no longer subject to a disciplinarian.

Galatians 3:19a, 22-25
optional: Joshua 2:15-24

Responsorial Psalm

One thing I asked of the LORD,
    that will I seek after:
to live in the house of the LORD
    all the days of my life,
to behold the beauty of the LORD,
    and to inquire in his temple.

For he will hide me in his shelter
    in the day of trouble.   Psalm 27:4-5a

Prayers, pp. 529-32

Closing Psalm Prayer

Wait for the LORD;
    be strong, and let your heart take courage;
    wait for the LORD!   Psalm 27:14

Week of the Sunday Closest to July 13   Wednesday

Theme: When we trust in Christ for our salvation we are made members
       of the family of God on earth.

Antiphon and Opening Prayer

Do not forsake me, O LORD;
    O my God, do not be far from me;
make haste to help me,
    O Lord, my salvation.   Psalm 38:21-22

Lord, my God,
you who called a family of people into being,
grant me a love for all who are in Christ.
Turn me away from all prejudice.

Scripture Reading

. . . For in Christ Jesus you are all children of God through faith.
As many of you as were baptized into Christ have clothed yourselves
with Christ. There is no longer Jew or Greek, there is no longer slave
or free, there is no longer male and female; for all of you are one in
Christ Jesus. And if you belong to Christ, then you are Abraham's
offspring, heirs according to the promise. . . .

So you are no longer a slave but a child, and if a child, then also an heir, through God.

Galatians 3:26-29; 4:7
optional: Joshua 3:1-13

Responsorial Psalm

I have chosen the way of faithfulness;
    I set your ordinances before me.
I cling to your decrees, O LORD;
    let me not be put to shame.
I run the way of your commandments,
    for you enlarge my understanding.   Psalm 119:30-33

Prayers, pp. 529-32

Closing Psalm Prayer

When I think of your ways,
    I turn my feet to your decrees;
I hurry and do not delay
    to keep your commandments.   Psalm 119:59-60

Week of the Sunday Closest to July 13   Thursday

Theme: There are always those who wish to put us in bondage again,
        but God calls us to the freedom of love and service.

Antiphon and Opening Prayer

Trust in the LORD, and do good. . . .
Take delight in the LORD,
    and he will give you the desires of your heart.   Psalm 37:3-4

Lord, you who loved me and gave your Son for my freedom,
keep me from hurting others with my liberty,
and turn me toward the love and service of others.

Scripture Reading

For freedom Christ has set us free. Stand firm, therefore, and do not submit again to a yoke of slavery. . . .

For you were called to freedom, brothers and sisters; only do not use your freedom as an opportunity for self-indulgence, but through love become slaves to one another. For the whole law is summed up in a single commandment, "You shall love your neighbor as yourself." If, however, you bite and devour one another, take care that you are not consumed by one another.

Galatians 5:1, 13-14, 15
optional: Joshua 3:14–4:7

Responsorial Psalm

Be still before the LORD, and wait patiently for him;
    do not fret over those who prosper in their way,
    over those who carry out evil devices.
Refrain from anger, and forsake wrath.
    Do not fret — it leads only to evil.
Trust in the LORD, and do good.   Psalm 37:7, 8, 3a

Prayers, pp. 529-32

Closing Psalm Prayer

Commit your way to the LORD;
    trust in him, and he will act.
He will make your vindication shine like the light,
    and the justice of your cause like noonday.   Psalm 37:5-6

Week of the Sunday Closest to July 13   Friday

Theme: God calls us to abandon all the works of the flesh, to turn away from them, and to live in the fruit of the Spirit.

Antiphon and Opening Prayer

Into your hand I commit my spirit;
    you have redeemed me, O LORD, faithful God.   Psalm 31:5

O Holy Spirit, you who fill us with the fruit of your Spirit,
turn me from all wickedness and vain deceit
and let me walk in your ways only.

Scripture Reading

Live by the Spirit, I say, and do not gratify the desires of the flesh. . . .
But if you are led by the Spirit, you are not subject to the law. . . .
    By contrast, the fruit of the Spirit is love, joy, peace, patience,
kindness, generosity, faithfulness, gentleness, and self-control. There
is no law against such things. And those who belong to Christ Jesus
have crucified the flesh with its passions and desires. If we live by
the Spirit, let us also be guided by the Spirit.

Galatians 5:16, 18, 22-25
optional: Joshua 4:19–5:15

Responsorial Psalm

O how abundant is your goodness
    that you have laid up for those who fear you,
and accomplished for those who take refuge in you,
    in the sight of everyone!
Blessed be the LORD,
    for he has wondrously shown his steadfast love to me
    when I was beset as a city under siege.   Psalm 31:19, 21

Prayers, pp. 529-32

Closing Psalm Prayer

Love the LORD, all you his saints.
    The LORD preserves the faithful. . . .
Be strong, and let your heart take courage,
    all you who wait for the LORD.   Psalm 31:23a, 24

Week of the Sunday Closest to July 13 Saturday

Theme: Sometimes we may feel that the good we do for others or our
service to the Lord is of no consequence.

Antiphon and Opening Prayer

Happy are those to whom the LORD imputes no iniquity,
    and in whose spirit there is no deceit.   Psalm 32:2

O Lord, you who have called me to live by your precepts
and to do good to all people,
keep me from growing weary in well-doing.

Scripture Reading

Do not be deceived; God is not mocked, for you reap whatever you
sow. If you sow to your own flesh, you will reap corruption from
the flesh; but if you sow to the Spirit, you will reap eternal life from
the Spirit. So let us not grow weary in doing what is right, for we
will reap at harvest time, if we do not give up. So then, whenever
we have an opportunity, let us work for the good of all, and especially
for those of the family of faith.

                                                    Galatians 6:7-10
                                              optional: Joshua 6:1-14

Responsorial Psalm

I will instruct you and teach you the way you should go;
    I will counsel you with my eye upon you.
Do not be like a horse or a mule, without understanding,
    whose temper must be curbed with bit and bridle,
    else it will not stay near you.   Psalm 32:8-9

Prayers, pp. 529-32

Closing Psalm Prayer

> . . . Steadfast love surrounds those who trust in the LORD.
> Be glad in the LORD and rejoice, O righteous,
>> and shout for joy, all you upright in heart.   Psalm 32:10-11

Week of the Sunday Closest to July 20   Sunday

Theme: This week we walk with Paul on his second missionary journey
through Asia and Greece and back to Jerusalem.

Antiphon and Opening Prayer

> Bless the LORD, O my soul,
>> and all that is within me,
>> bless his holy name.   Psalm 103:1

> O Lord, as you sent Paul and his companions out as heralds of
> the good news,
> so empower me to be your witness.

Scripture Reading

> After some days Paul said to Barnabas, "Come, let us return and
> visit the believers in every city where we proclaimed the word of the
> Lord and see how they are doing." . . .
>   As they went from town to town, they delivered to them for
> observance the decisions that had been reached by the apostles and
> elders who were in Jerusalem. So the churches were strengthened in
> the faith and increased in numbers daily.
>> Acts 15:36; 16:4, 5
>> optional: Joshua 6:15-27

Responsorial Psalm

> Bless the LORD, O my soul,
>> and do not forget all his benefits —
> who forgives all your iniquity,

> who heals all your diseases,
> who redeems your life from the Pit,
> who crowns you with steadfast love and mercy.
>
> Psalm 103:2-4

Prayers, pp. 529-32

Closing Psalm Prayer

> Bless the LORD, O you his angels. . . .
> Bless the LORD, all his hosts. . . .
> Bless the LORD, all his works,
>   in all places of his dominion.
> Bless the LORD, O my soul.   Psalm 103:20a, 21a, 22

Week of the Sunday Closest to July 20   Monday

Theme: A mark of the Christian faith is warmth and hospitality, the kind that the convert Lydia expressed.

Antiphon and Opening Prayer

> As a deer longs for flowing streams,
>   so my soul longs for you, O God.
> My soul thirsts for God. . . .   Psalm 42:1, 2a

> O Lord, you who came to give us abundant life,
> give me a heart of praise and hands of hospitality and love.

Scripture Reading

[In Philippi] on the sabbath day we went outside the gate by the river, where we supposed there was a place of prayer; and we sat down and spoke to the women who had gathered there. A certain woman named Lydia, a worshiper of God, was listening to us. . . . The Lord opened her heart to listen eagerly to what was said by Paul. When she and her household were baptized, she urged us, saying, "If you have judged me to be faithful to the Lord, come and stay at my home." And she prevailed upon us.

Acts 16:13-15
optional: Joshua 7:1-13

Responsorial Psalm

My soul thirsts for God,
    for the living God. . . .
These things I remember,
    as I pour out my soul:
how I went with the throng,
    and led them in procession to the house of God,
with glad shouts and songs of thanksgiving,
    a multitude keeping festival.
Psalm 42:2a, 4

Prayers, pp. 529-32

Closing Psalm Prayer

By day the LORD commands his steadfast love,
    and at night his song is with me,
    a prayer to the God of my life. . . .
Hope in God; for I shall again praise him,
    my help and my God.
Psalm 42:8, 11b

Week of the Sunday Closest to July 20   Tuesday

Theme: Are we among those who join Paul and Silas in believing that Jesus is the Christ and in singing praises to his name?

Antiphon and Opening Prayer

Clap your hands, all you peoples;
    shout to God with loud songs of joy.
For the LORD, the Most High, is awesome.
Psalm 47:1-2a

Lord, I have heard it proclaimed that you are the Christ.
Turn my heart toward faith in you,
and let my mouth sing out praise of you.

Scripture Reading

After Paul and Silas had passed through Amphipolis and Apollonia,
they came to Thessalonica, where there was a synagogue of the Jews.
And Paul went in, as was his custom, and on three sabbath days
argued with them from the scriptures, explaining and proving it was
necessary for the Messiah to suffer and to rise from the dead, and
saying, "This is the Messiah, Jesus whom I am proclaiming to you."
Some of them were persuaded and joined Paul and Silas, as did a
great many of the devout Greeks and not a few of the leading women.

Acts 17:1-4
optional: Joshua 8:1-22

Responsorial Psalm

God has gone up with a shout,
    the LORD with the sound of a trumpet.
Sing praises to God, sing praises;
    sing praises to our King, sing praises.
For God is the king of all the earth;
    sing praises with a psalm.   Psalm 47:5-7

Prayers, pp. 529-32

Closing Psalm Prayer

God is king over the nations;
    God sits on his holy throne.
The princes of the people gather
    as the people of the God of Abraham.
He is highly exalted.   Psalm 47:8-9

Week of the Sunday Closest to July 20   Wednesday

Theme: All too often we are like those who constantly seek new knowledge, but never truly come to an understanding.

Antiphon and Opening Prayer

Mortals cannot abide in their pomp;
>they are like the animals that perish.   Psalm 49:20

O Lord, revealer of all truth and judge of all peoples,
let me, your servant, not only seek the truth,
but find it in you.

Scripture Reading

While Paul was waiting for them in Athens, he was deeply distressed to see that the city was full of idols. So he argued in the synagogue with the Jews and the devout persons, and also in the marketplace every day with those who happened to be there. Also some Epicurean and Stoic philosophers debated with him. . . . So they took him and brought him to the Areopagus and asked him, "May we know what this new teaching is that you are presenting?"

>Acts 17:16-18a, 19
>optional: Joshua 8:30-35

Responsorial Psalm

God looks down from heaven on humankind
>to see if there are any who are wise,
>who seek after God.
They have fallen away, they are all alike perverse;
>there is no one who does good,
>no, not one.   Psalm 53:2-3

Prayers, pp. 529-32

Closing Psalm Prayer

Fools say in their hearts, "There is no God."
They are corrupt, they commit abominable acts;
   there is no one who does good. . . .
O that deliverance for Israel would come from Zion!

Psalm 53:1, 6a

Week of the Sunday Closest to July 20   Thursday

Theme: Although the works of the Lord are everywhere evident in his
        creation, we too frequently shut our ears and close our eyes to
        his presence.

Antiphon and Opening Prayer

Make a joyful noise to God, all the earth;
   sing the glory of his name.   Psalm 66:1-2a

O Lord, you created all that is
and you work in the world that you have made.
Let me see you in all your works.

Scripture Reading

Then Paul stood in front of the Areopagus and said, "Athenians, I
see how extremely religious you are in every way. For as I went
through the city and looked carefully at the objects of your worship,
I found among them an altar with the inscription: 'To an unknown
god.' What therefore you worship as unknown, this I proclaim to
you. . . ."

    When they heard of the resurrection of the dead, some scoffed;
but others said, "We will hear you again about this."

Acts 17:22-23, 32
optional: Joshua 9:3-21

Responsorial Psalm

Come and see what God has done:
   he is awesome in his deeds among mortals.
He turned the sea into dry land;
   they passed through the river on foot.
There we rejoiced in him,
   who rules by his might forever. . . .
Bless our God, O peoples.   Psalm 66:5-7a, 8a

Prayers, pp. 529-32

Closing Psalm Prayer

Come and hear, all you who fear God,
   and I will tell what he has done for me. . . .
Blessed be God,
   because he has not rejected my prayer
   or removed his steadfast love from me.   Psalm 66:16, 20

Week of the Sunday Closest to July 20   Friday

Theme: If we would seek the Lord and find him, we must come in
   repentance of our sin and turn toward him.

Antiphon and Opening Prayer

Purge me with hyssop, and I shall be clean;
   wash me and I shall be whiter than snow.

Lord, my Master and Savior,
let me see my sins and shortcomings,
so that I might turn away from them in repentance and faith
toward you.

Scripture Reading

From one ancestor he made all nations to inhabit the whole earth, and he allotted the times of their existence and the boundaries of the places where they would live, so that they would search for God and perhaps grope for him and find him — though indeed he is not far from each one of us. For "In him we live and move and have our being"; as even some of your own poets have said,
"For we too are his offspring."

Acts 17:26-28
optional: Joshua 9:22–10:15

Responsorial Psalm

Have mercy on me, O God,
    according to your steadfast love;
according to your abundant mercy,
    blot out my transgressions.
Wash me thoroughly from my iniquity,
    and cleanse me from my sin.   Psalm 51:1-2

Prayers, pp. 529-32

Closing Psalm Prayer

Restore to me the joy of your salvation,
    and sustain in me a willing spirit.
Then I will teach transgressors your ways,
    and sinners will return to you.   Psalm 51:12-13

Week of the Sunday Closest to July 20   Saturday

Theme: Paul ends his second missionary journey with plans to go up to Jerusalem for the feast, a dangerous choice.

Antiphon and Opening Prayer

Give ear to my prayer, O God;
     do not hide yourself from my supplication.   Psalm 55:1

Lord, you govern the world and all that are in it.
Protect me in the choices I make
and keep me in the palm of your hand.

Scripture Reading

After staying there for a considerable time, Paul said farewell to the
believers and sailed for Syria, accompanied by Priscilla and Aquila.
At Cenchreae he had his hair cut, for he was under a vow. When
they reached Ephesus, he left them there, but first he himself went
into the synagogue and had a discussion with the Jews. When they
asked him to stay longer, he declined; but on taking leave of them,
he said, "I will return to you, if God wills."

Acts 18:18-21
optional: Joshua 23:1-16

Responsorial Psalm

But I call upon God,
     and the LORD will save me.
Evening and morning and at noon
     I utter my complaint and moan,
     and he will hear my voice.
He will redeem me unharmed
     from the battle that I wage.   Psalm 55:16-18a

Prayers, pp. 529-32

Closing Psalm Prayer

Cast your burden on the LORD,
     and he will sustain you;
he will never permit
     the righteous to be moved. . . .
But I will trust in you.   Psalm 55:22, 23b

Week of the Sunday Closest to July 27   Sunday

Theme: The Lord God has singled us out to be examples of his name
throughout the world.

Antiphon and Opening Prayer

O LORD, our sovereign,
how majestic is your name in all the earth!   Psalm 8:1

Lord God, you whose name is above every name,
you whose name I bear,
grant that I should be a worthy example.

Scripture Reading

Paul, Silvanus, and Timothy,
To the church of the Thessalonians. . . .
We always give thanks to God for you and mention you in our
prayers, constantly remembering before our God and Father your
work of faith and labor of love and steadfastness of hope in our
Lord Jesus Christ. . . . And you became imitators of us and of the
Lord, for in spite of persecution you received the word with joy
inspired by the Holy Spirit, so that you became an example to all
the believers in Macedonia and in Achaia.

I Thessalonians 1:1-3, 6, 7
optional: Joshua 24:1-15

Responsorial Psalm

When I look at your heavens, the work of your fingers,
the moon and the stars that you have established;
what are human beings that you are mindful of them,
mortals that you care for them? . . .
You have given them dominion over the works of your hands;
you have put all things under their feet.   Psalm 8:3-4, 6

Prayers, pp. 529-32

Closing Psalm Prayer

Yet you have made them a little lower than God,
    and crowned them with glory and honor. . . .
O LORD, our Sovereign,
    how majestic is your name in all the earth!   Psalm 8:5, 9

Week of the Sunday Closest to July 27   Monday

Theme: Although death is the final enemy of the body, we do not need
    to live in fear of it.

Antiphon and Opening Prayer

. . . In God I trust; I am not afraid.
    What can a mere mortal do to me?   Psalm 56:11

O Lord God, you faced death in the person of your Son Christ
and overcame it.
Release me from the fear of death
and let me live in your confidence.

Scripture Reading

But we do not want you to be uninformed, brothers and sisters,
about those who have died, so that you may not grieve as others do
who have no hope. For since we believe that Jesus died and rose
again, even so, through Jesus, God will bring with him those who
have died. . . . For the Lord himself, with a cry of command, with
the archangel's call and with the sound of God's trumpet, will descend
from heaven, and the dead in Christ will rise first. . . . Therefore
encourage one another with these words.

I Thessalonians 4:13, 14, 16, 18
optional: Joshua 24:16-23

Responsorial Psalm

Be gracious to me, O God. . . .
When I am afraid,
    I put my trust in you.
In God, whose word I praise,
    in God I trust; I am not afraid;
    what can flesh do to me?   Psalm 56:1, 3, 4

Prayers, pp. 529-32

Closing Psalm Prayer

For you have delivered my soul from death,
    and my feet from falling,
so that I may walk before God
    in the light of life.   Psalm 56:13

Week of the Sunday Closest to July 27   Tuesday

Theme: We do not know when the end will come. Therefore God calls
us to watch, to be sober, and to live in hope.

Antiphon and Opening Prayer

Hear my cry, O God; when my heart is faint.
Lead me to the rock that is higher than I.
        adapted from Psalm 62:1-2

Lord God, you who will come again to complete your work on
earth,
let me live in such a way that your coming will find me ready.

Scripture Reading

Now concerning the times and the seasons, brothers and sisters. . . .
For you yourselves know very well that the day of the Lord will
come like a thief in the night. . . . So then let us not fall asleep as

others do, but let us keep awake and be sober. . . . But since we belong to the day, let us be sober, and put on the breastplate of faith and love, and for a helmet the hope of salvation. . . . Therefore encourage one another and build up each other, as indeed you are doing.

I Thessalonians 5:1, 2, 6, 8, 11
optional: Judges 2:1-13

Responsorial Psalm

For you, O God, have heard my vows;
    you have given me the heritage of those who fear your name.
Prolong the life of the king;
    may his years endure to all generations!
May he be enthroned forever before God;
    appoint steadfast love and faithfulness to watch over him!

Psalm 61:5-7

Prayers, pp. 529-32

Closing Psalm Prayer

. . . For you are my refuge,
    a strong tower against the enemy.
Let me abide in your tent forever,
    find refuge under the shelter of your wings.   Psalm 61:3-4

Week of the Sunday Closest to July 27   Wednesday

Theme: When we are in Christ, we are called to be attentive to the teachings of Christ, to follow him, and to do good to all people.

Antiphon and Opening Prayer

Oh, how I love your law!
    It is my meditation all day long. . . .
Through your precepts I get understanding.   Psalm 119:97, 104a

Lord God, you who gave us your law,
grant that I should listen to your teaching
and pattern my life after your will.

Scripture Reading

But we appeal to you, brothers and sisters, to respect those who
labor among you, and have charge of you in the Lord and admonish
you. . . . See that none of you repays evil for evil, but always seek
to do good to one another and to all. Rejoice always, pray without
ceasing, give thanks in all circumstances; for this is the will of God
in Christ Jesus for you. Do not quench the Spirit. Do not despise the
words of prophets, but test everything; hold fast to what is good;
abstain from every form of evil.

I Thessalonians 5:12, 15-22
optional: Judges 3:12-30

Responsorial Psalm

Your hands have made and fashioned me;
Give me understanding that I may learn your commandments.
Those who fear you shall see me and rejoice,
because I have hoped in your word.
I know, O LORD, that your judgments are right,
and that in faithfulness you have humbled me. . . .
May my heart be blameless in your statutes,
so that I may not be put to shame.   Psalm 119:73-75, 80

Prayers, pp. 529-32

Closing Psalm Prayer

. . . Your word is firmly fixed in heaven. . . .
I will never forget your precepts,
for by them you have given me life.
I am yours; save me,
for I have sought your precepts.   Psalm 119:89, 93-94

Week of the Sunday Closest to July 27 Thursday

Theme: God will always sustain us through the trials and difficulties of life, even through misunderstanding and rejection by family and friends.

Antiphon and Opening Prayer

In you, O LORD, I take refuge;
    let me never be put to shame. . . .
    For you are my rock and my fortress.   Psalm 71:1, 3b

Lord Jesus, you who were misunderstood and reviled for my sake,
give me grace to endure those who turn against me
and malign me for your sake.

Scripture Reading

We must always give thanks to God for you, brothers and sisters, as is right, because your faith is growing abundantly, and the love of everyone of you for one another is increasing. Therefore we ourselves boast of you among the churches of God for your steadfastness and faith during all your persecutions and the afflictions that you are enduring. . . .

To this end we always pray for you, asking that our God will make you worthy of his call and will fulfill by his power every good resolve and work of faith.

II Thessalonians 1:3-4, 11
optional: Judges 4:4-23

Responsorial Psalm

Rescue me, O my God, from the hand of the wicked,
    from the grasp of the unjust and cruel.
For you, O Lord, are my hope,
    my trust, O LORD, from my youth.
Upon you I have leaned from my birth. . . .
My praise is continually of you.   Psalm 71:4-6

Prayers, pp. 529-32

Closing Psalm Prayer

All day long my tongue will talk of your righteous help;
    for those who tried to do me harm
    have been put to shame, and disgraced.   Psalm 71:24

Week of the Sunday Closest to July 27   Friday

Theme: God, who is good to us, calls us to be faithful to him, to hold
fast to the teachings we have embraced.

Antiphon and Opening Prayer

My flesh and my heart may fail,
    but God is the strength of my heart and my portion forever.
           Psalm 73:26

O God, my strength,
enable me to be grateful
for the truth and fellowship that you have given me with your
people.

Scripture Reading

But we must always give thanks to God for you, brothers and sisters
beloved by the Lord, because God chose you as the first fruits for
salvation through sanctification by the Spirit and through belief in
the truth. For this purpose he called you through our proclamation
of the good news, so that you may obtain the glory of our Lord
Jesus Christ. So then, brothers and sisters, stand firm and hold fast
to the traditions that you were taught by us, either by word of mouth
or by our letter.

        II Thessalonians 2:13-15
        optional: Judges 5:1-18

Responsorial Psalm

> Truly God is good to the upright,
> > to those who are pure in heart.
> But as for me, my feet had almost stumbled;
> > my steps had nearly slipped.
> For I was envious of the arrogant;
> > I saw the prosperity of the wicked. Psalm 73:1-3

Prayers, pp. 529-32

Closing Psalm Prayer

> Whom have I in heaven but you?
> > And there is nothing on earth that I desire other than you.
> My flesh and my heart may fail,
> > but God is the strength of my heart and my portion forever.
> > > Psalm 73:25-26

Week of the Sunday Closest to July 27   Saturday

Theme: It is Jesus who establishes us before his Father and calls us to speak good words and do good works.

Antiphon and Opening Prayer

> We give thanks to you, O God;
> > we give thanks; your name is near.
> People tell of your wondrous deeds. Psalm 75:1

> Lord Jesus Christ, you have brought me to the Father
> through your good work of salvation.
> Now let me do works of love that will glorify your name.

Scripture Reading

> Now may our Lord Jesus Christ himself and God our Father, who loved us and through grace gave us eternal comfort and good hope,

comfort your hearts and strengthen them in every good work and word.

Finally, brothers and sisters, pray for us, so that the word of the Lord may spread rapidly and be glorified everywhere, just as it is among you.

The grace of our Lord Jesus Christ be with all of you.

II Thessalonians 2:16-17; 3:1, 18
optional: Judges 5:19-31

Responsorial Psalm

One thing I asked of the LORD,
    that will I seek after:
to live in the house of the LORD
    all the days of my life,
to behold the beauty of the LORD,
    and to inquire in his temple.
For he will hide me in his shelter
    in the day of trouble.   Psalm 27:4-5a

Prayers, pp. 529-32

Closing Psalm Prayer

The LORD is my light and my salvation;
    whom shall I fear?
The LORD is the stronghold of my life;
    of whom shall I be afraid? . . .
Yet I will be confident.   Psalm 27:1, 3b

Week of the Sunday Closest to August 3   Sunday

Theme: Sometimes we do not know the blessing of God that is in store
      for us. If we would only be open to his power, we would see it.

Antiphon and Opening Prayer

> I will bless the LORD at all times. . . .
> O magnify the LORD with me,
> > and let us exalt his name together.   Psalm 34:1a, 3

> Lord, my God, you who give freely of yourself to all who believe,
> bring to me those blessings of which I am unaware,
> that I might glory in you.

Scripture Reading

> While Apollos was in Corinth, Paul passed through the interior
> regions and came to Ephesus, where he found some disciples. He
> said to them, "Did you receive the Holy Spirit when you became
> believers?" They replied, "No, we have not even heard that there is
> a Holy Spirit." . . . When Paul had laid his hands on them, the Holy
> Spirit came upon them, and they spoke in tongues and prophesied.
> > Acts 19:1, 2, 6
> > optional: Judges 6:1-24

Responsorial Psalm

> O taste and see that the LORD is good;
> > happy are those who take refuge in him!
> O fear the LORD, you his holy ones,
> > for those who fear him have no want.
> The young lions suffer want and hunger,
> > but those who seek the LORD lack no good thing.
> > Psalm 34:8-10

Prayers, pp. 529-32

Closing Psalm Prayer

> When the righteous cry for help, the LORD hears,
> > and rescues them from all their troubles.
> The LORD is near to the brokenhearted,
> > and saves the crushed in spirit.   Psalm 34:17-18

Week of the Sunday Closest to August 3   Monday

Theme: When we turn away from our sin and trust in the work of Christ,
        God can do great things in our lives.

Antiphon and Opening Prayer

Restore us, O God;
    let your face shine, that we may be saved.   Psalm 80:3

Lord Jesus Christ, you who conquered the power of evil
and drove the enemy away,
turn my heart toward you in faith and simple trust.

Scripture Reading

God did extraordinary miracles through Paul, so that when the
handkerchiefs or aprons that had touched his skin were brought to
the sick, their diseases left them, and the evil spirits came out of
them. . . . A number of those who practiced magic collected their
books and burned them publicly; when the value of these books was
calculated, it was found to come to fifty thousand silver coins. So
the word of the Lord grew mightily and prevailed.

                                        Acts 19:11-12, 19-20
                                        optional: Judges 6:25-40

Responsorial Psalm

Turn again, O God of hosts;
    look down from heaven, and see;
have regard for this vine. . . .
But let your hand be upon the one at your right hand,
    the one whom you made strong for yourself.
Then we will never turn back from you;
    give us life, and we will call on your name.

                                        Psalm 80:14, 17-18

Prayers, pp. 529-32

Closing Psalm Prayer

O LORD God of hosts,
    how long will you be angry with your people's prayers?
Restore us, O God of hosts;
    let your face shine, that we may be saved!   Psalm 80:4, 7

Week of the Sunday Closest to August 3   Tuesday

Theme: Our God is not like an idol made with hands. He is the One
    who acts to redeem us and care for us.

Antiphon and Opening Prayer

Give ear, O my people, to my teaching;
    incline your ears to the words of my mouth.   Psalm 78:1

Lord, you who acted in history
to redeem Israel and your church,
act now to cast down the darkness of paganism
and let the light of your Christ shine.

Scripture Reading

A man named Demetrius, a silversmith who made silver shrines of
Artemis, brought no little business to the artisans. These he gathered
together, with the workers of the same trade, and said, "Men, you
know that we get our wealth from this business. You also see and
hear that not only in Ephesus but in almost the whole of Asia this
Paul has persuaded and drawn away a considerable number of people
by saying that gods made with hands are not gods."

Acts 19:24-26
optional: Judges 7:1-18

Responsorial Psalm

In the sight of their ancestors he worked marvels
    in the land of Egypt, in the fields of Zoan.
He divided the sea and let them pass through it,
    and made the waters stand like a heap.
In the daytime he led them with a cloud,
    and all night long with a fiery light.   Psalm 78:12-14

Prayers, pp. 529-32

Closing Psalm Prayer

I will utter dark sayings from of old,
we will tell to the coming generation the glorious deeds of the
Lord,
and the wonders that he has done.   adapted from Psalm 78:2, 4

Week of the Sunday Closest to August 3   Wednesday

Theme: God calls us to live our lives in such a way that we are a sign
       of his work.

Antiphon and Opening Prayer

Sing aloud to God our strength;
    shout for joy to the God of Jacob.   Psalm 81:1

Lord God, you showed yourself
in the lives of Moses, David, Paul, and John.
Now let me, your servant, witness to you in my life.

Scripture Reading

From Miletus he sent a message to Ephesus, asking the elders of the
church to meet him. When they came to him, he said to them:
    "You yourselves know how I lived among you the entire time
from the first day I set foot in Asia, serving the Lord with all humility

and with tears, enduring the trials that came to me through the plots of the Jews. I did not shrink from doing anything helpful, proclaiming the message to you and teaching you publicly and from house to house."

Acts 20:17-20
optional: Judges 7:19–8:12

Responsorial Psalm

Hear, O my people, while I admonish you;
    O Israel, if you would but listen to me!
There shall be no strange god among you;
    you shall not bow down to a foreign god.
I am the LORD your God,
    who brought you up out of the land of Egypt.
Open your mouth wide and I will fill it.   Psalm 81:8-10

Prayers, pp. 529-32

Closing Psalm Prayer

O that my people would listen to me,
    that Israel would walk in my ways!
Then I would quickly subdue their enemies,
    and turn my hand against their foes.   Psalm 81:13-14

Week of the Sunday Closest to August 3   Thursday

Theme: When God touches us by his grace and gives us his Holy Spirit, we are freed from the burden of our sin and built up in the faith.

Antiphon and Opening Prayer

Give ear, O LORD, to my prayer;
    listen to my cry of supplication.   Psalm 86:6

O Lord, you have heard my prayer of confession.
Receive me into the life of your Son,
and grant me the joy of your countenance.

Scripture Reading

And now I commend you to God and to the message of his grace,
a message that is able to build you up and to give you the inheritance
among all who are sanctified. . . . In all this I have given you an
example, that by such work we must support the weak, remembering
the words of the Lord Jesus, for he himself said, "It is more blessed
to give than to receive."

When he had finished speaking, he knelt down with them all
and prayed.

Acts 20:32, 35-36
optional: Judges 8:22-35

Responsorial Psalm

Incline your ear, O LORD, and answer me,
     for I am poor and needy.
Preserve my life, for I am devoted to you;
     save your servant who trusts in you.
You are my God; be gracious to me, O Lord,
     for to you I cry all day long.
Gladden the soul of your servant,
     for to you, O Lord, I lift up my soul.   Psalm 86:1-4

Prayers, pp. 529-32

Closing Psalm Prayer

Teach me your way, O LORD,
     that I may walk in your truth;
     give me an undivided heart to revere your name. . . .
     And I will glorify your name forever.
For great is your steadfast love toward me.

Psalm 86:11, 12b-13a

Week of the Sunday Closest to August 3   Friday

Theme: Paul's third missionary journey ends on a note of sadness as his impending imprisonment is prophesied.

Antiphon and Opening Prayer

O LORD, God of my salvation, . . .
let my prayer come before you;
    incline your ear to my cry.   Psalm 88:1a, 2

O God, you who have redeemed the world and renewed humankind,
help me accept what I cannot change,
and give me courage to go on serving you.

Scripture Reading

The next day we left and came to Caesarea; and we went into the house of Philip the evangelist, one of the seven, and stayed with him. . . . He came to us and took Paul's belt, bound his own feet and hands with it, and said, "Thus says the Holy Spirit, 'This is the way the Jews in Jerusalem will bind the man who owns this belt and will hand him over to the Gentiles.'"

                         Acts 21:8, 11
              optional: Judges 9:1-21

Responsorial Psalm

For my soul is full of troubles,
    and my life draws near to Sheol.
I am counted among those who go down to the Pit;
    I am like those who have no help,
like those forsaken among the dead,
    like the slain that lie in the grave,
like those whom you remember no more,
    for they are cut off from your hand.   Psalm 88:3-5

Prayers, pp. 529-32

Closing Psalm Prayer

Every day I call on you, O LORD;
I spread out my hands to you.
Do you work wonders for the dead?
Do the shades rise up to praise you? . . .
But I, O LORD, cry out to you.   Psalm 88:9b-10, 13a

Week of the Sunday Closest to August 3   Saturday

Theme: God calls us to a commitment so strong that we are willing
either to die or to live so long as we are doing his will.

Antiphon and Opening Prayer

Let the favor of the Lord our God be upon us,
    and prosper for us the work of our hands —
    O prosper the work of our hands!   Psalm 90:17

Lord Jesus Christ, you who have called me to be your servant,
lead me in that path of your calling,
and give me the grace to remain faithful.

Scripture Reading

When we heard this, we and the people there urged him not to go
up to Jerusalem. Then Paul answered, "What are you doing, weeping
and breaking my heart? For I am ready not only to be bound but
even to die in Jerusalem for the name of the Lord Jesus." Since he
would not be persuaded, we remained silent except to say, "The
Lord's will be done."

Acts 21:12-14
optional: Judges 9:22-25, 50-57

Responsorial Psalm

Turn, O LORD! How long?
    Have compassion on your servants!
Satisfy us in the morning with your steadfast love,
    so that we may rejoice and be glad all our days.
Make us glad as many days as you have afflicted us,
    and as many years as we have seen evil.   Psalm 90:13-15

Prayers, pp. 529-32

Closing Psalm Prayer

Lord, you have been our dwelling place
    in all generations.
Before the mountains were brought forth,
    or ever you had formed the earth and the world,
    from everlasting to everlasting you are God.   Psalm 90:1-2

Week of the Sunday Closest to August 10   Sunday

Theme: Christ is not and cannot be divided. There is only one Christ,
        one church, one faith.

Antiphon and Opening Prayer

God is our refuge and strength,
    a very present help in trouble.
Therefore we will not fear.   Psalm 46:1-2a

O Lord God, you who called the church into being,
look on our divisions,
and cause us to turn from our judgmental spirit to your glory.

Scripture Reading

Paul . . . to the church of God that is in Corinth. . . . Now I appeal
to you, brothers and sisters, by the name of our Lord Jesus Christ,

that all of you be in agreement and that there be no divisions among you, but that you be united in the same mind and the same purpose. . . . What I mean is that each of you says, "I belong to Paul," or "I belong to Apollos," or "I belong to Cephas," or "I belong to Christ." Has Christ been divided?

I Corinthians 1:1a, 2a, 10, 12-13
optional: Judges 11:1-11, 29-40

Responsorial Psalm

There is a river whose streams make glad the city of God,
    the holy habitation of the Most High.
God is in the midst of the city; it shall not be moved;
    God will help it when the morning dawns.
The nations are in an uproar, the kingdoms totter;
    he utters his voice, the earth melts.   Psalm 46:4-6

Prayers, pp. 529-32

Closing Psalm Prayer

"Be still, and know that I am God!
    I am exalted among the nations,
    I am exalted in the earth."
The LORD of hosts is with us;
    the God of Jacob is our refuge.   Psalm 46:10-11

Week of the Sunday Closest to August 10   Monday

Theme: God is not known through intellectual arguments and syllo-
    gisms, but through the demonstration of his power.

Antiphon and Opening Prayer

I will sing of your steadfast love, O LORD, forever;
with my mouth I will proclaim your faithfulness to all generations.
Psalm 89:1

Lord, you who are full of mercy,
reveal yourself to me through the power of your cross and
resurrection,
to the glory of your name.

Scripture Reading

When I came to you, brothers and sisters, I did not come proclaiming
the mystery of God to you in lofty words or wisdom. For I decided
to know nothing among you except Jesus Christ, and him crucified.
And I came to you in weakness and in fear and in much trembling.
My speech and my proclamation were not with plausible words of
wisdom, but with a demonstration of the Spirit and of power.

I Corinthians 2:1-4
optional: Judges 12:1-7

Responsorial Psalm

O LORD God of hosts,
who is as mighty as you, O LORD?
Your faithfulness surrounds you.
You rule the raging of the sea;
when its waves rise, you still them.
You crushed Rahab like a carcass;
you scattered your enemies with your mighty arm.

Psalm 89:8-10

Prayers, pp. 529-32

Closing Psalm Prayer

The heavens are yours, the earth also is yours. . . .
You have a mighty arm;
strong is your hand, high your right hand.   Psalm 89:11a, 13

Week of the Sunday Closest to August 10   Tuesday

Theme: When we see ourselves and others in the light of God's greatness,
we gain a true perspective on our work for the Lord.

Antiphon and Opening Prayer

The LORD is king! Let the earth rejoice;
    let the many coastlands be glad!   Psalm 97:1

Lord, you who reign over all things and people,
receive my humble efforts in the work of your kingdom.

Scripture Reading

What then is Apollos? What is Paul? Servants through whom you
came to believe, as the Lord assigned to each. I planted, Apollos
watered, but God gave the growth. So neither the one who plants
nor the one who waters is anything, but only God who gives the
growth. The one who plants and the one who waters have a common
purpose, and each will receive wages according to the labor of each.
For we are God's servants, working together; you are God's field,
God's building.

I Corinthians 3:5-9
optional: Judges 13:1-15

Responsorial Psalm

The LORD is king! Let the earth rejoice. . . .
His lightnings light up the world;
    the earth sees and trembles.
The mountains melt like wax before the LORD,
    before the Lord of all the earth.
The heavens proclaim his righteousness;
    and all the peoples behold his glory.   Psalm 97:1a, 4-6

Prayers, pp. 529-32

Closing Psalm Prayer

> The LORD loves those who hate evil;
> > he guards the lives of his faithful. . . .
> Rejoice in the LORD, O you righteous,
> > and give thanks to his holy name!   Psalm 97:10a, 12

Week of the Sunday Closest to August 10   Wednesday

Theme: If we are to serve the Lord and do his work, we must commit
    ourselves to rigorous discipline.

Antiphon and Opening Prayer

> I will sing of loyalty and of justice;
> > to you, O LORD, I will sing.
>
> Lord, you who have set before me the prize of your high calling,
> turn me away from my self-indulgent life.
> Let me take up my cross and follow you.

Scripture Reading

> Do you not know that in a race the runners all compete, but only
> one receives the prize? Run in such a way that you may win it.
> Athletes exercise self-control in all things; they do it to receive a
> perishable wreath, but we an imperishable one. . . . But I punish my
> body and enslave it, so that after proclaiming to others I myself
> should not be disqualified.
> > I Corinthians 9:24-25, 27
> > optional: Judges 13:15-24

Responsorial Psalm

> I will study the way that is blameless.
> > When shall I attain it?
> I will walk with integrity of heart
> > within my house;

I will not set before my eyes
>   anything that is base. . . .
Perverseness of heart shall be far from me;
>   I will know nothing of evil.   Psalm 101:2-3a, 4

Prayers, pp. 529-32

Closing Psalm Prayer

I will look with favor on the faithful in the land,
>   so that they may live with me;
whoever walks in the way that is blameless
>   shall minister to me.   Psalm 101:6

Week of the Sunday Closest to August 10   Thursday

Theme: Of all the gifts that God could give us, the greatest and the one
>   we ought to desire most is the gift of love.

Antiphon and Opening Prayer

O give thanks to the LORD, call on his name,
>   make known his deeds among the peoples.   Psalm 105:1

O Lord, you are love and you have shown us how to love.
Give me the gift of a loving heart and a caring soul.

Scripture Reading

If I speak in the tongues of mortals and of angels, but do not have
love, I am a noisy gong or a clanging cymbal. And if I have prophetic
powers, and understand all mysteries and all knowledge, and if I
have all faith, so as to remove mountains, but do not have love, I
am nothing. If I give away all my possessions, and if I hand over my
body so that I may boast, but do not have love, I gain nothing.

> I Corinthians 13:1-3
> optional: Judges 14:1-19

Responsorial Psalm

Sing to him, sing praises to him;
> tell of all his wonderful works.

Glory in his holy name;
> let the hearts of those who seek the LORD rejoice.

Seek the LORD and his strength;
> seek his presence continually.

Remember the wonderful works he has done.   Psalm 105:2-5

Prayers, pp. 529-32

Closing Psalm Prayer

O offspring of his servant Abraham,
> children of Jacob, his chosen ones.

He is the LORD our God;
> his judgments are in all the earth.   Psalm 105:6-7

Week of the Sunday Closest to August 10   Friday

Theme: The love of God remains the same year after year even though
all else changes.

Antiphon and Opening Prayer

Hear my prayer, O LORD. . . .
Incline your ear to me;
> answer me speedily in the day when I call.   Psalm 102:1a, 2b

Lord, you who love me with an endless and enduring love,
give me a steady heart that I might love with your love.

Scripture Reading

Love is patient; love is kind; love is not envious or boastful or
arrogant or rude. It does not insist on its own way; it is not irritable
or resentful; it does not rejoice in wrongdoing, but rejoices in the

truth. It bears all things, believes all things, hopes all things, endures all things.

Love never ends. But as for prophecies, they will come to an end; as for tongues, they will cease; as for knowledge, it will come to an end.

I Corinthians 13:4-8
optional: Judges 14:20–15:20

Responsorial Psalm

Long ago you laid the foundation of the earth,
  and the heavens are the work of your hands.
They will perish, but you endure;
  they will all wear out like a garment.
You change them like clothing, and they pass away.

Psalm 102:25-26

Prayers, pp. 529-32

Closing Psalm Prayer

. . . But you are the same, and your years have no end.
The children of your servants shall live secure;
  their offspring shall be established in your presence.

Psalm 102:27-28

Week of the Sunday Closest to August 10   Saturday

Theme: All the enemies of God will be put under his feet, but he is merciful to those who trust in him.

Antiphon and Opening Prayer

O give thanks to the LORD, for he is good;
  for his steadfast love endures forever.   Psalm 107:1

O Lord my God, you who shatter your enemies,
turn me toward yourself,
and let me trust in your power to rule with equity.

Scripture Reading

For since death came through a human being, the resurrection of the
dead has also come through a human being; for as all die in Adam,
so all will be made alive in Christ. But each in his own order: Christ
the first fruits, then at his coming those who belong to Christ. Then
comes the end, when he hands over the kingdom of God to the
Father, after he has destroyed every ruler and every authority and
power. For he must reign until he has put all his enemies under his
feet.

I Corinthians 15:21-25
optional: Judges 16:1-14

Responsorial Psalm

Then they cried to the LORD in their trouble,
     and he saved them from their distress;
he brought them out of darkness and gloom,
and broke their bonds asunder.
Let them thank the LORD for his steadfast love. Psalm 107:13-15a

Prayers, pp. 529-32

Closing Psalm Prayer

Let the redeemed of the LORD say so,
     those he redeemed from trouble
and gathered in from the lands,
     from the east and from the west,
     from the north and from the south.   Psalm 107:2-3

Week of the Sunday Closest to August 17   Sunday

Theme: Our suffering is not an end in itself, but a way of participating
        in the sufferings of Christ.

Antiphon and Opening Prayer

I will extol you, my God and King,
    and bless your name forever and ever.   Psalm 145:1

Lord Jesus, you who suffered for me and for all people,
know my suffering and free me to praise your name.

Scripture Reading

Paul, an apostle of Jesus Christ. . . . To the Church of God that is
in Corinth. . . . Blessed be the God and Father of our Lord Jesus
Christ, the Father of mercies and the God of all consolation, who
consoles us in all our affliction, so that we may be able to console
those who are in any affliction with the consolation with which we
ourselves are consoled by God. For just as the sufferings of Christ
are abundant for us, so also our consolation is abundant through
Christ.

II Corinthians 1:1, 3-5
optional: Judges 16:15-31

Responsorial Psalm

All your works shall give thanks to you, O LORD,
    and all your faithful shall bless you.
They shall speak of the glory of your kingdom,
    and tell of your power,
to make known to all people your mighty deeds. . . .
Your kingdom is an everlasting kingdom,
    and your dominion endures throughout all generations.

Psalm 145:10-12a, 13

Prayers, pp. 529-32

Closing Psalm Prayer

> Every day I will bless you,
>   and praise your name forever and ever.
> Great is the LORD, and greatly to be praised;
>   his greatness is unsearchable.   Psalm 145:2-3

Week of the Sunday Closest to August 17   Monday

Theme: God has manifested his true self in the person of Christ, the
person whom we believe and follow.

Antiphon and Opening Prayer

> Praise to the LORD!
>   O give thanks to the LORD, for he is good;
>   for his steadfast love endures forever.   Psalm 106:1

> Father, you who sent your Son to reveal yourself,
> let your countenance shine upon me that I may glory in your
> name.

Scripture Reading

And even if our gospel is veiled, it is veiled to those who are perishing.
In their case the god of this world has blinded the minds of the
unbelievers, to keep them from seeing the light of the gospel of the
glory of Christ, who is the image of God. For we do not proclaim
ourselves; we proclaim Jesus Christ as Lord and ourselves as your
slaves for Jesus' sake. For it is the God who said, "Let light shine
out of darkness," who has shone in our hearts to give the light of
the knowledge of the glory of God in the face of Jesus Christ.

II Corinthians 4:3-6
optional: Judges 17:1-13

Responsorial Psalm

> Remember me, O LORD, when you show favor to your people;
>> help me when you deliver them;
> that I may see the prosperity of your chosen ones,
>> that I may rejoice in the gladness of your nation,
>> that I may glory in your heritage.   Psalm 106:4-5

Prayers, pp. 529-32

Closing Psalm Prayer

> Save us, O LORD our God,
>> and gather us from among the nations,
> that we may give thanks to your holy name
>> and glory in your praise.
> Blessed be the LORD, the God of Israel,
>> from everlasting to everlasting.   Psalm 106:47-48a

Week of the Sunday Closest to August 17   Tuesday

Theme: The problems and afflictions we have in life can result in
       strengthening our interior person if we allow this to happen.

Antiphon and Opening Prayer

> In my distress I cry to the LORD,
>> that he may answer me:
> "Deliver me, O LORD,
>> from lying lips,
>> from a deceitful tongue."   Psalm 120:1-2

> O Lord, my protector,
> in all that life brings,
> let me never lose my confidence in you.

Scripture Reading

So we do not lose heart. Even though our outer nature is wasting away, our inner nature is being renewed day by day. For this slight momentary affliction is preparing us for an eternal weight of glory beyond all measure, because we look not at what can be seen but at what cannot be seen; for what can be seen is temporary, but what cannot be seen is eternal.

II Corinthians 4:16-18
optional: Judges 18:1-15

Responsorial Psalm

He will not let your foot be moved;
    he who keeps you will not slumber.
He who keeps Israel
    will neither slumber nor sleep.
The LORD is your keeper;
    the LORD is your shade at your right hand.
The sun shall not strike you by day,
    nor the moon by night.

Psalm 121:3-6

Prayers, pp. 529-32

Closing Psalm Prayer

The LORD will keep you from all evil;
    he will keep your life.
The LORD will keep
    your going out and your coming in
    from this time on and forevermore.

Psalm 121:7-8

Week of the Sunday Closest to August 17   Wednesday

Theme: Although the judgment of God is sure, his mercy and love are our comfort and hope.

Antiphon and Opening Prayer

> Lord, hear my voice!
> Let your ears be attentive
> to the voice of my supplications! Psalm 130:2

> Lord, you who judge all persons for their sin and rebellion,
> turn toward me in your mercy and love
> and grant me your peace.

Scripture Reading

So whether we are at home or away, we make it our aim to please him. For all of us must appear before the judgment seat of Christ, so that each may receive recompense for what has been done in the body, whether good or evil.

Therefore, knowing the fear of the Lord, we try to persuade others; but we ourselves are well known to God, and I hope that we are also well known to your consciences.

> II Corinthians 5:9-11
> optional: Judges 18:16-31

Responsorial Psalm

> If you, O LORD, should mark iniquities,
> Lord, who could stand?
> But there is forgiveness with you,
> so that you may be revered.
> I wait for the LORD, my soul waits,
> and in his word I hope;
> my soul waits for the Lord. Psalm 130:3-6a

Prayers, pp. 529-32

Closing Psalm Prayer

> O Israel, hope in the LORD!
> For with the LORD there is steadfast love,
> and with him is great power to redeem.
> It is he who will redeem Israel
> from all its iniquities. Psalm 130:7-8

Week of the Sunday Closest to August 17   Thursday

Theme: God, by giving us his Son, has shown to all people the meaning
        of sacrificial giving.

Antiphon and Opening Prayer

"Let us go to his dwelling place;
    let us worship at his footstool."
Rise up, O LORD, and go to your resting place,
    you and the ark of your might.   Psalm 132:7-8

Lord God, you who gave your only Son to redeem the world,
work within me a spirit of generosity, to the glory of your name.

Scripture Reading

The point is this: the one who sows sparingly will also reap sparingly,
and the one who sows bountifully will also reap bountifully. Each
of you must give as you have made up your mind, not reluctantly
or under compulsion, for God loves a cheerful giver. And God is
able to provide you with every blessing in abundance, so that by
always having enough of everything, you may share abundantly in
every good work. . . . Thanks be to God for his indescribable gift!
        II Corinthians 9:6-8, 15
        optional: Job 1:1-22

Responsorial Psalm

O LORD, my heart is not lifted up,
    my eyes are not raised too high;
I do not occupy myself with things
    too great and too marvelous for me.
But I have calmed and quieted my soul,
    like a weaned child with its mother;
    my soul is like the weaned child that is with me.
        Psalm 131:1-2

Prayers, pp. 529-32

Closing Psalm Prayer

Praise the LORD!
> Praise the name of the LORD;
> > give praise, O servants of the LORD,
> you that stand in the house of the LORD,
> > in the courts of the house of our God,
Praise the LORD, for the LORD is good.   Psalm 135:1-3a

Week of the Sunday Closest to August 17   Friday

Theme: Our battle in this life is with the powers of evil that continually
> try to turn us from our commitment to Christ.

Antiphon and Opening Prayer

I call upon you, O LORD; come quickly to me;
> give ear to my voice when I call to you.   Psalm 141:1

Lord Jesus, you who overcame the power of the evil one at the
temptation,
give me grace to spurn the power of evil and turn to you in faith.

Scripture Reading

Indeed, we live as human beings, but we do not wage war according
to human standards; for the weapons of our warfare are not merely
human, but they have divine power to destroy strongholds. We
destroy arguments and every proud obstacle raised up against the
knowledge of God, and we take every thought captive to obey Christ.
We are ready to punish every disobedience when your obedience is
complete.

> II Corinthians 10:3-6
> optional: Job 2:1-13

Responsorial Psalm

Set a guard over my mouth, O LORD;
    keep watch over the door of my lips.
Do not turn my heart to any evil,
    to busy myself with wicked deeds
in company with those who work iniquity;
    do not let me eat of their delicacies.   Psalm 141:3-4

Prayers, pp. 529-32

Closing Psalm Prayer

But my eyes are turned toward you, O GOD, my Lord;
    in you I seek refuge; do not leave me defenseless.
Keep me from the trap that they have laid for me,
    and from the snares of evildoers.   Psalm 141:8-9

Week of the Sunday Closest to August 17   Saturday

Theme: Although we go through troubles and trials in this world, our
    ultimate response should be to praise God.

Antiphon and Opening Prayer

Bless the LORD, O my soul.
    O LORD my God, you are very great.
You are clothed with honor and majesty.   Psalm 104:1

Lord Jesus, you who suffered and died on the wood of the cross,
teach me to accept my trials with grace,
and let me praise your holy name.

Scripture Reading

Five times I have received from the Jews the forty lashes minus one.
Three times I was beaten with rods. Once I received a stoning. Three
times I was shipwrecked; for a night and a day I was adrift at sea;

on frequent journeys, in danger from rivers, danger from bandits,
danger from my own people, danger from the Gentiles, danger in
the city, danger in the wilderness, danger at sea, danger from false
brothers and sisters.

II Corinthians 11:24-26
optional: Job 32:1-26

Responsorial Psalm

You make springs gush forth in the valleys;
    they flow between the hills,
giving drink to every wild animal;
    the wild asses quench their thirst.
By the streams the birds of the air have their habitation;
    they sing among the branches.
From your lofty abode you water the mountains;
    the earth is satisfied with the fruit of your work.

Psalm 104:10-13

Prayers, pp. 529-32

Closing Psalm Prayer

I will sing to the LORD as long as I live;
    I will sing praise to my God while I have my being.
May my meditation be pleasing to him,
    for I rejoice in the LORD.   Psalm 104:33-34

Week of the Sunday Closest to August 24   Sunday

Theme: Salvation does not come from anything we do, but from the gift
    of God's righteousness through Jesus Christ.

Antiphon and Opening Prayer

I will praise the LORD as long as I live;
    I will sing praises to my God all my life long.   Psalm 146:2

Lord God, you who accept the righteousness of your Son Jesus
Christ,
be pleased to see me through him,
and grant me the gift of everlasting life.

Scripture Reading

Paul, a servant of Jesus Christ. . . . To all God's beloved in Rome. . . .

First, I thank my God through Jesus Christ for all of you, because
your faith is proclaimed throughout the world. . . . For I am not
ashamed of the gospel; for it is the power of God for salvation to
everyone who has faith, to the Jew first and also to the Greek. For
in it the righteousness of God is revealed through faith for faith; as
it is written, "The one who is righteous will live by faith."

Romans 1:1a, 7a, 8, 16-17
optional: Job 4:1-21

Responsorial Psalm

Happy are those whose help is the God of Jacob,
    whose hope is in the LORD their God,
who made heaven and earth,
    the sea, and all that is in them;
who keeps faith forever;
    who executes justice for the oppressed;
    who gives food to the hungry.
The LORD sets the prisoners free.   Psalm 146:5-7

Prayers, pp. 529-32

Closing Psalm Prayer

Do not put your trust in princes,
in mortals, in whom there is no help.
When their breath departs, they return to the earth;
    on that very day their plans perish.   Psalm 146:3-4

Week of the Sunday Closest to August 24   Monday

Theme: All God asks of us is simple faith and trust in the work of his
       Son on the cross.

Antiphon and Opening Prayer

Answer me when I call. . . .
Be gracious to me, and hear my prayer.   Psalm 4:1

Lord Jesus, you who died on the cross to save humankind from
sin,
teach me to rest in your work,
and to turn from my vain striving.

Scripture Reading

What then are we to say was gained by Abraham, our ancestor
according to the flesh? . . . For what does the scripture say?
"Abraham believed God, and it was reckoned to him as
righteousness." Now to one who works, wages are not reckoned as
a gift but as something due. But to one who without works trusts
him who justifies the ungodly, such faith is reckoned as righteousness.
                                              Romans 4:1, 3-5
                                              optional: Job 5:1-11

Responsorial Psalm

"Let the light of your face shine on us, O LORD!"
You have put gladness in my heart
     more than when their grain and wine abound.
I will both lie down and sleep in peace;
     for you alone, O LORD, make me lie down in safety.
                                              Psalm 4:6b-8

Prayers, pp. 529-32

Closing Psalm Prayer

When you are disturbed, do not sin;
> ponder it on your beds, and be silent.
Offer right sacrifices,
> and put your trust in the LORD.   Psalm 4:4-5

Week of the Sunday Closest to August 24   Tuesday

Theme: Our choice to believe in and follow Jesus is no mere intellectual
decision, but a life-changing event.

Antiphon and Opening Prayer

Give ear to my words, O LORD;
> give heed to my sighing.
Listen to the sound of my cry.   Psalm 5:1-2a

Lord God, you who give peace to those who follow you,
work in my heart and life those virtues that are becoming to your
children,
to your glory.

Scripture Reading

Therefore, since we are justified by faith, we have peace with God
through our Lord Jesus Christ, through whom we have obtained
access to this grace in which we stand; and we boast in our hope of
sharing the glory of God. And not only that, but we also boast in
our sufferings, knowing that suffering produces endurance, and
endurance produces character, and character produces hope, and
hope does not disappoint us, because God's love has been poured
into our hearts through the Holy Spirit that has been given to us.
                                          Romans 5:1-5
                                      optional: Job 6:1-15

Responsorial Psalm

But let all who take refuge in you rejoice;
> let them ever sing for joy.
Spread your protection over them,
> so that those who love your name may exult in you.
For you bless the righteous, O LORD;
> you cover them with favor as with a shield.   Psalm 5:11-12

Prayers, pp. 529-32

Closing Psalm Prayer

Listen to the sound of my cry,
> my King and my God,
> for to you I pray.
O LORD, in the morning you hear my voice;
> in the morning I plead my case to you, and watch.

Psalm 5:2-3

Week of the Sunday Closest to August 24   Wednesday

Theme: Our baptism into Jesus is a symbol of our death to sin and our
> birth to the resurrected life.

Antiphon and Opening Prayer

O LORD, who may abide in your tent?
> Who may dwell on your holy hill?   Psalm 15:1

Lord God Almighty, you who gave your Son in death to redeem
the human race from sin,
cause me to live in my baptism by turning from sin to
righteousness.

Scripture Reading

What then are we to say? Should we continue in sin in order that grace may abound? By no means! How can we who died to sin go on living in it? Do you not know that all of us who have been baptized into Christ Jesus were baptized into his death? Therefore we have been buried with him by baptism into death, so that, just as Christ was raised from the dead by the glory of the Father, so we too might walk in newness of life.

Romans 6:1-4
optional: Job 7:1-21

Responsorial Psalm

Those who walk blamelessly, and do what is right,
    and speak the truth from their heart;
who do not slander with their tongue,
    and do no evil to their friends,
      nor take up a reproach against their neighbors.   Psalm 15:2-3

Prayers, pp. 529-32

Closing Psalm Prayer

But I trusted in your steadfast love;
    my heart shall rejoice in your salvation.
I will sing to the LORD,
    because he has dealt bountifully with me.   Psalm 13:5-6

Week of the Sunday Closest to August 24   Thursday

Theme: The law of God shows us the exceeding sinfulness of our sin and drives us to Christ, our only hope.

Antiphon and Opening Prayer

I love you, O LORD, my strength.
The LORD is my rock, my fortress, and my deliverer.

Psalm 18:1-2a

O Lord Jesus, you who took on yourself my penalty for breaking the law,
let me turn from the works of the flesh,
and live by your Spirit.

Scripture Reading

There is therefore now no condemnation for those who are in Christ Jesus. For the law of the Spirit of life in Christ Jesus has set you free from the law of sin and death. For God has done what the law, weakened by the flesh, could not do: by sending his own Son in the likeness of sinful flesh, and to deal with sin, he condemned sin in the flesh.

Romans 8:1-3
optional: Job 8:1-10

Responsorial Psalm

It is you who light my lamp;
  the LORD, my God, lights up my darkness.
By you I can crush a troop,
  and by my God I can leap over a wall.
This God — his way is perfect;
  the promise of the LORD proves true;
  he is a shield for all who take refuge in him.   Psalm 18:28-30

Prayers, pp. 529-32

Closing Psalm Prayer

The LORD is my rock, my fortress, and my deliverer,
  my God, my rock in whom I take refuge,
  my shield, and the horn of my salvation, my stronghold.
I call upon the LORD, who is worthy to be praised.

Psalm 18:2-3a

Week of the Sunday Closest to August 24   Friday

Theme: Sometimes we cannot identify the longing that is deep within
our hearts, but the Spirit can and does.

Antiphon and Opening Prayer

Hear a just cause, O LORD; attend to my cry;
give ear to my prayer from lips free of deceit.   Psalm 17:1

Lord Jesus, you who cried from the depths of your soul on the
cross,
turn your ear toward me,
hear my cries and answer me for your name's sake.

Scripture Reading

Likewise the Spirit helps in our weakness; for we do not know how
to pray as we ought, but that very Spirit intercedes with sighs too
deep for words. And God, who searches the heart, knows what is
the mind of the Spirit, because the Spirit intercedes for the saints
according to the will of God.

We know that all things work together for good for those who
love God, who are called according to his purpose.

Romans 8:26-28
optional: Job 9:1-15

Responsorial Psalm

I call upon you, for you will answer me, O God;
incline your ear to me, hear my words.
Wondrously show your steadfast love,
O savior of those who seek refuge
from their adversaries at your right hand.   Psalm 17:6-7

Prayers, pp. 529-32

Closing Psalm Prayer

> Guard me as the apple of the eye;
> > hide me in the shadow of your wings,
> from the wicked who despoil me,
> > my deadly enemies who surround me.   Psalm 17:8-9

Week of the Sunday Closest to August 24   Saturday

Theme: We are called to shun the goals and ambitions of worldly people
        and to present our whole lives as a sacrifice to God.

Antiphon and Opening Prayer

> Happy are those who fear the LORD,
> who greatly delight in his commandments.   Psalm 112:1

> Lord Jesus, you who turned from seeking power
> and gave up all worldly ambition,
> turn me toward a life of self-giving to your glory.

Scripture Reading

> For from him and through him and to him are all things. To him be
> the glory forever. Amen.
> > I appeal to you therefore, brothers and sisters, by the mercies of
> God, to present your bodies as a living sacrifice, holy and acceptable
> to God, which is your spiritual worship. Do not be conformed to
> this world, but be transformed by the renewing of your minds, so
> that you may discern what is the will of God — what is good and
> acceptable and perfect.
> > Romans 11:36; 12:1-2
> > optional: Job 10:1-9

Responsorial Psalm

> Praise the LORD!
> > Happy are those who fear the LORD. . . .

Their descendants will be mighty in the land;
    the generation of the upright will be blessed.
Wealth and riches are in their houses,
    and their righteousness endures forever.
They rise in the darkness as a light for the upright.

Psalm 112:1a, 2-4a

Prayers, pp. 529-32

Closing Psalm Prayer

    Happy are those who fear the LORD. . . .
They are not afraid of evil tidings;
    their hearts are firm, secure in the LORD.
Their hearts are steady, they will not be afraid.

Psalm 112:1a, 7-8a

Week of the Sunday Closest to August 31   Sunday

Theme: After Paul's third missionary journey he returned to Jerusalem
       where he was soon put into prison and later sent to Rome.

Antiphon and Opening Prayer

    Not to us, O LORD, not to us, but to your name give glory,
        for the sake of your steadfast love and your faithfulness.

Psalm 115:1

    O Lord, you who guide your servants and watch over them in
peril,
watch over my life and guide me in the path you would have me
take.

Scripture Reading

    After these days we got ready and started to go up to Jerusalem. . . .
       The next day Paul went with us to visit James; and all the elders

were present. After greeting them, he related one by one the things that God had done among the Gentiles through his ministry. When they heard it, they praised God. Then they said to him, "You see, brother, how many thousands of believers there are among the Jews, and they are all zealous for the law."

Acts 21:15, 18-20
optional: Job 11:1-9

Responsorial Psalm

Our God is in the heavens;
    he does whatever he pleases.
Their idols are silver and gold,
    the work of human hands.
They have mouths, but do not speak;
    eyes, but do not see.
They have ears, but do not hear,
    noses, but do not smell.   Psalm 115:3-6

Prayers, pp. 529-32

Closing Psalm Prayer

The LORD has been mindful of us; he will bless us;
    he will bless the house of Israel;
    he will bless the house of Aaron;
he will bless those who fear the LORD,
    both small and great.   Psalm 115:12-13

Week of the Sunday Closest to August 31   Monday

Theme: The preaching of the gospel is not always met with success, but God himself remains King regardless of the response.

Antiphon and Opening Prayer

The earth is the LORD's and all that is in it,
    the world, and those who live in it.   Psalm 24:1

O Lord God, you who are the King of the universe,
you who rule over all that you have made,
rule in my heart and life to your glory.

Scripture Reading

While they were trying to kill him, word came to the tribune of the
cohort that all Jerusalem was in an uproar. Immediately he took
soldiers and centurions and ran down to them. When they saw the
tribune and the soldiers, they stopped beating Paul. Then the tribune
came, arrested him, and ordered him to be bound with two chains;
he inquired who he was and what he had done.

Acts 21:31-33
optional: Job 12:1-6

Responsorial Psalm

Who shall ascend the hill of the LORD?
And who shall stand in his holy place?
Those who have clean hands and pure hearts,
who do not lift up their souls to what is false,
and do not swear deceitfully.
They will receive blessing from the LORD,
and vindication from the God of their salvation.

Psalm 24:3-5

Prayers, pp. 529-32

Closing Psalm Prayer

Lift up your heads, O gates!
and be lifted up, O ancient doors!
that the King of glory may come in.
Who is the King of glory?
The LORD, strong and mighty,
the LORD, mighty in battle.

Psalm 24:7-8

Week of the Sunday Closest to August 31   Tuesday

Theme: Even though we walk with integrity toward the Lord, our message and person will not always be received.

Antiphon and Opening Prayer

Vindicate me, O LORD,
   for I have walked in my integrity,
   and I have trusted in the LORD without wavering.   Psalm 26:1

O God my Father, you whose Son walked with integrity yet was
despised and rejected by people,
let me stand fast in your truth and service, to your praise.

Scripture Reading

. . . Paul stood on the steps and motioned to the people for
silence. . . . He addressed them . . . , saying:
   "Brothers and fathers, listen to the defense that I now make
before you."
   When they heard him addressing them in Hebrew, they became
even more quiet. . . .
   Up to this point they listened to him, but then they shouted,
"Away with such a fellow from the earth! For he should not be
allowed to live!"

Acts 21:40–22:1-2, 22
optional: Job 13:3-17

Responsorial Psalm

Prove me, O LORD, and try me;
   test my heart and mind.
For your steadfast love is before my eyes,
   and I walk in faithfulness to you.
I do not sit with the worthless,
   nor do I consort with hypocrites;

I hate the company of evildoers,
    and will not sit with the wicked.   Psalm 26:2-5

Prayers, pp. 529-32

Closing Psalm Prayer

But as for me, I walk in my integrity;
    redeem me, and be gracious to me.
My foot stands on level ground;
    in the great congregation I will bless the LORD.

                                                      Psalm 26:11-12

Week of the Sunday Closest to August 31   Wednesday

Theme: Even though our own consciences are clear before God and
    people, there are some who will always accuse us of wrong.

Antiphon and Opening Prayer

O LORD, do not rebuke me in your anger,
    or discipline me in your wrath.   Psalm 38:1

O Lord, your Son endured the hardship of being misunderstood
and reviled.
Look upon me your servant and grant me peace in spite of my
accusers.

Scripture Reading

Since he wanted to find out what Paul was being accused of by the
Jews, the next day he released him and ordered the chief priests and
the entire council to meet. He brought Paul down and had him stand
before them.

While Paul was looking intently at the council he said, "Brothers,
up to this day I have lived my life with a clear conscience before

God." Then the high priest Ananias ordered those standing near him
to strike him on the mouth.

Acts 22:30; 23:1-2
optional: Job 14:1-22

Responsorial Psalm

> I am utterly bowed down and prostrate;
>> all day long I go around mourning.
> For my loins are filled with burning,
>> and there is no soundness in my flesh.
> I am utterly spent and crushed;
>> I groan because of the tumult of my heart. Psalm 38:6-8

Prayers, pp. 529-32

Closing Psalm Prayer

> O LORD, do not rebuke me in your anger. . . .
> Do not forsake me, O LORD;
>> O my God, do not be far from me;
> make haste to help me,
>> O Lord, my salvation. Psalm 38:1a, 21-22

Week of the Sunday Closest to August 31 Thursday

Theme: Paul had every reason to be bitter over his jail sentence, con-
sidering how he served Christ with distinction and enthusiasm.

Antiphon and Opening Prayer

> Trust in the LORD, and do good. . . .
> Take delight in the LORD,
>> and he will give you the desires of your heart.

Psalm 37:3a, 4

Lord Jesus Christ, you who had nowhere to lay your head,
teach me not to expect creaturely comforts as a reward of
following you,
to your glory.

Scripture Reading

Some days later when Felix came with his wife Drusilla, who was
Jewish, he sent for Paul and heard him speak concerning faith in
Christ Jesus. And as he discussed justice, self-control, and the coming
judgment, Felix became frightened and said, "Go away for the
present; when I have an opportunity, I will send for you." . . .

After two years had passed, Felix was succeeded by Porcius
Festus; and since he wanted to grant the Jews a favor, Felix left Paul
in prison.

Acts 24:24-25, 27
optional: Job 16:16-22

Responsorial Psalm

Be still before the LORD, and wait patiently for him;
    do not fret over those who prosper in their way,
    over those who carry out evil devices.
Refrain from anger, and forsake wrath.
    Do not fret — it leads only to evil.
Psalm 37:7-8

Prayers, pp. 529-32

Closing Psalm Prayer

Commit your way to the LORD;
    trust in him, and he will act.
He will make your vindication shine like the light,
    and the justice of your cause like the noonday.
Psalm 37:5-7

Week of the Sunday Closest to August 31　　　　Friday

Theme: For years Paul had wanted to go to Rome. Now he was being
　　　 sent as a prisoner.

Antiphon and Opening Prayer

In you, O LORD, I seek refuge. . . .
Be a rock of refuge for me,
　　a strong fortress to save me.　　　　　　　　Psalm 31:1a, 2b

O Lord God, you who control the destinies of all people,
work your will in the events of my life to bring glory to your
name.

Scripture Reading

When it was decided that we were to sail for Italy, they transferred
Paul and some other prisoners to a centurion of the Augustan Cohort,
named Julius. Embarking on a ship of Adramyttium that was about
to set sail. . . .
　　Since much time had been lost and sailing was now dangerous,
because even the Fast had already gone by, Paul advised them, saying,
"Sirs, I can see that the voyage will be with danger and much heavy
loss, not only of the cargo and the ship, but also of our lives."

　　　　　　　　　　　　　　　　　　　　　　Acts 27:1-2a, 9-10
　　　　　　　　　　　　　　　　　　　　　　optional: Job 19:1-7

Responsorial Psalm

You are indeed my rock and my fortress;
　　for your name's sake lead me and guide me,
take me out of the net that is hidden for me,
　　for you are my refuge.
Into your hand I commit my spirit;
　　you have redeemed me, O LORD, faithful God.　　Psalm 31:3-5

Prayers, pp. 529-32

Closing Psalm Prayer

Love the LORD, all you his saints.
The LORD preserves the faithful. . . .
Be strong, and let your heart take courage,
all you who wait for the LORD. Psalm 31:23, 24

Week of the Sunday Closest to August 31 Saturday

Theme: When God purposes to do a work through us, that work will
be accomplished despite the obstacles.

Antiphon and Opening Prayer

Happy are those to whom the LORD imputes no iniquity,
and in whose spirit there is no deceit. Psalm 32:2

O Lord, my God and Maker,
you who watch over the designs of our lives,
guide my coming and my going to your glory.

Scripture Reading

But striking a reef, they ran the ship aground. . . . The soldiers' plan
was to kill the prisoners, so that none might swim away and escape;
but the centurion, wishing to save Paul, kept them from carrying out
their plan. He ordered those who could swim to jump overboard
first and make for the land, and the rest to follow, some on planks
and others on pieces of the ship. And so it was that all were brought
safely to land.

Acts 27:41a, 42-44
optional: Job 22:1-21

Responsorial Psalm

I will instruct you and teach you the way you should go;
I will counsel you with my eye upon you.

Do not be like a horse or a mule, without understanding,
    whose temper must be curbed with bit and bridle,
    else it will not stay near you.   Psalm 32:8-9

Prayers, pp. 529-32

Closing Psalm Prayer

But steadfast love surrounds those who trust in the LORD.
Be glad in the LORD and rejoice, O righteous,
and shout for joy, all you upright in heart.   Psalm 32:10b-11

Week of the Sunday Closest to September 7   Sunday

Theme: Regardless of the problems we face in this life, the proper
    response to life — because of God's work for us — is "Bless the
    LORD, O my soul!"

Antiphon and Opening Prayer

Bless the LORD, O my soul,
    and all that is within me,
        bless his holy name.   Psalm 103:1

Lord God Almighty, you who fill the earth with your presence
and bless your creation,
turn my heart to sing your praise forever.

Scripture Reading

Paul, an apostle of Jesus Christ . . . ,
    To the saints who are in Ephesus . . . :
        . . . Blessed be the God and Father of our Lord Jesus Christ,
who has blessed us in Christ with every spiritual blessing in heavenly
places. . . . In him we have redemption through his blood, the
forgiveness of our trespasses, according to the riches of his grace. . . .
In Christ we have also obtained an inheritance, having been destined

according to the purpose of him who accomplishes all things according to his counsel and will, so that we, who were first to set our hope on Christ, might live for the praise of his glory.

Ephesians 1:1, 3, 7, 11-12
optional: Job 25:1-6

Responsorial Psalm

Bless the LORD, O my soul,
   and do not forget all his benefits —
who forgives all your iniquity,
   who heals all your diseases,
who redeems your life from the Pit,
   who crowns you with steadfast love and mercy,
who satisfies you with good as long as you live
   so that your youth is renewed like the eagle's.   Psalm 103:2-5

Prayers, pp. 529-32

Closing Psalm Prayer

Bless the LORD, O you his angels,
   you mighty ones who do his bidding,
   obedient to his spoken word. . . .
Bless the Lord, all his works,
   in all places of his dominion.
Bless the LORD, O my soul.   Psalm 103:20, 22

Week of the Sunday Closest to September 7   Monday

Theme: God's work of salvation within us is done completely by him
      and is dependent on nothing that we do.

Antiphon and Opening Prayer

For God alone my soul waits in silence;
   from him comes my salvation.
He alone is my rock and my salvation.   Psalm 62:1-2a

Lord God, you who call us by your grace out of sin,
turn me from the course of this world,
and direct my paths in obedience to your will.

Scripture Reading

You were dead through the trespasses and sins in which you once lived, following the course of this world, following the ruler of the power of the air, the spirit that is now at work among those who are disobedient. . . . But God, who is rich in mercy, out of the great love with which he loved us even when we were dead through our trespasses, made us alive together with Christ — by grace you have been saved.

Ephesians 2:1-2, 4-5
optional: Job 27:1-6

Responsorial Psalm

For God alone my soul waits in silence,
    for my hope is from him.
He alone is my rock and my salvation,
    my fortress; I shall not be shaken.
On God rests my deliverance and my honor;
    my mighty rock, my refuge is in God.   Psalm 62:5-7

Prayers, pp. 529-32

Closing Psalm Prayer

Trust in him at all times, O people;
    pour out your heart before him;
    God is a refuge for us. . . .
    Twice have I heard this:
that power belongs to God.   Psalm 62:8, 11b

Week of the Sunday Closest to September 7   Tuesday

Theme: Our extreme individualism has no place in the church, where, with others, we are members together in the body of Christ.

Antiphon and Opening Prayer

Clap your hands, all you peoples;
    shout to God with loud songs of joy.   Psalm 47:1

O Lord, you who called the church into being
and who fill every part of it with your Spirit,
create in me a spirit of belonging to your universal body.

Scripture Reading

So then you are no longer strangers and aliens, but you are citizens with the saints and also members of the household of God, built upon the foundation of the apostles and prophets, with Christ Jesus himself as the cornerstone. In him the whole structure is joined together and grows into a holy temple in the Lord; in whom you also are built together spiritually into a dwelling place for God.

Ephesians 2:19-22

optional: Job 29:11-20

Responsorial Psalm

God has gone up with a shout,
    the LORD with the sound of a trumpet.
Sing praises to God, sing praises;
    sing praises to our King, sing praises.
For God is the king of all the earth;
    sing praises with a psalm.
God is king over the nations.   Psalm 47:5-8a

Prayers, pp. 529-32

Closing Psalm Prayer

For the LORD, the Most High, is awesome,
a great king over all the earth.
He subdued peoples under us,
and nations under our feet. . . .
He is highly exalted.

Psalm 47:2-3, 9b

Week of the Sunday Closest to September 7   Wednesday

Theme: No matter how diligently we seek to stay on course, we stray
again and again from our calling in Christ.

Antiphon and Opening Prayer

With my whole heart I cry; answer me, O LORD.
I will keep your statutes.

Psalm 119:145

O Lord, you have instructed us through your words
and you lead us into the path of truth.
Turn my heart toward loving you and keeping your precepts.

Scripture Reading

I therefore, the prisoner in the Lord, beg you to lead a life worthy
of the calling to which you have been called, with all humility and
gentleness, with patience, bearing with one another in love, making
every effort to maintain the unity of the Spirit in the bond of peace.
There is one body and one Spirit, just as you were called to the one
hope of your calling, one Lord, one faith, one baptism, one God and
Father of all, who is above all and through all and in all.

Ephesians 4:1-6
optional: Job 30:1-2, 6-31

Responsorial Psalm

I cry to you; save me,
that I may observe your decrees.

I rise before dawn and cry for help.
    I put my hope in your words.
My eyes are awake before each watch of the night,
    that I may meditate on your promise.
In your steadfast love hear my voice;
    O Lord, in your justice preserve my life.   Psalm 119:146-149

Prayers, pp. 529-32

Closing Psalm Prayer

Preserve my life according to your steadfast love.
The sum of your word is truth;
    and every one of your righteous ordinances endures forever.
                                   Psalm 119:159b-160

Week of the Sunday Closest to September 7   Thursday

Theme: When we walk according to the teaching of Christ and fulfill
     his will for our lives we bring glory to his name.

Antiphon and Opening Prayer

O sing to the LORD a new song;
    sing to the LORD, all the earth.
Sing to the LORD, bless his name.   Psalm 96:1-2a

O Lord God, you who made the heavens and the earth
and cause the birds to sing,
turn my feet to walk in the path of your will
and let me sing your praises.

Scripture Reading

. . . You must no longer live as the Gentiles live. . . .
    So then, putting away falsehood, let all of us speak the truth to
our neighbors, for we are members of one another. Be angry but do

not sin; do not let the sun go down on your anger. . . . Put away from you all bitterness and wrath and anger and wrangling and slander, together with all malice, and be kind to one another, tenderhearted, forgiving one another, as God in Christ has forgiven you.

Ephesians 4:17b, 25-26, 31-32
optional: Job 31:1-23

Responsorial Psalm

Sing to the LORD, bless his name;
    tell of his salvation from day to day.
Declare his glory among the nations,
    his marvelous works among all the peoples.
For great is the LORD, and greatly to be praised.   Psalm 96:2-4

Prayers, pp. 529-32

Closing Psalm Prayer

The Lord made the heavens.
Honor and majesty are before him;
    strength and beauty are in his sanctuary.
Ascribe to the Lord glory and strength.
Ascribe to the Lord the glory due his name.

adapted from Psalm 96:5-8

Week of the Sunday Closest to September 7   Friday

Theme: When we turn from the Lord and fall away from his teaching, our return to him begins with a broken spirit and contrite heart.

Antiphon and Opening Prayer

Have mercy on me, O God,
    according to your steadfast love;

according to your abundant mercy
    blot out my transgressions.   Psalm 51:1

O Lord God, you who have called your people into righteousness,
receive my cry of repentance,
and turn me to walk in your ways through all my life.

Scripture Reading

Be careful then how you live, not as unwise people but as wise,
making the most of the time, because the days are evil. . . . Be filled
with the Spirit, as you sing psalms and hymns and spiritual songs
among yourselves, singing and making melody to the Lord in your
hearts, giving thanks to God the Father at all times and for everything
in the name of our Lord Jesus Christ.

Ephesians 5:15-16, 18b-21
optional: Job 31:24-40

Responsorial Psalm

Indeed, I was born guilty,
    a sinner when my mother conceived me.
You desire truth in the inward being;
    therefore teach me wisdom in my secret heart.
Purge me with hyssop, and I shall be clean;
    wash me, and I shall be whiter than snow.   Psalm 51:5-7

Prayers, pp. 529-32

Closing Psalm Prayer

O Lord, open my lips,
    and my mouth will declare your praise. . . .
The sacrifice acceptable to God is a broken spirit;
    a broken and contrite heart, O God, you will not despise.

Psalm 51:15, 17

Week of the Sunday Closest to September 7   Saturday

Theme: The power of evil is real and attacks us from every side, attempting to draw us into its clutches.

Antiphon and Opening Prayer

Give ear to my prayer, O God;
   do not hide yourself from my supplication.   Psalm 55:1

Lord God, you whose only Son has overcome the power of evil
by the cross,
turn me to faith in him
and grant me deliverance from the powers of evil.

Scripture Reading

Finally, be strong in the Lord and in the strength of his power. . . .
For our struggle is not against enemies of blood and flesh, but against
the rulers, against the authorities, against the cosmic powers of this
present darkness, against the spiritual forces of evil in the heavenly
places. Therefore take up the whole armor of God, so that you may
be able to withstand on that evil day, and having done everything,
to stand firm. . . .
   Grace be with all who have an undying love for our Lord Jesus
Christ.
                                             Ephesians 6:10, 12-13, 24
                                             optional: Job 38:1-17

Responsorial Psalm

My heart is in anguish within me,
   the terrors of death have fallen upon me.
And I say, "O that I had wings like a dove!
   I would fly away and be at rest;
truly, I would flee far away;
   I would lodge in the wilderness;
I would hurry to find a shelter for myself
   from the raging wind and tempest."   Psalm 55:4, 6-8

Prayers, pp. 529-32

Closing Psalm Prayer

But I call upon God,
    and the LORD will save me.
Evening and morning and at noon
    I utter my complaint and moan,
    and he will hear my voice.
He will redeem me unharmed
    from the battle that I wage.   Psalm 55:16-18a

Week of the Sunday Closest to September 14   Sunday

Theme: God's word, when it is allowed to do its work ·in one person's
    life, will change many lives and bring forth fruit.

Antiphon and Opening Prayer

Sing praises to the LORD, O you his faithful ones,
    and give thanks to his holy name.   Psalm 30:4

O Lord my God, you who revealed yourself and your will for all
humankind,
turn me to do your will, to your praise and glory.

Scripture Reading

Paul, an apostle of Jesus Christ. . . .
    To the saints and faithful brothers and sisters in Christ in
Colossae: . . .
    In our prayers for you we always thank God, the Father of our
Lord Jesus Christ, for we have heard of your faith in Christ Jesus and
of the love that you have for all the saints, because of the hope laid up
for you in heaven. You have heard of this hope before in the word of
the truth, the gospel that has come to you. Just as it is bearing fruit and

growing in the whole world, so it has been bearing fruit among
yourselves from the day you heard it and truly comprehended the grace
of God.

Colossians 1:1a, 2a, 3-6
optional: Job 38:18-41

Responsorial Psalm

Ascribe to the LORD, O heavenly beings,
    ascribe to the LORD glory and strength.
Ascribe to the LORD the glory of his name;
    worship the LORD in holy splendor.   Psalm 29:1-2

Prayers, pp. 529-32

Closing Psalm Prayer

The LORD sits enthroned over the flood;
    the LORD sits enthroned as king forever.
May the LORD give strength to his people!
    may the LORD bless his people with peace.   Psalm 29:10-11

Week of the Sunday Closest to September 14   Monday

Theme: God calls us to a life that is worthy of the name "Christian,"
    which we bear.

Antiphon and Opening Prayer

Make a joyful noise to God, all the earth;
    sing the glory of his name.   Psalm 66:1-2a

O Lord Jesus, you who left an example for all to follow,
let me walk in your ways
and do your will to your praise and glory.

Scripture Reading

For this reason, since the day we heard it, we have not ceased praying for you and asking that you may be filled with the knowledge of God's will in all spiritual wisdom and understanding, so that you may lead lives worthy of the Lord, fully pleasing to him, as you bear fruit in every good work and as you grow in the knowledge of God. May you be made strong with all the strength that comes from his glorious power, and may you be prepared to endure everything with patience.

Colossians 1:9-11
optional: Job 40:1-24

Responsorial Psalm

For you, O God, have tested us;
    you have tried us as silver is tried.
You brought us into the net;
    you laid burdens on our backs;
you let people ride over our heads;
    we went through fire and through waters;
yet you have brought us out to a spacious place.   Psalm 66:10-12

Prayers, pp. 529-32

Closing Psalm Prayer

Come and hear, all you who fear God,
    and I will tell you what he has done for me. . . .
Blessed be God,
    because he has not rejected my prayer
    or removed his steadfast love from me.   Psalm 66:16, 20

Week of the Sunday Closest to September 14   Tuesday

Theme: Christ is not only at the center of God's plan for the world, but is the One around whom all things revolve.

Antiphon and Opening Prayer

But let the righteous be joyful;
　　let them exult before God;
　　let them be jubilant with joy.　　　　　　　Psalm 68:3

Christ Jesus, you who are the glory of your Father,
you in whom all things consist,
I flee to you.
You are greatly to be praised.

Scripture Reading

For in him all the fullness of God was pleased to dwell, and through
him God was pleased to reconcile to himself all things, whether on
earth or in heaven, by making peace through the blood of his cross.
　　And you who were once estranged and hostile in mind, doing
evil deeds, he has now reconciled in his fleshly body through death,
so as to present you holy and blameless and irreproachable before
him.

　　　　　　　　　　　　　　　　　　　　Colossians 1:19-22
　　　　　　　　　　　　　　　　　　　　optional: Job 41:1-11

Responsorial Psalm

Your solemn processions are seen, O God,
　　the processions of my God, my King, into the sanctuary —
the singers in front, the musicians last,
　　between them girls playing tambourines:
"Bless God in the great congregation,
　　the LORD, O you who are of Israel's fountain!"

　　　　　　　　　　　　　　　　　　　　　　Psalm 68:24-26

Prayers, pp. 529-32

Closing Psalm Prayer

Ascribe power to God,
　　whose majesty is over Israel;
　　and whose power is in the skies.
Awesome is God in his sanctuary.　　　　　　Psalm 68:34-35a

Week of the Sunday Closest to September 14   Wednesday

Theme: The power of God is shown in Christ, who by his death has destroyed the powers of evil.

Antiphon and Opening Prayer

May all kings fall down before him,
    all nations give him service.
For he delivers the needy when they call.   Psalm 72:11-12a

Lord Jesus, you who by your death sent the powers of evil into flight,
release me from the influence of evil and direct my paths.

Scripture Reading

And when you were dead in trespasses and the uncircumcision of your flesh, God made you alive together with him, when he forgave us all our trespasses, erasing the record that stood against us with its legal demands. He set this aside, nailing it to the cross. He disarmed the rulers and authorities and made a public example of them, triumphing over them in it.

Colossians 2:13-15
optional: Job 42:1-17

Responsorial Psalm

May he judge your people with righteousness,
    and your poor with justice.
May the mountains yield prosperity for the people,
    and the hills, in righteousness.
May he defend the cause of the poor of the people,
    give deliverance to the needy,
    and crush the oppressor.   Psalm 72:2-4

Prayers, pp. 529-32

Closing Psalm Prayer

> He has pity on the weak and the needy,
>   and saves the lives of the needy.
> From oppression and violence he redeems their life;
>   and precious is their blood in his sight.   Psalm 72:13-14

Week of the Sunday Closest to September 14   Thursday

Theme: In Christ we are called to turn our backs on evil and live lives
in pursuit of God.

Antiphon and Opening Prayer

> In you, O LORD, I take refuge;
>   let me never be put to shame.
>   For you are my rock and my fortress.   Psalm 71:1, 3b

Lord Jesus Christ, you who did the will of your Father
and redeemed humanity from sin,
keep my mind and heart on the things of the spirit.

Scripture Reading

So if you have been raised with Christ, seek the things that are above,
where Christ is, seated at the right hand of God. Set your minds on
things that are above, not on things that are on earth, for you have
died, and your life is hidden with Christ in God. When Christ who
is your life is revealed, then you also will be revealed with him in
glory.

Put to death, therefore, whatever in you is earthly: fornication,
impurity, passion, evil desire, and greed (which is idolatry).

Colossians 3:1-5
optional: Job 28:1-28

Responsorial Psalm

> Rescue me, O my God, from the hand of the wicked,
>> from the grasp of the unjust and cruel.
> For you, O Lord, are my hope,
>> my trust, O LORD, from my youth.
> Upon you I have leaned from my birth;
>> it was you who took me from my mother's womb.
> My praise is continually of you.   Psalm 71:4-6

Prayers, pp. 529-32

Closing Psalm Prayer

> My lips will shout for joy
>> when I sing praises to you;
>> my soul also, which you have rescued.
> All day long my tongue will talk of your righteous help.
>
>   Psalm 71:23-24a

Week of the Sunday Closest to September 14   Friday

Theme: Those who have faith in Christ are called to put off the works
of the flesh and to put on the Spirit of Christ.

Antiphon and Opening Prayer

> Truly God is good to the upright,
>> to those who are pure in heart. . . .
> I have made the Lord GOD my refuge.   Psalm 73:1, 28b

Lord Jesus Christ, you who showed us what it means to live by
the Spirit,
help me to cast off the works of darkness and walk in the light.

Scripture Reading

As God's chosen ones, holy and beloved, clothe yourselves with compassion, kindness, humility, meekness, and patience. Bear with one another and . . . forgive each other. . . . Above all, clothe yourselves with love. . . . And let the peace of Christ rule in your hearts. . . . Let the word of Christ dwell in you richly; teach and admonish one another in all wisdom; and with gratitude in your hearts sing psalms, hymns, and spiritual songs to God.

Colossians 3:12-16
optional: Esther 1:1-19

Responsorial Psalm

Truly God is good to the upright,
    to those who are pure in heart.
But as for me, my feet had almost stumbled;
    my steps had nearly slipped.
For I was envious of the arrogant;
    I saw the prosperity of the wicked.   Psalm 73:1-3

Prayers, pp. 529-32

Closing Psalm Prayer

Whom have I in heaven but you?
    And there is nothing on earth that I desire other than you.
My flesh and my heart may fail,
    but God is the strength of my heart and my portion forever.
Indeed, those who are far from you will perish.   Psalm 73:25-27a

Week of the Sunday Closest to September 14   Saturday

Theme: Being in Christ affects our daily lives and our relationships at home and at work.

Antiphon and Opening Prayer

We give thanks to you, O God;
    we give thanks; your name is near.
People tell of your wondrous deeds.   Psalm 75:1

Lord God, you who rule in the heavens and over the earth,
rule in my heart and in my relationships, to your glory.

Scripture Reading

Wives, be subject to your own husbands, as is fitting in the Lord.
Husbands, love your wives and never treat them harshly.

    Children, obey your parents in everything, for this is your
acceptable duty in the Lord. Fathers, do not provoke your children,
or they may lose heart. Slaves, obey your earthly masters in
everything . . . wholeheartedly, fearing the Lord. Whatever your task,
put yourselves into it, as done for the Lord and not for your masters,
since you know that from the Lord you will receive the inheritance
as your reward; you serve the Lord Christ.

                                        Colossians 3:18-24
                                        optional: Esther 2:5-23

Responsorial Psalm

I say to the boastful, "Do not boast,"
    and to the wicked, "Do not lift up your horn;
do not lift up your horn on high,
    or speak with insolent neck."
For not from the east or from the west
    and not from the wilderness comes lifting up;
but it is God who executes judgment,
    putting down one and lifting up another.   Psalm 75:4-7

Prayers, pp. 529-32

Closing Psalm Prayer

But it is God who executes judgment,
    putting down one and lifting up another. . . .

But I will rejoice forever;
    I will sing praises to the God of Jacob.   Psalm 75:7, 9

Week of the Sunday Closest to September 21   Sunday

Theme: When God begins a good work in the life of his own, nothing
    can prevent him from completing his purpose.

Antiphon and Opening Prayer

The LORD is king. . . .
He has established the world; it shall never be moved. Psalm 93:1

O Lord God, you who reign over the world
and who guide the lives of your own,
do a good work in my life and bring me to everlasting life.

Scripture Reading

[Paul,] to all the saints in Christ Jesus who are in Philippi. . . .
    I thank my God every time I remember you, constantly praying
with joy in every one of my prayers for all of you, because of your
sharing in the gospel from the first day until now. I am confident of
this, that the one who began a good work among you will bring it
to completion by the day of Jesus Christ. It is right for me to think
this way about all of you, because you hold me in your heart.
                                    Philippians 1:1, 3-7a
                                    optional: Esther 3:1–4:3

Responsorial Psalm

The LORD is king, he is robed in majesty;
    the LORD is robed, he is girded with strength.
He has established the world; it shall never be moved;
    your throne is established from of old;
    you are from everlasting.   Psalm 93:1-2

Prayers, pp. 529-32

Closing Psalm Prayer

The floods have lifted up, O LORD,
    the floods have lifted up their voice. . . .
More majestic than the thunders of mighty waters,
    more majestic than the waves of the sea.   Psalm 93:3-4a

Week of the Sunday Closest to September 21   Monday

Theme: The adversaries of the gospel, whether visible or invisible, seek
    to terrorize the Christian into defeat.

Antiphon and Opening Prayer

I cry aloud to God,
    aloud to God, that he may hear me.   Psalm 77:1

O Lord Jesus, you who in the temptation spurned the power of
your adversary,
look upon me with your grace,
and grant me the power to stand against evil.

Scripture Reading

Only, live your life in a manner worthy of the gospel of Christ, so
that, whether I come and see you or am absent and hear about you,
I will know that you are standing firm in one spirit, striving side by
side with one mind for the faith of the gospel, and are in no way
intimidated by your opponents. For them this is evidence of their
destruction, but of your salvation. And this is God's doing. For he
has graciously granted you the privilege not only of believing in
Christ, but of suffering for him as well.

    Philippians 1:27-29
    optional: Esther 4:4-17

Responsorial Psalm

I cry aloud to God. . . .
"Will the Lord spurn forever,
    and never again be favorable?
Has his steadfast love ceased forever?
    Are his promises at an end for all time?
Has God forgotten to be gracious?
    Has he in anger shut up his compassion?   Psalm 77:1a, 7-9

Prayers, pp. 529-32

Closing Psalm Prayer

Your way was through the sea,
    your path, through the mighty waters,
    yet your footsteps were unseen.
You led your people like a flock
    by the hand of Moses and Aaron.   Psalm 77:19-20

The Week of the Sunday Closest to September 21   Tuesday

Theme: The incarnation forever stands as God's statement that he is
    willing to put himself in our situation.

Antiphon and Opening Prayer

Give ear, O my people, to my teaching;
    incline your ears to the words of my mouth.   Psalm 78:1

O Lord God, you who became one of us and experienced our life,
teach me to be compassionate to my neighbors, to your glory.

Scripture Reading

If then there is any encouragement in Christ, any consolation from
love, any sharing in the Spirit, any compassion and sympathy, make
my joy complete: be of the same mind, having the same love, being

in full accord and of one mind. Do nothing from selfish ambition or conceit, but in humility regard others as better than yourselves. Let each of you look not to your own interests, but to the interests of others.

Philippians 2:1-4
optional: Esther 5:1-14

Responsorial Psalm

I will open my mouth in a parable;
    I will utter dark sayings from of old,
things that we have heard and known,
    that our ancestors have told us.
We will not hide them from their children;
    we will tell to the coming generation
the glorious deeds of the LORD, and his might,
    and the wonders that he has done.   Psalm 78:2-4

Prayers, pp. 529-32

Closing Psalm Prayer

Then we your people, the flock of your pasture,
    will give thanks to you forever;
        from generation to generation we will recount your praise.

Psalm 79:13

The Week of the Sunday Closest to September 21 Wednesday

Theme: The Incarnation stands as a testimony of how much God is willing to give to his people.

Antiphon and Opening Prayer

Sing aloud to God our strength;
    shout for joy to the God of Jacob.   Psalm 81:1

O Lord, you who became incarnate and took upon yourself our life,
grant that I may willingly give of my time and life to those in need.

Scripture Reading

Let the same mind be in you that was in Christ Jesus,
who, though he was in the form of God,
    did not regard equality with God . . .
but emptied himself,
    taking the form of a slave,
    being born in human likeness.
And being found in human form,
    he humbled himself
    and became obedient to the point of death —
    even death on a cross.
Therefore God also highly exalted him
    and gave him the name
    that is above every name.   Philippians 2:5-9
                                              optional: Esther 6:1-14

Responsorial Psalm

O that my people would listen to me,
    that Israel would walk in my ways!
Then I would quickly subdue their enemies,
    and turn my hand against their foes. . . .
I would feed you with the finest of the wheat,
    and with honey from the rock I would satisfy you.
                                              Psalm 81:13-14, 16

Prayers, pp. 529-32

Closing Psalm Prayer

In distress you called, and I rescued you;
    I answered you in the secret place of thunder;
    I tested you at the waters of Meribah.   Psalm 81:7

The Week of the Sunday Closest to September 21   Thursday

Theme: God works in us to do his good pleasure, which is a life without
blame, a life that shines as a light.

Antiphon and Opening Prayer

Give ear, O LORD, to my prayer;
    listen to my cry of supplication.   Psalm 86:6

Lord God, you who work in the lives of people to conform them
to your Son,
work in me and make me a light of your love.

Scripture Reading

. . . For it is God who is at work in you, enabling you both to will
and to work for his good pleasure.

Do all things without murmuring and arguing, so that you may
be blameless and innocent, children of God without blemish in the
midst of a crooked and perverse generation, in which you shine like
stars in the world. It is by your holding fast to the word of life that
I can boast on the day of Christ that I did not run in vain or labor
in vain.

Philippians 2:13-16
optional: Esther 7:1-10

Responsorial Psalm

Incline your ear, O LORD, and answer me;
    for I am poor and needy.
Preserve my life, for I am devoted to you;
    save your servant who trusts in you.
You are my God; be gracious to me, O LORD,
    for to you do I cry all day long.
Gladden the soul of your servant,
    for to you, O Lord, I lift up my soul.   Psalm 86:1-4

Prayers, pp. 529-32

Closing Psalm Prayer

Teach me your way, O LORD,
  that I may walk in your truth;
    give me an undivided heart to revere your name.
I give thanks to you, O Lord my God, with my whole heart.

Psalm 86:11-12a

The Week of the Sunday Closest to September 21   Friday

Theme: The most important matter in life is to have a right relationship
       with God through Jesus Christ.

Antiphon and Opening Prayer

O LORD, God of my salvation . . .
let my prayer come before you;
    incline your ear to my cry.   Psalm 88:1a, 2

O Lord, you who gave your Son to enter into a relationship with
me,
turn me away from my attachments to the things of this world
and fill me with faith.

Scripture Reading

Yet whatever gains I had, these I have come to regard as loss because
of Christ. More than that, I regard everything as loss because of the
surpassing value of knowing Christ Jesus my Lord. For his sake I
have suffered the loss of all things, and I regard them as rubbish, in
order that I may gain Christ and be found in him, not having a
righteousness of my own that comes from the law, but one that comes
through faith in Christ, the righteousness from God based on faith.

Philippians 3:7-9
optional: Esther 8:1-17

Responsorial Psalm

> For my soul is full of troubles,
>> and my life draws near to Sheol.
> I am counted among those who go down to the Pit;
>> I am like those who have no help,
> like those forsaken among the dead,
>> like the slain that lie in the grave,
> like those whom you remember no more,
>> for they are cut off from your hand. Psalm 88:3-5

Prayers, pp. 529-32

Closing Psalm Prayer

> O LORD, God of my salvation,
>> when, at night, I cry out in your presence,
> let my prayer come before you;
>> incline your ear to my cry. Psalm 88:1-2

The Week of the Sunday Closest to September 21   Saturday

Theme: God, who desires the best for his creation, calls us to strive for the higher things of life.

Antiphon and Opening Prayer

> Lord, you have been our dwelling place
>> in all generations. . . .
> From everlasting to everlasting you are God. Psalm 90:1, 2b

> Lord God, you are complete perfection in whom no evil dwells.
> Cause me to contemplate your virtues
> and turn me toward your face.

Scripture Reading

Finally, beloved, whatever is true, whatever is honorable, whatever is just, whatever is pure, whatever is pleasing, whatever is commendable, if there is any excellence and if there is anything worthy of praise, think about these things. Keep on doing the things that you have learned and received and heard and seen in me, and the God of peace will be with you. . . .

The grace of the Lord Jesus Christ be with your spirit. Amen.

Philippians 4:8-9, 23

optional: Hosea 1:1–2:1

Responsorial Psalm

For a thousand years in your sight
　　are like yesterday when it is past,
　　or like a watch in the night.
You sweep them away; they are like a dream,
　　like grass that is renewed in the morning;
in the morning it flourishes and is renewed;
　　in the evening it fades and withers.　　　　Psalm 90:4-6

Prayers, pp. 529-32

Closing Psalm Prayer

Let the favor of the Lord our God be upon us,
　　and prosper for us the work of our hands —
　　O prosper the work of our hands!　　　　Psalm 90:17

The Week of the Sunday Closest to September 28　　Sunday

Theme: The memory of special people in the faith is always an encouragement to prayer and thanksgiving.

Antiphon and Opening Prayer

Blessed be God,
> because he has not rejected my prayer
> or removed his steadfast love from me.   Psalm 66:20

O Lord, my God,
you who have given to us the church and fellowship of Christian people,
let me bless you for the memory of those lives that have
intersected with mine.

Scripture Reading

Paul, a prisoner of Christ Jesus . . . ,
> To Philemon, our dear friend and co-worker . . . :
> Grace to you and peace from God our Father and the Lord Jesus
Christ.
> When I remember you in my prayers, I always thank my God
because I hear of your love for all the saints and your faith toward
the Lord Jesus. I pray that the sharing of your faith may become
effective when you perceive all the good that we may do for Christ.
>   Philemon 1, 3-6
>   optional: Hosea 2:2-14

Responsorial Psalm

Make a joyful noise to God, all the earth;
> sing the glory of his name;
> give to him glorious praise.
Say to God, "How awesome are your deeds!
> Because of your great power,
> your enemies cringe before you.
All the earth worships you;
> they sing praises to you,
> sing praises to your name."   Psalm 66:1-4

Prayers, pp. 529-32

Closing Psalm Prayer

> Bless our God, O peoples,
>> let the sound of his praise be heard,
> who has kept us among the living,
>> and has not let our feet slip.   Psalm 66:8-9

The Week of the Sunday Closest to September 28   Monday

Theme: It takes a supernatural love and compassion to forgive those who have wronged us and restore them to their former status.

Antiphon and Opening Prayer

> I will sing of your steadfast love, O LORD, forever;
>> with my mouth I will proclaim your faithfulness to all
>> generations.   Psalm 89:1

> Lord, you who were wronged by those who persecuted and put
> you to death,
> let me learn from your love to be forgiving and loving
> to those who have wronged me.

Scripture Reading

> I have indeed received much joy and encouragement from your love, because the hearts of the saints have been refreshed through you, my brother.
>
> For this reason, though I am bold enough in Christ to command you to do your duty, yet I would rather appeal to you on the basis of love — and I, Paul, do this as an old man, and now also as a prisoner of Christ Jesus. I am appealing to you for my child, Onesimus, whose father I have become during my imprisonment. Formerly he was useless to you, but now he is indeed useful both to you and to me.
>
>> Philemon 7-11
>> optional: Hosea 2:14-23

Responsorial Psalm

Let the heavens praise your wonders, O LORD,
　　your faithfulness in the assembly of the holy ones.
For who in the skies can be compared to the LORD?
　　Who among the heavenly beings is like the LORD?

Psalm 89:5-6

Prayers, pp. 529-32

Closing Psalm Prayer

The heavens are yours, the earth also is yours;
　　the world and all that is in it — you have founded them. . . .
You have a mighty arm. 　　　　　　　　Psalm 89:11, 13a

The Week of the Sunday Closest to September 28　　Tuesday

Theme:　Our Lord calls on us not only to forgive those who do wrong,
　　　　but to receive the restored one into our fellowship as a brother
　　　　or sister.

Antiphon and Opening Prayer

The LORD is king! Let the earth rejoice;
　　let the many coastlands be glad! 　　　　　　Psalm 97:1

Lord Jesus Christ, you who forgive all who come to you in faith,
work within me a heart full of love for all who trust in you.

Scripture Reading

I am sending him, that is, my own heart, back to you. I wanted to
keep him with me, so that he might be of service to me in your place
during my imprisonment for the gospel; but I preferred to do nothing
without your consent, in order that your good deed might be
voluntary and not something forced. Perhaps this is the reason he
was separated from you for a while, so that you might have him

back forever, no longer as a slave but more than a slave, a beloved brother — especially to me but how much more to you, both in the flesh and in the Lord.

Philemon 12-16
optional: Hosea 4:1-10

Responsorial Psalm

The LORD is king!
His lightnings light up the world;
   the earth sees and trembles.
The mountains melt like wax before the LORD,
   before the Lord of all the earth.
The heavens proclaim his righteousness;
   and all the peoples behold his glory.   Psalm 97:1a, 4-6

Prayers, pp. 529-32

Closing Psalm Prayer

The LORD loves those who hate evil;
   he guards the lives of his faithful;
   he rescues them from the hand of the wicked. . . .
Rejoice in the LORD, O you righteous,
   and give thanks to his holy name.   Psalm 97:10, 12

The Week of the Sunday Closest to September 28 Wednesday

Theme: If we are truly devoted to our brothers and sisters in the Lord, we will go far beyond what is expected of us in love.

Antiphon and Opening Prayer

I will sing of loyalty and of justice;
   to you, O LORD, I will sing. . . .
   When shall I attain it?   Psalm 101:1, 2b

Lord, you who went to the cross out of your deep love,
let me be motivated by self-giving love in my relationships with others,
for your sake.

Scripture Reading

So if you consider me your partner, welcome him as you would welcome me. If he has wronged you in any way, or owes you anything, charge that to my account. I, Paul, am writing this with my own hand: I will repay it. I say nothing about your owing me even your own self. Yes, brother, let me have this benefit from you in the Lord! Refresh my heart in Christ. Confident of your obedience, I am writing to you, knowing that you will do even more than I say.

Philemon 17-21

optional: Hosea 4:11-19

Responsorial Psalm

I will not set before my eyes anything that is base.
I hate the work of those who fall away;
    it shall not cling to me.
Perverseness of heart shall be far from me;
    I will know nothing of evil. . . .
Whoever walks in the way that is blameless
    shall minister to me.

Psalm 101:3-4, 6

Prayers, pp. 529-32

Closing Psalm Prayer

How very good and pleasant it is
    when kindred live together in unity! . . .
It is like the dew of Hermon,
    which falls on the mountains of Zion.
For there the LORD ordained his blessing,
    life forevermore.

Psalm 133:1, 3

The Week of the Sunday Closest to September 28   Thursday

Theme: Through prayer and supplication God calls us to responsible
support of those who rule our world.

Antiphon and Opening Prayer

O give thanks to the LORD, call on his name;
    make known his deeds among the peoples.   Psalm 105:1

Lord God, you who reign over rulers and authorities,
teach me to pray with intelligence and concern for those who rule
in this world.

Scripture Reading

Paul, an apostle of Jesus Christ . . . ,
    To Timothy, my loyal child in the faith: . . .
    First of all, then, I urge that supplications, prayers, intercessions,
and thanksgivings be made for everyone, for kings and all who are
in high positions, so that we may lead a quiet and peaceable life in
all godliness and dignity. This is right and is acceptable in the sight
of God our Savior, who desires everyone to be saved and to come
to the knowledge of the truth.

I Timothy 1:1a, 2; 2:1-4
optional: Hosea 5:8–6:6

Responsorial Psalm

For he remembered his holy promise,
    and Abraham, his servant.
So he brought out his people with joy,
    his chosen ones with singing.
He gave them the lands of the nations,
    and they took possession of the wealth of the peoples,
that they might keep his statutes
    and observe his laws.
Praise the LORD!   Psalm 105:42-45

Prayers, pp. 529-32

Closing Psalm Prayer

Sing to him, sing praises to him;
>   tell of all his wonderful works.
Glory in his holy name. . . .
Seek the LORD and his strength;
>   seek his presence continually.   Psalm 105:2-3a, 4

The Week of the Sunday Closest to September 28   Friday

Theme: God's love for us is a mystery that goes deeper than our feeble
understanding but touches our inner person through faith.

Antiphon and Opening Prayer

Hear my prayer, O LORD;
>   let my cry come to you. . . .
Incline your ear to me.   Psalm 102:1, 2b

Lord Jesus Christ,
you who came among us and dared to be one of us,
touch me by the mystery of your love and change me,
to your glory.

Scripture Reading

. . . I am writing these instructions to you so that, if I am delayed,
you may know how one ought to behave in the household of God,
which is the church of the living God, the pillar and bulwark of the
truth. Without any doubt, the mystery of our religion is great:
>   He was revealed in flesh,
>   vindicated in spirit,
>   seen by angels,
>   proclaimed among the Gentiles,
>   believed in throughout the world,
>   taken up in glory.

I Timothy 3:14-16
optional: Hosea 10:1-15

Responsorial Psalm

Long ago you laid the foundation of the earth,
and the heavens are the work of your hands.
They will perish, but you endure;
they will all wear out like a garment.
You change them like clothing, and they pass away;
but you are the same, and your years have no end.

Psalm 102:25-27

Prayers, pp. 529-32

Closing Psalm Prayer

Do not hide your face from me
in the day of my distress.
Incline your ear to me;
answer me speedily in the day when I call.   Psalm 102:2

The Week of the Sunday Closest to September 28   Saturday

Theme: The rich are called to share their goods and not merely to fill
their own bank accounts and secure their own futures.

Antiphon and Opening Prayer

Let all the earth fear the LORD;
let all the inhabitants of the world stand in awe of him.

Psalm 33:8

Lord God, you who create the stars
and concern yourself with the lily of the valley,
create in me a love for the poor and needy, giving to your glory.

Scripture Reading

As for those who in the present age are rich, command them not to
be haughty, or to set their hopes on the uncertainty of riches, but

rather on God who richly provides us with everything for our enjoyment. They are to do good, to be rich in good works, generous, and ready to share, thus storing up for themselves the treasure of a good foundation for the future, so that they may take hold of the life that really is life.

Timothy, guard what has been entrusted to you.

I Timothy 6:17-20a
optional: Hosea 11:1-9

Responsorial Psalm

By the word of the LORD the heavens were made,
    and all their host by the breath of his mouth.
He gathered the waters of the sea as in a bottle;
    he put the deeps in storehouses.   Psalm 33:6-7

Prayers, pp. 529-32

Closing Psalm Prayer

For the word of the LORD is upright,
    and all his work is done in faithfulness.
He loves righteousness and justice;
    the earth is full of the steadfast love of the LORD.

Psalm 33:4-5

The Week of the Sunday Closest to October 5   Sunday

Theme: We are all the servants of God in his church who are called to live lives that reflect our calling.

Antiphon and Opening Prayer

O give thanks to the LORD, for he is good;
    his steadfast love endures forever!   Psalm 118:1

O Lord, my God, you who called your church into being
and who called us to be a sign of your redemption,
fill me with your Spirit that I might be an example of your peace.

Scripture Reading

Paul, a servant of God . . . ,
    To Titus, my loyal child in the faith we share: . . .
    For a bishop, as God's steward, must be blameless; he must not
be arrogant or quick-tempered or addicted to wine or violent or
greedy for gain; but he must be hospitable, a lover of goodness,
prudent, upright, devout, and self-controlled. He must have a firm
grasp of the word that is trustworthy in accordance with the teaching,
so that he may be able both to preach with sound doctrine and to
refute those who contradict it.

Titus 1:1a, 4, 7-9
optional: Hosea 13:4-14

Responsorial Psalm

Save us, we beseech you, O LORD!
    O LORD, we beseech you, give us success!
Blessed is the one who comes in the name of the LORD.
    We bless you from the house of the LORD.
The LORD is God,
    and he has given us light.
Bind the festal procession with branches,
    up to the horns of the altar.   Psalm 118:25-27

Prayers, pp. 529-32

Closing Psalm Prayer

You are my God, and I will give thanks to you;
    you are my God, I will extol you.
O give thanks to the LORD, for he is good.   Psalm 118:28-29a

The Week of the Sunday Closest to October 5   Monday

Theme: God does not call us to mere abstract goodness — rather, his instructions for our life are specific, dealing often with relationships.

Antiphon and Opening Prayer

Happy are those who observe justice,
    who do righteousness at all times.   Psalm 106:3

Lord Jesus Christ, you who walked through our life and left us
an example to follow,
teach me to love my neighbor and especially to be good to my
family.

Scripture Reading

But as for you, teach what is consistent with sound doctrine. . . .
The young women [are] to love their husbands, to love their children,
to be self-controlled, chaste, good managers of the household, kind,
being submissive to their husbands, so that the word of God may
not be discredited.

    Likewise, urge the younger men to be self-controlled. Show
yourselves in all respects a model of good works, and in your teaching
show integrity, gravity, and sound speech that cannot be censured.
                            Titus 2:1, 4-8a
                        optional: Hosea 14:1-9

Responsorial Psalm

Remember me, O LORD, when you show favor to your people;
    help me when you deliver them;
that I may see the prosperity of your chosen ones,
    that I may rejoice in the gladness of your nation,
    that I may glory in your heritage.   Psalm 106:4-5

Prayers, pp. 529-32

Closing Psalm Prayer

> Save us, O LORD our God,
>   and gather us from among the nations,
> that we may give thanks to your holy name
>   and glory in your praise.   Psalm 106:47

The Week of the Sunday Closest to October 5   Tuesday

Theme: God calls us to a life that is above reproach, a life that is willing
       to look for the positive in all people and situations.

Antiphon and Opening Prayer

> Blessed be the LORD. . . .
> Our help is in the name of the LORD,
>   who made heaven and earth.   Psalm 124:6a, 8

> Lord Jesus, you who loved the unlovely
> and spoke words of comfort to the oppressed,
> guide my thoughts and the words of my lips,
> so that I will speak evil of no one.

Scripture Reading

> Declare these things; exhort and reprove with all authority. Let no
> one look down on you.
>   Remind them to be subject to rulers and authorities . . . to speak
> evil of no one, to avoid quarreling, to be gentle, and to show every
> courtesy to everyone. . . . The saying is sure.
>   I desire that you insist on these things, so that those who have
> come to believe in God may be careful to devote themselves to good
> works; these things are excellent and profitable to everyone.
>   Titus 2:15; 3:1-2, 8
>   optional: Micah 1:1-9

Responsorial Psalm

> Those who trust in the LORD are like Mount Zion,
>> which cannot be moved, but abides forever.
> As the mountains surround Jerusalem,
>> so the LORD surrounds his people,
>> from this time on and forevermore.   Psalm 125:1-2

Prayers, pp. 529-32

Closing Psalm Prayer

> May those who sow in tears
>> reap with shouts of joy.
> Those who go out weeping,
>> bearing the seed for sowing,
> shall come home with shouts of joy,
>> carrying their sheaves.   Psalm 126:5-6

The Week of the Sunday Closest to October 5   Wednesday

Theme: God promises that if we are obedient and faithful to him, we
will see the results of that faithfulness in our children.

Antiphon and Opening Prayer

> Happy is everyone who fears the LORD,
>> who walks in his ways.   Psalm 128:1

> O Lord God, you who chose the church to be your family on
> earth,
> let me be faithful to your calling,
> not only in my personal life but also in my family.

Scripture Reading

> Paul, an apostle of Jesus Christ . . . ,
>> To Timothy, my beloved child: . . .
>> I am grateful to God — whom I worship with a clear conscience,

as my ancestors did — when I remember you constantly in my prayers night and day. Recalling your tears, I long to see you so that I may be filled with joy. I am reminded of your sincere faith, a faith that lived first in your grandmother Lois and your mother Eunice and now, I am sure, lives in you.

II Timothy 1:1a, 2a, 3-5
optional: Micah 2:1-13

Responsorial Psalm

Your wife will be like a fruitful vine
    within your house;
your children will be like olive shoots
    around your table.
Thus shall the man be blessed
    who fears the LORD. . . .
Peace be upon Israel!   Psalm 128:3-4, 6b

Prayers, pp. 529-32

Closing Psalm Prayer

The LORD bless you from Zion.
    May you see the prosperity of Jerusalem
    all the days of your life.
May you see your children's children.   Psalm 128:5-6a

The Week of the Sunday Closest to October 5   Thursday

Theme: Because life is a battle with the powers of evil, we need to be
        continually praising the Lord, from whom our strength comes.

Antiphon and Opening Prayer

Come, bless the LORD. . . .
Lift up your hands to the holy place,
    and bless the LORD.   Psalm 134:1-2

Lord Jesus Christ,
you who sent the powers of evil to flight by your mighty deeds,
let us turn to you in faith and full confidence,
praising your name every day.

Scripture Reading

You then, my child, be strong in the grace that is in Christ Jesus;
and what you have heard from me through many witnesses entrust
to faithful people who will be able to teach others as well. Share in
suffering like a good soldier of Christ Jesus. No one serving in the
army gets entangled in everyday affairs; the soldier's aim is to please
the enlisting officer. And in the case of an athlete, no one is crowned
without competing according to the rules.

II Timothy 2:1-5
optional: Micah 3:1-8

Responsorial Psalm

Praise the LORD!
Praise the name of the LORD;
give praise, O servants of the LORD,
you that stand in the house of the LORD,
in the courts of the house of our God.
Praise the LORD, for the LORD is good;
sing to his name, for he is gracious. Psalm 135:1-3

Prayers, pp. 529-32

Closing Psalm Prayer

For I know that the LORD is great;
our Lord is above all gods.
Whatever the LORD pleases he does,
in heaven and on earth,
in the seas and all deeps. Psalm 135:5-6

The Week of the Sunday Closest to October 5   Friday

Theme: We have been both crucified and risen with Christ in our baptism; therefore faith compels us to live in him.

Antiphon and Opening Prayer

Let my prayer be counted as incense before you,
    and the lifting up of my hands as an evening sacrifice.

Psalm 141:2

Lord Jesus Christ, you who rose from the dead to life again,
let me rise above the old life
and enter into the life of joy and peace in you.

Scripture Reading

The saying is sure:
    If we have died with him, we will also live with him;
    if we endure, we will also reign with him;
    if we deny him, he will also deny us;
    if we are faithless, he remains faithful —
        for he cannot deny himself.
    Remind them of this.

II Timothy 2:11-14a
optional: Micah 3:9–4:5

Responsorial Psalm

Set a guard over my mouth, O LORD;
    keep watch over the door of my lips.
Do not turn my heart to any evil,
    to busy myself with wicked deeds
in company with those who work iniquity;
    do not let me eat of their delicacies.   Psalm 141:3-4

Prayers, pp. 529-32

Closing Psalm Prayer

I call upon you, O Lord;
    come quickly to me.
My eyes are turned toward you,
O God, my lord;
    in you I seek refuge.   adapted from Psalm 141:1, 8

The Week of the Sunday Closest to October 5   Saturday

Theme: God has given us his Word to guide our choices in this life, to
    direct our paths in the way of righteousness and peace.

Antiphon and Opening Prayer

Blessed be the LORD, my rock . . .
    my stronghold and my deliverer,
my shield, in whom I take refuge.   Psalm 144:1a, 2a

Lord God of heaven and earth,
you who reveal yourself to us in scripture,
let me honor your word by hearing it and acting on it.

Scripture Reading

But as for you, continue in what you have learned and firmly
believed, knowing from whom you learned it, and how from
childhood you have known the sacred writings that are able to
instruct you for salvation through faith in Christ Jesus. All scripture
is inspired by God and is useful for teaching, for reproof, for
correction, and for training in righteousness, so that everyone who
belongs to God may be proficient, equipped for every good work.
                                        II Timothy 3:14-17
                                    optional: Micah 5:1-4, 10-15

Responsorial Psalm

> O LORD, what are human beings that you regard them,
>   or mortals that you think of them?
> They are like a breath;
>   their days are like a passing shadow.
> Bow your heavens, O LORD, and come down;
>   touch the mountains so that they smoke.   Psalm 144:3-5

Prayers, pp. 529-32

Closing Psalm Prayer

> I will sing a new song to you, O God. . . .
> Happy are the people to whom such blessings fall;
>   happy are the people whose God is the LORD.
>
> Psalm 144:9a, 15

The Week of the Sunday Closest to October 12   Sunday

Theme: God's mercy extended to us not only restores our relationships
with God, but fills us with hope.

Antiphon and Opening Prayer

> Praise the LORD!
> How good it is to sing praises to our God;
>   for he is gracious, and a song of praise is fitting.   Psalm 147:1
>
> O Lord Jesus, you who rose from the grave on the third day
> and filled the world with hope,
> restore the joy of my salvation,
> and grant me peace.

Scripture Reading

> Peter, an apostle of Jesus Christ,
>   To the exiles of the Dispersion . . . :

. . . Blessed be the God and Father of our Lord Jesus Christ! By his great mercy he has given us a new birth into a living hope through the resurrection of Jesus Christ from the dead, and into an inheritance that is imperishable, undefiled, and unfading, kept in heaven for you, who are being protected by the power of God through faith for a salvation ready to be revealed in the last time.

I Peter 1:1a, 3-5
optional: Micah 6:1-8

Responsorial Psalm

The LORD builds up Jerusalem;
    he gathers the outcasts of Israel.
He heals the brokenhearted,
    and binds up their wounds.
He determines the number of the stars;
    he gives to all of them their names.
Great is our Lord, and abundant in power;
    his understanding is beyond measure.
The LORD lifts up the downtrodden;
    he casts the wicked to the ground.   Psalm 147:2-6

Prayers, pp. 529-32

Closing Psalm Prayer

Sing to the LORD with thanksgiving;
    make melody to our God on the lyre.
He covers the heavens with clouds,
    prepares rain for the earth,
    makes grass grow on the hills.   Psalm 147:7-8

The Week of the Sunday Closest to October 12   Monday

Theme: We are called to live in the light of the character of God. As he
    is holy, so we are to be holy.

Antiphon and Opening Prayer

Answer me when I call, O God of my right! . . .
Be gracious to me, and hear my prayer.   Psalm 4:1

Holy and immortal God,
you who are perfect in your person and actions,
grant that I might walk in your ways and do your will.

Scripture Reading

Therefore prepare your minds for action; discipline yourselves; set
all your hope on the grace that Jesus Christ will bring you when he
is revealed. Like obedient children, do not be conformed to the desires
that you formerly had in ignorance. Instead, as he who called you
is holy, be holy yourselves in all your conduct; for it is written, "You
shall be holy, for I am holy."

I Peter 1:13-16
optional: Micah 7:1-7

Responsorial Psalm

Happy are those
    who do not follow the advice of the wicked,
or take the path that sinners tread,
    or sit in the seat of scoffers;
but their delight is in the law of the LORD,
    and on his law they meditate day and night.   Psalm 1:1-2

Prayers, pp. 529-32

Closing Psalm Prayer

They are like trees
    planted by streams of water,
which yield their fruit in its season,
    and their leaves do not wither.
In all that they do, they prosper.   Psalm 1:3

The Week of the Sunday Closest to October 12   Tuesday

Theme: The Lord who is righteous calls us to meekness and lowliness
of heart.

Antiphon and Opening Prayer

For the LORD is righteous;
he loves righteous deeds;
    the upright shall behold his face.   Psalm 11:7

Holy and righteous Lord,
help me to come to you
and to reflect you purity in my life.

Scripture Reading

Rid yourselves, therefore, of all malice, and all guile, insincerity, envy,
and all slander. Like newborn infants, long for the pure, spiritual
milk, so that by it you may grow into salvation — if indeed you have
tasted that the Lord is good.
    Come to him, a living stone, though rejected by mortals yet
chosen and precious in God's sight, and like living stones, let
yourselves be built into a spiritual house, to be a holy priesthood,
to offer spiritual sacrifices acceptable to God through Jesus Christ.
                                              I Peter 2:1-5
                                        optional: Jonah 1:1-17

Responsorial Psalm

The LORD is in his holy temple;
    the LORD's throne is in heaven.
    His eyes behold, his gaze examines humankind.
The LORD tests the righteous and the wicked,
    and his soul hates the lover of violence.   Psalm 11:4-5

Prayers, pp. 529-32

Closing Psalm Prayer

> O LORD, you will hear the desire of the meek;
> you will strengthen their heart, you will incline your ear
> to do justice for the orphan and the oppressed.   Psalm 10:17-18a

The Week of the Sunday Closest to October 12   Wednesday

Theme: Our God is a good God, giving to us more than we deserve, heaping on us his bountiful mercies.

Antiphon and Opening Prayer

> I will sing to the LORD,
> because he has dealt bountifully with me.   Psalm 13:6

> Lord God, you who are full of mercy and kindness,
> let my heart turn to you in grateful praise and song.

Scripture Reading

> But you are a chosen race, a royal priesthood, a holy nation, God's own people, in order that you may proclaim the mighty acts of him who called you out of darkness into his marvelous light.
> Once you were not a people,
>   but now you are God's people;
> once you had not received mercy,
>   but now you have received mercy.
> Beloved, I urge you as aliens and exiles to abstain from the desires of the flesh that wage war against the soul. Conduct yourselves honorably among the Gentiles.
>   I Peter 2:9-12a
>   optional: Jonah 1:17–2:10

Responsorial Psalm

> Consider and answer me, O LORD my God!
>   Give light to my eyes, or I will sleep the sleep of death,

and my enemy will say, "I have prevailed";
    my foes will rejoice because I am shaken.   Psalm 13:3-4

Prayers, pp. 529-32

Closing Psalm Prayer

But I trusted in your steadfast love;
    my heart shall rejoice in your salvation.
I will sing to the LORD,
    because he has dealt bountifully with me.   Psalm 13:5-6

The Week of the Sunday Closest to October 12   Thursday

Theme: It is one thing to suffer for doing wrong, but quite another to
        suffer when we have done the right.

Antiphon and Opening Prayer

I call upon the LORD, who is worthy to be praised,
    so I shall be saved from my enemies.   Psalm 18:3

Lord Jesus, you who suffered at the hands of wrongdoers,
grant me patience when I suffer for doing good,
and cause me to continue in the way of truth.

Scripture Reading

Slaves, accept the authority of your masters with all deference, not
only those who are kind and gentle but also those who are harsh.
For it is a credit to you if, being aware of God, you endure pain
while suffering unjustly. If you endure when you are beaten for doing
wrong, what credit is that? But if you endure when you do right and
suffer for it, you have God's approval. For to this you have been
called, because Christ also suffered for you, leaving you an example,
so that you should follow in his steps.

                                        I Peter 2:18-21
                            optional: Jonah 3:1–4:11

Responsorial Psalm

> With the loyal you show yourself loyal;
> > with the blameless you show yourself blameless;
> with the pure you show yourself pure;
> > and with the crooked you show yourself perverse.
> For you deliver a humble people,
> > but the haughty eyes you bring down.   Psalm 18:25-26

Prayers, pp. 529-32

Closing Psalm Prayer

> The LORD is my rock, my fortress, and my deliverer,
> > my God, my rock in whom I take refuge,
> > my shield, and the horn of my salvation, my stronghold.
> > > > > > > > Psalm 18:2

The Week of the Sunday Closest to October 12   Friday

Theme: Hospitality to our brothers and sisters is an expression of the
love we have for God.

Antiphon and Opening Prayer

> As for me, I shall behold your face in righteousness;
> > when I awake I shall be satisfied, beholding your likeness.
> > > > > > > > Psalm 17:15

> O Lord Jesus,
> you to whom the religious leaders of the world were inhospitable,
> grant me a love for people,
> so that I may express my love for you through my hospitality.

Scripture Reading

The end of all things is near; therefore be serious and discipline yourselves for the sake of your prayers. Above all, maintain constant love for one another, for love covers a multitude of sins. Be hospitable to one another without complaining. Like good stewards of the manifold grace of God, serve one another with whatever gift each of you has received. Whoever speaks must do so as one speaking the very words of God.

I Peter 4:7-11a
optional: Hebrews 1:1-11

Responsorial Psalm

Hear a just cause, O LORD; attend to my cry;
    give ear to my prayer from lips free of deceit.
From you let my vindication come;
    let your eyes see the right.   Psalm 17:1-2

Prayers, pp. 529-32

Closing Psalm Prayer

If you try my heart, if you visit me by night,
    if you test me, you will find no wickedness in me;
    my mouth does not transgress.   Psalm 17:3

The Week of the Sunday Closest to October 12   Saturday

Theme: The Lord cares deeply for each of us and watches over us with a loving and caring eye.

Antiphon and Opening Prayer

The LORD answer you in the day of trouble!
    The name of the God of Jacob protect you!   Psalm 20:1

Lord God, you who rescued us from sin
and restored us to fellowship with you,
watch over my life that I may live to your praise.

Scripture Reading

Humble yourselves therefore under the mighty hand of God, so that
he may exalt you in due time. Cast all your anxiety on him, because
he cares for you. Discipline yourselves, keep alert. Like a roaring
lion your adversary the devil prowls around, looking for someone
to devour. Resist him, steadfast in your faith, for you know that your
brothers and sisters in all the world are undergoing the same kinds
of suffering.

I Peter 5:6-9
optional: Nehemiah 2:1-20

Responsorial Psalm

May he grant you your heart's desire,
    and fulfill all your plans.
May we shout for joy over your victory,
    and in the name of our God set up our banners.
May the LORD fulfill all your petitions.   Psalm 20:4-5

Prayers, pp. 529-32

Closing Psalm Prayer

Now I know that the LORD will help his anointed. . . .
Some take pride in chariots, and some in horses,
    but our pride is in the name of the LORD our God.

Psalm 20:6a, 7

The Week of the Sunday Closest to October 19   Sunday

Theme: God became one of us in order that we might be remade in his
likeness and become partakers of the divine.

Antiphon and Opening Prayer

Not to us, O LORD, not to us, but to your name give glory,
for the sake of your steadfast love.   Psalm 115:1

O Lord God, you who became incarnate,
and took on yourself the form of a servant,
let me live in the fullness of your power.

Scripture Reading

Simeon Peter, a servant and apostle of Jesus Christ,
To those who have received a faith as precious as ours . . . :
May grace and peace be yours in abundance in the knowledge
of God and of Jesus our Lord.

His divine power has given us everything needed for life and
godliness, through the knowledge of him who called us by his own
glory and goodness. Thus he has given us, through these things, his
precious and very great promises, so that through them you may
escape from the corruption that is in the world because of lust, and
may become participants of the divine nature.

II Peter 1:1-4
optional: Nehemiah 4:1-23

Responsorial Psalm

O Israel, trust in the LORD!
He is their help and their shield.
O house of Aaron, trust in the LORD!
He is their help and their shield.
You who fear the LORD, trust in the LORD!
He is their help and their shield.   Psalm 115:9-11

Prayers, pp. 529-32

Closing Psalm Prayer

>The LORD has been mindful of us; he will bless us;
>   he will bless the house of Israel . . .
>he will bless those who fear the LORD,
>   both small and great.   Psalm 115:12a, 13

The Week of the Sunday Closest to October 19   Monday

Theme: Conversion to Christ is only the beginning of a long spiritual journey in the new life.

Antiphon and Opening Prayer

>To you, O LORD, I lift up my soul.
>O my God, in you I trust.   Psalm 25:1-2a

>O Lord, my God,
>you who convert people by your Spirit,
>bring me into constant union with you and your Son and your Holy Spirit.

Scripture Reading

. . . You must make every effort to support your faith with goodness, and goodness with knowledge, and knowledge with self-control, and self-control with endurance, and endurance with godliness, and godliness with mutual affection, and mutual affection with love. For if these things are yours and are increasing among you, they keep you from being ineffective and unfruitful in the knowledge of our Lord Jesus Christ. For anyone who lacks these things is nearsighted and blind, and is forgetful of the cleansing of past sins.

II Peter 1:5-9

optional: Nehemiah 5:1-19

Responsorial Psalm

> Who are they that fear the LORD?
>> He will teach them the way that they should choose. . . .
> The friendship of the LORD is for those who fear him,
>> and he makes his covenant known to them.
> My eyes are ever toward the LORD,
>> for he will pluck my feet out of the net. Psalm 25:12-15

Prayers, pp. 529-32

Closing Psalm Prayer

> Make me to know your ways, O LORD;
>> teach me your paths.
> Lead me in your truth, and teach me,
>> for you are the God of my salvation;
>> for you I wait all day long. Psalm 25:4-5

The Week of the Sunday Closest to October 19   Tuesday

Theme: God's enemies are always at work attempting to tear down the truth and introduce falsehoods.

Antiphon and Opening Prayer

> Hear the voice of my supplication,
>> as I cry to you for help,
> as I lift up my hands
>> toward your most holy sanctuary. Psalm 28:2

Lord God, you whom the powers of evil oppose,
turn me from the way of the wicked one,
and let my feet be shod with the message of your gospel.

Scripture Reading

But false prophets also arose among the people, just as there will be false teachers among you, who will secretly bring in destructive opinions. They will even deny the Master who bought them — bringing swift destruction on themselves. Even so, many will follow their licentious ways, and because of these teachers the way of truth will be maligned. And in their greed they will exploit you with deceptive words. Their condemnation, pronounced against them long ago, has not been idle, and their destruction is not asleep.

II Peter 2:1-3
optional: Nehemiah 6:1-19

Responsorial Psalm

Do not drag me away with the wicked,
    with those who are workers of evil,
who speak peace with their neighbors,
    while mischief is in their hearts.
Repay them according to their work,
    and according to the evil of their deeds;
repay them according to the work of their hands;
    render them their due reward.   Psalm 28:3-4

Prayers, pp. 529-32

Closing Psalm Prayer

The LORD is my strength and my shield;
    in him my heart trusts;
so I am helped, and my heart exults,
    and with my song I give thanks to him.   Psalm 28:7

The Week of the Sunday Closest to October 19   Wednesday

Theme: The Lord who loves us with an everlasting love is always ready to forgive us and receive us back into fellowship with him.

Antiphon and Opening Prayer

> O my God, be not far from me!
> Make haste to help me,
> O Lord, my salvation!   adapted from Psalm 38:21-22

> Lord, you who are the Alpha and the Omega,
> remember your promise toward me
> and bring me back to full fellowship with your Spirit.

Scripture Reading

> But by the same word the present heavens and earth have been reserved for fire, being kept until the day of judgment and destruction of the godless.
>
> But do not ignore this one fact, beloved, that with the Lord one day is like a thousand years, and a thousand years are like one day. The Lord is not slow about his promise, as some think of slowness, but is patient with you, not wanting any to perish, but all to come to repentance.
>
> II Peter 3:7-9
> optional: Nehemiah 12:27-47

Responsorial Psalm

> I am utterly bowed down and prostrate;
>   all day long I go around mourning.
> For my loins are filled with burning,
>   and there is no soundness in my flesh.
> I am utterly spent and crushed;
>   I groan because of the tumult of my heart.   Psalm 38:6-8

Prayers, pp. 529-32

Closing Psalm Prayer

> O Lord, all my longing is known to you,
>   my sighing is not hidden from you.
> My heart throbs, my strength fails me. . . .

But it is for you, O LORD, that I wait;
it is you, O LORD my God, who will answer.

Psalm 38:9-10a, 15

The Week of the Sunday Closest to October 19   Thursday

Theme: The problems of this life are to be understood in light of all
eternity.

Antiphon and Opening Prayer

Commit your way to the LORD;
trust in him, and he will act.   Psalm 37:5

Lord, you who stretched forth the heavens and made all that is,
teach me to wait on you in patience and expectation.

Scripture Reading

But the day of the Lord will come like a thief, and then the heavens
will pass away with a loud noise, and the elements will be dissolved
with fire, and the earth and everything that is done on it will be
disclosed.

Since all these things are to be dissolved in this way, what sort
of persons ought you to be in leading lives of holiness and godliness,
waiting for and hastening the coming of the day of God.

II Peter 3:10-12a
optional: Nehemiah 13:4-22

Responsorial Psalm

Be still before the LORD, and wait patiently for him;
do not fret over those who prosper in their way,
over those who carry out evil devices.
Refrain from anger, and forsake wrath.
Do not fret — it only leads to evil.   Psalm 37:7-8

Prayers, pp. 529-32

Closing Psalm Prayer

Our steps are made firm by the LORD,
> when he delights in our way;
though we stumble, we shall not fall headlong,
> for the LORD holds us by the hand.   Psalm 37:23-24

The Week of the Sunday Closest to October 19   Friday

Theme: There are always those who would twist the simple gospel of
Christ into systems of thought that lose that truth.

Antiphon and Opening Prayer

In you, O LORD, I seek refuge. . . .
Be a rock of refuge for me,
> a strong fortress to save me.   Psalm 31:1a, 2b

O Lord, my God, you who alone are the God of the universe,
keep me faithful to your truth and steadfast in my commitment
to you.

Scripture Reading

Jude, . . .
> To those who are called, who are beloved in God the Father and
kept safe for Jesus Christ: . . .
> Beloved, . . . I find it necessary to write and appeal to you to
contend for the faith that was once for all entrusted to the saints.
For certain intruders have stolen in among you, people who long
ago were designated for this condemnation as ungodly, who pervert
the grace of our God into licentiousness and deny our only Master
and Lord, Jesus Christ.

Jude 1, 3-4
optional: Joel 1:1-13

Responsorial Psalm

> You are indeed my rock and my fortress;
> > for your name's sake lead me and guide me,
> take me out of the net that is hidden for me,
> > for you are my refuge.
> Into your hand I commit my spirit;
> > you have redeemed me, O LORD, faithful God.   Psalm 31:3-5

Prayers, pp. 529-32

Closing Psalm Prayer

> Love the LORD, all you his saints.
> > The LORD preserves the faithful,
> > but abundantly repays the one who acts haughtily.
> Be strong, and let your heart take courage.   Psalm 31:23-24a

The Week of the Sunday Closest to October 19   Saturday

Theme: Although our hearts and lives often turn away from the Lord
in indifference, when we turn to him and long for him, he is
ready to receive us.

Antiphon and Opening Prayer

> As a deer longs for the flowing streams,
> > so my soul longs for you, O God.
> My soul thirsts for God, for the living God.   Psalm 42:1-2a

> Father, you who long for every person to turn to you in faith,
> look upon my repentance with favor
> and let me rest in your everlasting arms.

Scripture Reading

But you, beloved, build yourselves up on your most holy faith; pray in the Holy Spirit; keep yourselves in the love of God. . . .

Now to him who is able to keep you from falling, and to make you stand without blemish in the presence of his glory with rejoicing, to the only God our Savior, through Jesus Christ our Lord, be glory, majesty, power, and authority, before all time and now and forever. Amen.

Jude 20-21a, 24-25
optional: Joel 1:15–2:2

Responsorial Psalm

My tears have been my food
    day and night,
while people say to me continually,
    "Where is your God?"
These things I remember,
    as I pour out my soul:
how I went with the throng,
    and led them in procession to the house of God,
with glad shouts and songs of thanksgiving.   Psalm 42:3-4

Prayers, pp. 529-32

Closing Psalm Prayer

By day the LORD commands his steadfast love,
    and at night his song is with me. . . .
Hope in God; for I shall again praise him,
    my help and my God.   Psalm 42:8a, 11b

The Week of the Sunday Closest to October 26   Sunday

Theme: God, who is light, calls on us to confess our sins and turn away from them to receive his mercy and forgiveness.

Antiphon and Opening Prayer

Bless the LORD, O my soul,
    and all that is within me,
    bless his holy name!   Psalm 103:1

Father in heaven,
you look on all people with pity,
and you offer your salvation through Christ.
Hear my confession and forgive me for Christ's sake.

Scripture Reading

This is the message we have heard from him and proclaim to you,
that God is light and in him there is no darkness at all. . . . But if
we walk in the light as he himself is in the light, we have fellowship
with one another, and the blood of Jesus his Son cleanses us from
all sin. If we say that we have no sin, we deceive ourselves, and the
truth is not in us. If we confess our sins, he who is faithful and just
will forgive us our sins and cleanse us from all unrighteousness.

I John 1:5, 7-9
optional: Joel 2:12-19

Responsorial Psalm

For as the heavens are high above the earth,
    so great is his steadfast love toward those who fear him;
as far as the east is from the west,
    so far he removes our transgressions from us.
As a father has compassion for his children,
    so the LORD has compassion for those who fear him.

Psalm 103:11-13

Prayers, pp. 529-32

Closing Psalm Prayer

Bless the Lord, O my soul,
and never forget his benefits:
He forgives all your sins,

he heals your diseases, and
he redeems your life from death.   adapted from Psalm 103:1-4

The Week of the Sunday Closest to October 26   Monday

Theme: Our love for God is demonstrated through our love for those
who are poor and oppressed.

Antiphon and Opening Prayer

But may all who seek you
    rejoice and be glad in you;
may those who love your salvation
    say continually, "Great is the LORD!"   Psalm 40:16

Lord Jesus, you who came among the poor to release them from
their oppression,
give me a love for the needy that results in action.

Scripture Reading

Yet I am writing you a new commandment that is true in him and
in you, because the darkness is passing away and the true light is
already shining. Whoever says, "I am in the light," while hating a
brother or sister, is still in the darkness. Whoever loves a brother or
sister lives in the light, and in such a person there is no cause for
stumbling. But whoever hates another believer is in the darkness,
walks in the darkness, and does not know the way to go, because
the darkness has brought on blindness.

I John 2:8-11
optional: Joel 2:21-27

Responsorial Psalm

Happy are those who consider the poor;
    the LORD delivers them in the day of trouble.
The LORD protects them and keeps them alive;
    they are called happy in the land.

You do not give them up to the will of their enemies.
The LORD sustains them on their sickbed;
    in their illness you heal all their infirmities.   Psalm 41:1-3

Prayers, pp. 529-32

Closing Psalm Prayer

But you have upheld me because of my integrity,
    and set me in your presence forever.
Blessed be the LORD, the God of Israel,
    from everlasting to everlasting.
        Amen and Amen.   Psalm 41:12-13

The Week of the Sunday Closest to October 26   Tuesday

Theme: Although the things of our world's spirit continually beckon us
        to sin, our God calls us to commit our lives to right living.

Antiphon and Opening Prayer

Great is the LORD and greatly to be praised
    in the city of our God.   Psalm 48:1a

Lord God,
you who have received the insults of the devil and all his powers,
turn me from the evil one
and let me walk in your ways, to your glory.

Scripture Reading

Do not love the world or the things in the world. The love of the
Father is not in those who love the world; for all that is in the world
— the desire of the flesh, the desire of the eyes, the pride in riches
— comes not from the Father but from the world. And the world
and its desire are passing away, but those who do the will of God
live forever. . . .

If you know that he is righteous, you may be sure that everyone who does right has been born of him.

I John 2:15-17, 29
optional: Joel 2:28–3:8

Responsorial Psalm

Your throne, O God, endures forever and ever.
Your royal scepter is a scepter of equity;
you love righteousness and hate wickedness.
Therefore God, your God, has anointed you
with the oil of gladness beyond your companions.

Psalm 45:6-7

Prayers, pp. 529-32

Closing Psalm Prayer

My heart overflows with a goodly theme. . . .
I will cause your name to be celebrated in all generations;
therefore the peoples will praise you forever and ever.

Psalm 45:1a, 17

The Week of the Sunday Closest to October 26   Wednesday

Theme: In his infinite mercy God has loved us with an everlasting love, a love that he places in our hearts for others.

Antiphon and Opening Prayer

The earth, O LORD, is full of your steadfast love;
teach me your statutes.   Psalm 119:64

O God, you who are love,
look upon me in your mercy,
and turn me away from my anger and hate,
so that I may love with the love you have given me.

Scripture Reading

Beloved, let us love one another, because love is from God; everyone who loves is born of God and knows God. Whoever does not love does not know God, for God is love. God's love was revealed among us in this way: God sent his only Son into the world so that we might live through him. In this is love, not that we loved God but that he loved us and sent his Son to be the atoning sacrifice for our sins. Beloved, since God loved us so much, we also ought to love one another.

I John 4:7-11
optional: Joel 3:9-17

Responsorial Psalm

The LORD is my portion;
    I promise to keep your words.
I implore your favor with all my heart;
    be gracious to me according to your promise.
When I think of your ways,
    I turn my feet to your decrees;
I hurry and do not delay
    to keep your commandments.   Psalm 119:57-60

Prayers, pp. 529-32

Closing Psalm Prayer

I remember your name in the night, O LORD,
    and keep your law.
This blessing has fallen to me,
    for I have kept your precepts.   Psalm 119:55-56

The Week of the Sunday Closest to October 26   Thursday

Theme: If we have really been born of God, we will overcome the power of evil at work in our lives through the victory of Christ over evil.

Antiphon and Opening Prayer

The heavens declare his righteousness,
    for God himself is judge.   Psalm 50:6

Lord Jesus Christ,
you who confronted the powers of evil at the cross
and overcame them in the resurrection,
grant me the power of your victory.

Scripture Reading

By this we know that we love the children of God, when we love
God and obey his commandments. For the love of God is this, that
we obey his commandments. And his commandments are not
burdensome, for whatever is born of God conquers the world. And
this is the victory that conquers the world, our faith. Who is it that
conquers the world but the one who believes that Jesus is the Son
of God?

I John 5:2-5
optional: Habakkuk 1:1-12

Responsorial Psalm

The mighty one, God the LORD,
    speaks and summons the earth
    from the rising of the sun to its setting.
Out of Zion, the perfection of beauty,
    God shines forth.
Our God comes and does not keep silence,
    before him is a devouring fire,
    and a mighty tempest all around him.   Psalm 50:1-3

Prayers, pp. 529-32

Closing Psalm Prayer

Mark this, then, you who forget God. . . .
Those who bring thanksgiving as their sacrifice honor me;
    to those who go the right way
    I will show the salvation of God.   Psalm 50:22, 23

The Week of the Sunday Closest to October 26   Friday

Theme: The love that God calls us to live by is simple and clear; it is to
walk in his commandments and to love one another.

Antiphon and Opening Prayer

Create in me a clean heart, O God,
    and put a new and right spirit within me.   Psalm 51:10

Lord God, you who gave us the commandments
and sent your Son to show us how to live,
work within me an obedience to truth and a love for others.

Scripture Reading

I was overjoyed to find some of your children walking in the truth,
just as we have been commanded by the Father. But now, dear lady,
I ask you, not as though I were writing you a new commandment,
but one we have had from the beginning, let us love one another.
And this is love, that we walk according to his commandments; this
is the commandment just as you have heard it from the beginning
— you must walk in it.

II John 4-6
optional: Habakkuk 2:1-4, 9-20

Responsorial Psalm

O Lord, open my lips,
    and my mouth will declare your praise.
For you have no delight in sacrifice;
    if I were to give a burnt offering, you would not be pleased.
The sacrifice acceptable to God is a broken spirit;
    a broken and contrite heart, O God, you will not despise.

Psalm 51:15-17

Prayers, pp. 529-32

Closing Psalm Prayer

Restore to me the joy of your salvation,
   and sustain in me a willing spirit.
Then I will teach transgressors your ways,
   and sinners will return to you. Psalm 51:12-13

The Week of the Sunday Closest to October 26   Saturday

Theme: It brings joy to the heart of our Lord when his people walk
   according to his truth.

Antiphon and Opening Prayer

I give you thanks, O LORD, with my whole heart;
   before the gods I sing your praise. Psalm 138:1

Lord God, you who long for the obedience of your children,
let me fulfill your desires by walking in your truth
and keeping your commandments.

Scripture Reading

Beloved, I pray that all may go well with you and that you may be
in good health, just as it is well with your soul. I was overjoyed when
some of the friends arrived and testified to your faithfulness to the
truth, namely how you walk in the truth. . . .
   Beloved, you do faithfully whatever you do for the friends, even
though they are strangers to you; they have testified to your love
before the church.

III John 2-3, 5-6
optional: Habakkuk 3:1-10

Responsorial Psalm

All the kings of the earth shall praise you, O LORD,
   for they have heard the words of your mouth.
They shall sing of the ways of the LORD,

for great is the glory of the LORD.
For though the LORD is on high, he regards the lowly;
but the haughty he perceives from far away.   Psalm 138:4-6

Prayers, pp. 529-32

Closing Psalm Prayer

The LORD will fulfill his purpose for me;
Your steadfast love, O LORD, endures forever.
Do not forsake the work of your hands.   Psalm 138:8

The Week of the Sunday Closest to November 2   Sunday

Theme: Jesus Christ, who is the glory of the Father, is worshiped as the
fullness of the deity.

Antiphon and Opening Prayer

The earth is the LORD's and all that is in it,
the world, and those who live in it.   Psalm 24:1

Lord God, you who revealed yourself in Jesus Christ, your Son,
let me turn from my preoccupation with things to see the vision
of your Son.

Scripture Reading

Long ago God spoke to our ancestors in many and various ways by
the prophets, but in these last days he has spoken to us by a Son,
whom he appointed heir of all things, through whom he also created
the worlds. He is the reflection of God's glory and the exact imprint
of God's very being, and he sustains all things by his powerful word.
When he had made purification for sins, he sat down at the right
hand of the Majesty on high.

Hebrews 1:1-3
optional: Malachi 1:1, 6-14

Responsorial Psalm

Who shall ascend the hill of the LORD?
    And who shall stand in his holy place?
Those who have clean hands and pure hearts,
    who do not lift up their souls to what is false,
    and do not swear deceitfully.
They will receive blessing from the LORD,
    and vindication from the God of their salvation. Psalm 24:3-5

Prayers, pp. 529-32

Closing Psalm Prayer

Lift up your heads, O gates!
    and be lifted up, O ancient doors!
    that the King of glory may come in.
Who is this King of glory?
    The LORD of hosts,
    he is the King of glory.   Psalm 24:9-10

The Week of the Sunday Closest to November 2   Monday

Theme: We are called to pursue actively the salvation that our Lord
    brings and to turn from our indifference.

Antiphon and Opening Prayer

Be gracious to me, O God.
I trust in you,
and I am not afraid.   adapted from Psalm 56:1, 11

Lord, you who are faithful and keep covenant with those you call
by name,
keep me steadfast in the word and in faith.

Scripture Reading

Therefore we must pay greater attention to what we have heard, so that we do not drift away from it. For if the message declared through angels was valid, and every transgression or disobedience received a just penalty, how can we escape if we neglect so great a salvation? It was declared at first through the Lord, and it was attested to us by those who heard him, while God added his testimony by signs and wonders and various miracles, and by gifts of the Holy Spirit, distributed according to his will.

Hebrews 2:1-4
optional: Malachi 2:1-16

Responsorial Psalm

My vows to you I must perform, O God;
　　I will render thank offerings to you.
For you have delivered my soul from death,
　　and my feet from falling,
so that I may walk before God
　　in the light of life.　　　　　　　　Psalm 56:12-13

Prayers, pp. 529-32

Closing Psalm Prayer

When I am afraid,
　　I put my trust in you.
In God, whose word I praise,
　　in God I trust; I am not afraid.　　　　Psalm 56:3-4

The Week of the Sunday Closest to November 2　　Tuesday

Theme:　Our Lord Jesus suffered for us in order to bring us to the Father
　　　　　and to ultimate perfection.

Antiphon and Opening Prayer

On God rests my deliverance and my honor;
    my mighty rock, my refuge is in God.   Psalm 62:7

O Lord Jesus, you who suffered on the wood of the cross for my sake,
turn me to you that I might grow toward maturity in the faith.

Scripture Reading

. . . But we do see Jesus, who for a little while was made lower than the angels, now crowned with glory and honor because of the suffering of death, so that by the grace of God he might taste death for everyone.

    It was fitting that God, for whom and through whom all things exist, in bringing many children to glory, should make the pioneer of their salvation perfect through sufferings. For the one who sanctifies and those who are sanctified all have one Father.
                          Hebrews 2:9-11a
                    optional: Malachi 3:1-12

Responsorial Psalm

Those of low estate are but a breath,
    those of high estate are a delusion;
in the balances they go up;
    they are together lighter than a breath.
Put no confidence in extortion,
    and set no vain hopes on robbery;
        if riches increase, do not set your heart on them.
                          Psalm 62:9-10

Prayers, pp. 529-32

Closing Psalm Prayer

Once God has spoken;
    twice have I heard this: that power belongs to God. . . .
Trust in him at all times, O people;

pour out your heart before him;
God is a refuge for us.   Psalm 62:11, 8

The Week of the Sunday Closest to November 2   Wednesday

Theme: Through the work of his Son Jesus Christ, God makes us partakers of his heavenly calling.

Antiphon and Opening Prayer

From oppression and violence he redeems their life;
and precious is their blood in his sight.   Psalm 72:14

Lord God, you who sent your Son to redeem my soul,
let me hear your calling to do his will to your glory.

Scripture Reading

Therefore, brothers and sisters, holy partners in a heavenly calling,
consider that Jesus, the apostle and high priest of our confession,
was faithful to the one who appointed him, just as Moses also "was
faithful in all God's house." Yet Jesus is worthy of more glory than
Moses, just as the builder of a house has more honor than the house
itself. (For every house is built by someone, but the builder of all
things is God.)

Hebrews 3:1-4
optional: Malachi 3:13–4:6

Responsorial Psalm

May he live while the sun endures
and as long as the moon, throughout all generations.
May he be like rain that falls on the mown grass,
like showers that water the earth.
In his days may righteousness flourish
and peace abound, until the moon is no more.   Psalm 72:5-7

Prayers, pp. 529-32

Closing Psalm Prayer

Blessed be the LORD, the God of Israel,
    who alone does wondrous things.
Blessed be his glorious name forever;
    may his glory fill the whole earth.
        Amen and amen. Psalm 72:18-19

The Week of the Sunday Closest to November 2   Thursday

Theme: God calls us to persevere in the Christian life and not to grow
    weary or indifferent to the power of his Word.

Antiphon and Opening Prayer

In you, O LORD, I take refuge;
    let me never be put to shame. . . .
    for you are my rock and my fortress. Psalm 71:1, 3b

Father, you who revealed yourself through your word,
let me love your truth and live by it,
to your glory and my benefit.

Scripture Reading

Let us therefore make every effort to enter that rest, so that no one
may fall through such disobedience as theirs.

Indeed, the Word of God is living and active, sharper than any
two-edged sword, piercing until it divides soul from spirit, joints
from marrow; it is able to judge the thoughts and intentions of the
heart. And before him no creature is hidden, but all are naked and
laid bare to the eyes of the one to whom we must render an account.
        Hebrews 4:11-13
        optional: Isaiah 63:7-14

Responsorial Psalm

Rescue me, O my God, from the hand of the wicked. . . .
For you, O Lord, are my hope,
    my trust, O LORD, from my youth.
Upon you I have leaned from my birth;
    it was you who took me from my mother's womb.
My praise is continually of you.   Psalm 71:4-6

Prayers, pp. 529-32

Closing Psalm Prayer

But I will hope continually,
    and will praise you yet more and more.
My mouth will tell of your righteous acts,
    of your deeds of salvation all day long.   Psalm 71:14-15

The Week of the Sunday Closest to November 2   Friday

Theme: The Christian life requires constant attention in the face of
    repeated temptations to fall away from the faith.

Antiphon and Opening Prayer

Answer me, O LORD, for your steadfast love is good. . . .
Draw near to me, redeem me.   Psalm 69:16, 18a

Lord Jesus Christ,
you who endured to the end,
empower me by your Spirit
to hold fast to my profession of faith and commitment to
Christian living.

Scripture Reading

Since, then, we have a great high priest who has passed through the
heavens, Jesus, the Son of God, let us hold fast to our confession.

For we do not have a high priest who is unable to sympathize with our weaknesses, but we have one who in every respect has been tested as we are, yet without sin. Let us therefore approach the throne of grace with boldness, so that we may receive mercy and find grace to help in time of need.

Hebrews 4:14-16
optional: Isaiah 63:15–64:9

Responsorial Psalm

But as for me, my prayer is to you, O LORD.
   At an acceptable time, O God,
   in the abundance of your steadfast love, answer me.
With your faithful help rescue me
   from sinking in the mire.

Psalm 69:13-14

Prayers, pp. 529-32

Closing Psalm Prayer

Answer me, O LORD, for your steadfast love is good;
   according to your abundant mercy, turn to me. . . .
Draw near to me, redeem me,
   set me free because of my enemies.

Psalm 69:16, 18

The Week of the Sunday Closest to November 2   Saturday

Theme: It is altogether too easy to convert to Christ and then neglect the food necessary for normal growth.

Antiphon and Opening Prayer

We give thanks to you, O God;
   we give thanks; your name is near.
People tell of your wondrous deeds.

Psalm 75:1

Lord Jesus Christ, you who grew in stature and wisdom,
let me not be satisfied with the milk of the word only,
but turn me toward its solid food of faith.

Scripture Reading

For though by this time you ought to be teachers, you need someone
to teach you again the basic elements of the oracles of God. You
need milk, not solid food; for everyone who lives on milk, being still
an infant, is unskilled in the word of righteousness. But solid food
is for the mature, for those whose faculties have been trained by
practice to distinguish good from evil.

Hebrews 5:12-14
optional: Isaiah 65:1-12

Responsorial Psalm

I say to the boastful, "Do not boast,"
and to the wicked, "Do not lift up your horn;
do not lift up your horn on high,
or speak with insolent neck."
For not from the east or from the west
and not from the wilderness comes lifting up;
but it is God who executes judgment,
putting down one and lifting up another.   Psalm 75:4-7

Prayers, pp. 529-32

Closing Psalm Prayer

But I will rejoice forever;
I will sing praises to the God of Jacob.
All the horns of the wicked I will cut off,
but the horns of the righteous shall be exalted.   Psalm 75:9-10

The Week of the Sunday Closest to November 9   Sunday

Theme: Jesus Christ is a better high priest than those of the Old Testament because his sacrifice for sin is once and for all.

Antiphon and Opening Prayer

Your decrees are very sure;
    holiness befits your house,
    O LORD, forevermore.   Psalm 93:5

O Lord Jesus Christ,
you who gave yourself in sacrifice for the sins of the world,
accept my praise and adoration, to your glory.

Scripture Reading

For it was fitting that we should have such a high priest, holy, blameless, undefiled, separated from sinners, and exalted above the heavens. Unlike the other high priests, he has no need to offer up sacrifices day after day, first for his own sins, and then for those of the people; this he did once for all when he offered himself. For the law appoints as high priests those who are subject to weakness, but the word of the oath, which came later than the law, appoints a Son who has been made perfect forever.

Hebrews 7:26-28
optional: Isaiah 66:1-6

Responsorial Psalm

The LORD is king, he is robed in majesty;
    the LORD is robed, he is girded with strength.
He has established the world; it shall never be moved;
    your throne is established from of old;
    you are from everlasting.   Psalm 93:1-2

Prayers, pp. 529-32

Closing Psalm Prayer

The floods have lifted up, O LORD,
    the floods have lifted up their voice. . . .
More majestic than the thunders of mighty waters,
    more majestic than the waves of the sea.   Psalm 93:3a, 4a

The Week of the Sunday Closest to November 9   Monday

Theme: The blood of Christ exceeds that of bulls and goats, for his
    once-for-all sacrifice cleanses us from sin and frees us to do
    God's will.

Antiphon and Opening Prayer

Restore us, O God;
    let your face shine, that we may be saved!   Psalm 80:3

Father in heaven,
you who were pleased to accept the sacrifice of your Son for the
sin of the world,
stir up in me faith and works of charity.

Scripture Reading

But when Christ came as a high priest of the good things that have
come, then through the greater and perfect tent (not made with
hands, that is, not of this creation). . . . For if the blood of goats
and bulls, with the sprinkling of the ashes of a heifer, sanctifies those
who have been defiled so that their flesh is purified, how much more
will the blood of Christ, who through the eternal Spirit offered
himself without blemish to God, purify our conscience from dead
works to worship the living God!

Hebrews 9:11, 13-14
optional: Isaiah 66:1-6

Responsorial Psalm

> O LORD God of hosts,
>> how long will you be angry with your people's prayers?
> You have fed them with the bread of tears,
>> and given them tears to drink in full measure.
> You make us the scorn of our neighbors;
>> our enemies laugh among themselves.   Psalm 80:4-6

Prayers, pp. 529-32

Closing Psalm Prayer

> Give ear, O Shepherd of Israel,
>> you who lead Joseph like a flock!
> You who are enthroned upon the cherubim, shine forth. . . .
> Stir up your might
>> and come to save us!   Psalm 80:1, 2b

The Week of the Sunday Closest to November 9   Tuesday

Theme: The Lord God not only stood beside Israel, he also stands with
        us and leads us into the fulfillment of our faith.

Antiphon and Opening Prayer

> Give ear, O my people, to my teaching;
>> incline your ears to the words of my mouth.   Psalm 78:1

> O Lord, my God,
> you who brought Israel through the wilderness into the promised
> land,
> let me cling to you and follow your will without wavering.

Scripture Reading

> Therefore, my friends, since we have confidence to enter the sanctuary
> by the blood of Jesus, by the new and living way that he opened for us

through the curtain (that is, through his flesh), and since we have a great priest over the house of God, let us approach with a true heart in full assurance of faith, with our hearts sprinkled clean from an evil conscience and our bodies washed with pure water. Let us hold fast to the confession of our hope without wavering, for he who has promised is faithful.

Hebrews 10:19-23
optional: Isaiah 66:7-14

Responsorial Psalm

I will open my mouth in a parable;
    I will utter dark sayings from of old,
things that we have heard and known,
    that our ancestors have told us.
We will not hide them from their children;
    we will tell to the coming generation
the glorious deeds of the LORD, and his might,
    and the wonders that he has done.   Psalm 78:2-4

Prayers, pp. 529-32

Closing Psalm Prayer

Even though he struck the rock so that water gushed out
    and torrents overflowed,
can he also give bread,
    or provide meat for his people?   Psalm 78:20

The Week of the Sunday Closest to November 9   Wednesday

Theme: More than anything else God wants us truly to believe that he is and that he will act favorably for us.

Antiphon and Opening Prayer

Sing aloud to God our strength;
>   shout for joy to the God of Jacob. Psalm 81:1

O Lord God, you who are,
turn my doubts to belief,
and cause me to turn from the worship of things and success
to follow after you.

Scripture Reading

Now faith is the assurance of things hoped for, the conviction of things not seen. Indeed, by faith our ancestors received approval. By faith we understand that the worlds were prepared by the word of God, so that what is seen was made from things that are not visible. . . .

And without faith it is impossible to please God, for whoever would approach him must believe that he exists, and that he rewards those who seek him.

>   Hebrews 11:1-3, 6
>   optional: Ezekiel 33:1-11

Responsorial Psalm

Hear, O my people, while I admonish you;
>   O Israel, if you would but listen to me!
There shall be no strange god among you;
>   you shall not bow down to a foreign god.
I am the LORD your God,
>   who brought you up out of the land of Egypt.
>   Open your mouth wide, and I will fill it. Psalm 81:8-10

Prayers, pp. 529-32

Closing Psalm Prayer

O that my people would listen to me,
>   that Israel would walk in my ways!
Then I would quickly subdue their enemies,
>   and turn my hand against their foes. Psalm 81:13-14

The Week of the Sunday Closest to November 9   Thursday

Theme: Not only does the Lord make salvation possible through the
work of Jesus, he also helps us through the host of heavenly
angels.

Antiphon and Opening Prayer

Incline your ear, O LORD, and answer me,
    for I am poor and needy. . . .
You are my God.   Psalm 86:1, 2

O Lord God, you who made heaven and earth
and who chart the course of the stars,
protect and guide me by the host of angels
prepared for my endurance in the faith.

Scripture Reading

Therefore, since we are surrounded by so great a cloud of witnesses,
let us also lay aside every weight and the sin that clings so closely,
and let us run with perseverance the race that is set before us, looking
to Jesus the pioneer and perfecter of our faith, who for the sake of
the joy that was set before him endured the cross, disregarding its
shame, and has taken his seat at the right hand of the throne of God.
Hebrews 12:1-2
optional: Ezekiel 33:21-33

Responsorial Psalm

There is none like you among the gods, O Lord,
    nor are there any works like yours.
All the nations you have made shall come
    and bow down before you, O Lord,
    and shall glorify your name.
For you are great and do wondrous things;
    you alone are God.   Psalm 86:8-10

Prayers, pp. 529-32

Closing Psalm Prayer

Teach me your way, O LORD,
> that I may walk in your truth;
> give me an undivided heart to revere your name.
I give thanks to you, O Lord my God, with my whole heart,
> and I will glorify your name forever.   Psalm 86:11-12

The Week of the Sunday Closest to November 9   Friday

Theme: In this world, relationships come and go, but our Lord has
> promised to be faithful to the end.

Antiphon and Opening Prayer

It is good to give thanks to the LORD,
> to sing praises to your name, O Most High.   Psalm 92:1

God of our fathers and mothers,
you who remain steadfast and faithful to Israel,
remain at my side and deliver me from the power of evil.

Scripture Reading

Let mutual love continue. Do not neglect to show hospitality to
strangers, for by doing that some have entertained angels without
knowing it. . . . Keep your lives free from the love of money, and be
content with what you have; for he has said, "I will never leave you
or forsake you." So we can say with confidence,
> "The Lord is my helper;
>> I will not be afraid.
> What can anyone do to me?"

Hebrews 13:1-2, 5-6
optional: Ezekiel 34:1-16

Responsorial Psalm

>The righteous flourish like the palm tree,
>   and grow like a cedar in Lebanon.
>They are planted in the house of the LORD;
>   they flourish in the courts of our God.
>In old age they still produce fruit;
>   they are always green and full of sap,
>showing that the LORD is upright;
>   he is my rock, and there is no unrighteousness in him.
>
> Psalm 92:12-15

Prayers, pp. 529-32

Closing Psalm Prayer

>It is good to give thanks to you, Lord,
>to declare your steadfast love in the morning.
>For you, Lord, have made me glad by your work;
>at the work of your hands I sing for joy.
>
> adapted from Psalm 92:1-4

The Week of the Sunday Closest to November 9   Saturday

Theme: God calls us to offer a continual sacrifice of praise, not only by
our words but also through our deeds.

Antiphon and Opening Prayer

>Satisfy us in the morning with your steadfast love,
>   so that we may rejoice and be glad all our days.   Psalm 90:14

>Lord God Almighty,
>you who give us life through your Son,
>turn me away from the things of self
>so that I may speak of your glory.

Scripture Reading

Therefore Jesus also suffered outside the city gate in order to sanctify the people by his own blood. Let us then go to him outside the camp and bear the abuse he endured. For here we have no lasting city, but we are looking for the city that is to come. Through him, then, let us continually offer a sacrifice of praise to God, that is, the fruit of lips that confess his name. Do not neglect to do good and to share what you have, for such sacrifices are pleasing to God.

Hebrews 13:12-16
optional: Ezekiel 37:21-28

Responsorial Psalm

Satisfy us in the morning with your steadfast love,
 so that we may rejoice and be glad all our days. . . .
Let your work be manifest to your servants,
 and your glorious power to their children.
Let the favor of the Lord our God be upon us,
 and prosper for us the work of our hands.

Psalm 90:14, 16-17a

Prayers, pp. 529-32

Closing Psalm Prayer

Lord, you have been our dwelling place
 in all generations.
Before the mountains were brought forth,
 or ever you had formed the earth and the world,
 from everlasting to everlasting you are God. Psalm 90:1-2

The Week of the Sunday Closest to November 16 Sunday

Theme: As Advent now approaches, God calls us to meditate on Christ's coming in glory at the end of time.

Antiphon and Opening Prayer

> Make a joyful noise to God, all the earth;
>> sing the glory of his name.   Psalm 66:1-2a

> Lord God, you who called into being all things
> and move history toward its end,
> help me to prepare for your coming again
> by being diligent in love and service.

Scripture Reading

> The revelation of Jesus Christ, which God gave him to show his
> servants what must soon take place; he made it known by sending
> his angel to his servant John, who testified to the word of God and
> to the testimony of Jesus Christ, even to all that he saw.
>> Blessed is the one who reads aloud the words of the prophecy,
> and blessed are those who hear and who keep what is written in it;
> for the time is near.
>
>> Revelation 1:1-3
>> optional: Isaiah 19:19-25

Responsorial Psalm

> Come and see what God has done:
>> he is awesome in his deeds among mortals.
> He turned the sea into dry land;
>> they passed through the river on foot.
> There we rejoiced in him. . . .
> Bless our God, O peoples,
>> let the sound of his praise be heard.   Psalm 66:5-6, 8

Prayers, pp. 529-32

Closing Psalm Prayer

> But truly God has listened;
>> he has given heed to the words of my prayer.
> Blessed be God,
>> because he has not rejected my prayer
>> or removed his steadfast love from me.   Psalm 66:19-20

The Week of the Sunday Closest to November 16   Monday

Theme: When the Lord comes in glory all the inhabitants of the earth
will see him and know that he is God.

Antiphon and Opening Prayer

I will sing of your steadfast love, O LORD, forever;
with my mouth I will proclaim your faithfulness to all
generations.   Psalm 89:1

Lord Jesus Christ,
you who sit enthroned on high,
come and rule with truth and justice over your earth,
and let us sing your praises.

Scripture Reading

John to the seven churches that are in Asia:
Grace to you and peace from him who is and who was and who
is to come, and from the seven spirits who are before his throne. . . .
Look! He is coming with the clouds;
every eye will see him,
even those who pierced him;
and on his account all the tribes of the earth will wail.
So it is to be. Amen.
"I am the Alpha and the Omega," says the Lord God, who is
and who was and who is to come, the Almighty.

           Revelation 1:4, 7-8
           optional: Joel 3:1-2, 9-17

Responsorial Psalm

Then you spoke in a vision to your faithful one, and said:
"I have set the crown on one who is mighty. . . .
My arm also shall strengthen him.
The enemy shall not outwit him,
the wicked shall not humble him.

I will crush his foes before him,
    and strike down those who hate him."

                              Psalm 89:19a, 21b, 22-23

Prayers, pp. 529-32

Closing Psalm Prayer

O LORD God of hosts,
    who is as mighty as you, O LORD? . . .
The heavens are yours, the earth also is yours;
    the world and all that is in it — you have founded them.

                                        Psalm 89:8a, 11

The Week of the Sunday Closest to November 16   Tuesday

Theme: On the final day of judgment all evil will be exposed and
    disarmed and the whole earth will rejoice.

Antiphon and Opening Prayer

The LORD is king! Let the earth rejoice;
    let the many coastlands be glad!   Psalm 97:1

O Lord Jesus, you who defeated the powers of evil
and tread upon the devil,
rule over the earth and turn my heart to sing your praise
forevermore.

Scripture Reading

When he opened the sixth seal, I looked, and there came a great
earthquake; the sun became black as sackcloth, and the full moon
became like blood, and the stars of the sky fell to the earth as the
fig tree drops its winter fruit when shaken by a gale. The sky vanished
like a scroll rolling itself up, and every mountain and island was

removed from its place. . . . "For the great day of wrath has come, and who is able to stand?"

Revelation 6:12-14, 17
optional: Nahum 1:1-13

Responsorial Psalm

Clouds and thick darkness are all around him;
righteousness and justice are the foundation of his throne.
Fire goes before him,
and consumes his adversaries on every side.
His lightnings light up the world;
the earth sees and trembles.
The mountains melt like wax before the LORD,
before the Lord of all the earth.   Psalm 97:2-5

Prayers, pp. 529-32

Closing Psalm Prayer

The heavens proclaim his righteousness;
and all the peoples behold his glory. . . .
The LORD loves those who hate evil. . . .
Rejoice in the LORD, O you righteous,
and give thanks to his holy name!   Psalm 97:6, 10a, 12

The Week of the Sunday Closest to November 16 Wednesday

Theme: The judgment of the Lord over all things will surely come at the end of history.

Antiphon and Opening Prayer

I will sing of loyalty and of justice;
to you, O LORD, I will sing.   Psalm 101:1

O Lord, you who gather together all things from the four corners
of the world,
let me prepare for your judgment with a good life and faith.

Scripture Reading

After this I saw four angels standing at the four corners of the earth,
holding back the four winds of the earth so that no wind could blow
on earth or sea or against any tree. I saw another angel ascending
from the rising of the sun, having the seal of the living God, and he
called with a loud voice to the four angels who had been given power
to damage earth and sea, saying, "Do not damage the earth or the
sea or the trees, until we have marked the servants of God with a
seal on their foreheads."

Revelation 7:1-3
optional: Obadiah 15-21

Responsorial Psalm

I will not set before my eyes
    anything that is base.
I hate the work of those who fall away;
    it shall not cling to me.
Perverseness of heart shall be far from me;
    I will know nothing of evil.
One who secretly slanders a neighbor
    I will destroy.
A haughty look and an arrogant heart
    I will not tolerate.   Psalm 101:3-5

Prayers, pp. 529-32

Closing Psalm Prayer

I will look with favor on the faithful in the land,
    so that they may live with me;
whoever walks in the way that is blameless
    shall minister to me.   Psalm 101:6

The Week of the Sunday Closest to November 16   Thursday

Theme: The worship of eternity praises God for the work of salvation
that he has accomplished through his Son.

Antiphon and Opening Prayer

O give thanks to the LORD, call on his name;
    make known his deeds among the peoples.   Psalm 105:1

O Lord God, you who sit on the throne of heaven
surrounded by the praise of the heavenly throne,
hear my shouts of praise to your holy name.

Scripture Reading

After this I looked, and there was a great multitude that no one
could count, from every nation, from all tribes and peoples and
languages, standing before the throne and before the Lamb, robed
in white, with palm branches in their hands. They cried out in a loud
voice, saying,
    "Salvation belongs to our God who is seated on the throne,
    and to the Lamb!"
And all the angels stood around the throne and around the elders
and the four living creatures, and they fell on their faces before the
throne and worshiped God.

Revelation 7:9-11
optional: Zephaniah 3:1-13

Responsorial Psalm

He is the LORD our God;
    his judgments are in all the earth.
He is mindful of his covenant forever,
    of the word that he commanded, for a thousand generations,
the covenant that he made with Abraham,
    his sworn promise to Isaac,

which he confirmed to Jacob as a statute,
>   to Israel as an everlasting covenant.   Psalm 105:7-10

Prayers, pp. 529-32

Closing Psalm Prayer

O give thanks to the LORD, call on his name. . . .
Sing to him, sing praises to him;
>   tell of all his wonderful works.
Glory in his holy name.   Psalm 105:1a, 2-3a

The Week of the Sunday Closest to November 16   Friday

Theme: Judgment awaits those who rebel against God, but peace and
>   hope remain with those who trust in him.

Antiphon and Opening Prayer

O give thanks to the LORD, for he is good;
>   for his steadfast love endures forever.   Psalm 107:1

Father Almighty,
you who bring to judgment all those who rebel against your holy
name,
work in me a spirit of submission to your holy will.

Scripture Reading

Then I looked, and I heard an eagle crying with a loud voice as it
flew in midheaven, "Woe, woe, woe to the inhabitants of the earth,
at the blasts of the other trumpets that the three angels are about to
blow!"
>   And the fifth angel blew his trumpet, and I saw a star that had
fallen from heaven to earth, and he was given the key to the shaft
of the bottomless pit; he opened the shaft of the bottomless pit, and
from the shaft rose smoke like the smoke of a great furnace.
>   Revelation 8:13; 9:1-2a
>   optional: Isaiah 24:14-23

Responsorial Psalm

> Some sat in darkness and in gloom,
>   prisoners in misery and in irons,
> for they had rebelled against the words of God,
>   and spurned the counsel of the Most High.
> Their hearts were bowed down with hard labor;
>   they fell down, with no one to help.   Psalm 107:10-12

Prayers, pp. 529-32

Closing Psalm Prayer

> Let the redeemed of the LORD say so,
>   those he redeemed from trouble
> and gathered in from the lands,
>   from the east and from the west,
>   from the north and from the south.   Psalm 107:2-3

The Week of the Sunday Closest to November 16   Saturday

Theme: The Lord's power extends over his whole creation over which
       he will rule with equity and justice.

Antiphon and Opening Prayer

> I will give thanks to you, O LORD, among the peoples. . . .
> For your steadfast love is higher than the heavens.
>
> Psalm 108:3a, 4a

> Father God, you who execute justice and call us to righteousness,
> look on me with your mercy
> and lead me in your paths of truth.

Scripture Reading

> And I saw another mighty angel coming down from heaven, wrapped
> in a cloud, with a rainbow over his head; his face was like the sun,

and his legs like pillars of fire. He held a little scroll open in his hand. Setting his right foot on the sea and his left foot on the land, he gave a great shout, like a lion roaring. And when he shouted, the seven thunders sounded.

Revelation 10:1-3
optional: Micah 7:11-20

Responsorial Psalm

My heart is steadfast, O God, my heart is steadfast;
   I will sing and make melody.
   Awake, my soul!
Awake, O harp and lyre!
   I will awake the dawn.
I will give thanks to you, O LORD, among the peoples,
   and I will sing praises to you among the nations.
For your steadfast love is higher than the heavens,
   and your faithfulness reaches to the clouds.   Psalm 108:1-4

Prayers, pp. 529-32

Closing Psalm Prayer

Be exalted, O God, above the heavens,
   and let your glory be over all the earth.
Give victory with your right hand, and answer me,
   so that those whom you love may be rescued.   Psalm 108:5-6

The Week of the Sunday Closest to November 23   Sunday

Theme: That Christ is victor over all the powers of evil will be the theme of praise throughout eternity.

Antiphon and Opening Prayer

O give thanks to the LORD, for he is good;
   his steadfast love endures forever.   Psalm 118:1

Lord Jesus Christ,
you who triumphed over the powers of evil,
create in me a spirit of joy
and the shout of gladness to your holy name.

Scripture Reading

Then the seventh angel blew his trumpet, and there were loud voices
in heaven, saying,
"The kingdom of the world has become the kingdom of our
Lord
and of his Messiah,
and he will reign forever and ever!"
Then the twenty-four elders who sit on their thrones before God
fell on their faces and worshiped God, singing,
"We give you thanks, Lord God Almighty,
who are and who were."

Revelation 11:15-17a
optional: Zechariah 9:9-16

Responsorial Psalm

Out of my distress I called on the LORD;
the LORD answered me and set me in a broad place.
With the LORD on my side I do not fear.
What can mortals do to me?
The LORD is on my side to help me.   Psalm 118:5-7

Prayers, pp. 529-32

Closing Psalm Prayer

It is better to take refuge in the LORD
than to put confidence in mortals.
It is better to take refuge in the LORD
than to put confidence in princes.   Psalm 118:8-9

The Week of the Sunday Closest to November 23   Monday

Theme: God will cast down all the powers of evil and destroy them, to
        his glory and his praise.

Antiphon and Opening Prayer

Praise the LORD!
O give thanks to the LORD, for he is good;
    for his steadfast love endures forever.   Psalm 106:1

Lord God,
you who cast down the dragon and all his works of evil,
fill my heart with praises and let my lips speak of your glory.

Scripture Reading

The great dragon was thrown down, that ancient serpent, who is
called the Devil and Satan, the deceiver of the whole world — he
was thrown down to the earth, and his angels were thrown down
with him.
    Then I heard a loud voice in heaven proclaiming,
    "Now have come the salvation and the power
        and the kingdom of our God
        and the authority of his Messiah,
    for the accuser of our comrades has been thrown down,
        who accuses them day and night before our God."
                                        Revelation 12:9-10
                                        optional: Zechariah 10:1-12

Responsorial Psalm

Remember me, O LORD, when you show favor to your people;
    help me when you deliver them;
that I may see the prosperity of your chosen ones,
        that I may rejoice in the gladness of your nation,
        that I may glory in your heritage.   Psalm 106:4-5

Prayers, pp. 529-32

Closing Psalm Prayer

Who can utter the mighty doings of the LORD,
>   or declare all his praise?
Happy are those who observe justice,
>   who do righteousness at all times.   Psalm 106:2-3

The Week of the Sunday Closest to November 23   Tuesday

Theme: The powers of evil cannot harm those who are chosen by God,
since he watches over them and cares for them.

Antiphon and Opening Prayer

I lift up my eyes to the hills —
>   from where will my help come?
My help comes from the LORD.   Psalm 121:1, 2a

Lord God, you who created the heavens and the earth
and love all that you have made,
watch over my life and protect me from the powers of evil.

Scripture Reading

So when the dragon saw that he had been thrown down to the earth,
he pursued the woman who had given birth to the male child. . . .
But the earth came to the help of the woman; it opened its mouth
and swallowed the river that the dragon had poured from his mouth.
Then the dragon was angry with the woman, and went off to make
war on the rest of her children, those who keep the commandments
of God and hold the testimony of Jesus.
>   Revelation 12:13, 16-17
>   optional: Zechariah 11:4-17

Responsorial Psalm

> He will not let your foot be moved;
>   he who keeps you will not slumber.
> He who keeps Israel
>   will neither slumber nor sleep.
> The LORD is your keeper;
>   the LORD is your shade at your right hand.
> The sun shall not strike you by day,
>   nor the moon by night.   Psalm 121:3-6

Prayers, pp. 529-32

Closing Psalm Prayer

> The LORD will keep you from all evil;
>   he will keep your life.
> The LORD will keep
>   your going out and your coming in
>   from this time on and forevermore.   Psalm 121:7-8

The Week of the Sunday Closest to November 23 Wednesday

Theme: In heaven a new song is being sung because the Lamb rules over
        all the powers of evil.

Antiphon and Opening Prayer

> Those who trust in the LORD are like Mount Zion,
>   which cannot be moved, but abides forever.   Psalm 125:1

> Lord Jesus Christ,
> to whom is sung the new song of power and might,
> fill my heart with laughter
> that my mouth can sing your praises.

Scripture Reading

Then I looked, and there was the Lamb, standing on Mount Zion! And with him were one hundred forty-four thousand, who had his name and his Father's name written on their foreheads. And I heard a voice from heaven like the sound of many waters and like the sound of loud thunder; the voice I heard was like the sound of harpists playing on their harps, and they sing a new song before the throne and before the four living creatures and before the elders.

Revelation 14:1-3a
optional: Zechariah 12:1-10

Responsorial Psalm

When the LORD restored the fortunes of Zion,
    we were like those who dream.
Then our mouth was filled with laughter,
    and our tongue with shouts of joy;
then it was said among the nations,
    "The LORD has done great things for them."
The LORD has done great things for us,
    and we rejoiced.   Psalm 126:1-3

Prayers, pp. 529-32

Closing Psalm Prayer

May those who sow in tears
    reap with shouts of joy.
Those who go out weeping,
    bearing the seed for sowing,
shall come home with shouts of joy,
    carrying their sheaves.   Psalm 126:5-6

The Week of the Sunday Closest to November 23   Thursday

Theme: The heavens break forth in loud shouts of joy and praise to the Lord, for he has saved us from the evil one.

Antiphon and Opening Prayer

Praise the LORD!
> Praise the name of the LORD;
> give praise, O servants of the LORD!   Psalm 135:1

Lord Jesus Christ,
you who bring down the powers of evil and judge them,
fill my heart to sing your praises forevermore.

Scripture Reading

After this I heard what seemed to be the loud voice of a great
multitude in heaven, saying,
> "Hallelujah!
> Salvation and glory and power to our God,
>> for his judgments are true and just;
> he has judged the great whore
>> who corrupted the earth with her fornication,
> and he has avenged on her the blood of his servants."
Once more they said,
> "Hallelujah!
> The smoke goes up from her forever and ever!"
>
> Revelation 19:1-3
> optional: Zechariah 13:1-9

Responsorial Psalm

For I know that the LORD is great;
> our Lord is above all gods.
Whatever the LORD pleases he does,
> in heaven and on earth,
> in the seas and all deeps.
He it is who makes the clouds rise at the ends of the earth;
> he makes lightnings for the rain
> and brings out the wind from his storehouses.
>
> Psalm 135:5-7

Prayers, pp. 529-32

Closing Psalm Prayer

Praise the LORD!
>Praise the name of the LORD;
>give praise, O servants of the LORD,
you that stand in the house of the LORD,
>in the courts of the house of our God.
Praise the LORD, for the LORD is good;
>sing to his name, for he is gracious.   Psalm 135:1-3

The Week of the Sunday Closest to November 23   Friday

Theme: The Lord God has overcome the powers of evil and set us free
because he loves us with an everlasting love.

Antiphon and Opening Prayer

O LORD, what are human beings that you regard them,
>or mortals that you think of them?   Psalm 144:3

Lord God, you who love us and redeem us from all evil,
look on me with your favor and hear the praises that I lift up to
you.

Scripture Reading

Then I saw an angel coming down from heaven, holding in his hand
the key to the bottomless pit and a great chain. He seized the dragon,
that ancient serpent, who is the Devil and Satan, and bound him for
a thousand years, and threw him into the pit, and locked and sealed
it over him, so that he would deceive the nations no more, until the
thousand years were ended. After that he must be let out for a little
while.

Revelation 20:1-3
optional: Zechariah 14:1-11

Responsorial Psalm

Blessed be the LORD, my rock,
   who trains my hands for war, and my fingers for battle;
my rock and my fortress,
   my stronghold and my deliverer,
my shield, in whom I take refuge,
   who subdues the peoples under me.   Psalm 144:1-2

Prayers, pp. 529-32

Closing Psalm Prayer

One generation shall laud your works to another,
   and shall declare your mighty acts.
On the glorious splendor of your majesty,
   and on your wondrous works, I will meditate.   Psalm 145:4-5

The Week of the Sunday Closest to November 23   Saturday

Theme: The Lord, who began to make all things new at the resurrection,
         will complete his work in the new heavens and earth.

Antiphon and Opening Prayer

Bless the LORD, O my soul.
   O LORD, my God, you are very great.
You are clothed with honor and majesty.   Psalm 104:1

Lord God Almighty, you who make all things new,
help me to live in expectation of the day
when all will be well in heaven and on earth.

Scripture Reading

Then I saw a new heaven and a new earth; for the first heaven and
the first earth had passed away, and the sea was no more. And I saw
the holy city, the new Jerusalem, coming down out of heaven from

God, prepared as a bride adorned for her husband. And I heard a
loud voice from the throne saying,
> "See, the home of God is among mortals.
> He will dwell with them as their God;
> they will be his peoples,
> and God himself will be with them;
> he will wipe every tear from their eyes."

Revelation 21:1-3
optional: Zechariah 14:12-21

Responsorial Psalm

> You set the earth on its foundations,
>> so that it shall never be shaken.
> You cover it with the deep as with a garment;
>> the water stood above the mountains.
> The earth is satisfied with the fruit of your work. . . .
> May the glory of the LORD endure forever.

Psalm 104:5-6, 13b, 31a

Prayers, pp. 529-32

Closing Psalm Prayer

> May my meditation be pleasing to him,
>> for I rejoice in the LORD.
> Let sinners be consumed from the earth,
>> and let the wicked be no more.
> Bless the LORD, O my soul!
> Praise the LORD!

Psalm 104:34-35

The Prayers

These prayers are adapted for private prayer from *The Book of Common Prayer* of the Episcopal Church (1979), pp. 360, 356, 101, and 383-85. Use one or more of them every day, returning after the prayers to the closing psalm prayer of the day. The Prayer of Confession below is especially suitable for every day during Advent, Lent, and Holy Week.

A Prayer of Confession

> Most merciful God,
> I confess that I have sinned against you
> in thought, word, and deed,
> by what I have done,
> and by what I have left undone.
> I have not loved you with my whole heart;
> I have not loved my neighbor as myself.
> I am truly sorry and I humbly repent.
> For the sake of your Son Jesus Christ,
> have mercy on me and forgive me,
> that I may delight in your will,
> and walk in your ways,
> to the glory of your Name.

A Prayer of Adoration

Glory to God in the highest,
  and peace to his people on earth.

Lord God, heavenly King,
almighty God and Father,
  I worship you, I give you thanks,
  I praise you for your glory.

Lord Jesus Christ, only Son of the Father,
Lord God, Lamb of God,
you take away the sin of the world:
  have mercy on us;
you are seated at the right hand of the Father:
  receive our prayer.

For you alone are the Holy One,
you alone are the Lord,
you alone are the Most High,
  Jesus Christ,
  with the Holy Spirit,
  in the glory of God the Father.

Prayer of General Thanksgiving

Almighty God, Father of all mercies,
I your unworthy servant give you humble thanks
for all your goodness and loving-kindness
to me and to all whom you have made.
I bless you for creation, preservation,
and all the blessings of this life;
but above all for your immeasurable love
in the redemption of the world by our Lord Jesus Christ;
for the means of grace, and for the hope of glory.
And, I pray, give me such an awareness of your mercies,
that with a truly thankful heart I may show forth your praise,
not only with my lips, but in my life
by giving up myself to your service,
and by walking before you
in holiness and righteousness all my days;

through Jesus Christ our Lord,
to whom, with you and the Holy Spirit,
be honor and glory throughout all ages.

A Prayer of Intercession

With all my heart and with all my mind I pray to you, O Lord:
For the peace from above, for the loving-kindness of God, and
for the salvation of my soul.
Add your own intercessions

For the peace of the world, for the welfare of the holy Church of
God, and for the unity of all peoples.
Add your own intercessions

For our nation's leaders, for the leaders of other nations, and for
all in authority throughout the world.
Add your own intercessions

For this place, for every city and community, and for those who
live in them.
Add your own intercessions

For seasonable weather, and for an abundance of the fruits of the
earth.
Add your own intercessions

For the good earth which God has given and for the wisdom and
will to conserve it.
Add your own intercessions

For the aged and infirm, for the widowed and orphans, and for
the sick and the suffering.
Add your own intercessions

For the poor and the oppressed, for the unemployed and the
destitute, for prisoners and captives, and for all who remember
and care for them.
Add your own intercessions

For deliverance from all danger, violence, oppression, and degradation.

Add your own intercessions

That I may end my life in faith and hope, without suffering and without reproach. Defend me, deliver me, and in your compassion protect me, O Lord, by your grace.